Bright Eyes

The Story of Susette La Flesche,
an Omaha Indian

DOROTHY CLARKE WILSON

McGRAW-HILL BOOK COMPANY
New York   Toronto   London   Sydney

Book design by Marcy J. Katz

1 2 3 4 5 6 7 8 9 B A B A 7 9 8 7 6 5 4

Library of Congress Cataloging in Publication Data

Wilson, Dorothy Clarke.
  Bright Eyes; the story of Susette La Flesche.

  1. La Flesche, Susette, 1854–1903. I. Title.
E99.04W54   970.3 [B]   73-15636
ISBN 0-07-070752-9

Excerpts from *Buckskin and Blanket Days* by Thomas Henry Tibbles.
Copyright © 1957 by Vivien K. Barris. Reprinted by permission
of Doubleday & Company, Inc.

Prologue

The time was December 1879, the place a sumptuous home in Cambridge, Massachusetts, the occasion a selective little dinner given by Mr. Henry O. Houghton for some unusual guests of honor.

Mr. Houghton's little dinners were always selective and his guests of honor unusual, for, as one-time mayor of Boston, owner of the distinguished Riverside Press, and chief partner of one of Boston's foremost publishing firms, soon to become Houghton, Mifflin and Company, his friends and associates included most of the social, political, educational, business, and literary giants of the period. Placecards bearing the names of Whittier, Lowell, Holmes, Bryant, Longfellow, Emerson, Howells, Samuel Clemens, Harriet Beecher Stowe, Helen Hunt Jackson, the Alcotts, were repeatedly interspersed with those of public officials like Mayor Prince and Governor Talbot, editors such as Edward Everett Hale, distinguished clergymen like Wendell Phillips, college presidents like Seelye of Amherst, such eminent businessmen as William H. Lincoln, the importer, and S. D. Warren, the paper magnate. However, this dinner–reception was unique. Until a few days earlier probably nothing like it had occurred in New England society since the time of the first Thanksgiving. For the guests of honor were three American Indians.

The stage for their arrival was set. In the dining room damask shone, silver and crystal glittered under blazing candelabra. Stagehands wearing caps and aprons hovered nervously or soft-footed about making last-minute checks of the props. The audience, including a preponderance of literary figures, was assembled. Only the chief actors, the guests of honor, had not yet arrived—except one.

Many eyes were watching him with curiosity, anticipation—a slight yet impressive figure with long white silken hair and patriarchal beard, but with remarkably young and fresh-looking features. Even now in his seventies, Henry Wadsworth Longfellow was vigorous in appearance, blue eyes sparkling with interest and energy, deep baritone voice as full and sonorous as ever. His presence at this party was unusual, for, since his affliction with neuralgia in the last half-dozen years, he seldom appeared at social gatherings. There was a reason tonight for his coming, and everybody knew it.

"Where is she?" he demanded, looking eagerly about the room, face clouding with disappointment. "Why isn't she here? When is she coming?"

His two daughters, Alice and Annie, at either side to support his slight unsteadiness, looked both amused and indulgent.

"Don't worry, Father, she'll be here."

"Don't be so impatient."

Henry Houghton, tall, gaunt, distinguished in black dinner dress, always the perfect host, gave further reassurance.

"Our guests of honor have undoubtedly been delayed. They say there is a terrific snarl of traffic, lines of carriages drawn up for blocks around, all the way to Harvard Square."

Leaving his daughters, Longfellow made his way a bit unsteadily to a window, pushed back the curtains, and stood watching, eyes fixed on the long walk leading to the street, nose pressed to the glass with all the eagerness of a child.

"I've seldom seen him so excited," laughed one of his daughters. "He has been looking forward to meeting this Bright Eyes for days. He's brought one of his books of poems to autograph and give her, including, of course, *Hiawatha*. I believe he thinks she may be the incarnation of his precious Laughing Water! I just hope he won't be disappointed."

"He won't be," said one of the guests confidently. "I've seen and heard her."

There were nods of agreement, for many of the others had seen and heard the young Omaha Indian woman named Bright Eyes, who had arrived in Boston the month before, with her brother Wood Worker, Standing Bear, a Ponca Indian, and Thomas Tibbles, an Omaha newspaperman, to plead the case of the wronged Poncas, who had been forcefully driven from their reservation in violation of a treaty. They had taken the staid cultural city by storm. The names of Bright Eyes and Standing Bear were bandied from Harvard campus to Haymarket Square. Churches, hotels, homes, even Faneuil Hall and the Merchants' Exchange, were being crowded for their lectures. Headlines championing the "poor Poncas" flared side by side with scurrilous denunciations of the "savage bloodthirsty Utes" in Colorado. The city was aroused to a fervor of moral indignation seldom evinced since the days of the Boston Tea Party.

Longfellow's interest in the young Indian woman was understandable. Since the writing of *Hiawatha* a quarter century before, involving extensive study of the legends and customs of many tribes, he had been admired as a romantic poet, humored as a sentimental idealist, cursed as a "bloody Indian lover." His "Indian maiden" was a synthesis of every imaginable quality of perfection—virtue, grace, intelligence, beauty. Now he was to meet face to face the only red-skinned heroine who had come within the orbit of Eastern culture for generations, perhaps since Pocohontas. No wonder all his friends were agog with curiosity and expectation.

"They're coming!" He turned from the window and, scorning the helping hands of his daughters, made straight for the front door. Flinging it open, he stood waiting, many of the guests crowding into the hall behind him.

The little party came up the front walk—a giant of a white man with a mane of thick hair, two tall Indians in proper dinner dress, and a slight young woman in a black coat and small modish hat. Seeing the impressive figure in the open door, and understanding, the white man pushed her forward, and with a timid little gasp she started up the steps alone. Longfellow stepped forward to meet her, took both her hands in his, and looked long and hard into her face. She gazed back at him steadily. The group in the hall behind held its breath, fearing his disappointment. No long braids, no beaded headband, no feathers, no moccasins, no fringed and gayly embroidered skin tunic. But the light from the open door spread a bronze glow over the softly rounded cheeks, cast a blue sheen on the sable winds of hair framing the broad forehead, kindled unquenchable fires in the great dark eyes.

The poet nodded with satisfaction.

"This," he said in a loud clear voice, "is Minnehaha."

From the wigwam he departed,
Leading with him Laughing Water;
Hand in hand they went together
Through the woodland and the meadow;
Left the old man standing lonely
At the doorway of his wigwam,
Heard the Falls of Minnehaha
Calling to them from the distance,
Crying to them from afar off,
"Fare thee well, O Minnehaha!"

Henry W. Longfellow.

Cambridge. Dec. 3.
1879.

*(One of the earliest and most treasured
entries in Bright Eyes' autograph album)*

Part One

1

Spring was early that year. The seven geese who returned at the end of the "Moon of Blinding Snow" to see if the waterways were open did not go back south to bid the flocks wait until after the "Moon of Little Frogs." The rest soon followed, and after the geese came back things began to happen. Wakonda spoke. With the voice of the First Thunder he wakened Earth from its long winter's sleep.

Hearing his command the medicine men took out their sacred bundles, opened them, and, going to a high hill, offered their prayers and songs, blowing smoke from their pipes to the four winds. Freed from its imprisoning bonds, the swollen river set a quickened rhythm. The tips of willows and cottonwoods kindled with pale fire. Birds that had stayed through the winter, cardinals, woodpeckers, blue jays, chickadees, burst into joyous sound. Nights came alive with the chattering and shrieking of owls and the mating cries of coyotes. And, as the sun grew stronger and the "gone-down" birds returned, the gurgling flute notes of the meadowlark announced loud and clear in the Omaha language, "It is spring! It is spring!" It was the awaited signal. A large tent was erected and made *xube*, sacred. The tribal herald proclaimed the approaching ceremonies called Turning of the Child.

Susette, daughter of Joseph La Flesche, head chief of the Omahas, was ready for this rite. She was old enough to walk unassisted, to speak clearly, to understand and be understood. *Indádi*, Father, tried to explain its meaning.

"Now, my little one, you are part of a family. You belong to us, here in this lodge, to Mother Mary, Grandmother Nicomi, your other mother Tainne, the 'oldest grandmother,' your brother Louis. But the world you must live in is more than a family. You are old enough now to belong to our tribe and to take your place in it. You will be sent into the midst of the winds, to give you life and health. Your feet will be set on a stone, emblem of long life and wisdom. The fire will give you power to live a long life of service in our tribe. You understand, *chérie?*"

She didn't, but she nodded soberly. It was Louis, who had lived nine winters and seemed to her wise, strong, admirable above all human beings, who made matters clearer.

"You go into this big tent, you know? And there's a big man there all dressed up and painted, he's the priest of the Thunder, you know? And there's a fire in the middle and a stone and a ball of grass. And they sing songs and beat drums, making believe they're the winds and thunder, and you just have to do what the big man tells you."

"Do—do I have to go in all alone?" she quavered.

"*Dho*, yes, of course you do, you little mouse." It was a term of affection, not of contempt. "There's nothing to be afraid of. You're a chief's daughter. Don't you dare be afraid."

But Susette watched the preparations with mounting anxiety: the huge pile of presents for the priest, robes and shawls and skins, to say nothing of two of Father's best horses; the tunic she would wear of soft deerskin all embroidered with beads; the new moccasins. These, it seemed, were of special importance. She was to carry them in her hand into the tent. Grandmother Nicomi had spent many days making them, choosing the softest skins and embroidering them in the ancient fashion with designs of dyed porcupine quills instead of the newfangled beads bought from the traders. Susette watched fascinated as she made black dye by cutting the inner bark of the maple into strips, added mashed leaves and roasted earth and boiled all

2

together; yellow from early buds of cottonwood; red from the root of a small plant that grew in the marshes.

"We Omahas call this 'feather dye,'" Grandmother explained. "It has to be done early in the morning to come out well. Not many people know how to get a good red."

Grandmother did. The quills that emerged from the kettle were cardinal bright. She used fine quills to embroider the line around the upper part of the moccasins, larger ones to decorate the flaps about the ankles. When they were finished the child turned one of them over and over in her hand, as if looking for something.

Grandmother smiled. "No, *Tushpáha*.[1] There's no hole in the bottom as in your baby moccasins. You know why we cut the hole in them?" The child shook her head. "It was so that if a messenger should come from the spirit world and say to you, 'I have come for you,' you could answer, 'I cannot go on a journey. See, my moccasins are worn out.' But now that turning time is come, you will be prepared for the journey of life, and, please Wakonda, it will be a long one."

The day came. Susette was dressed in the skin tunic, made in two pieces and fringed at both sides. She liked the feeling of it, so much softer than her long calico skirt with its Mother Hubbard tunic buttoned down the back. Mother combed and combed her hair with the stiff grass brush until it was as glossy black as a raven, then braided it on either side and looped the ends together at the back of her neck. She patted the round, anxious little face.

"Don't look so frightened, *Wízhungeha*.[2] There's nothing to fear. It's beautiful, this thing that is going to happen."

The big new tent was about a mile away, between Joseph's lodge and the Big Village. Here also were the two sacred tents, the Tent of the White Buffalo Hide and the Tent of the Sacred Pole. Even Susette, young though she was, knew vaguely the awful implications of their sanctity. One must not go near them or touch them. If an animal or even a tent pole, much less a person, came in contact with one of them, it must be taken to

1. Grandaughter, as spoken to by Grandmother.
2. Daughter, as spoken to by mother.

3

the keeper of the tent and be cleansed ceremonially. If a horse should tread on one of the tent poles, its legs must be broken.

The Sacred Pole looked harmless enough, a long stick of cottonwood bound with leather in the middle, a great tuft of human hair at one end. On fair days like this it was in full view outside its tent, fastened at an angle to one of the tent poles. Nothing to show that it was centuries old, that its origin was shrouded in holy legend, that it symbolized the provider and protector and unifying spirit of a people! Yet there were reverence and respect as well as fear in the caution of the assembling people to keep their distance.

The crowds took Susette's breath away. Never had she seen so many people at once. All her fears returned. Yet it was more shyness than fear that made her hide her face in Mother's voluminous skirt.

"Come, *Wizhungeha.*" Taking one of the child's hands, Mary placed the new moccasins in the other. "You are a chief's daughter, so you must go first."

They moved toward the tent. When some distance away, Mother stopped and called out, "Venerable man! I desire my child to wear moccasins," After a moment she spoke again. "I desire my child to walk long on the earth; I desire her to be content with the light of many days."

Susette felt hands on her shoulders, pushing her forward, heard Mother whisper, "Go now. You must go in alone." Obediently, clutching the moccasins, heart pounding, she moved toward the tent. *Don't you dare be afraid!* She wouldn't, she *couldn't* let Louis be ashamed of her! Suddenly in the tent's entrance loomed a figure, giant-tall, a huge animal skin over one shoulder, a towering thing of furs and feathers on its head. With a little shriek she turned and fled.

It was Grandmother Nicomi who caught her, took her hand, led her back to the tent's entrance. "See, little one. There's nothing to fear. This man is your friend."

The face between the frightening skin and headdress became suddenly familiar. She had seen it often in Father's lodge, ridden laughing on the powerful shoulders. She went forward willingly.

The priest looked down at her, smiling. "You shall reach the fourth hill sighing," he said gently. "You shall be bowed over.

4

You shall have wrinkles. Your staff shall bend under your weight. I speak to you that you may be strong."

A bright fire glowed in the center of the tent. He led her to it, then spoke again. This time his voice was deep and strong, not gentle. She looked up at him trustingly. "I bring to you the power of thunder, whose priest I am. I breathe from my lips over you. Listen now, while I call the four winds to help us."

He began to sing. "*Duba ha ti nozhinga she nozhinga* . . . Ye four, come hither and stand, near shall ye stand . . ."

Susette would remember little or nothing of the long ritual which followed, its roots buried deep in the primeval strata of tribal rites which are the heritage of all peoples, a quest for relationship with the basic cosmic forces—earth and wind and fire. She was too young to understand either the words or the symbolic action, but the essence of both instilled itself into her whole being.

She was lifted by the shoulders, faced toward the east, her feet placed on a stone, then turned from left to right, to face the south; turned again toward the west, and toward the north. With each turning a song was sung. She yielded herself willingly, responding as instinctively to the rhythm of motion as to the glow of fire, the thunder-roll of drums, the age-old cadences of her people. Had she resisted, turned ever so little in the wrong way, the watchers symbolizing the four winds would have cried out in alarm. As disastrous to make a false motion as to intone a wrong note or syllable in the songs handed down for generations!

Standing once more on the stone facing the east, she could almost sense in the vigorous music the strengthening power of the winds which the song invoked.

"Turned by the winds goes the one I send yonder;
Yonder goes she who is whirled by the winds;
Goes where the four hills of life and the four winds are standing;
There, in the midst of the winds do I send her,
Into the midst of the winds standing there."

The new moccasins were put on her feet. She was lifted again, set down, and made to take four steps to symbolize entrance into a long and fruitful life. Then her new name, her *nikie,* tribal name, was announced, after which the priest cried aloud, "Ye hills, ye grass, ye trees, ye creeping things both great and small, I bid you hear! This child has thrown away its baby name. Ho!"

It was over. She went out wearing the new moccasins. She was still shy of the crowd. She would always be that. But she was no longer afraid, and even the crowd had lost some of its strangeness. She belonged to it. She was part of it. In her childish way she realized vaguely that she had become part of something much bigger, akin to fire and wind and earth and the whole family of living things.

And she had a new name, one aptly suited to the radiant liveliness which sent her running with open arms to Mary and Nicomi. *Inshtatheamba.* Bright Eyes.

2

The year of her birth had been one of crisis and transition for her people. In 1854 the Omaha tribe maintained their central village near Bellevue, a few miles south of the settlement soon to become the city of Omaha. Called by early explorers the Mahas (for so the name *U-ma-ha*, with its accent on the second syllable, sounded to the white men in the soft-spoken native tongue), they camped and hunted and held undisputed claim over a territory far to the west and north—undisputed that is, save by increasing swarms of white squatters hungry for rich new land.

The "country of the Mahas," as defined by three commissioners appointed by the Secretary of War in 1834, was bounded by the Platte River on the south, the Niobrara on the north, Pawnee country on the west, and the Missouri on the east, and it had been occupied by no other tribe for the last 450 years. Lewis and Clark had found them living in villages on Omaha Creek at the beginning of the nineteenth century, and a hundred years earlier explorers and hunters had spoken of the Mahas located near the Missouri or at the mouth of the Big Sioux.

The history of the Omahas was buried deep in legend. Until a few hundred years ago they were apparently part of a much larger group which included the Poncas, the Osages, the Kansas, and the Quapaws. Their legends recalled an early home far to the east, near a great body of water.

"In the beginning," Shúdenathi, one of the old men, would relate, "the people were in water. They opened their eyes, but they could see nothing. As they came out of the water they beheld the day. They were naked and without shame. But after many days passed they desired covering. They took the fiber of weeds and grass and wove it about their loins for covering."

Migrations westward through hundreds of years were remembered in other legends, the finding and cutting of the Sacred Pole, the discovery of maize, the building of earth lodges.

"It was the women who saved the life of the people. They built the sod houses, they made them by their labor. The work was divided. Men cut the poles and fixed the frame and tied the opening for the smoke hole. The women brought the willows and sod and finished the building."

The name "Omaha" means "upstream, or against the current." Perhaps on the banks of the Mississippi in the sixteenth century the Omahas parted from the Quapaws, whose name means "downstream." It was farther north near the Missouri, at a place where they "could step over the water," that the Poncas separated from them and went southward. Apparently the Omahas lingered long in northern territory covered later by Minnesota, North Dakota, South Dakota, and between the Mississippi and Missouri Rivers. It was sometime and somewhere in this breadth of time and space that they first encountered the white man.

"One day the people discovered white objects on the waters, and they knew not what to make of them. The white objects floated toward the shores. The people were frightened. They abandoned their canoes, ran to the woods, climbed the trees, and watched. The white objects reached the shore, and men were seen getting out of them. For several days they watched; then the strangers entered into the white objects and floated off. But they left one man. Seeing that he was starving, the people approached him, extending a stalk of maize having ears

7

on it, and bade him eat and live. They treated him kindly until his companions returned. Thus the white people became acquainted with the Omaha by means of one whom the latter had befriended. In return they gave the Indians implements of iron. It was in this way that we gained iron among us."

Waxe, the Omahas called the white man because his skin was the color of the *waxoha*, the inner layer of the corn husk. The French traders who came and went without disturbing Indian lands or customs they called *Waxe Ukethin*, Not Strange or Uncommon—unlike the English, who came to possess land, often by force, first with swords, then with guns, and were called *Monhin Tonga*, Big Knives. The French often took Omaha women as their wives according to tribal law, respecting them as equals and honoring their own responsibility as fathers. It was from one of these marriages that Bright Eyes' father, Joseph La Flesche, was born.

Joseph was the son of a wealthy young Frenchman also named Joseph, who had run away from his home in France, gone to Canada, and become a trader for the Hudson Bay Company. He had married an Indian woman named Watunna. Accounts vary as to whether she was an Omaha or a Ponca, but even after their separation the two tribes were closely related. At least the boy Joseph was born among the Omahas. Unhappy with the prolonged absences of her husband, Watunna left him and married a man of the Omaha tribe. The boy's childhood was spent with two aunts, who took him to live for some years among the Sioux, so that Joseph became acquainted with both the Omaha and the Dakota language and cultures. When Joseph Senior returned to trade among the Omahas, the boy went with him and shared his father's life of hunting and trading, learning to speak not only French but several other Indian languages. It was during these years that he met and fell in love with Mary Gale, whose Indian name aptly signified "the one woman."

Mary was the child of Nicomi, an Omaha–Iowa Indian girl, daughter of an Iowa chief whose tribe was camped outside Fort Atkinson on the bluffs above the Missouri. Nicomi's beauty and intelligence captured the heart of the handsome and respected army surgeon, Dr. John Gale, who was assigned to the Fort, and in proper Indian fashion he married her, approaching her nearest relative and giving and receiving presents. She bore him two little girls, Mary and a younger child who died as a baby.

The troops were ordered away in 1827. Knowing Nicomi's passionate loyalty to her people and to her beloved river—her name meant "Voice of the Waters"—John Gale left his wife and children, but he could not forget them. Returning later to take Mary away to be educated, he found Nicomi in mourning for the baby, and he could not deprive her of her only child. However, becoming ill and knowing he would soon die, he made one more attempt. This time he bribed an Indian to bring the child to the landing post just as the boat was about to leave. He reckoned without the proud and strong-willed Nicomi. Warned by the messenger of the plan, she fled to the woods with the child and stayed until the boat had gone. Before John Gale died, however, he gave his friend Peter Sarpy, whose life he had once saved, a trust fund, bidding him care for his wife and child. Honoring the commitment, Sarpy built a little house for them at his own rich trading post at Bellevue, fell captive himself to Nicomi's charms, and, after the four-year interval prescribed by Indian custom, married her.

Beautiful, imperious, high-spirited, she was no mean match for the rich and despotic Sarpy, acknowledged ruler of the area through his post with the great American Fur Company. She braved his fiery tongue more than once. When he upbraided her for showing generosity to her people at the post's expense, she turned on him furiously, snatched up a bolt of his fine cloth, worth perhaps twenty dollars a yard, and, marching to the river, flung it into the water.

"Say any more," she challenged, "and I'll do the same to everything in your precious trading post!" She always used the Omaha language, refusing to speak a word of English.

Nor would she suffer the slightest hint of feminine rivalry. Once when Sarpy planned to impress a visiting female by a ride in his carriage and ordered his spirited mare Starlight harnessed to the rig, Nicomi appeared, brandished a knife, and ordered the groom and the whole equipage back into the stables. Meekly the groom obeyed mistress instead of master. She was in fact as well as in name the "first lady" of what was to become Sarpy County.

But she was as faithful in service to her husband as to her own people. Once, it was told, she carried him, ill with mountain fever, many miles through the wilderness to find medical aid. She even yielded to his insistence that she go to St. Louis with him and live as the mistress of his fine city house—but only after he promised that she could return to visit her people each year. A few months of city life and white culture were all she could tolerate. Even the proximity of Mary, who was there in school, could not assuage her homesickness. She went back to Bellevue and remained. Many years later, however, when Sarpy sent for her in his last illness, she went to him, nursed him, comforted him until his death in 1865.

Such was "the beautiful Omaha, Voice of the Waters," who bore and reared the wife of Joseph La Flesche and bequeathed to their daughter Bright Eyes something of her beauty, pride, strong will, and passionate loyalty to her people.

3

Young Joseph was an employee of Peter Sarpy. His knowledge of several Indian languages made him invaluable as an interpreter. Occasionally he returned from trips into the wilderness to the Bellevue trading post. It was there that he saw Mary Gale after her return from school in St. Louis and fell in love with her. Was it an incident that happened on one of these visits which softened her heart toward Joseph? At least she remembered to tell it to her oldest daughter long afterward.

At that time the Omahas were living in mud lodges scattered along the river bank between Bellevue and the site of their ancient Big Village, in the vicinity of the future town of Homer. An Omaha Indian, returning to a straw hut which he had built, found a Frenchman taking refuge there and, out of some mistaken idea of revenge, killed him, or so he thought. He went and told his brother, Waoga, who went with him to the hut. They found the Frenchman still alive, though mortally wounded, and out of pity Waoga put an end to his suffering. Chief Big Elk, always desirous of peace with the white men, realized that the offenders must be punished or vengeance might fall on the whole tribe. Joseph and his father were commissioned to accompany the prisoners, with Big Elk and the

Agent, to St. Louis (called by the Omahas "Town of the Red-hair"). With them were to go five Spanish boys who had been taken captive by a band of Pawnees along with the horses they were herding far to the west. The Omaha Agent had rescued them and brought them to Bellevue. The two youngest, only about eight and ten years old, had aroused all the mother instincts of the tender-hearted Mary.

"Please—take care of them," she begged young Joseph. "They're so frightened! Please see that they are delivered to their own people."

Joseph fervently promised to guard them with his life.

It was a beautiful day in early spring when Mary stood on the balcony of the two-story house close to the river and saw the two Indian prisoners being led in chains to the dock, where a raft built across two great log boats was moored. As she watched, one of the captives stopped, looked up at the sky and began to sing:

> "Un winwata btha dan,
> Gunata ha hata dan? . . .
> Where can I go
> That I might live forever?
> The old fathers have gone to the spirit-land,
> Where can I go
> That we might live together?"

It was the Indian death song. The haunting, mournful melody brought tears to her eyes. When the raft started on its long treacherous journey down the river, she was filled with confused emotion—pity for the captives, concern for the little Spaniards, and, perhaps, a sudden knowledge of her love for the stalwart and gallant young Joseph La Flesche.

The death song was prophetic. Close to St. Louis, the boat capsized in a storm. Big Elk, the Agent, and some others swam to safety. Young Joseph ordered the Spanish boys to cling to the boat, but the three older ones struck out for the shore and sank. The two little ones obeyed and were saved. The Indian captive considered most guilty, when he saw the others jump, managed to break his handcuffs. Taking his free hands, he threw the

11

heavy log chain binding his feet over his shoulders and prepared to jump.

"The iron will make you sink," shouted Joseph, but the captive jumped. As he was sinking Joseph grasped him by the hair and pulled him back to the raft. But perhaps the man remembered his death song. He gave a mighty jump and sank. Joseph and his father, with the two Spanish boys, drifted safely to land. A passing steamer, bound for the Yellowstone, threw them a ham, a box of crackers, and some blankets. Without them the party could never have reached St. Louis, for there were no settlements between that city and Bellevue.

In St. Louis the other prisoner, Waoga, was put under guard, to be fed only bread and water. Joseph managed to flout the order. Cutting open a loaf of bread and hollowing it, he would put in a sizable piece of cooked meat and take it to the prisoner. Waoga was finally released and, with the two Josephs, walked back to Bellevue, a distance of nearly two hundred miles. At least Joseph had kept his promise to Mary. The two youngest boys had been safely delivered to friends and restored to their people.

From that time on Joseph spent less time trading and trapping with his father and more with his friends the Omahas. "*Folie de jeunesse!*" chided Joseph Senior, half vexed, half amused. "Dallying with those pretty Omaha maids, I'll wager!" But Joseph was not dallying. He had eyes for only one pretty maid, Mary. His interest in the Omahas was rooted in a deep concern for their future and a growing conviction that someone must try to save them from annihilation. On the one hand they were being constantly harassed by raiding parties from the Sioux who invaded their hunting territory. More deadly far than this threat was the relentless westward thrust of the white man. Big Elk the First, the noble head chief of the Omahas, descendant of the mighty and arrogant Blackbird, had comprehended the danger well. After returning from Washington, where in the treaty of 1836 the Omahas had made large concessions of lands, the chief had assembled the tribal council and delivered a tragic prophecy.

"My chiefs, braves, and young men, I have just returned from a visit to a far-off country and have seen many strange things. I bring to you news which it saddens my heart to think of. There is a coming flood which will soon reach us, and I advise you to prepare for it. Soon the animals which Wakonda has given us for sustenance will disappear beneath this flood to return no more, and it will be very hard for you. Look at me; you see I am advanced in age, I am near the grave. I can no longer think for you and lead you as in my younger days. You must think for yourselves what will be best for your welfare. I tell you this that you may be prepared for the coming change. You may not know my meaning. Many of you are old, as I am, and by the time the change comes we may be lying peacefully in our graves; but these young men will remain to suffer. Speak kindly to one another. Do what you can to help each other, even in the troubles with the coming tide. Now, my people, this is all I have to say. Bear these words in mind, and when the time comes think of what I have said."

Joseph, called in Omaha Inshtámaza, Iron Eye, sat at the feet of Big Elk, absorbing his wisdom. He visited the lodges of other chiefs, listening to their conflicting reactions as the flood predicted by the old chief roared louder and louder. There was no escaping it. The tribe must ride on its crest or vanish in its swelling torrent. The white men were coming with their new ways, their deadly weapons, their thirst for land, their inexorable will for conquest. Indeed, they were already here. Indians must change and learn the new ways rather than fight against them. Yet except for Big Elk the chiefs seemed undecided, helpless. They listened to Big Elk now, with the respect due their head chief, third of his name, leader of the powerful Wezshinshte Clan, keepers of the Tent of War, but when he was gone—what? Big Elk's son Cross Elk was a mere child and sickly. Who?

The answer came slowly to Joseph but with a terrible certainty. It meant irrevocable choice. He was the son of a wealthy Frenchman. Relinquish this half of his heritage? And suppose the other half rejected him? An Indian tribe was a closed society. Could a half-breed rise to leadership? Still more disturbing, what about Mary? Would John Gale's daughter, who had gone to school in St. Louis, lived in the luxurious houses of Peter Sarpy, consent to share life in an earth lodge?

Joseph made his decision before asking her. Looking into her great dark eyes, waiting for her answer, he had never been so conscious of her lovely fragility, her regal beauty. She could have graced the grandest château in France with dignity and poise. "The beautiful Omaha"? It was daughter, not mother, who should wear the title! Now, more than ever, in this moment when he was likely to lose her, she became "the one woman."

There was nothing fragile about the firm lips which framed her answer.

"*Dho!*" She spoke in Omaha, scorning the French she had learned in St. Louis. "It is what you—what we—must do."

His relief was explosive. "You mean—you *will*—you don't *mind?*"

"Of course. How could you doubt me? I am an Indian, not a Frenchwoman."

They were married in 1843, in Mary's seventeenth year, and Joseph cast his lot irrevocably with the Omahas. Immediately he began to observe the necessary ceremonies, the accumulation of honors which must precede an election to chieftainship. Though the office was partly hereditary, it was possible for a man to attain it through other designated means. Good fortune was with Joseph. He had won the favor of Big Elk. Two years after his marriage the great chief "pipe-danced" Mary, a formal ceremony which included dancing, visiting, feasting, the giving of valuable presents. Then for Joseph himself Big Elk performed the Calumet Dance, or adoption ceremony.

"I wish to dance for Inshtámaza," he informed the other chiefs gathered for the preliminary feast. "See for me if he is the proper one."

The chiefs gave their approval. A messenger was sent to Joseph's lodge with a buffalo bladder containing tobacco. Joseph received it with all the prescribed formalities. Then came four days of elaborate ceremonies, featuring dancers who imitated the wild swooping grace of the war eagle to the rhythm of gourd rattles and waving calumets. Afterward Big Elk proclaimed by public crier that Inshtámaza, Iron Eye, was his "oldest son," taking precedence over all others.

Joseph served the tribe in myriad capacities: interpreter,

14

soldier, hunter, trader. Like Big Elk, he was deeply troubled. The Omahas seemed beset with enemies—the encroaching white settlers, the warlike Sioux (who had been displaced from their previous lands), disease, starvation. The semi-annual hunts which provided food, clothing, and shelter were proving less and less productive. Fur-bearing animals which could be traded for goods were becoming increasingly scarce.

"The Omahas are a poor dispirited people," reported an Indian agent in the decade of the forties, "nearly starving and beset by enemies and diseases."

For the giving of the white man had been as destructive to the ancient culture as his taking. With iron, beads, calico, guns, and sturdy half-breed children he had brought also the decadence of drunkenness, the ravages of disease. The tribe, which had numbered nearly three thousand at the end of the eighteenth century, had been reduced by smallpox to fifteen hundred at the beginning of the nineteenth and numbered only about a thousand at mid-century.

Added to these problems was that of tribal disorganization. "Chiefs" were being created at the whim of government agents or traders merely by presenting a cheap medal and a scrap of paper to men who could be used for their purposes. These "paper chiefs," as the Indians called them, often brash young braves who knew nothing of the age-old process of discipline and ceremony by which chieftainship was attained, claimed equal authority and rank with the genuine chiefs.

"I feel like an old scabby buffalo," complained Big Elk bitterly, "separated from his own band on the prairie!"

And even the prairie was being taken away. In the centuries since the coming of the white man there had been many relinquishments of land, some of them by treaty. At Prairie du Chien in 1830 the Omahas had ceded to the United States claim to all lands in the future state of Iowa. In 1836 at Bellevue were added all lands lying between the state of Missouri and the Missouri River. Now they were being asked, though *asked* was hardly the' word, to sell most of their remaining land that it might be included in the huge new Nebraska Territory.

The whole idea was as incomprehensible to an Indian as the name "Indian" itself. *Buy* or *sell* land? It was an act unheard of.

15

Land was like water and wind, "what could not be sold." Not like horses, clothing, lodges, and such, which were personal property and could be, not sold, but given away. Certainly a tribe claimed a defined territory as its own, to occupy, to cultivate, to hunt in and fish. And of course each head of a household held a possessory right to the tract his family cultivated, and he could cultivate any unoccupied land and add it to his own. It was his to use as long as he cultivated it. But to *sell* it! However, if the white man said so, he must do it. He would consent . . . as a white man would "consent" to hand his wallet to a robber who demanded his money or his life.

Late in 1853 Major·James M. Gatewood was appointed Agent to the tribes near Bellevue with instructions to arrive at an understanding with the Omahas on terms for a treaty. The tribe should appoint a delegation with full power to act "as if the whole nation were present." The delegation was to go to Washington to sign a treaty. All would be for the good of the tribe. Their Great Father in Washington would see to that. They would be given land to their liking and full protection on it. They would receive large payments. Details were outlined, but the delegation was to have power to "ratify, confirm, to slightly modify, alter or amend any of the stipulations."

Big Elk was not happy. He had been to Washington before. He shook his massive head with its crown of short thick black hair and fingered the medal given him by the Great Father and worn about his neck—a true chief's medal earned by wise and just service to his people. This was not the proper way to decide important issues, by a select few, but by all the Council, head men, warriors, and braves reaching a consensus together. And he had had experience with the white men's promises of payments.

Leaving for the winter hunt, Joseph was concerned over the change in Big Elk. His heavy-lidded eyes, usually eagle sharp, seemed focused on something far away, his ears attuned to inaudible sounds. So worried was Joseph that he could not share the excitement of five-year-old Louis, reluctantly permitted by Mary to join his father for the first time in the winter hunt.

The chief went out one afternoon and killed a deer, not with a gun but with a tomahawk, as if he were trying to recapture lost realities. A few hours later he was stricken with fever. He called Joseph to his side. "My son—give me some medicine!" Immediately Joseph dispatched a runner to Bellevue, but it was a three days' journey, and long before the messenger could return with medicine or a doctor Joseph knew it was too late. He watched over the old chief day and night, but there was little he could do.

"My son—" At the end Big Elk was so weak he could hardly speak. "I give you—all my papers—from Washington—make you—head chief—you occupy—my place. When your—brother Cross Elk is of age—do with him as is best. I leave him—in your charge." Louis had crept into the tipi. The chief recognized him, lifted his hand, and smiled. "My—grandson—" They were his last words. He was taken to the banks of the Missouri and buried in the region known to white men as the Blackbird Hills. Not to the Omahas. For them it would long be called *Onpontonga Xaithon*, "Where Big Elk Is Buried."

4

Joseph mourned Big Elk as he would never mourn his own father. But there was no time for brooding. He must try to fill the chief's moccasins and keep his people from annihilation in the coming flood.

The following year he went with a group of chiefs and other leading men to Washington, a long tedious journey down the Missouri and up the Ohio by boat, over the Allegheny mountains by slow stages and on by railroad to the capital. There the Treaty of 1854 was executed on April 17th. There were seven signers. The first was Logan Fontenelle, who, like Joseph, was half French, half Indian, and one of Sarpy's traders. A grandson of Big Elk the First, the son of one of his daughters, Logan Fontenelle occupied a chief's position. His facility with English as well as with French and Omaha gave him prime influence and prominence, although Louis Sansouci was the official interpreter. Joseph's name came second. Others were Standing

Hawk, Little Chief, Village Maker, Noise, and Yellow Smoke.

But it was Joseph who argued with the officials against payment being made in goods, demanding that the tribe receive money for their land, for with money the people could buy what they needed, tools, food, clothing. Goods they knew well—clothes they did not need or want, food unsuited to their taste and often arriving spoiled, tools they could not use. The silver dime he used to illustrate his argument was to become a cherished symbol of tribal victory—symbol also of the enmity of some trading factions which would have made outrageous profits had payment been made in goods.

The tribe ceded to the United States their vast hunting grounds, keeping for their own use a tract of 300,000 acres in the far northeast bordering the Missouri River. They had not wanted to move so far north, fearing the Sioux, but they were promised protection. Moneys for the land ceded were to be held by the government, payments to extend through forty years. All claims for money under preceding treaties were released, except for one long-unpaid balance of $25,000, which would come "later." It was this sum which Joseph insisted must be paid in cash instead of goods.

It took months for the treaty to be ratified, years for the money to be paid. It was a time of trouble. Uncertainty kept the tribe from planting crops on the old lands because they expected to be moved before harvest. Their fear of moving so far north became terror when on their summer hunt into the area in 1855 Logan Fontenelle was attacked by Sioux, killed, and scalped. So this was the promised protection! They retreated in panic without an adequate winter's supply of meat. Months of hunger and destitution followed. The annuities did not come. Many would have starved had Joseph not taken his own savings, purchased beef and other supplies, and shared them with his neighbors. Though there was always enough for his family, he seldom satisfied his own hunger, preferring to give his share to others.

"It is our way," he told Reverend William Hamilton, the Presbyterian missionary, when the latter remonstrated. "As long as one Indian has food, none of his tribe goes hungry."

"I know." Father Hamilton, as he was always called, had

spent many years among the Iowas before crossing the river to take charge of the Mission at Bellevue and was almost as familiar with Indian culture as with his own. He could converse fluently with Joseph in the Iowa language, and the latter often served as his interpreter into Omaha.

Management of the school which the government promised to provide on the new reservation was delegated to the Presbyterian Board of Foreign Missions. Hamilton set about the task of building immediately. With Joseph he explored the new area for a desirable site and chose a high bluff overlooking the river not far north of Blackbird Hills. The Council of Chiefs approved the choice. A man of swift action, Hamilton soon had a garden planted, plans for a building drawn, lumber secured, wagons and teams and laborers hired, and by the time the tribe was moved to its new location in 1856 the building was under construction.

Not without opposition! Though the Great Father in Washington and his lieutenant, George Manypenny, Commissioner of Indian Affairs, were doubtless diligent (if remote), guardians of the treaty, their henchmen in the field were far less scrupulous. The newly appointed agent had set his sights on the same parcel of land for the Agency, his intent, so Hamilton deduced, to secure a foothold for speculation when it should be sold. Powerful interests were working to have the Omahas placed with the Poncas, ostensibly for the good of both tribes, in reality to get possession of this extra 300,000 acres of their land for a pittance. Hamilton wrote urgently to Walter Lowrie, the secretary of his board in Philadelphia.

"When it is once thought advisable to purchase them out, once the department is persuaded to move in the matter, the next step will be to persuade the Indians to consent. That's not hard if they make a chief or two. All that's necessary is to appoint some political favorite as Agent, and for a consideration he takes all the trouble and responsibility. The interpreter advises it, the chiefs are anxious for it. Government thinks it well to grant the request. The tribe knows little about it until they find they are without a home. Our building there may prevent their plans."

"If they sell the land," Joseph told Hamilton hotly, "it will be over my dead body. Yet," he added helplessly, "the chiefs can be easily persuaded."

The walls of the Mission continued to rise, and the chiefs remained surprisingly firm in their decision. "It will be a great disappointment to the Company " men in Council Bluffs were reported as saying. "The missionaries are always thrusting themselves into these places, and they are pretty hard to get out."

Thanks to counterinfluences—to Hamilton; to Lowrie, who had the ear of Colonel Manypenny; certainly to Joseph La Flesche, whose honesty was unimpeachable—the crisis passed. Joseph was recognized as a chief by the Bureau in Washington. The Omahas, though still half starving through delay of their annuity payment, were permitted to remain on the small section of land which had been allocated to them, in the usual verbiage of Indian treaties, "as long as the grass shall grow and the waters flow."

Meanwhile Joseph worked tirelessly to bring Big Elk's hopes to fruition. He had long conversations with Father Hamilton. He gathered about him active young members of the tribe and imbued them with progressive spirit.

"We must not go on in the old ways." It was the soul of Big Elk which looked out of his brilliant dark eyes, but the words were Joseph's. He spoke not of a vague coming flood but of crops to be grown, houses to be built, children who must be sent to school, the sawmill and blacksmith shop the government had promised to build, a police force which must be organized. The group he gathered about him was soon dubbed "the Young Men's Party."

The same group joined him on the new reservation when he built an earth lodge for his family, forty feet in diameter, about a mile south of where the Mission was being constructed on the bluffs above the Missouri. But most of the older conservative members of the tribe settled in what was called Big Village, about three miles away, on Blackbird Creek. The separation involved more than distance. They were as far apart as two ways of life, one looking toward the past, the other toward the future.

It was sometime during this period that Joseph was formally installed as one of the two *níkagahi úzhu*, head chiefs, to serve jointly with Standing Hawk, who had been head chief with Big Elk. The ceremony was as old as the Sacred Pole and the dawn of tribal organization. It was performed in summer, when the tribe was on the hunt and the tent of each clan was in its proper place in the *huthuga*, circle. A large tent was erected in the middle, and the two sacred tribal pipes, feared by all but their keepers and the chiefs, were carried four times around the circle, stopping on the last round at Joseph's tent.

"Are you willing to become a chief?"

"I am willing."

In token of his agreement Joseph put the pipestem to his lips, its mouthpiece of bison hide signifying Earth, from which man came and at whose breast he sucks. He was led to the tent where the chiefs were assembled. The people thronged outside but at a distance, so great was their fear of the sacred pipes. Even the horses were sent to the rear of the encampment.

Inside the tent the two pipes were set in their place of honor, the one ornamented with seven woodpecker heads, one for each of the seven chiefs, the other with but one woodpecker head representing the chiefs' unity of authority. Though their keeping belonged to the Inkethabe Clan, whose dwelling was on the Earth side of the circle, the office of filling them belonged to the Inshtathunda Clan, representing the sky half. Earth and sky, male and female, the dual nature of the universe was thus portrayed in the *huthuga*, the human circle.

It was the duty of Monhinsi, an old man, to fill them. Only he knew the ritual, given him by his father. It was a long recitation, and his voice quavered with weariness as he finished. He lifted the sacred objects to fill them, and as he did so his hands trembled. *One of the pipes fell to the ground!*

A gasp of horror, like a breath of winter wind, swept the circle of chiefs and braves. It was more than an ill omen. It was an act of desecration, almost as grave as dishonor to the Sacred Pole. All looked apprehensively at Monhinsi, half expecting him to be struck down on the spot. The ceremony was at an end. Law forbade that after such a violation it should continue. No one was surprised when in the fall of that same year Monhinsi died.

It was the last time the ancient ritual was ever repeated, for he had not imparted it to his son.

Though not properly initiated, Joseph took his place as one of the two head chiefs. But, like all men who try to change the inbred ways of centuries, he soon made enemies. And they never forgot that in his moment of ascending triumph one of the pipes had fallen.

Two

1

The new baby was a red wizened thing, with a head like a big dried chokecherry. As it lay on the cradle board, its shock of hair a black smutch against the soft deerskin pad, Bright Eyes regarded it with mingled curiosity and distaste. Her brother, she was told. But Louis was her brother. She wanted no other. Its name was Francis, like her *winegi*, uncle, who lived a long way off with the Poncas, and whose other name was White Swan. And how could this be her brother when it didn't belong to Mother, like herself and Louis, but to Tainne, whom she had been taught to call Other Mother? It was confusing and would remain so for some years, until she was old enough to understand that Father, after the custom of the Omahas, had more than one wife.

There were things happening that year of 1857 more exciting than the birth of the head chief's manchild. Joseph was building a house. Not a tipi, not a lodge, a *house*, square, made of logs cut into planks, with doors and windows and floors, the kind white men lived in. The government had not yet supplied the promised sawmill, but Father Hamilton had bought one and set it up on the bluffs where the Mission was being built. Members of the Young Men's Party cut the logs and hauled them to the mill, which Joseph operated with his own oxen, paying for the use of the mill in cash. Then he hired white carpenters to build his house, after which they were to supervise the building of other houses by the men of his village.

People swarmed from all over the reservation to watch the work. They came from Big Village, from the Sacred Tents, from the settlement ten miles away at the southern end called the Wood-eaters' Village, after an insect which lived under the bark of trees in their vicinity. They came to stare, to admire, to deride, to marvel, to wag their heads in scorn.

"Like the crowd that watched Noah build the ark," joked Father Hamilton to Charles Sturges, the new principal at the Mission School.

"What are you trying to do?" taunted one of the scoffers. "Make believe you're white men?"

The idea spread, and all over the reservation the new settlement came to be known as the "Village of Make-Believe White Men."

Joseph was planning more than houses. He and his young men laid out roads, to the new Agency close by, to the Mission, to the steamboat landing, and one through the center of their village. He fenced a tract of 100 acres in the bottom lands and furnished the oxen to plow it, dividing it into separate fields so each man could have a tract of his own. Here the first wheat on the reservation was planted. Soon large crops of corn and sorghum were being harvested, and in the winter men would haul their produce on the ice to Sioux City, a newly formed settlement on the Iowa side of the river to the north. Another of his projects was even more ambitious. The idea had been sparked in his mind many years ago. So vivid was his memory of a certain incident that it might have happened only yesterday.

It was back in the 1830s, when he was about seventeen, acting as clerk for his father. Late one afternoon he was alone in the trading hut, where Omaha came to exchange their pelts for the white man's goods—cloth, beads, guns, tools, and especially liquor. A drunken quarrel started, during which another man came in with his little son, and, fearing to become involved, retreated into a corner. One of his quarreling tribesmen,

24

intoxicated to belligerence, drew his knife, rushed at him, and buried it in his throat, then, suddenly sobered, burst into horrified cries of remorse. Screaming, the boy ran out to spread the news of his father's murder. Joseph found himself alone with the murderer.

"You'd better stay here," he warned. "It's the only place you can be safe."

But in his agony of guilt the man rushed out of the hut and had gone but a few steps when an arrow struck him down.

Joseph's horror turned to swift realization. Of all the evils which the white man brought the red man, *pede-ni*, fire water, was the most deadly. Whites had partially inured themselves to the effects of liquor through the centuries, but the Indian had never known intoxicating drink. It loosed his restraints, set him on fire with thirst. Being a trader, Joseph well knew the power of the liquor interests. Far cheaper than goods in barter, whiskey was the trader's most profitable unit of exchange. All the big companies exploited it. That afternoon in the hut Joseph made a vow. If he ever rose to power in the tribe, he would use his authority to break the habit of drinking. Now, twenty years later, the time had come.

In 1856 he organized a tribal police force. With the consent of the Council he took about $1,000 from tribal funds for the pay and equipment of thirty selected men. He paid for their uniforms himself, and Mary made them out of green broadcloth, trimmed with red facings. They were as smartly appareled as the Great Father's soldiers and fully as dedicated. A tribal law was passed prohibiting drinking under penalty of a severe whipping. Even the Omaha proven drunk when away from the reservation was not exempt, nor were the noblest braves or Joseph's closest friends.

Two Crows was both. Not only was he a respected chief, but Joseph and he were like brothers. One day Two Crows was missing. Joseph feared that he might have met with an accident and sent out scouting parties into the surrounding country to find him, but without success. After four days a runner came with a message. Two Crows had returned. Much relieved, Joseph looked out of his lodge and saw his friend coming slowly toward him.

"*Ah ho!*" he shouted in greeting. "*Ah hó kagay,* hello friend!"

Two Crows made no reply but stalked into the lodge with head hanging. "Where have you been?" asked Joseph.

"Drunk," replied Two Crows. "Four days drunk, alone in the hills."

Joseph stared at him aghast. What to do? He would gladly have borne the penalty himself, but that would have defeated his purpose. Friendship must not interfere with duty.

"You know the penalty?" he asked sadly.

"I know," replied Two Crows steadily.

Chief Iron Eye ordered his friend flogged. A big member of the police force took the rawhide whip and approached the culprit with misgivings. Punish this respected brave, this best friend of the head chief? No, he could not! But Two Crows faced him with head held high, eyes arrow-sharp and lips clamped in a down-curve like a taut bow. "Do your duty," he ordered calmly. "The law was made for *all* men. I broke it and must take my punishment. And dare not spare your blows."

Two Crows was flogged—hard. He made not a murmur, though the rawhide made great welts and bloody gashes on his back. After the whipping he went silently to his lodge. His action not only enhanced his own reputation and influence in the tribe but strengthened the chief in his efforts to eradicate the demoralizing habit. Under the leadership of Chief Iron Eye the Omahas remained a sober people for many years. His police force, first among Indians, became a model copied by agents on most other reservations.

2

The new house was completed in the "Moon When the Deer Shed Their Antlers," November. Already winter was sounding stern warnings, the wail of the north wind bringing hints of the dead, desperate days ahead. The storm called "the hiding of the moon" which preceded the new moon's appearance had brought blinding fits of snow, and, when the thin sickle appeared, its horns were turned upward, a sure sign of bitter weather ahead.

"*Ou-daa,* good!" said Joseph. "A hard winter should teach

the tribe a lesson. When the lodges are turned into white mounds and the snow mounts to the poles of the tipis, they will see our high stout walls and resolve to build themselves just such a house."

But, as with Noah and his ark, there were scoffers, some in his own household. One was the Oldest Grandmother, Memetage, Nicomi's half-sister, who somehow—probably through missionary influence—had acquired the alternate name of Madeline Wolf.

"*Pe-áh-zhi*, it is bad! Ugly! All straight lines going this way, that way, like sharp arrows! Has not Wakonda made all things round—sky, moon, sun, trees, whirling wind, circle of the seasons? Yes, even the birds he taught to make their nests round, not square! And did he not give us the sacred hoop in which we should set our tipis and lodges, round also like a nest, and in which we should move always in a circle, like the sun, from east to west? *Pe-áh-zhi*, not good this square thing of wood. I will have none of it."

She meant it. Bright Eyes watched, entranced, while Oldest Grandmother, with Mother and Nicomi helping, made herself an earth lodge, like the one the family lived in now, only much smaller, after the manner of the women of her people for centuries. First they set up two circles of vertical poles, one inside the other, crotched to hold the roof beams, which were made out of long slender tapering willow stocks stripped of their bark and tied at their large ends with cords. At the small end they were cut to form a round opening for the smoke. A wall was made with upright slabs of wood all around the outer posts. Outside the woodwork of the walls and roof, branches of willow were laid crosswise and bound tightly to each slab and pole. Bright Eyes helped Nicomi and the Oldest Grandmother gather grass to cover the rafters at least a foot thick. Then over the grass was put a heavy coating of sod, cut to lap like shingles, and over the whole structure earth was piled—hundreds of baskets full, it seemed—over a foot deep. A passageway was made with a curtain of skins hung at its inner and outer entrances.

"*Ou-daa!*" pronounced Oldest Grandmother. "It should last twenty winters. Now for the floor."

Bright Eyes kept watching, speechless. A floor made of dirt so hard to make! It took longer than the wooden ones in the new house. Oldest Grandmother was fussy. Because Mother and Nicomi had lived in white men's houses, she thought they could not make a proper floor, and she insisted on doing it herself. First she removed all the loose earth from the inside and tamped every inch with a big pestle. Then she flooded it with water. Over this she spread dried grass which she set on fire. Then she tamped again. Not once she did all this, but three times. When she had finished, it was hard and level, smooth as wood planks and easy to sweep. The hole in the middle for the fire was just deep enough so the smoke went straight up through the opening. And when thick winter hides, dried with the hair on, were piled between the inner posts for couches and stacked with pillows made from *ibehin*, the soft thin skin of deer killed when the spring grass was about three inches high, and stuffed with goose feathers, it was far cosier and more homelike than the new big house.

In fact, Bright Eyes did not like the house at all. It was too big, too tall, too square, too hard, too cold, too bare, too everything that the familiar lodge was not. There were two stories, for it was intended not only for a family home but for a trading post and stopping place for travelers. It was frightening to think of climbing the long wooden hill to get to one's sleeping mat. She was relieved when Father decided to wait until spring to move into the new house. Winters were cold, and the new iron fire-box had not arrived.

Never again would a winter bring such happiness. Life was simple and had no sharp edges. It moved in circles, like the round walls of the lodge and the hollow in its center, like days and nights. She liked nights best. There were usually guests for the evening meal, and the smells of boiling corn and beans and meat and baking bread, mingling with the rich aromas of woodsmoke and kinnikinnick, made one's mouth water along with one's eyes. There were few rules for a child to remember. You must never run around the fireplace, which was sacred, or walk between the fire and a guest. You must not make noises or grimaces when you ate. You should sit sidewise, with legs drawn round closely to the right, and when you rose you should spring up lightly, using only one hand to help.

It was hard keeping awake after the meal, but Bright Eyes tried, especially when the old men started to tell stories about Beginnings. Yellow Smoke's were the best. When he started talking, she propped her eyes open with her fingers. The firelight shone on his huge dark eyes and made shadow pools under his high cheekbones as he told about the Finding of the Sacred Pole or the Giving of the Peace Pipes or the Finding of the Maize or the Meeting with the First Horses.

"It happened that a man in his wanderings discovered some animals. At first he thought they were elk . . ."

When there were no guests, Grandmother told stories as they sat about the fire. But Bright Eyes liked best the few minutes after bedtime when she lay on her thick buffalo robe, another robe pulled over her feet toasted by the warmth of the fire. Her place was always beside Grandmother at the back of the lodge, just as Mother's and Father's was on the right side of the fireplace and Tainne's and the new brother's on the left. *Chunka*, make-believe stories, could be told only in winter and at night, because in summer snakes were supposed to come around to listen.

"Tell me a story," she would whisper. "Tell me the one about how the turkeys got red eyes!"

"Don't bother Grandmother," Mother would murmur. "Go to sleep, *Wizhungeha*."

But Grandmother was never bothered. "An old woman was living all alone with her grandson, Rabbit, and one day the old woman said to him . . ."

Tingling with delight, the child would snuggle closer to the enthralling whispers.

Life would have been perfect that winter but for one heart-breaking loss. Louis was away from home. The new boarding school had opened at the Mission. At Joseph's urging many families in the village had sent their children. Others came from Henry Fontenelle's village ten miles to the south. None were sent from Big Village, whose leaders gave but grudging acceptance of the missionaries. Some, like White Cow, were actively belligerent.

"Make little Waxes out of our children, would they? We want none of this House of Teaching run by the white chests." The missionaries were often called "white chests" because of their stiff white shirtfronts.

Even Yellow Smoke, who lived at the place of the Sacred Tents, was doubtful, if more tolerant. "Better to have the Mission on that fine high place of land than the Agency that tried so hard to get it! At least the Mission Waxes are our friends. Not like the government which makes chiefs they can get to betray us. Still—I will not send my children—yet."

Joseph was vehement in his support of the school. The flood was coming, and the tribe must flow with it or be drowned. He even became a pupil himself, going for an hour each day to study English with Dr. Sturges. One day he took Bright Eyes with him.

They climbed a big hill high above the river valley. On the hill was a huge square mountain of stone with great staring eyes all over its front. She knew what they were—windows. There were some in the new house, but not big like these or so many. She clutched Father's hand tightly and hid her face in his robe.

"Come, little one. There's nothing to be afraid of. See, here's Louis!"

She opened her eyes wide, heart pounding, then shrank back in horror. This wasn't *Witinu*, Older Brother, this strange figure with hair cut short, even his scalp lock gone, and dressed in Waxe coat and pants! But he ran to her, picked her up in his arms, and lifted her high, crying the familiar exultant "*Choo-ie!*"

A smiling woman with a pale face came toward her, began jabbering in a strange tongue. Then a big girl came and took her hand.

"She says you must be Susette. Her name is Mrs. Sturges. I am Mary Fontenelle, one of the pupils. I'm ten years old. Come, I'll show you over the school while your father has his lesson."

Taking the child firmly by the hand, she led her on a tour of the building. "See, here on the first floor is the schoolroom. We sit there at those desks and learn our lessons. In the middle is the dining room. We sit at those three long tables and eat. Here on the other side is the chapel. We go here every morning and on Sundays to hear stories from the white chests' holy book.

Now we'll go upstairs . . . This is where the principal and teachers all live, except this room, which we girls use for a playroom. Now we'll go up some more stairs. . . . On this third floor is the boys' sleeping room. They call it a dormitory. I can't show you that, but here is our girls' dormitory. See all the beds? There are twelve of us girls now. One of them, Mary Ellen, is only four, just about your age. You'll be here soon . . ." Bright Eyes felt the hand holding hers tighten, and she was dragged swiftly past another long wooden hill. "We won't go up there. That's the attic. The boys all say there are ghosts up there, or maybe it's where the Devil lives that the white chests talk so much about. Ask Louis to tell you about the big black hole at the head of the stairs . . ."

It seemed an eternity before Father came and they were trudging the mile-long road toward home. Her small head whirled with bewildering, frightening shapes, all drawn in straight lines, squares, and jagged angles—walls, desks, tables, chairs, beds, staring eyes of windows, a great square moutain of stone. And *three* long terrifying wooden hills to climb! But even more alarming than the shapes were words still dinning in her ears like drum beats. *"You'll be here soon. . . . You'll be here soon. . . ."*

"Eh bien, you saw the House of Teaching, little one. How did you like it?"

Even at four she was not one to evade issues. "Will—will I have to go there?"

"Dho." Father's hand clasping hers was warm and firm. "We must learn all that the missionaries can teach us, little one. Our daughters must learn as well as our sons. You will be able to speak their language, to understand even when they talk with forked tongues, saying one thing and meaning another. I am too old to learn. You must learn about Wakonda from their lips, for perhaps they know him better than we do. I am not sure. Sometimes I wonder. Yes, you must go to the school."

"When?" she demanded. "How soon?"

His clasp tightened. "Ho! Not for a long time yet. The missionaries would have you go now, but *non*, I do not agree. A little girl child should be with her mother, not with strangers. Besides, who would help Other Mother take care of little

31

brother? You are almost old enough now to have his cradle board tied to your back!"

She breathed a long sigh of relief. Back at the village she ran straight to the lodge, refusing even to glance at the big square house into which they were soon to move. All was as it should be—round walls, round glowing fireplace, round kettle in which Mother was mixing roasted corn with dried pumpkin and strips of jerked buffalo meat. Nothing had changed—and everything. For life was not longer simple and of one piece. Child though she was, she knew now that there was not one world, but two. And she must live in both of them.

3

Bright Eyes was five winters old when she went on her first hunt.

Joseph was trying to discourage the annual tribal hunt, as ancient as the Sacred Tribal Pipes and the Council of Seven. Well did he know what damage such a position might cause to his prestige, for the whole tribal structure—its economy, its political and social organization, its religous ritual—was involved in this annual activity. From time immemorial the buffalo had been synonymous with survival. It was the sacred gift of Wakonda to his people. Even its emergence from the womb of Mother Earth was buried deep in legend.

"The buffalo was underground. A young bull browsing about found his way to the surface of the earth. The herd followed him. As they went they came to a river. The water looked shallow, but it was deep. As the buffalo jumped in, the water splashed and looked gray in the air. The herd swam on and over the stream, where on the other side they found good pasture and remained on the earth."

Joseph cared less for prestige than for saving his people. Already the buffalo were becoming scarce. Harassment by other displaced tribes as well as by white settlers made each hunt more dangerous. More important, Omahas must become a thrifty agricultural people. To plant corn, then go off on the hunt and leave it to mature, was no longer enough. Cultivation must become a full-time occupation. In 1857 Joseph had agreed to join the hunt on the condition that he would not be asked again. Now, in 1859, his close friends were begging him to reconsider.

"Just this once," pleaded Thangeska (White Horse). "It would silence some of the wagging tongues that say you are the tool of the white chests."

Joseph shook his head stubbonrly. "I work with the missionaries, yes. They are our friends. But I am no tool, and I care not for wagging tongues."

Two Crows, one of the bravest and most outspoken of the tribal leaders, was more blunt. "The tongues do more than wag. They dart forth with the poison of vipers."

Joseph's eyes flashed fire. Never had his name Iron Eye more suited him. "And you think I am afraid?"

Wajapa, the son of Joseph's mother's sister, Watunna, knew his cousin better. Though little more than twenty, he was wise beyond his years. He also had been raised by Big Elk. "Better if the course of the river is changed slowly, else there be a flood and all one has planted be swept away. It is only the Waxes who destroy when they build. Let us not be like them, my brother."

Joseph agreed to go on the hunt once more and take his family, all but Louis, of course. On this point he was adamant. Children must remain in school.

As for countless generations, before the hunt came the planting of the corn. Like the buffalo, maize was the sacred gift of Wakonda, so essential to sustenance that the Omahas called it "Mother." When the grass came up and the oak leaves had uncurled to the size of rabbits' ears, the ancient ritual began. The songs were chanted while members of the Inkethabe Clan distributed four grains of red corn to each household—red, the color of life.

"With firm roots I stand . . . with one leaf I stand, with two leaves I stand . . . " and so on up to seven. "With one joint I stand . . ."

So sang the corn through all stages of its growth, glossy hair, yellow hair, dark hair; glossy tassel, pale tassel, yellow tassel. "With fruit I stand possessed, pluck me, roast by fire my fruit, rip from the cob, eat me."

Delighted, Bright Eyes fingered the different kinds of kernels, white, blue, yellow, red, reddish blue, striped. Before planting, she helped put them to soak overnight with three or four buffalo apples, "to keep gophers from eating them." When the earth was heaped into hills, with little trenches around them for water, she was allowed to drop some of the beautiful colored bits into each mound, one for each finger of her right hand. Then came the waiting. When the corn came up it must be hoed. Stubbornly Oldest Grandmother refused to use the white man's iron tool. The old kind was better, made from the shoulder bone of the elk, its handle a pole fastened on by sinew. A second time the corn was hoed. Then, when the shoestring with its purple flower bloomed—in the "Moon When the Buffalo Bulls Hunt the Cows," called June by the white man—it was time for *Taune,* the summer hunt.

The huge procession started, at least two miles long. Only the aged and infirm were left behind with their protectors—and the *wathon,* leader of the hunt. For four days he had fasted. Now, carrying no weapons, he followed on bare feet, praying constantly. He would reach camp after all others, go to his tent alone. During all the hunt he must eat little, live apart, continue to pray. For children the hunt might be a holiday, for the women drudgery; but for the hunters and their leader it was a sacrament.

At first Bright Eyes rode, but soon she was off and away with the other children, scampering through tall grass, picking flowers, playing the game of *uhebashonshon,* crooked path, each one repeating the pranks of the leaders, dashing through gaps in the procession, galloping, backtracking, the line kept by each child holding to a string about the waist of the one in front, singing a song handed down for countless generations. They were free as air, save for one awful tabu. In the center of the procession, walking alone, was a solitary old man with a heavy robe wrapped around him. About his shoulders was a leather strap, to the ends of which was attached a dark object that was long and black. From one end hung what looked like a scalp with long hair. He looked tired, and sweat dropped from his face as he struggled to keep pace. Even the children, careless in their play, gave the space a wide berth. For the old man was carrying the Sacred Pole.

They had gone perhaps five miles and the day was well past

"sun high" when a cloud of dust appeared far to the rear. Presently ponies emerged. Bright Eyes' heart began to hammer. "It's Louis," intuition told her. It was—not only Louis but four others of his schoolmates, who had run away from school, sneaked home to their villages, seized their ponies, and dashed in hot pursuit after the cavalcade.

Bright Eyes was close to Joseph when a sheepish but hopeful Louis dismounted to face his father. "Please," his great dark eyes silently pleaded. They were startlingly alike as they stood facing each other, heads flung back, feet wide apart, firm chins and strongly arched noses belying the full, habitually smiling lips, brows beetling like clumps of *lahu-hi* weeds overhanging black pools.

"My son has disobeyed me. Did I not tell him to remain in the House of Teaching?"

The boy's lips quivered, but his eyes did not waver. "Yes, Dadíha."

"Then what is he doing here?"

"I would go on the hunt. I am not white man. I am Omaha. It is my right."

Bright Eyes looked from one to the other, Her heart seemed to stop beating. Father's lips quirked. His gaze wavered between amusement and anger, as he felt a small soft hand steal into his.

It was Two Crows, Louis' uncle by adoption, who clinched the argument. "Let him go, Brother. He will have many winters to become like the white man. But who knows how many summers will be left him to live as an Omaha?"

Louis was "punished" by having to drive his father's horses, a task he had long secretly coveted. His school uniform was exchanged for his buckskin shirt and short leggings which Grandmother, canny in her knowledge of boys, had just happened to bring along. He performed his duties well, only once with near disaster.

Accompanied by one of his friends, he was driving the horses near the middle of the caravan when they stopped to nibble some grass. Impatiently Louis jerked at the lariat with all the force he could muster. The end of it came with a resounding whack against the side of a gray. Startled, all the horses broke into a swift gallop toward the open space where walked the old man with his sacred burden. The gray and a black, one after the other, ran against the old man, nearly knocking him over. The two boys were horrified. They had desecrated the Sacred Pole! Would they or the horses be struck dead? That night in camp Louis could eat no supper. He finally decided he had to tell his father. To his immense relief Father only smiled. "Eat your supper, son," he said, "and don't worry."

After the meal Father told Louis what to do. "Go to the sacred tent. Take both horses with you, and this piece of scarlet cloth. When you reach the entrance you must say, 'Venerable man, without any intention of disrespect we have touched you and have come asking to be cleansed from the wrong we have done.'"

Still terrified, Louis did as he was told. The old man came out, took the scarlet cloth, reentered the tent. Soon he returned, carrying a wooden bowl filled with warm water. He lifted his right hand to the sky and wept, then sprinkled both boy and horses with the water, using a spray of artemisia. So was the anger of the "Venerable Man," the Sacred Pole, washed away.

Each sundown they stopped at an appointed place, usually a level spot near a stream. The ritual of making camp was as old as the giving of the sacred hoop by Wakonda. Though in the home village tents and lodges need be placed in no particular order, on the hunt there was always the *huthuga*, tribal circle, its two arcs symbolic of the cosmic unity of earth and sky, its entrance open to the east.

Bright Eyes loved the nights in camp. Their beauty made her throat smart and her eyes ache. Though the tops of the conical tents, black with smoke, were lost in darkness, the lower parts, glowing with fires, were alive with shadow pictures. Her fingers itched to capture the scene forever. Later, wrapped in her blanket, she watched the stars wink through the smoke hole and went to sleep to the music of rippling waters. Even when swarms of fireflies presaged rain and she lay listening to drops pattering on the skins, delight was undimmed. The dark night was soft, black, and safe; dampness softened the footsteps, and one could dream in comfort.

Sometimes there was a bright jewel on the golden chain of days.

One evening when Mother and the other women were cooking supper she was playing near Father. There was a soft yellow sunset, with no wind. A small boy, one of her playmates, came and gave her a little bird that he had found.

"*Ou-daa, ou-daa!*" she cried in delight. Holding the trembling creature, she showed it to Father, then filled a bowl with water and, taking some kernels of corn, tried to make it eat and drink. No use. It cowered against her palm, quivering with fright.

"Daughter," called Father suddenly, "bring your bird to me."

He held it in his hand, smoothing the feathers gently. "Daughter, I will tell you what you might do with it. Take it carefully out yonder where there are no tents, where the high grass is, put it softly down on the ground, and say as you put it down, 'Wakonda, I give you back your little bird. Have pity on me, as I have pity on your bird.'"

She looked up at him wonderingly. "Does it belong to Wakonda?"

"Yes, little one. And he will be pleased if you give it back to him to take care of."

Carefully she did as she was told. In the years that followed many memories of her father would become blurred, but not this. Nearly forty years later she would record it verbatim, though in words of another language. With this little incident she would climax her story of his life, placing beneath it as a symbol of finality the drawing of an arrow with an unstrung bow.

4

As the caravan neared buffalo country on the broad plains of *Ni-btha-thka*, Land of the Flat Water, anxieties mounted. The *wathon* rose long before dawn to pray. Watchmen became more alert. Twenty young "runners" were selected by the *wathon* to search for a suitable herd. When their signal came from a high hill, a herald rushed about the camp.

"It is reported that dust is rising from the earth as far as the eye can reach!"

In spite of the excitement, all must be done according to the prescribed ritual. There must be no haste. Two young men were selected to lead the attack, one to carry the sacred pipe, the other the *wathon's* ceremonial staff, the *washabe*. A herald passed around the tribal circle, calling in the name of the *wathon*:

"You are to go upon the chase, bring in the horses,
Braves of the Sky People, the Earth people, pity me who belong to you!"

Thus did the *wathon* appeal to the honor and compassion of the tribe, that all dissension and misdeeds might be avoided. Only so would Wakonda bless the sacrament.

Silently and in perfect order the camp moved toward the herd. Four times the procession halted, while chiefs and *wathon* made prayer offerings of smoke. Still in silence the new camp was pitched. Divesting themselves of all save moccasins and breechcloths, the hunters rode forth in two parties to surround the herd, the two youths bearing the pipe and staff leading the way.

About to mount, Joseph looked down into a pair of wide eager eyes. "Come!" On an impulse he hoisted Bright Eyes up in front of him. "Don't worry," he told the horrified Mary, "we'll watch at a distance. I promise to bring her back safe."

Bright Eyes trembled with excitement. Like all Omaha children she had ridden horses almost from infancy, and the big spirited gray was no more intimidating than her own pony. Besides, Father's long arm was about her waist. But she sensed that for some unknown reason she was being accorded a unique privilege, and she knew she was the envy of every other small girl in camp. As they rode past the place where the packhorses were tethered, Louis ran toward them.

"Let me ride out with the hunters and shoot," he begged his father.

Joseph smiled but shook his head. "No, son—perhaps in another summer, when you are twelve. The horse might throw you suddenly, and the buffalo might gore you."

Louis went back to the horses, sulking, and they rode on to the top of a small hill. Bright Eyes caught her breath. The yellow plain below was mottled with black splotches, ugly in shape yet strangely beautiful. There was grace in their very awkwardness of motion. Their black hides glistened in the sun, and the long yellow grass flowed and rippled about them like waves. Father dismounted and lifted her down.

"Look well, little one," he told her, "and remember. For the thing you see now will soon be gone forever."

She watched, fascinated, as the two parties of hunters appeared and circled the grazing herd, so silently and unobtrusively that the big black shapes seemed unaware of their presence. When the two young men met, the *washabe* was thrust in the ground and the sacred pipestem tied to it. The air was so clear that Bright Eyes could see clearly the golden eagle feathers hung on the crook of the *washabe*. There was a long silence, then—

"*O-we-ya!*" came a wild cry, and the plain burst into life.

Bright Eyes clutched her father's hand. The world turned suddenly into a welter of confusion—dashing horses, flying arrows, yells, exploding gunpowder, flashing knives, slashes of bright crimson, screams of dying animals. Shuddering, she hid her face in her father's robe, but he turned it firmly about.

"No, I want you to see—and remember."

"But they're killing them," she sobbed, "the poor animals!"

"So that you and all the rest of our people can eat and grow strong. They will kill only as many as will be needed to last the winter, and not a scrap will be wasted. Not like the white man," his voice grew harsh with bitterness, "who kills for the sport of killing, or for the delicate taste of a heart or tongue, leaving the carcass to rot on the plain."

She tried to close her eyes, but the strong hands were insistent.

"That's right. Look, my little one. Never turn your back. See everything in the world just as it is."

She looked, eyes wide open, nerves quivering. Hard to remember that the iron fingers clamped about her forehead had held the little bird so gently! Louis ran up and stood by their side. His face was still dark and sulking. Beneath them, at the foot of the hill, a big buffalo bull was charging, a man with a bow and arrow in hot pursuit. Now and then the bull would turn to attack, and the man would duck just in time.

"If I were only down there with a gun—" muttered Louis angrily.

"*Eh bien*, go," said Joseph. "Take this little gun of mine and the big red mare. Show us what you can do."

Louis was off with a glad cry and presently reappeared, looking very straight and brave, riding hard toward the man and the savage bull. Bright Eyes watched, torn between pride and terror, as the boy circled warily, aiming his gun. Suddenly the hunter shot an arrow, wounding the bull in the back. Snorting, he charged blindly, nose to the ground, weak little eyes under the curly mat of hair unable to spot his tormentors, great black flanks upreared. Horrified, Bright Eyes saw the red mare leap—leap again—four times, flinging Louis high into the air. The fingers on her forehead tightened in a painful grip. Straight toward the prostrate figure the bull charged, then, just before reaching it, wheeled and trotted away, snorting. Bright Eyes felt the taut fingers slowly relax, but her forehead still smarted as they mounted the horse and returned to camp.

Mother knew Louis had been thrown when the red mare came in alone, nervously aquiver and with bridle hanging, and she gave Father a great scolding, which he endured in silence. She was still berating him when Louis arrived, meek and crestfallen.

"Well," inquired Father with apparent innocence, "and did you kill the big buffalo bull?"

Louis grinned sheepishly and handed over the gun without reply.

When the meat came into the camp on the pack ponies, there was great rejoicing. A feast of hearts and tongues was held in the Tent of the White Buffalo Hide, and the long Ritual of the Hide was sung far into the night. Wakonda had hearkened to his children's supplications and given food. There was feasting too around all the little camp fires. After the butchering the meat had been distributed, the *ha*, hide, given to the man who had killed the animal, together with a portion of the brains and *tezhu*, the choice parts between the end of ribs and breast. Other portions were graded and allotted to the helpers according to the time they had arrived to work on the carcass. All received some parts. The large intestines were stripped, turned inside out, washed and boiled. Every member of the tribe feasted that night on this succulent delicacy. Young braves who had killed their first buffalo went about boasting, the taste of its raw liver and gall still bitter on their lips.

Fixing her eyes on a star blinking through the smoke hole, Bright Eyes tried to keep awake, wanting to ponder the events of this strange-awful-wonderful day with all its paradoxes—joy and terror, gentle hands that could turn iron-hard, life that had to be secured through death. But her small body was too replete with fried bread and the first fresh meat in many months, so much more satisfying than wild turnips.

Day dawned on a flurry of activity. The huge piles of meat must be stripped and hung to dry before they spoiled. Already the *wámonshihas*, drying racks, were set up beside each tent. A holiday spirit eased the drudgery. All day the women sat in little circles, their sharp knives unwinding the great chunks, vying to see whose strip would be thinnest and longest. Outside the camp rawhides were pegged out everywhere, and the old women sat scraping and beating them to make them soft and pliable as cloth. These were *teshnaha*, summer hides without hair, used for clothing, moccasins, tent covers. It was the winter hide, *moha*, tanned on one side only, which was used for rugs or robes or wraps. Some hides would be tanned with the skin left so hard that they could be used for packing cases, gayly painted on the outside. The sinews would make thread and the bones handles of tools and implements. Nothing would be thrown away.

The long thin strips turned brown in the bright sunlight, the brown turned black. In the dry bracing air of the prairie, with its constant breezes, it took little time for the meat to dry. It was taken in at night if there was a dew, put out again in the morning. Other herds were located and surrounded. The "Moon When the Buffalo Bellow" passed, and there came the "Moon When the Elk Bellow." That too passed. When the wind blew open the jaqcazi and the sunflowers, the first of the "Moon When the Deer Paw the Earth" (September), it was time to return home to the banks of the Smoky Waters. The results of the hunt were meager, not enough to last the winter. They dared not venture too far for fear of the Sioux. And the white man had often gone before them. Many buffalo had been found diseased, dead, or dying. The decimation of the great herds had long since begun.

But Wakonda had been good and must be thanked. Hedewachi, the Ceremony of Thanksgiving, was one of the most solemn and sacred of all rituals, for it paid homage to the Sacred Pole. A huge tent was constructed by throwing together the two sacred tents of the Honga Clan and adding a dozen or more tent skins.

"Come on," said Louis to Bright Eyes the evening after it appeared. "Some of us boys are going to see what's in the big tent. You can come too if you like."

She went, of course. Anywhere with Louis! The tent was big, all right. It would have held two or three hundred people. No one stopped them, so they went inside. Other children soon joined them, and they had great fun playing "Follow My Leader" and hide and seek among the folds. The next night they did it again. But on the third two officers were waiting at the entrance with whips. "No playing here tonight," they were told sternly.

"*Ah hé, ah hé!*" announced the crier. "The day of the ceremony approaches. Conduct yourselves with dignity."

Early the next morning Mother wakened Louis. "Listen!" she said. Soon he heard an old man calling the names of boys, his playmates. Suddenly he heard his own name called. Regardless of his good skin tunic, Mother put in his arms a large piece of meat, with no wrappings. "Go," she said, "take it to the holy tent." Her black eyes twinkled. "You'd better. The old men say that anyone who refuses to bring an offering will be struck by lightning, wounded in battle, or will lose a limb by a splinter running into his foot!"

Louis ran out. Anxiously Bright Eyes watched. An old man wearing a band of buffalo skin about his head and a buffalo robe about his body came to meet Louis. He took the meat and laid it on the grass in front of the Sacred Pole, which stood aslant in front of the holy tent. After boys from all the tents had brought their offerings, many songs were sung.

"The people cry aloud—tho ho! before thee.
Here they prepare for sacred rites—tho ho!
Their Sacred, Sacred Pole,
With reverent hands, I say, they touch the Sacred Pole before
thee."

The ceremony lasted several days. Its climax came with the anointing of the pole. The night before, sent to bed early but too excited to sleep, Bright Eyes heard Father and Standing Hawk, the other head chief, talking outside the tent.

"Are you sure you were wise, my brother? There was much opposition to your words in the Council. To suggest that they should not anoint the Pole—!"

"Some of our ways are not good." It was Father's voice, low but insistent. "You know it as well as I. Thanksgiving to Wakonda, yes. All things come from him. But to daub a piece of wood with blood and clay—how can such a thing please the Great Spirit?"

"I fear you have been listening too much to the white chests at the House of Teaching. Many of the people do not like it."

"They don't like many things—houses of wood, working hard in the fields, saving a little instead of giving everything away. But—" Bright Eyes heard her father give a long sigh "—even much that is good they must sacrifice if they would survive."

It was a hot night, but she shivered in the darkness. What did it all mean? Why did some people hate Father? And—suppose he had done something to offend the Venerable Man, like the horses which had run against him? Would he be struck by lightning, wounded in battle, or . . . Mercifully she drifted off to sleep.

The ceremonies proceeded. Fat from the best *tezhu* was cut off, dropped into a wooden bowl, pounded to a paste, and mixed with red clay—fat, emblem of abundance, red, the color of life. With reverent fingers the priest took a brush and rubbed the mixture over the pole, already crusted thick and dark from the accumulations of centuries. The Venerable Man, symbol of tribal unity and authority, was again given his proper homage.

"I cause the paint to adhere . . . I make him to be red . . . I make him beautiful!"

5

It was soon after the return from the hunt that Joseph had the accident. He stepped on a nail while helping a member of the Young Men's Party to build his house. It penetrated his moccasin and stabbed painfully into his flesh. He was too busy to give the wound any attention or a chance to heal itself. The corn on the bottom lands must be harvested. Already the length of the hunt and the prolonged ceremonies of the Hedewachi had postponed the ingathering beyond the time of best fruition, and Iron Eye was anxious to prove to the tribe that abundant crops could partially atone for the inevitable curtailment of the hunts.

Then, too, the Village of Make-Believe White Men was growing fast. Thangeska, Two Crows, Village Maker, and others of his party had houses either built or under construction, and he wanted to see them finished. Disregarding the painful foot, he hobbled about in fields or store all day, then helped with the building as long as there was daylight, continuing sometimes by lantern light. He felt driven by a fierce compulsion. Opposition to his ideas was strong and growing. Little Chief, White Cow, Yellow Smoke—all had big followings among the more conservative members of the tribe. How long his own influence could prevail he did not know. He lived each day as if the survival of the tribe depended on how much he could accomplish—as perhaps it did. Nothing must interrupt his labors.

But something did. The foot became too painful even to hobble. One Sunday when the missionary, Charles Sturges, who was a doctor as well as superintendent of the Mission, came to hold services in the village, he found the head chief on his bed, sick with fever. He examined the swollen and blackened foot with distress and alarm. Though he gave what treatment he could, he shook his head.

"Tell your father," he told Louis, who had learned enough English to act as interpreter, "that he must have a doctor come from Bellevue—at once. This may have serious complications. *Pe-áh-zhi!*" he simplified as Louis looked bewildered. "Bad!"

A message was dispatched, and finally a doctor came, prescribed soakings, also shook his head. But the Omahas too had their priests of healing, members of *Te Ithathe*, "those to whom the buffalo has shown compassion," a society made up of persons of both sexes to whom the buffalo had appeared in dreams. Two Crows' father was a member, and to him through countless generations had been transmitted knowledge of medicines for the curing of wounds. At Two Crows' urging Joseph consented to have the buffalo men called. They came, galloping over the hills on their horses, one or two at a time, their long hair flowing over their naked backs. Dismounting, they entered the house one by one and made a circle around Joseph, who lay on a pile of robes in the center of the room.

Crouched within the folds of Mother's skirt, Bright Eyes watched from the doorway. Strange, frightening, to see Father, the all-wise, all-powerful, lying there, tossing with pain, helpless! Mother was frightened too. The child could tell by the coldness of the hands closed about her bare upper arms, the way the fingers quivered as they moved nervously up and down.

The buffalo men looked very old, but their eyes gleamed brightly in their wrinkled faces. One of them, Two Crows' father, began in a low voice to tell how in a vision he had seen the buffalo which had revealed to him the secret of the medicine and taught him the song he must sing when using it. Then he took bits of roots from his skin pouch and started to sing at the top of his voice. The other doctors, perhaps twenty in all, joined in. The sound was so loud that surely it could be heard up at the Mission nearly a mile away! While the others sang, one blew on a bone whistle, imitating the cry of an eagle. The man who had started the song took the roots in his mouth, ground them between his teeth; then, taking a mouthful of water, he approached Father, bellowing and pawing at the floor like an angry buffalo, and with a great whizzing sound blew the water into the wound in Father's foot.

"*Hi! Hi! Hi!*" he exclaimed in a loud voice.

A second doctor began the treatment and started a song, then a third, a fourth. There were few words, but somehow they made a picture of the prairie, the round wallow with its pool of water, a wounded buffalo being healed by its companions. All that day and night and for four days following the men remained, continuing their treatment. Bright Eyes fell asleep to the sound of their singing, and it was in her ears when she wakened. Long afterward she would learn the nature of the medicine they had used: roots of the wild anise, the hop vine, the *Physalis viscora*, wild rose, pleurisy root, ground cherry— all of them fully as efficacious as the remedies known at that time by the white man. And they tried other remedies, sprinkled over the sick man ground powders of malachite and turquoise, the pollen of a cattail weed called *thá-hin*; gave him a decoction of red grass for his fever. But this time there was no triumphal ceremonial dance to crown their success.

"We were too late," said the troubled Two Crows. "He should have followed the ways of our people, kept the wound clean and applied poultices."

Members of the Pebble Society, *Inkugthi Athin*, also tried to heal their chief. These were they who in dream or vision while fasting had beheld water or its symbol, the pebble, or the fabulous water monster, a huge creature in animal form that lashed the water with a mighty tail. The society had acquired many new members of late, for in the previous year there had been stories all along the Smoky Waters of a flying serpent that had hovered over a river steamboat slowing for a landing. Like an undulating serpent it had looked—so white men said as well as Omahas—moving in and out of lowering clouds and breathing fire.

Before attempting the rite of healing, the leader, Wakidezhinga, entered the sweat lodge to prepare himself, its stones representing that primal rock from which creation had sprung, its steam symbolic of the water which had power to wash away impurities.

"*He!* Aged One," he addressed the rock. "*Ethka*, I desire, I crave! Your children being in sore distress, *ethka!*"

His manner of treatment was different from that of the buffalo men. The members of the Pebble Society used mechanical means—bleeding, sucking out a disturbing object, practicing a kind of massage which consisted of kneading and pulling on the region below the ribs with motions severe and painful. Joseph was in even greater agony when he had finished.

46

There were those in the tribe who could suggest a reason for his misfortune—and did.

"Remember how he spoke against the anointing? One cannot insult the 'Venerable Man' and go unpunished."

"Is it not said that he who offends the Sacred Pole will be struck by lightning, wounded in battle, or—*lose a limb by a splinter running into his foot?*"

On November 4, 1859, Dr. Sturges wrote to Dr. Lowrie: "La Flesche is very sick. He injured his foot by stepping on a nail and neglecting it. Several doctors and surgeons have been called and it appears amputation will be necessary. His mind is somewhat interested in religion."

It was, indeed, but not for the reason Sturges first suspected, fear for his soul in the presence of death.

"Pray for me," he begged during one of their almost daily interviews.

"What shall I pray for?" asked Sturges.

"That if God sees fit to take me out of this world, he will be my friend, and, if I get well, that he will help me to live in the good road."

"God has afflicted me," he said again. "God is good. I love God."

Joseph asked to have the religion of the book explained, but not because he was afraid to die. And he had no need of the white man's book to assure him that Wakonda was good. The red man had known that from the time he had first lifted his eyes to the sun and felt the rain on his face. But, if the book was the secret of the white man's power, he wanted to know about it for the good of his people.

The leg was amputated below the knee, and he did not die. But the surgery was crude, and he continued to suffer. Not that it mattered. He soon put in a request to the government to send him to New York or Washington, but only incidentally that he might receive more expert surgery. The Treaty of 1854 was still far from fulfillment, and he wanted to find influential friends, perhaps on the Mission Board, who could exert pressure on the Indian Bureau.

There was fire that fall on the bottoms by the Smoky Waters. It whipped through the dry stubble of cornfields, raged under a

47

high wind through the tops of trees, threatened to climb the wooded bluffs and obliterate the Mission and the cluster of new wooden houses. Men returned helpless from fighting it, wheezing, faces blackened—until the wind changed, driving the flames toward the river. Bright Eyes watched from the hilltop, throat choked from fear as well as smoke. But fear was slight compared with dismay over the desolate fields and the gaunt black tree stumps. And neither fear nor dismay was half as poignant as sorrow over Father's loss. Never to run again, to race with the wind, to jump, to climb, to walk long strides through the tall grass—the thought was almost more than she could bear!

Three

1

Sometimes, it seemed, she was two people. One day she was what the white chests called an "Indian" (though she couldn't understand why), and the next she was some kind of make-believe white person, like Father's village. She even had a different name to go with each identity. For six days in the week she was Susette La Flesche, shy, dutiful, often frightened, one pupil in a school of forty, twenty-six boys and fourteen girls, dressed like all the other girls, in a wide calico skirt and loose blouse with long sleeves and high neck, buttoned up the back. But on Saturday, when she was allowed to go home, she was once more Inshtatheamba, Bright Eyes, free as the wind and happy as the sunshine, where even the work she had to do seemed like play—fetching wood for the fire, pounding corn in the mortar, keeping three-year-old Frank out of mischief, carrying other Mother's new baby, a tiny girl, on the board cradle strapped to her back.

At least it was her own name she was called by in the House of Teaching, the name Father had given her, not some queer-sounding words that the white chests handed out. Among the twenty-six boys were George Washington, Daniel Webster, Jonathan Edwards, James Madison, Thomas Macaulay.

"What name shall we give him?" Superintendent Burtt

(called "Graybeard" by the pupils) asked one day when a new boy appeared.

There were eager suggestions, based on information recently acquired in history class and chapel. "Gideon . . . Samson . . . Henry Clay . . . Lewis and Clark . . ." This was followed by an explosive titter, sternly quashed by smart raps of Graybeard's ruler. It was finally decided to name the newcomer James Buchanan, in deference to the incumbent Grand Father in Washington.

Susette had acquired enough English to know what was happening. She felt both bewilderment and resentment. Why give him a new name when he already had one? His own name, Ka-gay-ha (Friend) sounded much better. And she felt like weeping with him when they cut off his little braided scalp lock and he saw it lying like a small dead snake on the floor. She was sorry, too, when they took away his little buckskin robe, beautifully ornamented with porcupine quills dyed in many different colors, and he appeared looking like all the other boys, in short pants, cap, jacket with brass buttons, long stockings, and heavy black shoes that squeaked when he walked.

"Why?" she asked Father when she went home the next Saturday.

It was a long time before he answered. He seemed almost apologetic, and he did not look straight at her when he spoke. "They mean it for our good, little one. They want us to be able to take our place in the world that is coming. And—they find our names hard to pronounce." He did not add, "Besides, they think them heathenish."

The child nodded, reluctantly. "Same as we do theirs," she agreed.

Only English must be spoken at the House of Teaching. It was hard when you were a new pupil. At first you could not talk at all, and you felt like a little dummy, smiling at people to show you meant to be friendly, but unable to even say "Hello" or "How are you?" until you knew the words. If you made a mistake and said something in Omaha, and you were a boy, you were whipped with a hickory rod, and if you were a girl you got your hand slapped with a ruler. If it happened to be Miss Smith who caught you, your palm showed the red marks for days.

Susette was quick to learn English words. In no time at all she was saying "Good morning" instead of "*Umba-ouda*," "Good-bye" for "*An-ga-tha*," and "Thank you" instead of "*Ou-dha*." In some ways English was easier. For instance, you said "Come and eat," whether you were man or woman talking. In Omaha, if you were a woman, it was "*Wa la te ghia*," but if you were a man, "*Wa lá te ghi ga ho*." Even harder to learn was the custom of addressing anyone by his personal name. Omahas always used the proper term of relationship when speaking to each other—father, uncle, nephew, daughter-in-law—and it was considered respectful and proper to call almost any male person, even Wakonda and the president in Washington, "Grandfather." But when a new boy, intending to be most polite, used the term in addressing Graybeard, the latter turned red as a chokecherry and reached for his hickory stick.

Adjustment to the new language was far easier than to new ways of living. For the first few days she nearly starved. Her introduction to the dining room was an ordeal. "Come quick!" a big girl told her, seizing her hand. "Time for supper." With a crowd of milling children they pushed their way into a big room in the middle of the first floor. Bright Eyes had seen tables before, but there was none as yet in the village houses. Here there were four long ones with benches at each side. She sat on one of them, feet dangling, clutching at the edge of the table which was covered with something smooth and cold, to keep from falling. There was a pounding sound, and everybody became quiet. A man with gray hair and whiskers, who sat at the end of one of the tables, muttered something—then there was a clatter of tin plates and cups. Young women came from the kitchen carrying big pans of steaming food. Some of it was put on her plate: a boiled potato, a chunk of meat, something that looked like wild turnip, but wasn't. She tasted it gingerly, and it was all she could do not to spit it out. The meat was better, not sweet and tangy like jerked buffalo, but edible. She looked for Louis over on the boys' side of the room but could not see him. Everything was strange, and curiosity kept her eyes wandering—to the flickering lamps fastened to the walls and posts, to a big clock ticking noisily on a shelf, to a cupboard with a tin door pricked all over into queer patterns. She had barely begun to eat when the meal was over. Those on the inner sides of the tables turned around to face the center of the room. She folded her arms like the rest. Everybody started singing, queer sounds, not at all like the music played and sung at feasts and dances. Then the benches were pushed back with loud grindings and scrapings. Everybody stood up, but instead of going somewhere, they all dropped to their knees. The older girl beside her pulled her down.

"Why—?" Susette whispered in Omaha. "Are they looking for something?"

"Ssh!" The girl pushed her head toward the bench. "They're going to pray. And you musn't talk in Omaha."

Pray! How could you pray like this, with your face toward the ground? When people prayed, they lifted their eyes, stretched their arms to the four winds, to the skies, looking always upward. Wakonda wasn't down there, was he, under this dusty wooden floor! But she bowed dutifully, pressed her forehead against the hard bench—and, before the voice had finished talking in the strange language, fell sound asleep. She awoke to find the pupils gone and a kind white face, eyes rimmed with glasses, looking down at her. The woman, whom she soon came to know as Mrs. Burtt, took her by the hand, led her up the two wooden hills, and put her to bed.

The first nights were pure torture. She was terrified of falling out of the high corded bed, and she longed for the comfort of her thick buffalo robe and soft deerskin pillow. All the girls slept in this big room on the third floor. They ranged in age from five to mid-teens. Mary Ellen Smith, seven, was one of those nearest her age, and they soon became close friends. Susan Fontenelle, ten, and her sister Mary seemed very grown up, comfortingly so, for Mary understood her fears and took her hand when they climbed the long wooden hills at night. Even Mary, she discovered, was afraid of the stairs that led to the huge ghostly attic and hustled her past them.

It was Louis' presence in the school that made those first days bearable, though Susette saw him only at a distance, across the dining room or over the fence which separated the boys' and girls' playgrounds. Even the few times they passed each other she dared not speak to him because she didn't know enough English. Instead of playing games with the other girls, she would linger by the fence between the playgrounds, watching for a glimpse of his tall, darting figure, his bright face like a gleam of sunshine, listening for his merry laughter.

There was another boy whom her eyes often followed. His name was Matzhezinzah, but the white chests said it was Francis Vinton Brush. Though he was only seven, a year older than herself, he had been in the House of Teaching since he was four and was already in the Second Reader class. He could repeat what the Superintendent called "The Lord's Prayer" and "The Ten Commandments" and knew many words in Webster's Elementary Spelling Book. Even the white children who had known English all their lives could do not better.

For there were white children too in the school. They belonged to some of the missionary teachers and to the government workers who ran the saw and grist mills, the blacksmith and carpenter shops, and lived in a long wooden house built by the government. It had taken a long time for the mills and shops to come, but at last this part of the treaty of 1854 had been fulfilled—part of the price the Grand Father in Washington had paid to his "Red Children" for hundreds of thousands of acres of their fine land.

Another of the white man's gifts arrived in that year of 1860—measles. "Little smallpox," almost as dreaded as its namesake which had reduced the once powerful Omahas to a few hundreds, descended on the tribe in the spring, displaying a virulence unknown to the comparatively immune white race. The herbs and roots accompanied by the rituals of centuries, remarkably effective in the treatment of wounds, fevers, and many other ailments, were powerless against this mysterious scourge, though perhaps their decoctions of the bark of red cedar, with which they attempted to treat smallpox and cholera, were as efficacious as the white men's remedies. Certainly the school's medicine chest was sadly deficient.

"Our only reliable drugs," complained Superintendent Burtt to his superiors, "are one bottle of castor oil, a half ounce of calomel and a half ounce of laudanum and a little camphor." No rhubarb, senna, manna, jalap, aloes, sweet oil, salts. No mortar, weights, measures, or spatula. Nothing for the coughs and diseases to which such a place was exposed.

The scourge took its toll, leaving two small mounds in the tiny cemetery on the hill above the Mission, one of them the grave of Burtt's own small daughter Lillie, the other that of a little girl whom Susette sorely missed. She could not understand why the Burtts did not mourn their little Lillie like the Omahas, whose wails for their dead children could be heard from the village just as the sun was sinking beyond the hills, or at daybreak when the first red rays streaked the sky to the east beyond the Smoky Waters.

"She has gone to be with Jesus," Mr. Burtt said in chapel, his eyes very bright and shining.

Susette knew about Jesus. She heard the name often, sitting in the big room at the north end of the building on a high backless bench, feet dangling. Sunday morning, afternoon, and evening, and Thursday evening the pupils sat there in long rows listening to sermons of extreme length and sleep-inducing power. More than once Susette would have fallen off the bench if Mary Fontenelle, who sat beside her, had not firmly grasped the yoke of her Mother Hubbard. But, as her knowledge of English increased, the semi-consciousness of these hours became peopled with figures even more adventurous than the fabulous Ictinike or Wahanthicige, the Orphan—Samson with his jawbone club, David killing Goliath with his sling, Moses and his plagues, Elisha killing the children who laughed at him. The people of the white man's book, she decided, must be a fierce and warlike tribe, like some of the Sioux. She dreamed about them at night, waking in a cold sweat. But other dreams were delightful, of little Samuel who heard Wakonda speak, Joseph and his coat of many colors.

"Like Louis," she thought happily, "with his deerskin jacket all embroidered with red and blue and yellow porcupine quills."

Jesus, Wakondizhinge, the son of Wakonda, was both fascinating and frightening. Until the white chests had come the Omahas had not known that Wakonda had a son. In fact, as Louis carefully explained to her, that was why they had come. They believed that, if you didn't know about Wakondizhinge, you were what they called "heathen" and when you died you would go to a terrible place called hell, where you burned forever. It was all hard to understand, for Wakondizhinge inspired both sweet dreams and nightmares. He had loved children and been a very powerful medicine man, but he had died and come back to life again, which was frightening, like the ghosts in the attic.

Bright Eyes shivered. She was Bright Eyes again now, for it was Saturday and she and Louis were on their way home by the path which led over the hill. For a whole day they could eat familiar food and ride their ponies and talk Omaha. The path led by a small burial place on the bluffs. Suddenly her mouth watered, for there on a freshly made mound was a wooden bowl filled with pemmican. The *papa*, dried lean buffalo meat pounded into cakes with fat, was one of her favorite foods.

"*Choo-ie!*" she cried, running toward it. "I'm going to have some."

"*Nonshtán*, stop!" Horrified, Louis pulled her back just in time. "If you eat that, you'll die before another winter is gone!"

She was still trembling when they reached home. She ran to her mother, crying. Would she really have died if she had touched the food? "Of course not," said Mother, smiling. She had them sit down on the floor and placed a bowl of pemmican in front of them.

"Let me tell you," said Mother, "why the food was put on the grave. People love their dead relatives. When they gather to eat, they long for their presence. So they put a share of the food on the grave, not because they think the spirit can come back and eat it, but just out of love and remembrance. Do you understand?"

Bright Eyes nodded. She dipped her hand into the bowl and ate with relish. No one could make pemmican like Mother.

2

It was in the "Moon When the Frogs Sing"—April—when Nishuda, Smoky Water, was beginning to throb again with life, that Louis went on his vision quest. *Non-zhin-zhin*, it was called, trial of endurance, literally "to stand sleeping." It symbolized the birth of night into day, youth into manhood. It was a battle between the spirit of man and his flesh.

"He will go to the high hill," explained Two Crows, eyes

remote with reminiscence, "the hill of the Sacred Fireplace. He will go alone. Four days he will fast and sing and pray. Always before praying he must lift both hands high with the pipe in his right and send forth his voice four times, 'Hey-a-hey!' First he shall pray at the place where the sun goes down, then at the place whence comes cleansing and healing, then toward the place from which light comes, after that toward where lives the power to grow. 'Wakonda,' he will pray, 'here, poor and needy, I stand.' He will weep. Then—if he is strong—if he can endure—"

"Oh, he can," Bright Eyes breathed. "Louis can!"

"Then, when he becomes so weak that his body is near dying and his soul is at one with Wakonda, he will have his vision. It may be a cloud, rain, wind, bird, beast, but it will bring with it a song. All through life this object will be his help."

The day came. Bright Eyes saw Father put clay on Louis' head, place a bow and arrow and a pipe in his hands. She watched him leave the village alone. She knew where he was going, to the hill of the Sacred Fireplace, high on the bluffs toward "where the great white giant lives." Father had taken her there once. They had found some arrow heads, roughly chipped, and bits of pottery. "From a culture long before ours," Father had mused. "We are here now, but for how long?" Child though she was, she had understood, and for a moment she had felt suspended in time, had heard drums beating, seen a child like herself watching an old man patiently chipping at an arrowhead.

The four days seemed endless. Food choked her, thinking how hungry Louis must be. She awoke in the middle of the night and wondered if he was still standing there, shivering perhaps with cold. In the daytime she would go off by herself, seeing how long she could stand without moving, trying vainly to weep. The fourth day came. Would he give up and come home, unable to bear the strain and hunger? Other boys had done so, to their eternal disgrace. Came the fourth night. Was he already lying in the deep sleep, spirit at one with the mysterious Wakonda? And what would his vision be? Surely not a snake or a burden strap, which were unlucky, or the moon, most unlucky of all! Oh, let it be a lovely bird or a fleecy cloud or a graceful elk, or, most lucky of anything, a bear!

Louis returned. He looked thin and gaunt, but he walked with a firm step, and his eyes shone like an animal's in firelight. She ran toward him, but he went past on the path toward Big Village, as if he did not see her.

"No, little one." Father answered her troubled, beseeching gaze, "we must not follow him. He has gone to tell his vision to some old man who had one like it. Don't worry, your brother will be back."

Louis came back, and they returned to school, a few days late after what the white chests called "Easter vacation." Soon he was ordered to the superintendent's room above the chapel. Susette, toeing the line for the primary reading class, stumbled over the simplest words. What had Louis done? She had peered into the superintendent's room once when the door was open. It had cloth curtains at the windows, pictures with gold frames, heavy dark shiny furniture. Unlucky victims reported there was a chair that rocked back when you sat in it, sending your feet into the air, then tipped front so you almost fell on your face. The room was almost more intimidating than the whipping rod.

It was recess when Louis emerged. Susette stood by the fence and waited until he came toward her. She knew enough English now so they could talk together.

"What happen?" she asked anxiously. "Bad? Get whipping?"

"No. He just talk. He not like me going on *Non-zhin-zhin.*" Then Louis said something she did not understand. His eyes looked hard, and his voice was bitter. "Their Isaiah go to temple and have vision. Fine. He holy man, prophet. But Indian go to high hill and have vision, he heathen savage."

3

Chief Iron Eye was beset with problems. Pain from his badly amputated leg was constant, the infection spreading. Continued applications to go east remained unheeded. Many of the provisions of the treaty were still unfulfilled. Incursion of white settlers, pressure from unfriendly bands of Sioux, themselves driven from their ancestral hunting grounds by the hordes of prospectors and colonizers, the increasing scarcity of game—all combined to make the summer hunts more dangerous and futile. Other tribes, closely related or traditionally friendly, the

Poncas and Pawnees, were equally harassed. Though he had discouraged the custom of intertribal visits, time consumed in ceremonial feasting and dancing, he suddenly decided to make one himself.

"I shall go to the Pawnees," he told the other chiefs, meeting in council after a terrifying incident which had set the tribe wild with excitement. Four Omahas had gone out to gather dry sumac for their pipes when four Sioux had fallen on them within a mile of the Mission, killing one. Another, old Mark who worked at the Mission, had barely escaped. "We have many enemies. We must make even more secure the alliance with our friends. Next summer the Pawnees should go with us on our hunt."

It was in the "Moon When the Deer Paw the Earth" that he left, taking all the family except Louis and Bright Eyes, who must remain in school, and Grandmother Nicomi, who preferred to stay at home—not in the new house, but in Oldest Grandmother's lodge. A house reminded her too much of that unhappy year as Sarpy's first lady in St. Louis. Henry Fontenelle, Joseph's partner, was left in charge of the trading post.

Susette loved the autumn. Bright colors quickened her blood, made her fingers itch with inexplicable desire. When she drew pictures of flying geese and cranes instead of ABC's in her copy-book, Miss Smith first poised her ruler, then, looking more closely at the graceful, swooping figures, expressed grudging approval.

"Why—that's very good, Susette. You have a real gift for drawing. But back to work now. No more doodling."

It was while Father was away that Susette's world turned from gold to black.

One day Louis did not appear in the dining room for breakfast. He was not in the schoolroom for morning classes. Perhaps he had been sent on an errand, she thought. But, no, since the attack by the Sioux the older boys had not been allowed to ride their ponies to the Agency or the post office. One of the farm men even went with them to the spring down the hill to draw water. When he did not appear at dinner, she summoned courage to approach Mrs. Burtt. "Please, ma'am, where Louis?"

"He isn't feeling well," the superintendent's wife told her kindly. "Just a little stomach upset, I'm sure. We thought it best to let him spend the day in bed."

Louis sick! The beauty of the golden autumn suddenly paled. Susette longed to go to him, but it was an unpardonable offense for a girl to approach the boys' dormitory. Another day passed, and another. Still no Louis. Saturday, day of recreation when one did not go home, was agony; Sunday with its Bible class and long sermons pure torture. Even the slice of brown ginger-cake given for Sunday lunch, usually a rare treat, tasted like sand.

"He's still not feeling well"—Mrs. Burtt's smile was reassuring— "but it's not serious. Don't worry, dear. We're sure it's a little childish ailment."

Usually timid and circumspect, Susette determined to do an unheard-of thing, break rules. She waited her chance. It came the next afternoon when the girls were all in sewing class learning to make comforters for next winter, and the boys were at their usual work outdoors with Mr. Betz, the farmer. She asked to leave the room, but instead of going to the outhouse she crept up the two flights of stairs, tiptoed to the boys' dormitory, and opened the door. It was a big bare room with a post in the middle and double beds ranged side by side. All were empty except one. Fearless now of discovery, she ran to it. "*Tinuhá*, brother!"

He gave her a wan smile. "Wihe, little sister! How did you get here?"

Recklessly she spoke in Omaha. How was he? What was the matter? Were they taking care of him? Did he hurt very much? What could she do to help?

He looked feverish, and his voice sounded weak. He was—all right, he guessed. No, he didn't hurt now—not much. He did have a pain—down here—but it was gone now. Just a stomach-ache, they said. He'd soon be—well—maybe tomorrow. And she must go down—before—someone found her—

She went back downstairs, still wary, but not from fear of punishment. She must not get caught this time, for she intended to commit a much graver offense. She was going to run away! She would find the path to the Village—yes, even go alone through the dark, tree-shaded glen past the graves where even the big boys ran fast—and she would tell Two Crows or Grandmother—

Later on the playground she waited for an opportunity, but none came. One of the teachers was always watching. Then suddenly her heart leaped. There on the boys' side of the playground was Kaghaumba, a man from her own village, one of Father's friends. He had come to the Mission and was just leaving. She ran to the fence. The boy called Brush was sitting on the other side, whittling something out of wood. Recklessly she called to him in Omaha.

"*Matzhezinzah! Ehna gi ya*, come here!"

He jumped up and came to the fence. "Please," she begged, "go tell that man about Louis being sick. Quick—before he goes!"

Brush ran after Kaghaumba. They talked. Kaghaumba turned and went back toward the Mission. Susette waited, tense with excitement. Presently he reappeared, carrying Louis in his arms, wrapped in a blanket. Mr. Burtt came out of the Mission, ran after him, and remonstrated.

Kaghaumba was not a big man, but he could look imposing when angry. He was angry now. He knew not a word of English, but he could express himself volubly in Omaha, and did. He had found the child of his chief sick, up in a bare cold room, with no one to attend him. Perhaps the white man's medicine was more powerful than the Indian's, but when a boy was sick he needed his family. And whether the white chest liked it or not, Kaghaumba was taking Louis to his Grandmother.

He turned and strode toward the path that led over the hills. Susette felt weak with relief. Far away though she was, she had caught the word "*Ikon*", Grandmother. Everything would be all right now.

But everything was not all right. A few days later Susette was called out of the schoolroom by a stricken Mr. Burtt. "Your father is waiting for you. God bless you, my child."

"*Indádi!*" she cried, rushing into his arms.

But it was not Father. He had the same features. His arms enfolded her with the same tender strength. He walked with the same crutches. But his face looked drawn and old, and the vigorous sparkle was gone from his eyes. He lifted her in front of him on his horse, and they rode to the Village. She dared not ask questions, afraid of what he would tell her, but her whole body felt cold, as if it were the "Moon When the Little Black Bears Are Born" instead of the "Moon When the Deer Rut." Long before they reached the Village they could hear the keen, long-drawn sound of wailing.

Later, much later, Mary told Susette what had happened. "We were on our way home. We still had a day's journey to go. A runner came out to meet us. He told us that—that our beautiful boy, whom we had left so strong and healthy, so full of life, was—dead! We came home. That night—that night your father lay all night with his dead son in his arms. From that time he has been a changed man."

No longer were some of the old customs of burial observed in the Omaha tribe. It was said, probably without foundation, that the great Chief Blackbird was buried on the hill called "Ompon-tongah Xaithon" astride his horse. The last traditional Omaha ceremonies had been observed in full for Zhinga gahige, Little Chief, who had died soon after the treaty of 1854 was made. His horse, led to the grave, covered with blankets and other personal belongings of the chief, had been strangled, together with his favorite dog, and buried with him, that they might accompany him on his long journey.

But two worlds joined in performing their sacred rites for the son of Chief Iron Eye, Joseph La Flesche. His body was clothed in his best deerskin jacket and leggings and wrapped in a blanket. On his feet were placed moccasins of elkskin, tabu to his clan in life. He was laid in his grave on a hilltop, facing east, the source of all life. Reverend Mr. Burtt conducted a service over the grave. He read from the white man's book and preached a long sermon.

"I am sure Louis was a believer," he told Joseph, "and has gone to heaven. It must be a satisfaction to you that he received a sort of Christian baptism." Even though it was a Catholic one, he implied, for Louis had been baptized by a Catholic priest, Father Hoechen, on December 27, 1850.

For four days a light was kept burning at the grave, to cheer the spirit during the time it might be lingering. Food and water were placed there, not that the spirit could partake of them, but an act of homage, as a bit of food was offered before each meal to Wakonda. All weeping and wailing ceased during these four days, that the loved one might enter the spirit land in a happy state. But when the four days were over the wailing resumed. Only one mourner remained silent. Going apart by himself, Joseph drew his blanket over his head and sat motionless, refusing to speak or eat, displaying grief far more eloquent than sound.

"Where"—Susette wandered about in numbed misery, trying to find someone to answer her agonized question—"where has Louis gone?" Mother, her long black hair flowing, unbraided, looked at her with unseeing eyes and began again to wail. Grandmother Nicomi shook her head. "Who knows, child? The white man says to heaven, but it seems only a few can go there. Our people say . . . But who can tell?"

It was Memetage, the Oldest Grandmother, who tried to answer her question. "To the spirit world, child. Some say that there are seven spirit worlds, each higher than the one before, and that a man passes from one to the other."

"But *where?*" the child persisted.

Memetage pointed upward. "You know the path of light that crosses the sky on a dark night, that which the white men call the Milky Way?" The child nodded. "Our people call it the path of the dead. It is said that at the forks of the path there sits an old man wrapped in a buffalo robe, and when the spirits of the dead pass along he turns the steps of the good toward the short path which leads to the abode of their loved ones, but he allows the wicked to take the long path, over which they wearily wander."

Bright Eyes was satisfied. That night she looked up at the broad belt of light arching the blue-black sky. Louis would like that, she thought, much better than the white man's "heaven" with its streets of hard shiny gold. And anybody could see that he was good, so he would follow the short path. Perhaps he was running along it already, leaping from star to star.

But of all the events of that sad time one was to remain so indelibly burned into memory that many decades later, when she wrote about it, it would seem to have occurred only yesterday. It happened in one of the intervals when the wailing had ceased for a time and there was quiet. Looking out over the prairie, perhaps a mile away, she saw men emerge from the hillsides. They seemed to be advancing in a line. Then she heard a far-off singing. They and their singing came nearer and nearer. There was something strange about the way they moved, half walking, half running. As they came up the slope toward the house, she saw that each of them was dragging an unstripped willow branch, trailing behind him on the ground. She stared, eyes wide with shock. Their bodies were bare except for the breechcloths, and blood flowed in long crimson streams from their left arms. She ran weeping to her father.

"Don't cry, little one." It was the first time he had spoken in many days. "It is the way of our people. See, each one has taken the broken end of a willow branch and thrust it through the thick flesh of his upper arm, letting the boughs and leaves trail on the ground. They are all young men and boys, friends of our Louis, and they have walked a mile like this, singing the death song, to show how they loved him. It is not a sad thing. How can a man show his love better than by giving of himself?"

Nor was the song a sad one. It had no words, only vocal sounds, but the tune and rhythm were blithe and happy, almost triumphant.

At the close of the song Father advanced toward the singers and, raising his hand in an attitude of thanks, withdrew the willow branches from the young men's arms and threw them on the ground.

Thus at an early age did Bright Eyes learn what her people thought about the stern realities of existence. Grief and joy, suffering and love, death and life—all were inseparably intermingled, part of an eternal unity and continuity.

"We see death everywhere," the old men would say. "Plants, trees, animals die, and man dies. No one can escape death, and no one should fear death, since it cannot be avoided. Yet do we not pray in all our sacred ceremonies 'to reach the fourth hill'? Life is good, and death is good, for both are part of the great mystery which is Wakonda."

One day Mary went to the big oak chest in which she kept the family's best clothes and other treasured articles. From the very bottom she drew out a piece of paper. "See, *Wizhungeha*." She held it out to Bright Eyes but jealously retained her hold on it.

It was a rough sketch of a chubby baby face.

"Louis!" the child exclaimed wonderingly.

Mary nodded, tears streaming down her face. She had been standing one day at the landing place by the Smoky Waters at Bellevue, with Louis in her arms. It was at the time of the Mormon migration to Utah, when many of the emigrants had passed through on their way to the west. Among the passengers on a steamboat was a wandering artist. While the boat was unloading its passengers he had gotten off, made the sketch, torn the leaf out of a book, and handed it to her as he stood on the gangplank, just as the whistle sounded. Still weeping, Mary put it back in the chest, at the very bottom, her tender, careful fingers attesting it to be the dearest of all her treasures.

"My mother must be over seventy years of age, as near as we can make out," Susette was to write many years later in an article which included the little sketch, "and yet to this day she cannot speak of my brother Louis' death without her eyes filling with tears."

Four

1

It was an apt coincidence that the name La Flesche should signify "the arrow," for it was symbolic both of Joseph's chosen people and of his own straight singleness of purpose. Nothing, certainly not an ugly stump of leg, must keep him from shooting toward his goal.

"La Flesche wants you to state his case to the Commissioner," Burtt wrote to Lowrie in March 1861. "He is very desirous of going east on account of his leg. It must cost him his life in a year's time unless a second amputation is effected. All that he desires to live for is to see his people on the road to improvement, money matters straight, and the Mission in favor."

Though government permission to make the trip did not come, and did not come, there were a few small signs that the arrow was pursuing its course. There were now nineteen inhabited frame houses in the Village of Make-Believe White Men, eight built that very year—seven more than there were in the predominantly white settlement at Decatur ten miles to the south. The number of children in school had increased to forty, twenty-six boys and fourteen girls. "Mission good," was the common report. Even in Big Village Burtt was meeting with more friendly response. At one Sunday service in April there were thirty present, including three chiefs, Noise, Hard Walker, and Standing Hawk.

"We know it is Sunday only when we see you come to our village," he was told through the interpreter.

Dutifully the tribe proclaimed its loyalty to the new Great Father, whose problems of national unity were far more grievous than the Omahas'. Independence Day, an anomaly for an Indian celebration, was observed on the Reservation with great fanfare, doubly significant for it marked the appointment of a new Agent, Orasmus H. Irish. There was always hope that a fresh arm of government would extend a hand less crafty and grasping, and with the Civil War ablaze it was especially desirable for a tribe to arouse no suspicion of disloyalty. It had proved altogether too easy in the past to confuse Indians with the current enemy.

"The whole tribe turned out in its best attire," reported Burtt. "Many whites assembled from thirty miles around, such another sight was never seen. Several addresses were made and the Union flag hoisted. Among the speakers, La Flesche gave us quite a treat."

"My white and red Friends." Chief Iron Eye spoke with dignity and authority. "This flag, I understand, signifies freedom and equal rights. When we were at Washington at our Great Father's we saw this flag floating in the breeze. Our Great Father gave us this flag at our departure. As long as it waves over us, I think we will be a people. When it is torn down we will go with it also. By it we stand and with it we fall."

Joseph was fighting against time, not only for his own life but for the survival of his people. The roar of the flood was mounting. Land to the west, their old hunting grounds, had been opened to homesteaders. The buffalo was near extermination. Time was running out—and fast. A whole culture must be transformed—and overnight. It was no wonder that he met opposition. Sometimes the most violent resistance was in himself. No one knew better than he the loss of values that must be incurred. For the white man's culture decreed that the tribe be subordinated to the individual, cooperation to competition, communal sharing to self-interest. How could a man to whom land had been as free as fresh air and sunshine compress his life into the "ownership" of an acre? It was like imprisoning a meadowlark in a cage and expecting it to sing! Yet to save it from the deadly hawks it must be done.

The Mission, Joseph was convinced, was his best ally, for it meant education—learning the white man's skills, the farmer's, the carpenter's, the blacksmith's; knowledge of reading and writing, necessary tools to combat the dishonest trader's unscrupulous manipulations, as with the collection of debts at the time of annuity payments. Many times white men would list an Indian's debts at an increased figure and enter the side door of the Agency to be first in line as each member of the tribe came for his allotted payment. And how was a man to know when he was being cheated if he could not read or write? Add to this prevalent cheating his ignorance of money values, and his small allotment was gone with little to show that it had passed through his hands.

Joseph promoted the school constantly, sending his own children and urging others to do so. He often went there to visit. When children ran away, he sent Ma-ha-thin-gay, No Knife, captain of the tribal police, to find them and bring them back. He saw that minor offenses were punished.

Not that Joseph's relations with the Mission were always without constraint. Sometimes he had more money than he needed, and he had learned the white man's technique of loaning surplus funds at the prevailing high interest rates. He had loaned $1,800 to Father Hamilton back in 1857, not understanding that the missionary was borrowing for the organization and not for himself. When Hamilton was unable to pay, Joseph was persuaded by certain white men hostile to the Mission to place the matter in a lawyer's hands, only to find that an Indian had no legal rights in a court of law. It was years before a reconciliation was effected between him and the beloved missionary. Then, too, the staff at the Mission was often in dissension. Personalities clashed. The paradox of isolation and close proximity fostered suspicion and gossip. Rumors, later proved false, of an improper affair between the superintendent and one of the unmarried woman teachers reached Joseph's ears.

Perhaps it was this seeming discrepancy between faith and

practice which made him slow to accept the missionaries' religion. Moreover, acceptance would have meant putting away his second wife, Tainne, mother of his only living son, Frank. Perhaps it was these rumors which seemed to justify his taking another wife a bit later, a concession to the deep-seated Indian custom that, when a man's wife died, it was a commendable act for him to marry her sister. Joseph, it was reported, had long ago been married to an Otoe woman, who had died with her son, and he had promised her father at her grave that some day he would take her sister to wife.

"If the missionary can do it, so can I," he insisted stoutly.

In spite of his reluctance and reservations the Mission remained his chief hope for the necessary conformance of his people to white men's ways. An event in the late summer of 1861 confirmed the imperative need for haste.

The Omahas were visited by a band of their related tribe, the Poncas, who had been persuaded by their Agent to go on a hunt. In less than a month, unable to find game, they had come straggling back, begging provisions for their women and children, whom they had left on the plains half starved. The Agent had no food to give them—in spite of the fact that the Great Council in Washington had appropriated $20,000 of its debts to the tribe for provision and house-building! The Poncas had traded away most of their blankets and horses for provision; then some had gone to the Pawnees to ask help, others to the Omahas.

Bright Eyes returned from school one Saturday to find a familiar figure seated on a pile of blankets in the dining-living-sleeping room. She ran to it with a glad cry of welcome. *"Winegi!* Uncle!"

It was White Swan, or Frank, Joseph's half brother, who was a chief of the Poncas. She had been to visit him more than once in his village far up the Smoky Waters at the mouth of the Niobrara. She had had much fun playing with his two little girls, her cousins.

"Rosalie? Susanne?" she inquired, looking about eagerly.

No, White Swan's daughters had not come. The women and children had been left near the Agency on the Ponca reservation, where they would at least have protection, if not food. Most of them had been too weak to travel.

Already Joseph and the other chiefs had sent messengers with provisions to the tribe at the Ponca Agency. White Swan and the other Poncas had been feasted. That night Bright Eyes lay on her blanket in the shadows and listened to the talk of men sitting in a circle of lantern light. She longed for the old days in the lodge when there had been a glowing fire flickering on dark intent faces, wood smoke mingling with the pungent, curling plumes of the pipe being passed from hand to hand. Lantern light was colder, steadier. It threw the features of the squatting men into bold relief.

Bright Eyes could not help staring at one of them. So tall was he that most of the other heads came only to his shoulders. He wore a red blanket trimmed with broad blue stripes, a wide beaded belt, and a long necklace of bear claws. Yet even without his colorful regalia his face would have arrested one's attention. The eyes were dark and piercing beneath a high forehead and heavy brows, lips curved strongly downward like a bow, nose sharply aquiline. The light cast deep shadows in the hollows of hunger-thinned cheeks and made overhanging crags of high cheekbones. She knew who he was, Ma-chu-nah-zhay, Standing Bear, one of the leading Ponca chiefs. His wife was named Susette, like herself, and she had played with his little daughter, Prairie Flower, who was pretty and dainty and graceful, like a plum blossom blowing in the wind. Bright Eyes was fascinated by Standing Bear. Little did either of them guess that night, the man of forty-odd and the child of about seven, how closely their lives were to be linked.

It was Standing Bear who did much of the talking, telling a story of long treks, fear and hunger, patient waiting and broken promises. His voice was low but musical and penetrating. Captured more by the magnetism of the man than by his words, Bright Eyes absorbed every one of them.

"Ah, yes, we were once a great people, more than the leaves on a *waga chun*, the rustling tree. *A-sha-tun-ah-tha!* It is so indeed. That was when we lived on the Red River far to the north beyond the big lake, before the buffaloes which the Great

Spirit had given us for food were all driven away or killed, and before our young men, obliged to penetrate into the countries of their enemies for game, were cut to pieces. Ah, yes, and before our people became foolishly fond of the white man's fire water and died like flies from his plague called *di-xe*, smallpox. Now who knows how few we have become? Perhaps seven hundred."

The Poncas, like the Omahas, had been a peaceable people, never taking up arms against the encroaching white man. In 1817 they had made a treaty of peace and friendship with the United States. Another in 1825 had admitted that "they reside within the territorial limits of the United States, acknowledge their supremacy, and claim their protection." After that they had been left alone for some thirty winters, while other tribes on the Upper Missouri had been troublesome and warlike. But all the time men from the steamboats had been cutting down their trees, white settlers taking away their lands. Just three winters ago they had agreed to another treaty, in which they had yielded up all their lands except a small portion between the Ponca and Niobrara rivers.

"So we abandoned our villages and hunting grounds," said Standing Bear, "and moved to the new small portion of land. But we were too late to plant corn, and the summer hunt brought no meat. We were destitute."

Since the promises of the treaty were not kept, they had believed it void and had prepared to move back to their old settlements. Too late! Already the land had been overrun by white settlers like grasshoppers.

The treaty, it seemed, had been submitted to the Great Council in Washington but not ratified. Only a year later, when forced to "incur a great expense" in furnishing food to keep the Poncas from starving, had the Senate decided to ratify it. By it the government of the Great Father had agreed to "protect the Poncas in the possession of this tract of land, and their persons and property thereon, during good behavior on their part; to pay them annuities annually for thirty years; to expend $20,000 for their subsistence during the first year, for building houses, etc.; to establish schools, and to build mills, mechanics' shops, etc; to give $20,000 for the payment of the existing obligations to the tribe."

Now, two years laters, the Poncas were half starving. There was no protection from their old enemies, the Sioux. In fear they huddled their tents close to the Agency. And in spite of the promised $20,000 the Agent had no food to give them. But they did not despair. They had been able to plant a little corn on the new land, and soon it would produce roasting ears. Meanwhile, with the wild turnips and cherries and plums they could gather, and the help of their friends, they would somehow survive.

Bright Eyes understood nothing of "treaties," "annuities," "reservations," but she knew well the meaning of "hunger" and "fear." Somebody, she got the message clearly, had broken a promise. A wrong had been done. She stared at Standing Bear in amazement. He did not look angry. On the rugged, craglike face there was only a vast patience. Then her eyes were drawn to the man beside him, his brother Big Snake. If Standing Bear was a towering crag, Big Snake was the solid mountain beneath it. His powerful shoulders filled the space where two men might have sat. His hands looked as though they could easily crush rocks. Yet one of them was resting gently on the head of little Frank, who had crawled in between him and Uncle White Swan and gone to sleep. There was no patience on Big Snake's face. His eyes smoldered with anger.

Bright Eyes sensed that Big Snake, like all the others, was looking at Joseph, hopefully, expectantly. That was why they had come here for a council. It was why people usually came. Father would tell them what to do. He was always helping to right wrongs. Perhaps he would go to that far-off mysterious somewhere called Washington and make government, whatever that was, keep its promises to the Poncas. She twisted around on her blanket so she could see Father's face. And suddenly she knew dismay and disbelief. Even before he spoke, she sensed that he had no answer.

"We are one people," he said at last. "Rather than starve at the hands of government or be destroyed by your old enemies, the Sioux, you—you could always come here and join us."

Bright Eyes found it hard to sleep that night. Her dreams

were peopled with faces—sad, patient, angry, but all helpless. And Father's, most helpless of all. He was not all-wise, all-powerful, all problem-solving. Somebody was cheating the poor Poncas, doing them a terrible wrong, and—all Father could tell them was that they might run away!

2

It was 1861, and blessings as well as problems came to the house of Joseph.

"Wihe, Wihe!" Bright Eyes crooned ecstatically over the cradle board. The words "Little Sister" were sweet as honey on her lips. Neither Francis, the robust male, nor Tainne's frail girl baby who had not lived had been as dear to her heart as this child of her own mother Mary. Rosalie, they called her, like Uncle White Swan's daughter. It was a name familiar to the Omahas, for it had belonged to the daughter of an Omaha woman Mitain, who, like Oldest Grandmother, had been a relative of the romantic Chief Blackbird.

On school holidays Bright Eyes often went to Memetage's lodge. The house with its square walls, iron stove, staring windows, was too much like school. Living there, she was still part Susette. For at least one day in the week she wanted to be completely Inshtatheamba. The round walls, glowing fire, soft curtains of skin, roof poles rising to a point high in the shadows—all satisfied some primal need of her being. Besides, no one could cook like Oldest Grandmother. Her cakes of parched ground corn mixed with wild honey and buffalo marrow were mouth-watering. And her loaves of bread, browned quickly on one side over an open fire, then set against the coals to rise, were bigger and fluffier even than Grandmother Nicomi's. Even better were her stories.

"Tell me about Chief Blackbird," Bright Eyes would plead over and over.

The fabulous chief had been Memetage's grandfather. Proud, majestic, handsome, shrewd, ambitious, he had both ruled his people with tyrannical skill and been more than a match for the crafty Waxes. But he had been cruel, too. Learning that his beautiful young wife had been keeping tryst with a lover, he had burst into a rage and stabbed her.

Memetage's eyes grew dark with memory. "I was there. I saw it happen. I was a child, younger than you. He went to look at his tobacco growing in the field and—and found her there. Afterward he covered his head with a buffalo robe and wept. Some say he was so stricken with guilt that he starved himself to death, others that he died of the white man's poison. I know better. The white man's poison, yes, but not the kind that comes in a bottle. He died of the spotted sickness that took away two out of every three of our people. He was buried on the great hill which bears his name. And they say that in the 'Moon When the Deer Rut, on the seventeenth day, if you go to that hill, you can hear the cry of his beautiful wife, like a lost soul."

Bright Eyes was fiercely proud of Chief Blackbird, resentful when she heard one of the white chests call him an ungodly savage. He compared very well, she thought, with Samson and David and Joshua, whom they considered such wonderful heroes. Why, she wondered, did they believe all the stories in their book were holy, but all the sacred Indian stories heathen? Like Adam and Eve. Secretly she thought the Omahas' idea of how man came to be was just as good or better.

"In the beginning all things were in the mind of Wakonda." Once old Waki-des-chinga, leader of the Pebble Society, had gathered the children about him and told them all about the Creation. "All creatures, including men, were spirits. They were seeking a place where they could come into bodily existence. They descended to the earth and saw it was covered with water. Suddenly from the midst of the water uprose a great rock. It burst into flames and the waters floated into the air in clouds. Dry land appeared, the grasses and the trees grew. The host of spirits descended and became flesh and blood. The land vibrated with their joy and gratitude to Wakonda, the maker of all things."

It was 1862, and a young nation "dedicated to the proposition that all men are created equal" was fighting for its life. So was a much older nation called the Sioux. While generals named Sherman and Sheridan and Grant were battling for land which its owners wished to wrest away, chiefs named Little Crow, Big Eagle, and Medicine Bottle were battling to avenge ten years of broken treaties, the massacre of a whole tribe for the murder of a white man by one Indian, near starvation while a trader with a full warehouse remarked contemptuously, "So far as I am concerned, if they are hungry, let them eat grass or their own dung."

The Homestead Act was passed, opening to white settlers at $1.25 an acre 160 acres each of fine land purchased from its previous owners at from three to nine cents an acre, much of which still remained unpaid. In September, the "Moon When the Deer Shed Their Horns," the Great Father in Washington boldly issued his proclamation freeing all slaves in territories at war with the Union (black men, not red.) And in the "Moon When the Little Black Bears Are Born," December, thirty-eight Santee Sioux who had been promised leniency if they surrendered—some of whom had never killed, wounded, or injured a white man—sang the Indian death song and were hanged. But for the intercession of the Great Father, whose conscience was sorely troubled, the number would have been three hundred.

It was 1863. The names allotted to new Indian boys in school acquired contemporary pertinence. Ulysses S. Grant, William T. Sherman, Edwin M. Stanton, and Philip Sheridan shared desks with the more obsolete Alexander, Gideon, and Joshua. Many older boys donned the Union blue and went off to fight Confederates instead of Sioux, brass buttons replacing war paint and eagle feathers as status symbols. At age nine Bright Eyes was rapidly acquiring seniority, especially with little Frank, now six, in attendance. On his first day she agonized for him, knowing the awful strangeness of transition. Through her fingers during the long prayers she could see his round black head, shorn of its scalp lock, droop lower and lower toward the bench. *Nunh he!* Like herself the first time, he had gone to sleep!

It was 1863. In May, the "Moon in Which the Tribe Plant," the Poncas hoed their corn and went hopefully on their hunt—only to learn that the Yankton Sioux, sent south by one of the generals, occupied their hunting grounds. They returned without meat, to find their corn dried up by drought. Meanwhile the plains had been burned over, and there were no wild turnips or other roots to dig. Even the wild plums were withered. Their agent, who had been sent no provisions for them, marveled at their restraint.

"They have behaved well," he reported, "quite as well, if not better than the same number of whites would have done under like circumstances. I have known whole families to live for days together on nothing but half-dried corn stalks, and this when there were cattle and sheep in their sight."

Their patience was sorely tried when what government reported as "an unfortunate occurrence" took place in Nebraska. The news of it even reached Susette, safe in the square impregnability of school, and she lay awake that night, trembling. It could so easily have happened to Uncle White Swan!

A party of Poncas were on their way home from a visit to the Omahas, four men, six women, three boys, and two girls. One night a party of white soldiers came to their camp, making advances to the women with both money and guns. The Indians fled, hiding in a willow copse. The soldiers despoiled all their goods, cutting the tent skins, burning saddles and blankets, strewing over the ground the food given them by the Omahas. Fortunately the Poncas had hidden their ponies. In the morning they returned, picked up the remnants they could find, loaded their ponies, and set off for home. After a few miles they built a fire to parch the scavenged corn, and some of the women went to hunt for wild beans. The soldiers came on them again, and the Indians fled—too late. The soldiers fired on them, wounding two women and a child as they tried to cross the river on the ice. Taking the six ponies and all other articles they could find, the soldiers started away, but a barking dog revealed the hiding place of the other women. Wheeling, the soldiers shot them dead, three women and a little girl. One of the little boys dived into a hole in the ice. When his head appeared, the soldiers fired at him, but later he managed to escape. His mother, one of the murdered women, was found with three balls in her head and cheek, her throat cut, and her head half severed. Another woman, the youngest, was left naked. The soldiers belonged to Company B of the Seventh Iowa Cavalry.

The deed was investigated, but with no result. The soldiers were never punished.

3

It was 1863. Opposition toward Chief Iron Eye, fostered by white men who could not use him for their purposes, increased. It was not in the interest of white men that Indians should become intelligent farmers. Often the Agent, the Agent's employees, and the authorities behind them in Washington, as well as the "Chiefs' Party" in his own tribe, were opposed to his efforts to promote education. But he persisted.

"It is either civilization or extermination," he told the tribe repeatedly.

Many had not forgotten that the loss of his leg had followed his rejection of the ancient rite of annointing the Sacred Pole. Now, as his condition grew dangerously acute, the suspicion was revived. "See! The Venerable Man will have his revenge!"

But there came a time when Chief Iron Eye made the superstitions of his people an asset instead of a liability.

It was May 1863 when he finally secured permission to go east. Not only had certain terms of the treaty of 1854 remained unfulfilled, but others had been violated. Why, he wanted to demand of the Commissioner, were the more rebellious tribes around them paid their annuities in silver and gold, while the Omahas received theirs in paper currency? Not only a violation but an injustice, since the government would not receive treasury notes in payment for Indian taxes on the reservation! He asked Burtt to secure the assistance of Dr. Lowrie both in approaching the Bureau in Washington and in arranging for further surgery on his leg. Burtt was glad to comply, adding in his letter to Lowrie, "Would you lend him money if he needs it? He is honorable and meets his bills."

When Chief Iron Eye returned from New York and Washington he made a feast and invited all the chiefs and braves. The company was almost equally divided between his supporters and his opponents. The conservative Big Village was well represented by those consistently opposed to the adoption of white men's ways: Noise, Little Chief, White Cow, and their staunch adherents known as the Chiefs' Party. Wakonmonthin was there, Keeper of the White Buffalo Hide, and of course Yellow Smoke, lines of anxiety furrowing his fine high forehead and tensing the flesh beneath his heavy cheek bones, eyes still sorrowfully brooding with memory of the indignity to his Sacred Pole. But friends were as much in evidence: Wajapa, Two Crows, Thangeska, No Knife, John Big Elk, and the rest of the Young Men's Party *en masse*. After the sumptuous feast, served by two young men from great iron kettles, and the passing of the pipes, Chief Iron Eye rose from his seat at the left of the entrance of his house and invited all to go outside, that the whole tribe might hear what he had to say.

The chiefs again formed their circle, while curious onlookers pressed close. Word had gone out that Iron Eye was to make a speech and that he had brought something back with him from the land of the Great White Father. Necks craned. Was that the "something" which one of the young men was carrying, as if it were heavy like iron, a queer square thing like a box? The crowd coalesced into groups: men from Big Village, wary, watchful; the Young Men's Party, hopeful, anxious; leaders of the various medicine societies.

"So the chief has been to Washington. Let's see what his love of the Waxes has got for us!"

He has something in mind, but what? This crowd could easily turn into a mob!"

"They say he had more of his leg cut off. That's what comes of flouting the old ways and angering Wakonda. But listen! Let's hear what he has to say."

Chief Iron Eye remained close to the door of his house, the heavy black box at his feet. He stood on his one good leg, balancing himself on his crutches.

"*Ah ho!*" he greeted them. "*Ku-gay-ho!* Hello, my friends. I have come back to you from the land toward the coming of the sun. I have something to say to you. You all believe in the power of our medicine men. However much power they may have, I tell you it is nothing compared with that of the white men. Our medicine is but a breath that vanishes, when compared with theirs. We cannot resist them, it is useless to try. Now I will show you something of the power of the white men's medicine."

There was a brief burst of confusion, angry murmurs, shocked exclamations, muttered questions, anxious whispers. Then the groups dissolved, pressed forward in solid unity, tensed with curiosity.

Chief Iron Eye directed the circle of other chiefs to join hands. He asked the one on his right, Standing Hawk, to take hold of a handle on the square black box. He asked the one on his left, Yellow Smoke, to grasp a second handle. Then he pressed a small lever. An electric battery leaped into action. So did the circle of chiefs. Clinging to each other's hands, they writhed, jerked, grimaced, twitched, squirmed, in convulsions of amazed and tortured agony. Iron Eye watched their contortions for a moment, then turned the power off. While they struggled to regain their dignity he stumped into the house on his crutches, to reappear a few moments later walking like a normal man, having to all appearances grown a new leg.

Pandemonium burst. Women screamed. Some stumbled and fell in an attempt to flee. Horror, awe, terror, bewilderment, curiosity, all struggled for supremacy. But again curiosity won. Most remained rooted, staring, eyes wide and mouths agape while the chief sat down on a box, crossed his legs, moved his new foot up and down, rose from his seat and walked easily about. Then, while they were still rooted in astonishment, before fright could send them fleeing, he raised his hands in a gesture of command.

"*Ah ho!* My friends, sit down."

It was the voice of their chief, and they obeyed. He spoke to them then at length, simply, with deep sympathy and understanding. He showed them the new leg, made of cork and fitted to the stump, not a thing of magic but a creation of the white man's skill and knowledge. He explained to them the working of the electric battery.

"There is no such thing as 'big medicine,'" he said, "among either red men or white. The Waxes are not strong and powerful because of magic but because they have worked and sent their children to school. We also can have this power. It is this, my people, that all these years I have been trying to tell you."

Many were impressed. The new way of living gained a few converts. That fall the school was full. No Knife, captain of police, with two daughters already at the Mission, determined to send his wife also. Even Little Chief, an open foe to almost everything which white men would consider improvement, was for once active. "Like the wind that blows," wrote Burtt. A new hydraulic ram at the Mission aroused almost as much respect for the white man's skill as had the artificial leg.

But, though there was less open opposition to the head chief's authority, there were sullen looks and mutterings among the Keepers of the Sacred Tents and the Sacred Packs and the medicine men who were the sole guardians of ancient secrets, and in the lodges of Big Village fires often glowed on circles of troubled faces far into the night.

4

It was 1863. Snow piled high in the three villages, mounting to the poles of tipis, turning the round lodges into domes of glittering ice. The blizzard called "the geese come hidden by the storm" was even more severe than usual, and only a few birds came riding in its wake. In that same "Moon When the Geese Come Back," February, the Great Council in Washington passed an act authorizing the "peaceful and quiet removal of the Winnebago Indians from the state of Minnesota"—an act which was profoundly to affect the Omahas.

According to their treaty of 1859 many of the peaceful Winnebagoes had had farms allotted to them in severalty; the remainder of their rich lands, hundreds of thousands of acres, were to be sold to white settlers, the proceeds from which were to be expended partly on improvements for their farms, partly to be held in trust. They had begun farming energetically, planning to build houses and raise good crops, though with no sign of the promised funds for improvement. In 1862 white settlers had been so aroused by a ferocious attack of Sioux that they had turned against all Indians, even the peaceful Winnebagoes, and had begun shooting them on sight. Without the promised implements for agriculture and fearful of going on their annual hunt, the tribe had soon approached starvation. Now they were faced also with eviction.

They took their possessions to the bank of the Mississippi, where soldiers explained to them that their goods would be sent down the river and up the Missouri. They never saw them again. Marched across country, many dying on the way, they arrived in a barren country where no food or shelter was provided, and they faced starvation. Though there was an abundance of game, the new agent refused to let them go on a hunt. A missionary who had accompanied the tribe from Minnesota told the chief to assemble the hunters and go. He would take the consequences. When they returned with game, the angry agent appropriated all of it, doling it out in small quantities to the tribe in troughs and selling the remainder for his own profit. Their condition seemed hopeless.

Secretly, members of the tribe went to a heavy growth of cottonwoods, cut down trees, and built canoes, a hundred of them. Then one dark night the whole tribe boarded them and fled down the river. Freezing temperatures, starvation, and the guns of pursuing soldiers soon reduced the two thousand of their number to about twelve hundred, but the sorry remnant finally began arriving at the Omaha Agency, begging for food to keep them from starving.

Iron Eye and the other chiefs received them, sharing with them their scanty stores of meat from their unsuccessful summer hunt. But the Winnebagoes kept coming, canoe after canoe, until there were over 700 of the refugees on the reservation. Then in September almost the whole Ponca tribe arrived with no provisions except a little buffalo meat. Neither tribe had enough to last more than a few weeks. The new Omaha Agent, Colonel Furnas, was faced with the task of feeding over 3,000 Indians. Though emergency rations arrived from government, and the Poncas left before winter, months of acute hardship followed. Even the good earth turned hostile, freezing to a depth never before seen, bursting the pipes leading from the Mission's new hydraulic pump. The winter's hunting and trapping also produced little more than bitter complaints from the surrounding white settlers.

Chief Iron Eye, always incensed by injustice, was stirred to action. He set aside fields for the Winnebagoes to cultivate until a new home could be arranged for them, insisting, however, on a rigid code of conduct which especially prohibited gambling and the use of intoxicating liquors. He himself would go to Washington with a delegation, to lay the case of the Winnebagoes before the government.

The Department of the Interior professed itself shocked and astounded by these developments. It had "presumed that the Winnebagoes' agent would adopt such measures as would induce the tribe to remain on their reservation" and it had been "understood that ample arrangements had been made for their subsistence."

Chief Iron Eye was well pleased with the result of his efforts. The Winnebagoes were promised land on which they could make a living by farming—well pleased, that is, until he was told that the promised land was to be taken from their own Omaha reservation! It was the new agent's solution to a troublesome dilemma, and Colonel Furnas was a man of vigorous and aggressive action.

Iron Eye was outraged. A strip of land eight miles wide and twenty-five miles long, to be carved out of the pittance of acres which had been promised them forever! It was a flagrant violation of their treaty, which had promised that the lands would be surveyed and individual farms allotted. But the government representative was adamant. The decision had already been made.

"How much will the government pay us?" the chief demanded bluntly.

"Nothing," replied the emissary equably. "You had more than your people needed, and now a part of it belongs to the Winnebagoes."

The new treaty was signed in 1865 and ratified a year later. The Winnebagoes were no more pleased than the Omahas. They refused to live in the houses which the government built for them and to return to farming. They had been defrauded of their own homes in Minnesota, forced to take land from their friends, the Omahas. If they developed new farms, they feared, the white men would only take them away. Their ambition had been destroyed, their hopes broken. They erected shacks and tipis, and, once a highly civilized tribe, they would remain for many years shiftless and degraded, an easy prey to the white traders who, now that Iron Eye's rigid code no longer controlled them, were able to ply their trade in fire water unmolested.

The Omahas bitterly resented their proximity, and they found many ways to express their contempt. But not Chief Iron Eye. His code of justice permitted no personal prejudice. His children discovered that one day.

It was Saturday. As usual Susette and Frank were allowed to go home for the day. They took the path over the hill, Susette walking with the dignity befitting an older schoolgirl trained in manners by Miss Diament, not even scurrying, as did Frank, past the little graveyard. Frank went at once to the barns to fondle and feed his favorite horses, Kushas and Hintu, then was off to play with the village boys. Susette felt suddenly bereft. Each Saturday it was becoming harder to turn into In-shtatheamba, even for a single day. The Village of Make-Believe White Men, now usually called "Joe's Village," was much like the Mission. Most of the women and girls wore calico Mother Hubbards. And Susette had changed most of all. She thought now in terms of months, not moons; years, not winters; nights, not sleeps. Indeed, she was even beginning to think in English!

"Play with me!" begged little Rosalie.

A-ou-da! Very good! Why not? They played together while Marguerite, a year younger than Rosalie, gleefully tried to interfere, thrusting her plump fingers into the strings of the *wabaha* (which the white people called "cat's cradle"), jostling their hands when they tried painstakingly to pull one joint of prairie grass away from a big pile without moving the rest. When Rosalie ran away in disgust and Mother came to rescue the weeping Marguerite, Bright Eyes joined some of her village friends who were going to the fields to hunt "mouse beans." It was fun finding the mouse holes, whole cellars, where the little field rodents had stored wild beans, big like limas, and hazelnuts. You stole either the beans or the nuts, never both, which would have left the little animals without food. Bright Eyes was willing to hunt them, but she could not eat them, though they were just like regular cultivated beans when boiled. Somehow the thought of the little mouse with a bean in its mouth . . .!

"Kill him! Kill him!" The shrieks of boys at the west end of the village sent the children flying in that direction. A weasel? A big snake? Or—terrifying thought—a marauding Sioux? No. Reaching the small hillock, they looked down on a crowd of boys and young men swarming about a small lad and throwing sticks and stones at him. A little way off stood Frank and his friends, looking on but not participating in the attack. They must have been playing a game of "bone slides," for they still held the willow throw-sticks, the scorched stripes resembling a snake's skin.

"Kill him!" The shrieks became shriller. "He's just a thieving Winnebago!"

The boy was a pitiable object, legs and feet bare, a ragged blanket over one arm, a crust of bread clutched in his hand. Mud streaked his face from the barrage. Several boys took turns at kicking him. When he tried to run away, someone threw a big stick in front of him. He stumbled over it and fell. The crowd laughed hilariously. Some of the girls laughed, too, and clapped their hands.

"Oh! *Nonshtán*, stop!" Bright Eyes was crying. "Why doesn't somebody stop them!"

Her friends were indignant. "*Ho!* Serves him right! What's the matter with you? He's a Winnebago!"

Bright Eyes fell silent. She wished she were a boy, like Frank. She wouldn't just stand there clutching a stick. She would . . . but would she? After all, the boy *was* a Winnebago, and the Winnebagoes had been given their land, unjustly. Father said so.

A man came running up, No Knife, the chief of police. "You are commanded to cease molesting that boy!" he shouted.

Recognizing him as coming from the chief, the crowd dispersed, but reluctantly, angrily, in muttering groups. Bright Eyes saw someone else run up and touch Frank on the arm. It was the boy who ran errands for Father. Sheepishly Frank followed him toward the village.

When Bright Eyes arrived at home she found a circle of men sitting with Father on the floor of the downstairs room. They were passing a pipe from hand to hand. Frank stood at one side, apparently unnoticed by his father, who was talking. Wajapa was there and Dubamone, also other prominent men of the village: Kahenumba, Teokenha, and Wahonige, the fathers of some of Frank's school friends.

"Son," said Chief Iron Eye at last, "step to the middle of the floor."

Frank did so, and Father began talking in a low voice. "I speak not boastfully. All of you here have known me from boyhood, and will know that what I am about to say is true."

He spoke of his early struggles with hunger and poverty and how, remembering them, even after winning position and high honors, he had always given help to the poor. He had given them horses and sent them away singing for joy. The stranger who had entered his door had never gone away hungry. He had never tormented or abused a poor man.

He turned now and spoke directly to his son. "You came into existence and have reached the age when you should seek for knowledge. That you might profit by the teachings of your people and those of the white race, and that you might avoid the misery which accompanies ignorance, I placed you in the House of Teaching of the white chests, who are said to be wise and to have in their books the utterances of great and learned men. I had treasured the hope that you would seek and know the good deeds done by men of your own race, and by men of the white race, that you would follow their example and take pleasure in doing the things that are noble and helpful to those around you. Am I to be disappointed?"

The chief rose and pointed his finger at Frank. Never had his handsome features so exemplified the unyielding will which had inspired his name.

"Only today there crept to the door of my house a poor boy driven thither by hunger. He was given food by my command. He went away happy. Hardly had he left the village when a rabble gathered about him and persecuted him. They threw mud at him, pointed at him their fingers in derision, and laughed rudely at his poverty; and you, a son of Inshtamaza, joined the tormentor and smiled at the poor boy's tears."

No! That isn't fair. He didn't do that! Bright Eyes opened her mouth to do an unforgivable thing, interrupt her elders, but before she could speak a small boy cried out hesitantly, "Sir, he didn't join them!" She trembled with relief. But Father continued as if he had not heard.

"By your presence you aided and encouraged those wicked boys. He who is present at a wrongdoing and lifts not a hand to prevent it is as guilty as the wrongdoers. The persecution of the poor, the sneer at their poverty, is a wrong for which no punishment is too severe. I have finished. Go, and think of my words."

Frank went out, head bent, boyish features constricted with approaching tears. So deeply scored were the words on his conscience that years later he would write them down in a book, just as they had been spoken.

Five

1

It was 1864. After the terrible cold of the "Moon When the Geese Come Back," also called the "Moon of Storms," Nishuda, the Smoky Water, was even wilder than usual. Ice piled in great jams along all its 2,500 miles of snakelike bends, cracking with bursts like cannon fire. "Too thick to wade and too thin to walk on," as the traders said, its churning murk overspread the bottoms to twice, three times its six-mile width, disgorging trees, brush, dead buffalo, rabbits, and all manner of refuse. Every day the big school boys devised some errand down the river path to see what new treasures might have been washed up. But by now there were few big boys. Sixteen of them, including James Donaldson, Matthew and William Tyndall, Daniel Webster, Charles Morgan, and George Washington, had gone to join the Union army.

After the cold and the floods came drought and heat: two moons when not a drop of rain fell and even in the "Moon in Which One Plants," May, the thermometer at the Mission registered up to ninety-six. Measles raged through the tribe. There was no lodge or tipi at Big Village that remained unvisited. In one week, during the "Moon When the Buffalo Bellow," there were fifteen deaths, and the hunt had to be postponed. The mercury soared to 110 degrees in the shade, and men's passions mounted with it. One day the aunt and wife of Louis Sansouci, the interpreter, were riding quietly along a path of the reservation. The aunt was recklessly shot at by some white soldiers, the wife shot and sabered.

It was 1864. The war ground on toward Union victory. The Great White Father in Washington was reelected. To the west at Sand Creek in Colorado a Cheyenne Indian chief named Black Kettle gathered hundreds of his tribe around him, the American flag waving above his head, and assured his people that as long as that flag flew over them the soldiers would never fire on his followers. Such had been the pledge given by Colonel Greenwood, Commissioner of Indian Affairs. Unfortunately Greenwood had not heard the ultimatum of Colonel Chivington, a former Methodist preacher who directed the Colorado volunteers.

"Damn any man who sympathizes with Indians! I have come to kill Indians, and I believe it is right and honorable to use any means under God's heaven to kill Indians."

He meant it. Neither the stars and stripes nor a white flag raised over the band of Black Kettle prevented the massacre of Sand Creek, in which 105 Indian women and children and twenty-eight men were slaughtered, among them Chief One Eye, who had told a white officer with dignity, "The Cheyennes do not break their word. If they should do so, I would not care to live longer."

By that strange, often wordless communication which could sweep over the world of the Plains Indians like wind over prairie grass, the Omahas learned of this breach of faith with uneasiness and apprehension. "We have our treaty," the chiefs assured each other. But the Cheyennes also had had their treaty. Though by it they had relinquished no rights nor claims to their lands, the Pike's Peakers had descended on their country like a plague of grasshoppers, burrowed into it like armies of prairie gophers, staked hundred of claims, built towns and cities.

And that summer trouble came closer than Colorado Territory. In the "Moon When the Elk Bellow" some Winnebagoes crossed the river to get rushes for their mats, were set upon by Sioux, and eleven of their number were killed. The Omahas were driven in from their hunt by attacking Sioux, leaving two scalped bodies behind. Sioux? It was hard to tell, for the worst-feared guerillas on their hunting grounds were painted white men.

For many of the tribe's troubles Chief Iron Eye was held responsible. He was the apostle of change, therefore the scapegoat. Now also he encountered a new and powerful source of opposition, the new agent. Colonel Furnas, who had been appointed to the position through the influence of Samuel Daily, the territorial representative to Congress, in payment of a political debt, was a man of vigorous and dominating personality, accustomed to obedience. Iron Eye, also vigorous and dominating, was not accustomed to obey. Their ideas for the tribe's improvement soon clashed. An order requiring military passes for all who wished to leave the reservation for any purpose was especially galling. It was Furnas also who had maneuvered the sale of reservation lands for the Winnebagoes.

It was 1865. The Civil War ended. A week later the Great Father in Washington was assassinated. The Thirteenth Amendment to the Constitution became law, abolishing slavery (for Blacks). And early in the following year the Nebraska Territorial Legislature, in its lower house, passed an act memorializing the General Government to force the removal of all Indians from the Territory.

The Omahas were stunned. This could not happen to them! To the Cheyennes, the Winnebagoes, the Sioux, the Arapahoes, but not to them! They had their treaty, signed by the Great Council in Washington and all their seven chiefs. It promised them this small portion of their ancient heritage in perpetuity.

A-sha-tun-ah-tha, agreed Chief Iron Eye. It was so indeed. And had they forgotten that but a few moons ago their chiefs had been forced to sign another treaty selling a good portion of it to the Winnebagoes?

But they had been promised that each man would have his own little section, his allotment, with a certificate so it could not be taken away!

A-sha-tun-ah-tha. But over eleven years had passed since the treaty, and, in spite of all their reminders and requests and pleadings, had such an allotment ever been made?

Excitement seethed. A mass meeting was held at the Mission. A committee was appointed to wait on the Agent and ask him to call a Council of the chiefs and braves, a necessary preliminary under Furnas's stern rulings. A memorial was drawn up requesting an immediate survey of the tribal lands and the apportionment of farms, equipped with stock, wagons, and other necessary tools. In return the Omahas would promise to give up their annual hunts and try to live like white people. Feverishly they began cutting logs for houses, splitting rails for fences, even marking out their claims. Chief Iron Eye watched a little grimly and with tongue in cheek, for many had been the most ardent opponents of change. They still were. Their grudging compliance with his and Big Elk's advice only aggravated their opposition and resentment.

The antagonism of the Agent increased. Furnas had been promised on taking the Agency that he could appoint his own trader, though advised that this would be "a delicate matter." Joseph and Fontenelle were still the sole tribal traders, though they often lacked capital to make cash payments for goods and freight bills. Joseph had been loaned some funds by the Mission Board which he had scrupulously repaid. A white trader would have had more capital available and, if one could be found at the lowest possible pay, there would be more profits for the Agent, the Territorial Representative to Congress, and the Commissioner of Indian Affairs. Division of such profits among agents and their superiors was common practice.

Though Furnas ostensibly supported the Mission, presenting it with a Bible and other gifts, both Joseph and Superintendent Burtt sensed his covert opposition. Some of it was justified. Only a small percentage of Omaha children was being reached by the school. Even Joseph admitted that his daughter had made little progress in her studies for the last two years, and no one was more conscious of the school's inadequacies than Burtt himself. More schools should be established and the Mission school upgraded. Its contact was with the government, and it operated as efficiently as its funds and facilities permitted.

Susette was conscious of no deficiencies in her education. English had become almost as familiar as the Omaha language. With girls older than herself she was reading in the Fourth Eclectic Reader, studying Intermediate Geography, mental and written arithmetic, and writing. She could read long sentences glibly.

"To take what is not yours is a sin, for the word of God says, 'Thou shalt not steal.' . . . If you swear and lie and steal, you will live and die in shame. . . . Pray God to save you from all these sins."

Books were her closest companions. She was not like Frank, who belonged to a gang of boys calling themselves "The Middle Five," to distinguish themselves from "The Big Seven" and some gangs of lower age. She was too shy to make intimate friends among the girls, though she secretly adored some of them. When two of the most promising pupils, Julia Harvey and Susette Benjamin, died of consumption within a few months of each other, she cried herself to sleep for many nights in succession. But it was the boy Francis Vinton Brush who commanded her most passionate devotion. He was the leader of Frank's gang, the head of every recitation class, and as fluent a reader of English as Graybeard. There was nothing, it seemed, that he could not do, from whittling remarkably lifelike horses and buffaloes with his rusty jackknife to riding one of Father's most spirited horses in a race on the bottoms and winning. An orphan, grandson of a former chief, he sometimes came home with Frank on a Saturday, days of bliss for Susette, though she remained tonguetied and awkward in his presence. Her surreptitious glances in his direction at school were not unnoticed.

"Susette is sweet on Brush!" the girls began chanting one day on the playground.

Flushing hotly, she dashed up the steep steps to the porch, stumbling over her long skirt and skinning her knees, taking refuge in the dim bare schoolroom. For days she dared not glance across the wide aisle separating the boys' desks from the girls'.

It was one hot day in September that a flurry of excitement swept the boys' side of the aisle, where the windows faced the driveway. A tossed note soon transferred the news to the girls. A big black carriage had come up to the gate, and the Agent and three big fat men had alighted. Graybeard had also seen and was noticeably nervous. Presently the four men entered the room, conducted by Superintendent Burtt. They asked many questions of Graybeard, about the subjects taught and the progress of the children. Then Graybeard turned to face the pupils.

"Now, children," he said, "pay strict attention. These gentlemen want to see what you have learned. I will put some questions to you."

All sat as stiff as ramrods. One could have heard a pin drop.

"Who," asked Graybeard, "discovered America?"

Dozens of hands went up. Not Susette's. A hard little core constricted her throat, and her lips tightened. Sometime, she had long since resolved, she would be asked that question, and she would say exactly what she thought. Politely but firmly. *I don't know his name. Nobody does. It was too long ago. But it was one of the people you call Indians.*

"Columbus," replied Brush dutifully.

Susette relaxed. Sometime, but not now. The questions continued. There was a spelling match, with Brush and an older girl left standing. To Susette's anguish Brush went down first. The girl was given a gilt-edged book for a prize.

"Are they taught music?" asked one of the visitors.

No, the Superintendent admitted, but they could sing all the Sunday School songs. Would they like to hear "The Little Brown Church in the Wildwood"?

No, the visitors would like to hear an Indian song—that is, if the Indians had such things.

The Indians certainly did. Somebody started a Victory song, and soon the whole school was making the room ring. Though the visitors could not understand the words, they could not fail to sense the surging virulence of emotion, the patriotic exultancy of a people triumphant over their enemies.

"Savage!" muttered one of the visitors. "They must be taught real music."

That same afternoon they received their first singing lesson and soon they were intoning such acceptable tunes as "Daisy Lee" and "Laura, Laura, still we love thee, Though we see thy form no more."

Joseph also came to visit the school, not, like the Agent, to inspect and criticize, but to lend support. Once he and Mary rode over bringing five new pupils, one of them little Rosalie.

Within hours the four-year-old was the darling of the twenty-four girls in the dormitory, a favorite of all the teachers, and was permitted to chatter in Omaha to her heart's content. *Tapuka*, she called Superintendent Burtt, her version of *Tapuska*, teacher.

"I Tapuka's girl."

Her coming changed Susette's world. The bare bleak dormitory became bright with sunshine. The older girls, Mary and Marie and Jane, included her in their whispered confidences. The younger children, through Rosalie, discovered that she had a rare gift for story telling, and she was often surrounded at recess. At last Susette felt almost as much at home in the big square school as in the Oldest Grandmother's cozy round lodge. She could go from one to the other and feel that she belonged in both. That was why the disaster that soon came seemed to tear her world apart.

2

It was 1866. The Great Council in Washington passed a bill over the President's veto giving equal rights to all persons born in the United States—except Indians. The Fourteenth Amendment to the Constitution giving Blacks rights of citizenship was forwarded to the states for ratification. With the Civil War at an end the westward migration became a stampede. Permission to build roads and railroads across Indian land must be secured at all costs. Up in the Powder River country a Brûlé Sioux named Red Cloud was told that the government intended to open a road through his tribe's country regardless of their treaty. Red Cloud, joined by such chiefs as Sitting Bull and Crazy Horse, determined to resist. They succeeded. *"Hoka-hey! Hoka-hey!"* came the battle cries. "It's a good day to die!" This time it was not Indians who died but white men. The carnage the Indians inflicted near Fort Phil Kearney on Pino Creek when Captain Fetterman and eighty-one men were slaughtered was called by the white men the Fetterman Massacre. To the Indians it was the Battle of the Hundred Slain. "Savage! Pagan terrorism!" shuddered a white Colonel, shocked by the mutilation perpetrated by Indians on white bodies and doubtless forgetting that at the Sand Creek Massacre two years before the same mutilations had first been practiced by whites on Indians.

It was 1866. Agent Furnas appointed a new trader for the Omaha tribe, depriving Joseph La Flesche and his partner Henry Fontenelle of their means of livelihood. Efforts to compete with the authorized trader were doomed to failure. Joseph was forced to rely on his beef cattle and horses for his family's subsistence.

"White men are determined to ruin me," he told Father Hamilton when the beloved missionary came to the reservation that spring to conduct religious services. "They turn my own people against me. If—if only I could go away somewhere and find peace!"

"I advised him to continue with his people," Hamilton wrote Lowrie, "in the hope of doing them good. He is a man of no ordinary ability and of sterling integrity. I have known him for twelve years. Strong efforts have been made to turn my mind against him, but I think if anybody has had an opportunity to study his character, I have."

Joseph listened with grave interest to the missionary's teachings, but, unlike Mary, who professed a sense of her sins' forgiveness, he would not commit himself. There was still the matter of his three wives. He wanted to do right. He would be glad if all but his first wife left him, but—how could he drive them away? They were members of his family!

The Agent did not share Hamilton's opinion, and he also was in correspondence with Dr. Lowrie. "It is possible that I judge La Flesche too severely, but two years convince me that he is a corrupt man and has not the interests of the Omahas at heart. He became a chief accidentally. All the headmen agree but two of his relatives. . . . He is a shrewd, ambitious, cunning politician, has never been willing to subordinate himself to an Agent, or even the Honorable Commissioner of Indian Affairs. He has arrayed himself against every effort of mine or order of the Department calculated to benefit and elevate the whole tribe."

Like selling our land to the Winnebagoes? Joseph might have asked bitterly. Like appointing a white trader who would share more profits with the Agency?

It was inevitable that the Agent's opposition should extend to the school and its superintendent, so close was the relationship of both with Joseph. And Burtt also was no puppet. Yet never had the missionary seemed more accepted by the people. When he went out to the villages, even to Big Village, they saluted him with "*Han Kingi, Han Indadi*, My Friend, My Father." To her great delight Susette was asked to help Reverend Burtt with his language study. Already he was able to write the Omaha alphabet and, with her assistance, two hymns and the Lord's Prayer. She was helping him compose some short sermons so he could dispense with an interpreter.

Yet somehow she knew that all was not well. She sensed the presence of dissension in school during the week, at home on Saturdays: whisperings among the teachers and older girls, worried lines on Father's face, conversations of Wajapa and Two Crows quickly hushed at her approach. But life went on as usual, dressing each morning in the freezing dark, school prayers at five, breakfast at six, classes, dinner at twelve, sewing, a bit of play, farm work for the boys, supper at five, school worship at six, back to the cold dark again to undress, bed at seven. And always Saturdays to anticipate.

Then suddenly it came, the end of everything. First the fragments of gossip at school, the teachers not even bothering to hush when the pupils came near—

"Reverend Burtt—dismissed—letter from Dr. Lowrie—no reasons given—that old slander, do you think?—forgotten long ago, proved false. No, mark my word, it's the Agent's doing . . ." Then the sight of the superintendent's face at prayers, eyes reddened as if from weeping, cheeks bloodless, lips straight and hard as an arrow shaft above his black beard. For once there was no whispering, punching, or spitball snapping during prayers.

Then during classes the next morning Susette and Frank and Rosalie were called out of the schoolroom. Two Crows was waiting. "*Ithadi*, your father, sends me. You are to get all your belongings and come home."

Miss Mills, who had charge of the girls outside of school, helped Susette pack her few possessions. It took only a small parfleche case to hold them. The uniform must be left behind

—and her books! That was what hurt the most. And she had just begun reading in the Fifth Eclectic Reader! She stroked its hard covers lovingly, exclaimed in dismay when a tear raised a big blob on its smooth surface.

"It's all right, dear. You haven't hurt it. And you'll be coming back soon."

It was Mi-on-thi-ga-ke, the "Moon in Which Nothing Happens." Nothing? Everything! The whole village was gathered in the open space about Chief Iron Eye's house, and on the outskirts of the crowd stood groups of men from Big Village, wrapped in their blankets, faces watchful and noncommittal. Travoix were being loaded with goods; tent poles fastened to the sides of ponies by one end, the other left to trail on the ground; parfleche cases, food supplies, cooking utensils tied in great bundles to the backs of other ponies. Horses were everywhere, many already equipped for travel with the elaborately embroidered cruppers used by women or the wooden saddles wrapped around with soft green hide, easier on the horse's back than the white man's leather. Others, unsaddled, were being led about by the strips of hide which served for bridles. It looked as if all Father's corral had been emptied!

"It's like a hunt," thought Susette, bewildered, but it was not the time of year for hunting. And—she stared, even more puzzled—Father was giving away many of his horses!

"*Ah ho!* Dubamoni, *Kagaeha*, Friend! For you the bald face that won the last race on the bottoms . . ."

Not that there was anything strange about giving things away. Indians were always giving, even their best horses, at feasts, at funerals, when they went visiting, when guests left them to go home. But Dubamoni was going away, leading the horse, and weeping.

"It's like a funeral," she thought, terrified, suddenly aware of wailing women on the outskirts of the crowd. But—*who?* In a panic she looked about, accounting for one after the other of the family—Baby Susan held tightly by Marguerite high on the load of a pack horse; Grandmother, Other Mother on one of the travoix; Mother, looking strange in buckskin jacket and leggings, without her calico Mother Hubbard, and with the greatest strangeness in her face, which had grown suddenly old and colorless. Susette ran to her with an anguished cry.

"*Nonha!* What is it? Who—what—"

The familiar arms enfolded her. "It's all right, little one. Don't be frightened. We're going away, that's all."

"Where—"

"We don't know yet. Perhaps to the Pawnees. Father has friends there. Perhaps to the Poncas and your Uncle White Swan. Wouldn't you like to see Susanne?"

"But—why?"

"I—can't tell you now, Wizhungeha. You're too young now to understand."

But Susette did understand. Her eyes were sharp and her ears keen, and she had seen and heard many things. There were the men from Big Village, watchful and silent, Little Chief, White Cow, Noise, and others. They had never wanted Father for their head chief. There was Yellow Smoke, sad but still angry because Father had not wanted the Sacred Pole anointed. There was the Agent—yes, it was the Agent who was most to blame. He had gotten Reverend Burtt, Father's friend, dismissed. Susette was her father's daughter, and she understood only too well. He had to go.

"In regard to my ordering him off the reserve," Agent Furnas wrote Dr. Lowrie on May 29, 1866, "I solemnly declare that I never said anything to him, directly or indirectly, that would demand such. He went entirely of his own accord. He knew that I had or would prefer charges against him. When Mr. Burtt received his letter of dismissal from you, he went directly to La Flesche and informed him of his fate. La Flesche immediately packed up his household goods, took his children out of school, and left the reservation. I leave you to draw your own inference as to the reasons, motives, or influence. . . . I have no objection to his coming back, but he must return of his own accord. I will not compromise myself by inviting him. I will treat him kindly. He must, however, be subordinate to the Agent."

So it was that Iron Eye, head chief of the Omahas, left his Village of Make-Believe White Men with all his family.

3

Joseph came back. He had not intended to, and he never divulged the reason for his change of mind. Perhaps it was the influence of his wise and gentle brother White Swan, or the persuasion of members of the Young Men's Party who visited him in exile, or the knowledge that the beloved Father Hamilton was again in charge at the Mission. Or possibly, like another Joseph, it was a hope that with the passing of one "Herod" and the appointment of a new agent, he would encounter less opposition. More likely it was a deepening sense of commitment to his people which, he discovered in his absence, transcended the importance of personal authority and prestige. He returned with no illusions. His days as head chief of the Omahas were numbered.

Hope for a better relationship with government was soon dashed. The new Agent was as stern and unyielding as his predecessor. Opposition was as virulent as ever. But his Young Men's Party were his loyal and obedient henchmen. Mahathinga, captain of the police, obeyed his every command, a thorn in the flesh of the new trader, who had hoped to make the large profits from the sale of whiskey which were procurable on other reservations. It was Mahathinga, with others of the Young Men's Party, who suggested an action which might enhance the chief's influence among the more conservative tribesmen.

"Grandfather." It was the salutation of highest respect, applied often to the Great Spirit Wakonda. "Surely you have performed nearly enough deeds to gain honorary chieftainship in the Honhewachi, which is the highest honor an Omaha can achieve. We believe that with your daughter made a *Nikagahi wa-u*, woman chief, those who now oppose you would listen to you with more respect."

Joseph considered. There was logic in the suggestion. Surely he had accumulated enough *wathinethe*, acts receiving honor, to make up the required hundred. But—remember them all so he could recount them, all the acts promoting peace both within and without the tribe, the gifts made to the poor and to mourners, saving a life in battle, giving a *Weku* feast when two tribes wished to make peace? A full hundred—and none could be "counted" which had already been used toward the attainment of chieftainship! After long consideration and much soul-searching he determined to do it. He found a sponsor in the secret society of the Honhewachi. He secured the necessary food to entertain the chiefs and other guests for the initiatory ceremonies. His name was proposed and accepted as a candidate for membership. He had a lodge prepared for the ceremonies between his own village and Big Village, close to the Sacred Tents. And he summoned his oldest daughter, Bright Eyes, from the Mission to take her part as the maid in the coming ceremonies.

Father Hamilton was shocked and distressed. Joseph could not do this. It meant catering to the very heathen practices he was trying to eliminate. And Susette was just getting settled again in school. She was a born student, and the teachers were expecting great things of her. Her education must not be interrupted even for a few days. Joseph *could* not. . . .

But Joseph could and did. It was not a heathen ceremony, he told the missionary with dignity. It was sacred. It depicted the mysteries of creation. In fact, the word *Honhe* meant the creative acts of Wakonda, who through his mystical power had caused night to bring forth day. And his daughter, like himself, was an Omaha. It was right that she should share in the sacred ceremonies of her people.

Bright Eyes, no longer Susette, went with her father. What—why? As they rode home, Father explained it to her. She was to be greatly honored. She was to be a *Nikagahi wa-u*, a woman chief, and because of her Father would attain a new position of authority among the people. He could do more to help them.

Curiosity changed to fright. A woman chief! Honored! Eyes staring at her, fingers pointing at her? But—if it was to help her people . . .

"What will I have to do?" she asked Mother. But Mother only shook her head. "Ask Grandmother." Nicomi shook her head. "Ask the Oldest Grandmother. She is a *Nikagahi wa-u*. She knows."

Bright Eyes went to Memetage's lodge. "When the time comes," said the old woman, eyes sunk deep into the memories of nearly eight decades, "I will tell you."

The ceremonies lasted four days. At first Bright Eyes stood in the crowd outside the lodge which Father had prepared. She saw the seven chiefs and the members of the Honhewachi go in, wearing their ornate robes and bearing the sacred pipe. She saw Father enter with a great bundle of willow sticks, each signifying one of his hundred "counts," and take his place at the left of the entrance. All that first day he took the sticks, one after the other, and recounted the gift or deed it represented, a fearful ordeal, for some involved memory of ten, twenty, thirty years. His friends and relatives, Two Crows, Wajapa, Thangeska, Village Maker, Dubamoni, moved anxiously about outside, hoping to jog his memory or refute those who tried to controvert his statements. But at last this was over. The "count" of one hundred had been completed and proclaimed to the people.

The ceremony of smoking followed. Bowls of maize porridge prepared by Mary and Nicomi were handed into the lodge and passed around the circle from left to right, each man taking four spoonfuls, careful not to spill the sacred food or make a noise with his lips while eating. Then came the feast of the Honhewachi.

"*Wathkathin ho!*" The two heralds gave the invitation. The sacred drum was beaten, a privilege accorded only to the man who could count the highest war honors. The song of the Honhewachi was begun.

"Uthitha shaya ma,
Uthitha shaya ma . . ."

"Now!" said the Oldest Grandmother, pushing Bright Eyes toward the lodge's entrance. "Don't be afraid. Never has the chosen maid been more beautiful."

The dreaded moment had come. The eyes were staring, the fingers pointing. What matter if she was beautiful, if her new garments were of the finest fawn skin and embroidered like Joseph's coat of many colors? Her heart seemed to stop beating, her limbs felt encased in ice. She couldn't . . . yet somehow she did. Entering the lodge, she stood straight as the willow sticks symbolizing Father's count. She fixed her eyes on the glowing central fire, with the buffalo skin behind it and near it the two bunches of grass on which rested the sacred pipe, willing herself not to look once at the circle of staring faces. When the song moved into its final stanza, proclaiming the acceptance of the count, she moved to the beat of the drum, rhythmically, about the fire from right to left, a living embodiment of night merging into day, the fulfillment in tangible form of creation's life-giving power.

"*Ou-daa! Ou-daa!* Good!" The words seemed to echo from a distance as, almost fainting, she fell into Mother's arms. It was over. But, no, that night in the Oldest Grandmother's lodge she learned that there was more, much more, to come.

"See," said Memetage. She pointed to the round red spot in the center of her forehead. "That," she said, "represents the sun." Then she loosened the shawl from her neck, revealing the dark blue four-pointed star etched deeply into her throat, its points extending from her chin almost to the cleft of her withered breasts. "And that is emblematic of the night, the great mother-force of all creation. Would you like to know how I got them?"

"Yes," said Bright Eyes, for she had often wondered.

"It was one morning, early." The old woman's voice sounded low and muffled, for she had hidden her head and shoulders again in the shawl. "I was taken into a lodge and placed on a couch covered with costly robes, with a pillow placed toward the east. But I lay facing the west, for I was the emblem of life and must move with the sun. They put charcoal in a wooden bowl and outlined these figures on my neck and forehead. Then they pricked them in with flint needles. They put on more charcoal, then pricked again." She lowered the shawl, revealing the etched figures, and looked straight into the girl's eyes. "That was all. I had been given the 'mark of honor.' I had become a *Nikagahi wa-u,* a woman chief."

Bright Eyes stared at her with dawning comprehension. "You—you mean—"

"Yes, child. And now you must get some sleep. For they will come for you early in the morning."

The girl lay in the warm circle of the lodge watching the flame-lit wisps of smoke spiral upward. Occasionally the wisps cleared, and she caught a glimmer of stars. Her first shock and dismay at tomorrow's ordeal were gone. She was no longer frightened. If this was the way she could help her people, she would face the ordeal bravely, as Louis had faced his on the hill of vision. Drifting off to sleep she felt a strange relief. For after tomorrow she would never again be two persons. Susette in name, yes, but not as a separate identity. The conflict between two worlds would be over. With the "mark of honor" branded forever in her flesh, she would remain always Inshtatheamba, the Omaha Indian.

It was Iron Eye, Joseph, who could not sleep. Like Jacob in the white man's Book, he wrestled all night with an invisible adversary. Conscience? Ambition? Loyalty? And if so, to what, to whom? . . . Day was being created out of night when he came to his decision. His children would have to live in a white man's world. They must not be permanently marked with the traditions of the past. *No one of his daughters would ever be tattooed.*

The ceremonies ceased abruptly. The members of the Honhewachi were shocked and alienated. Since the "mark of honor" was the sole credential of membership in the society, his decision was tantamount to a rejection of one of the most coveted tributes his people could bestow. His popularity among the conservatives sank to a new low. Disappointment was all the more bitter because he believed implicitly in the beauty and verity of the age-old symbolism of creation.

But there were beauty and verity also in the white man's religion, and Father Hamilton's influence was profound. Joseph finally made another momentous decision. He sent his third and youngest wife away, a giddy woman who had won little favor with the family. Mary and Tainne had both evidenced the "change of heart" deemed essential in the Christian tradition. Father Hamilton was tolerant and understanding, and with this partial solution to his marital problems, Joseph was permitted to join the little Presbyterian church. The following Sunday, to the missionary's amazement, the tiny room would not hold a fifth of the Indians who attended. In subsequent weeks the influx continued, all the more baffling because it was winter, and some of the days were cold and stormy. They came *en masse* from the Village of Make-Believe White Men, some from Big Village, men, women, children, plus dogs and ponies.

"How? Why?" inquired the baffled Father Hamilton.

"It is good for my people to go to church," replied Joseph. "I want them to learn to be Christians, so I ordered them to go."

"But—" Hamilton tried to explain the Protestant ethic of voluntary loyalty, but Joseph would have none of it. "No. This new way that you teach us is good. The words of the book are good. When you read from it and explain what it means, it teaches people to walk in the right way."

For three days they argued, several hours a day. "*Bien!*" agreed Joseph at last. "Take God's book. Read it all through, and then tell me what it says about this matter."

Hamilton hunted up many texts and read them. Joseph merely shook his head, unconvinced, until one verse caught his attention. "My kingdom is not of this world. If my kingdom were of this world, then would my servants fight." He sat for some moments in deep thought, then rose and went away. After some days he returned. His handsome face, piercing-eyed, sternly resolute, had acquired a new mobility and gentleness.

"My friend," he said, "you have often read to me out of God's book, and I thought I understood its meaning, but I did not. Now I see it tells us about two things instead of one. It tells us how to do that we may get things to eat and drink, so that we may live here on the earth that Wakonda gave us. That refers only to the body. About such things, if I know a better way, I can give orders. But there is something different, pertaining to the heart and soul. I cannot make a man good by issuing an order. I can say to a man, 'You build a house and live in it and no longer live in a tent.' Perhaps he will go and do it. But I cannot say to a man, 'Your heart is bad, have a good heart hereafter.' There is something over which no man, however great his authority—even if it is as great as that of the Great Father in Washington—can have control. Over that Wakonda alone can rule."

The next Sunday Chief Iron Eye made an address to his friends who came to church. At no synod or general assembly, Father Hamilton reported, had he ever heard a more profound and philosophical discourse on the invisible Kingdom of God. The order to go to church was revoked, and after that the little church built up its membership from those who freely chose to attend.

Chief Iron Eye was asked by Agent Callon to resign, and, in spite of Father Hamilton's urging that he resist, he submitted his resignation as head chief of the Omahas. Surprisingly, his new status effected little change in his tribal relationships. If anything, his counsel was more widely accepted than before. He was still leader of the Young Men's Party. Many from Big Village came to seek his advice. Once he would have felt resentment, bitterness at his rejection, a sense of irreparable loss. Not now.

For out of his anguish of self-searching Joseph had learned another lesson. Men's wills and bodies could no more be controlled by command than their spirits. Henceforth he must try to *show* them, not *tell* them, the better way. It was a truth buried deep not only in the white man's religion but in the origins of the Omahas. For did not the Sacred Legend say, again and again, each time a mighty change took place, "And the people thought, what shall we do to help ourselves?" Now was coming the mightiest change of all, and it must be accomplished in the same way or not at all. *And the people thought . . .*

4

It was 1868, and the Great Council in Washington was having second (or third or fourth) thoughts about its Indian policy.

"The result of the year's campaign," stated Number 97, Series 1337, of its Documents and Reports, "satisfied all sensible men that war with Indians was both useless and expensive. Fifteen or twenty Indians had been killed, at an expense of more than a million dollars apiece, while hundreds of our soldiers had lost their lives, many of our border settlers been butchered, and much property destroyed. . . . If it be said that because they are savages they should be exterminated, we answer that, aside from the humanity of the suggestion, it will prove exceedingly difficult, and if money considerations are permitted to weigh, it costs less to civilize than to kill."

The "fifteen or twenty killed" was a slight understatement, for this was the year General Sheridan made his classic comment, "The only good Indians I ever saw were dead," later construed, "The only good Indian is a dead Indian," and in the course of the year he succeeded in making "good" Indians out of hundreds of "bad" ones, most of whom had kept their treaty obligations. In one foray on a single village his subordinate General Custer killed 103 Cheyennes, only eleven of them warriors. The rest were old men, women, and children.

It was 1868, and at last the school promised the Poncas in their treaty of 1859, by which the government vowed to "establish and maintain for ten years, at an annual expense of no more than $5,000, one or more schools for the education and training of the Ponca youth," had been in operation for nine months with an average attendance in the school of about fifty scholars. (Wonderful, thought Susette on hearing the news from Uncle White Swan. Now cousins Susanne and Rosalie and her playmate Prairie Flower could enter her enchanting world of books!) But that same year the Poncas were told that, since the ten years were about to expire, all funds for both school and agricultural purposes would cease at the end of that fiscal year. Nobody thought to inform them, however, that in violation of that same treaty, confirmed again in 1865, the government mapped out a large reservation for the Sioux which inadvertently included the area given to the Poncas "as long as the grass shall grow and the waters flow"—a minor blunder which was to shape the future life of a young girl and the destiny of a people and the policy of a nation.

It was 1868, and Susette was fourteen. Daughter of the "one woman," grandaughter of Nicomi, "the beautiful Omaha," already she gave promise of an equal beauty. Less angular and piquant of feature than Marguerite and little Susan, less intense than the fiery, volatile Rosalie, her maturing loveliness was peculiarly her own. The delicately rounded face with its fine even features was calmly serene, the slender body, slightly under average height, straight and poised yet supple. The wide-spaced eyes under the shining black wings of hair were brightly curious but softly luminescent as two glowing candles. Even the shapeless Mother Hubbard could not quite hide the lithe grace of moving limbs.

Fortunately she was indifferent to the covert admiring glances of big boys on the other side of the aisle, or she would have shrunk like a turtle into its shell. She still blushed painfully when called on to recite. Had the glance of Brush, her childhood hero, been among them, she might have noticed, but Brush had gone to join the other small victims of consumption, measles, pneumonia in the tiny cemetery on the hill. She had secretly mourned his loss as bitterly as had Frank.

It was 1868, and some of the Omaha chiefs, encouraged by their agent, sent a petition to the Superintendent of Indian Affairs in Omaha requesting the termination of the contract between the government and the Presbyterian Mission. It was signed by Fire Chief, Yellow Smoke, No Knife, Cahega, Noise, White Horse, and Hard Walker, each making his mark.

"Tell all the bad things you know about the Mission," the superintendent was reported saying, "and I will help you get them away." They did. The old gossip about Burtt was revived. Hamilton, they claimed, had interfered in local dissensions not as peacemaker but as partisan. It was Yellow Smoke, guardian of the Sacred Pole, who complained that the children did not get good food!

"The old quarrel," commented Joseph wearily, "between old and new. They think of me and the Mission as one."

Susette was terrified. The school be closed! Her lovely, pulsing, singing world suddenly lost its rhythm, freezing into an immobility as static as the icebound river. Even the coming of the *ma*, the snow, with its miracle of whiteness, its racing ice sleds, its feathered etching of the walnut branches in front of the Mission aroused no stirring of excitement. She began to read furiously in the Fifth Eclectic Reader, far ahead of her class, in case the end should come before she had absorbed all its treasures. Read! It was her favorite teacher's name—Miss Read. She loved the sound of it, said it over softly as she snuggled under her blankets in the cold dormitory before going to sleep, drew pictures of a gayly smiling face topped with a wealth of fluffy hair on her scratch paper for working sums; drawing was a much more interesting subject than arithmetic, which she hated. She was doing this one day when a hand reached down suddenly and lifted the paper. With horror she looked up into the same face with its frame of fluffy hair, only now it was not smiling. The likeness was unmistakable.

"Well—Susette! So this is the way you work problems in long division!"

Susette flushed and quivered in an agony of embarrassment and guilt. "I—I'm sorry—"

The smile was back, gayer than ever. "Don't be, child. I'm flattered. You have made me much prettier than I really am. But—where did you learn to draw like that? No, don't tell me. You didn't learn. It was born in those bright eyes and those long slender fingers."

After that the young *tapuska* from the East showed an increasing interest in the painfully shy but obviously gifted Indian girl. Timidly Susette produced other scraps of drawings —a baby on a cradle board, a woman pounding maize, a warrior in full panoply, the tent of the Sacred White Buffalo Hide with its mystic symbols—fearful that the white woman would frown at their "heathen" style and content. But the *tapuska* only nodded thoughtfully. "*Ou-daa*, good," she said once in surprising defiance of the school's ban on speaking Omaha. Her eyes twinkled. "You see I do know one word of your language."

It was 1869. A report from the Governor of Dakota Territory stated that the Ponca school had been "discontinued for lack of funds." Susette mourned in sympathy for her cousins Rosalie and Susanne, and their misfortune made the specter of her own fears more tangible. Letters from Uncle White Swan were doggedly optimistic. Cheerfully the Poncas were attempting to improve their reservation, building themselves sixteen comfortable houses and buying cookstoves, cows, and tools with their annuities. True, the crops they put in were unfortunately all destroyed by drought, and the tribe was practically starving. While digging wild roots to eat, they saw hordes of cattle being driven across their reservation to feed the recently hostile Sioux, but, always a peaceful people, they made no attempt to retaliate, certain that the government would keep its faith with them and reimburse them for their losses in accordance with their treaty.

It was 1869, and President Grant's "peace policy" went into effect, a plan of segregation of all Indian tribes on their respective reservations, by force if necessary, and, to prevent further revolts, all tribal organization was officially destroyed. It was the age of the vanishing frontier. Expulsion of Indians to unwanted lands was no longer possible, because there were no such lands. Consequently they must be enclaved, for their protection and the civilizing benefits of government control, preferably in remote areas whose undesirable features would tempt less encroachment by white settlers.

It was 1869, and the dread specter turned into a monster far more grim than the fabulous flying serpent, for with one blow it killed a young girl's dreams. The Agent and his henchmen had their way. Funds allotted to the Mission by government were withdrawn, necessitating the closing of the boarding school. There would be day schools at points on the reservation under the direction of the government and conducted by the Agent's own denomination, which was not Presbyterian. They would be for younger children. Not for Susette. On her bits of scrap paper now she drew pictures of arrows and unstrung bows, the mute symbols of death.

Surprisingly spring came as usual. The seven geese that were its harbingers must have found some waters open, for long before the "Moon When Nothing Happens" arrowlike wedges of geese and cranes were shooting north along the corridor. With a great rush and roar the river burst into life, setting free the sleeping world. Willows and cottonwoods turned smoky green and gold. Owls shrieked and coyotes cried to their mates in the night. The "gone-down" birds came back to fill the air with melody. And at last the voice of Wakonda, speaking in the first thunder, was heard. Obediently, as from time immemorial, the old men would be taking out their sacred bundles, opening them, going to the high hills to pray, to smoke their tobacco and scatter some of it to the four winds.

"I may be a good Presbyterian most of the year," thought Susette, "but when the first thunder sounds, I'll always be an Indian."

Strange that the world could be so beautiful when it was about to end! In spite of herself she found the scribbles of unstrung bows on the bits of paper turning into outspread wings. Yet no miracle of nature could avert the tragedy. Never would she forget the last day of school. She was not the only one to mourn. Many of the children cried and asked, "Are we never to come back any more?" Susette did not cry or voice complaint. Her grief was too deep for tears or words. Yet at its center was forming a hard little core of questioning resentment. *Why?* The Mission school was prospering. It had more pupils than ever before. Why should one white man who happened not to be a Presbyterian and had a different idea of doing things—? Not until ten years later would she be able to put the accumulating resentment into words.

"Every two or three years," she would tell a huge Boston audience, "a new agent has been provided by your government. Each new agent that comes has a new theory of his own to practice on us and we must take it meekly or be termed rebellious or sullen and incapable of being civilized. Even when our agents are good and try to help us in our efforts to help ourselves, they are as powerless as we are. It seems strange that they are *powerful* and are aided by the government when they try to do wrong, like the one who broke up the Mission school, and *powerless* when they try to do right, as in the case of one who really tried to help us."

It was 1869 . . . 1870 . . . 1871. Never had the inner conflict between Bright Eyes and Susette been more tumultuous, secret, hopeless. There was no one with whom she could share her torturing frustration. The girls of her age had thoughts of little except courtship and marriage, seemed to care not at all that the magic world of books had ended. Going with some of them to the spring in the early morning, she tried to join in their nervous giggles, their excited conjectures. Would such-and-such a young brave be lying hidden again in the grass in hopes of glimpsing So-and-So? Would he make known his presence in the age-old love call played on his flute? Should So-and-So yield to his pleadings for a whispered tête-à-tête? Try as she would, Susette could not share their excitement. Perhaps if it had been Brush lying in the grass. . . . But Brush, who would have understood her insatiable thirst for knowledge, was dead. While the soft flute notes and trilling vocables of the love songs stirred her as no "Annabelle Lee" or "Nellie Gray" could ever do, she was glad none was meant for her. Not that exploratory glances were not cast in her direction! But something more than her innate shyness, perhaps a protective shell of remoteness, discouraged such advances.

Except for two people the years of conflict would have been almost unbearable. One was Father Hamilton. Though the missionaries had all been ordered off the reservation, he had refused to go. His library was small, but Susette was given free use of it. She waded through huge volumes of ecclesiastical history and Calvinist theology. She read the Bible and Shakespeare from cover to cover. Sometimes parcels came to the Mission wrapped in old newspapers, and she would pore over them avidly. It was poor, cheap reading, but it was all she had.

And sometimes, in the care of the Mission, there would come a letter, for Miss Read, the beloved Tapuska, had not forgotten her shy pupil with the clever fingers and seeking eyes. At the holiday season she usually sent a small gift, perhaps a brooch or a lace collar or a necklace—never, as Susette passionately hoped, a book.

"What would you like for Christmas?" questioned one letter, when the school had been closed for more than three years.

What would she like? Susette sat down with a bit of carefully hoarded paper, chewed her pencil for a long time, then started to write. Usually her letters were shy stilted notes, their only spontaneous feature the quaint little drawings bordering the beautifully slanted handwriting. Now suddenly, almost against her will, the pencil flew across the paper. The frozen inner longings melted and flooded to the surface. What did she want? Nothing—nothing at all except to go to school again, to learn more and more and more. If only—! The words rushed across the page like speeding arrows, filling it full. When there was no more space, she folded the sheet, sprang up, and went straight to the Mission, running almost all the way. If Father Hamilton was startled by her flushed cheeks and blazing eyes, he gave no sign. Yes, he would see that the letter went East by the next boat.

There! Susette walked slowly home, the flood of emotion drained away. She would be getting no trinkets at Christmas. There would probably be no more letters. Such ingratitude as she had shown did not deserve them. She should be expressing thankfulness for what the white chests had done for the poor Indians, not wishing for more. It was autumn, and the river valley was a gold strip of magic wrapped in bluish haze. Already at night the moon was turning watery pale, a sign of the coming fall rains—"enough," so the old Omahas said, "to turn the fields to mud until the snows came." Clouds of ducks, geese, cranes were skimming overhead in long graceful V's, bound for a clime that held warmth and promise. Susette did not even see them.

Then, before earth became ice-bound, came the miracle. It was Father Hamilton who broke the news. His kindly face was beaming.

"A letter, my dear, from Miss Read back in the East. It seems she is teaching now in a school, a very fine school for girls in Elizabeth, New Jersey. She has found friends who want to help you get an education. The money is all arranged. As soon as we can find reliable persons going East, you may travel with them and attend this fine school. I have already spoken to your father, and he is willing. You will soon be receiving a letter from Miss Read yourself."

Susette needed no tattooed star and sun on her face to depict the creation of day out of night. It was all there in her *inshtatheamba*, bright eyes.

Part Two

1

It was 1875. Going out on their summer hunt, the Omahas found the plains strewn with rotting carcasses, their stench fetid on the blistering, rainless winds from the southwest, the silence a mocking sacrilege of the moons "when the buffalo and the elk bellow." The despoiling had not been done by red men. Of the nearly four million buffalo killed in the previous three years, only 150,000 had been killed by Indians. They viewed the carnage with bewilderment and horror. Killing just for skins or tongues! To a people who for centuries had killed only enough animals to supply their needs for winter, using every scrap— meat, marrow, fat, sinews, horns, hair, hides—such waste was incomprehensible.

"Let them kill, skin, and sell," General Sherman commended the wholesale slaughter, "until the buffalo is exterminated, as it is the only way to bring lasting peace and allow civilization to advance."

And not only buffalo, the words implied. In a letter some years before to his brother John, a United States Senator from Ohio, he had been more explicit. "The more we can kill this year, the less will have to be killed in the next war, for the more I see of these Indians the more convinced I am that all have to be killed or maintained as a species of pauper. Their attempts at civilization are simply ridiculous."

It was 1875, and the Poncas were continuing a three-year bout with misfortune. Secure in their treaty of 1859 by which the United States agreed and stipulated to protect the tribe in the possession of a designated tract of land on the Niobrara, "reserved for their future homes, and the persons and property thereon, during good behavior on their part," they were working industriously to improve their reservation. In 1873 a flood had washed away the site of their village. By working day and night for two weeks they had managed to carry most of their houses a half mile inland, often risking their lives in swift and turbid waters. A year later, having built twenty new houses, possessing over a hundred head of cattle and fifty wagons, with 300 acres under cultivation, they had experienced drought, then three visitations of locusts which had stripped their fields. Now locusts came again, destroying corn and oats. With only one reaper at the Agency, most of the wheat left had to be cut with butcher knives, a slow and tedious process, much of the crop drying up before it could be harvested.

"They are not only willing but extremely anxious," reported their agent, "to learn the arts by which they may become self-supporting and conform to the usages of white men. With the small advantages afforded them, their advancement has been very great."

It was 1875, and Susette La Flesche, honor graduate of a fine girls' boarding school in the East, came home. Home!

"How beautiful," she thought, riding over the green rolling hills of Ni-btha-thka, the Land of the Flat Water, "how beautiful is the country of my people!"

Her people! The words sang through her blood, quickened her pulse beats. For more than two years she had lived for this fulfillment of her dreams—to come home and share her new knowledge and experience with *her people*. She had pored over her books by flickering gaslight until her eyes burned, left her idly chattering schoolmates to attend lectures and concerts, absorbed the niceties of Eastern speech and manners with meticulous passion for detail—all for one purpose, to bring back the best of the white man's culture to *her people*. What Chief

Iron Eye had been unable to accomplish through authority and example, his daughter Bright Eyes would bring to fruition— through the only means possible, education.

The euphoria was short-lived. The Agent seemed unimpressed with her record of high scholastic achievement. The day schools were all supplied with teachers, and he foresaw no vacancy in the near future. Yes, it was true that not half of the tribe's children attended the schools, but that was due largely to their parents' inertia. No, there were no funds for any more schools and no buildings available. She walked home from the Agency sick at heart. Home? But she had already discovered that it was not home. She no longer belonged. All her life she had struggled for identity in two worlds. Now suddenly she belonged to neither.

The family were strangers. No, not the family. She was the stranger. They welcomed her joyfully, affectionately, tried to make her feel part of the close-knit group bulging the small bare house. Marguerite and Susan, thirteen and ten, listened rapturously to descriptions of the spacious school and life in the glamorous East. Rosalie, fourteen, grave, erect, slender, savored her handful of precious books with the insatiate appetite of the born student.

"'Presented to Susette La Flesche at Elizabeth, New Jersey,'" she read from the fly-leaf of a beautiful new volume titled *Yesterday with Authors,* "'on June 24, 1875, by N. C. Read.'" She lifted shining eyes. "You really got this for a prize?"

"Yes," said Susette, "and this one too."

Rosalie picked up a second volume, so new its pages were uncut. "*Personal Reminiscences of Cornelius Knight and Thomas Raikes,*" she read. "And they gave you this 'for observing the rules of the school.' Also from N. C. Read." She looked wistful.

"As you know, she's the principal of the Elizabeth Institute," said Susette. "Her father is a well-known Presbyterian minister, and I often went to her home for vacations, and to other beautiful homes." Remembering, she felt such a stab of homesickness that she had to turn away to hide her tears. But—*this* was her home! She had shed tears of homesickness often enough during her first months of strangeness at the school!

Beside the mansionlike building which housed the Elizabeth

Institute for Young Ladies at No. 521 North Broad Street in Elizabeth and the school's orderly regime, the crowded little house with its haphazard ways of living, half white and half Indian, was a trap filled with milling victims. Its bare walls bulged with human life. Besides Father, Mother, Grandmother, Other Mother, Oldest Grandmother (who had at last been persuaded to leave her lodge), there were Mary's three girls (four with herself) and Tainne's three children—Frank, a full-grown man at eighteen, astonishingly like his father, ten-year-old Lucy, and Carey, a dark mischievous little will-o'-the-wisp of three.

Susette longed for privacy, the quiet of the study hall, even the disciplined silences of the full dormitory. But even more she yearned for useful and satisfying occupation. With four mature women sharing household tasks, there was little room for a fifth, and the old methods of housekeeping now seemed appallingly strange and outmoded. Though the frame houses of the Village of Make-Belive White Men were a vast improvement over tents and lodges, their furnishing were still primitive beside the luxurious appointments in homes visited in the East—seats of skins and blankets mingled with the few wooden chairs, beds of handhewn posts and sideboards, with woven strips of willow branches tied together by willow bark, one table seldom used for meals. Strange to sit in a circle on the floor again to eat—as strange as her first meals at a table covered with white damask and set with a bewildering medley of china and silver and crystal! She found herself biting her lips to keep from bursting into comments.

"But we have forks and spoons! Surely the children should be taught . . ."

"Why bother to teach Lucy the polite way to sit on the floor and how to spring up using only one hand? She should be learning to sit on a chair!"

"You should taste real tea instead of this made with the leaves of *tabehi!*"

Even her favorite childhood foods tasted unfamiliar. Compared with fresh beef, dishes made with jerked buffalo meat had a strong unpleasant flavor. Parched corn was dry and tasteless. Corn, beans, jerked meat, pumpkin, even in their many combinations, were deadly monotonous. And she was repelled at the sight of a small child munching on a curl of animal intestine, once a rare and favorite delicacy. But she had dreamed longingly of all these foods back at school. What had happened to her!

She read her few precious books over and over, *Travels in Arabia* by Bayard Taylor, *Personal Reminiscences* edited by Henry Stoddard, especially *Within and Without*, a verse-drama by George MacDonald which Father Hamilton had given her just before she went East. Already its binding was worn, its pages thumbed and marked with pencilings. It fell open at one favorite passage, so often had she read it:

"And should the twilight darken into night
And sorrow grow to anguish, be thou strong.
Thou art in God, and nothing can go wrong
Which a fresh life pulse cannot set aright!
That thou dost know the darkness, proves the light!"

She was knowing the darkness now, and no light shone ahead. Father Hamilton was still at the Mission, and his little Presbyterian church had steadily increased in numbers. He sympathized with her restlessness and frustration but had little to suggest.

"Have faith, child. Pray. God will direct your path in his own good time."

The women of the household had their solution: marriage. She heard them talking. "Twenty-one! All the other girls her age with husbands and one or more children!" . . . "—shouldn't be hard to find a suitor of the proper clan. Have you noticed how much more beautiful she is?" . . . "If only she had the mark of honor, men would find her more desirable!" . . . "—have to be a widower or an older man, those of her age are all married." . . . *Witonde*, son-in-law, should say to the tribe, 'We have a single daughter, and it is our wish to get her married.'"

Susette's cheeks burned. She might be one of Father's horses they were trying to sell! She looked forward to being married sometime, yes, but not because it was the role expected of a woman, and not—not to some fellow tribesman who could barely write his name in English and probably had never heard of Shakespeare! This latter admission left her aghast. What had she done? Exiled herself from her own people? Now that she thought of it, since her return all her old school friends had shied away from intimacy. They spoke a different language.

She felt imprisoned. Her books were soon read and re-read. She made endless sketches. She did a little writing. Her courses in English literature and composition at Elizabeth had been exceptional, and she had so excelled that one of her last essays had been printed in a New York newspaper. But the effort was halfhearted. Of what use? The newspapers of Sioux City and Omaha were as far away as those of New York—and their libraries and concerts and lectures. She was not even allowed to leave the reservation without obtaining a pass from the Agent, three miles away!

She could not burden Father with her problems. He had too many of his own. Without his trading post he was finding it harder and harder to support his growing family. But personal worries were far outweighed by those for the tribe. Though after long delays some of the tribe had received certificates of title on the first allotment of lands in severalty, they felt no assurance of permanency. Government had failed them too many times before. Each new administration in Washington brought changes in Indian policy. The state continued to agitate for the removal of all Indians. White settlers were edging illegally into reservation land to the west, yet government did nothing about it. Already the Omahas had been coerced into selling part of their reservation to another tribe. Who could tell? Tomorrow their titles might become null and void, and, like the Pawnees, the Osages, the Cheyennes, they might be driven away to that death land "Toward the Heat," called by the white man the Indian Territory. A spirit of apathy and despair had settled on the tribe.

Joseph was helpless to counteract it. No longer a chief, he could only advise, not speak with authority. The police force he had instigated was becoming less able to enforce his rigid code of sobriety. The greed of the white traders was slowly winning. Liquor, the Red Man's poison, was seeping into the reservation.

Agents could no longer report that they had never seen a drunken Omaha. And of course Joseph was blamed for many of the tribe's misfortunes, even the slow disappearance of the buffalo. Had he not urged them to become like white men, to flout some of the most sacred traditions? Had he not refused to imprint on his daughter's flesh the "mark of honor"? No wonder the unmarried men of the tribe brought no gifts to her father's house! Had he not forbidden the anointing of the Sacred Pole? No wonder the Venerable Man was seeking his revenge.

Yet in spite of his worries it was Joseph who was most acutely aware of his daughter's frustration.

"I heard at the Agency," he remarked one day with apparent carelessness, "that they need teachers down in Indian Territory."

Susette's pulses leaped. Would they employ an Indian? Surely she was as well qualified as many white teachers! The graduates of Elizabeth Institute were employed in some of the foremost girls' schools in the East. And she could speak a little Pawnee and Osage. She rode to the Agency, learned the details, and secretly applied for a teacher's position in one of the displaced Indian tribes. Weeks passed and finally a letter of acceptance came. She broke the news with trepidation. Its reception by the other women was predictably one of horror. "*Na-he!* Not to that land of death!" . . . "A woman all alone among strange tribes!" . . . "No man of your family to protect you!" . . . "We won't let you!"

Susette waited tensely for Joseph's verdict. An unmarried Indian girl, even at twenty-one, was still subject to her father's rule. To her infinite relief he nodded. "*Bien*, we must let her go. A meadowlark shut up in a cage would soon break its wings."

Opposition came from an unexpected source. Two Crows, her uncle by adoption, had as much control over her actions as her parents. And he was adamant.

"No! *Pe-áh-zhi*, it is bad! Have you not heard that 800 Pawnees, more than a third of the tribe, died in their first two years there? She shall not go."

Another bubble of hope burst! The two years following her return to the reservation were the hardest and most frustrating of her life, just as the two preceding had been the happiest. Life was no longer a unity, man and nature a single creation. All was conflict, like the elements battling within herself.

A spring came, surprisingly, heartbreakingly beautiful, yet seeming an end, not a beginning. One day she walked along the path to the Mission, high on the bluffs, with ten-year-old Susan skipping and scuffing through the new grass beside her.

"*A-hun*, ouch!" exclaimed the child, nursing a bruised bare toe. Stooping, she picked up the offending object. "*Tam-be*, look!"

Susette took it from her, brushing away the dust, stroking the triangular bit of satin-smooth flint with her long sensitive fingers. "An arrow head," she said, "a very old one," trying to summon some of her childhood eagerness on that day long ago at the Sacred Fireplace. "See, Wihe, it's a hundred years old, maybe more. See how carefully somebody chipped it, making it so smooth and sharp. Who knows who or when? But it was one of our people. It's a part of our life, which goes deep into the past, making us one with everything that's gone before."

The child nodded, eyes aglow with understanding. It was with this youngest sister that Susette often felt the most intimate kinship. "Yes," responded Susan happily, "and it will keep going on and on even after we're gone, but we'll still be a part of it, won't we?"

Susette's hand clenched over the bit of flint, its sharp edges bruising her palm. The past, yes, but—what good was past without a future? Suddenly she flung the arrow head with all her strength over the edge of the bluff. They heard it strike with a dull thud far below.

"There!" She tried to answer the hurt perplexity in the child's eyes without betraying her own uncertainty. "We'll leave it, shall we, for someone else to find, maybe after we're gone?"

Again Susan nodded. "I just hope it didn't get broken."

It was dusk when they returned along the path from the Mission. A great golden globe—the "Moon When the Frogs Sing"—hung low over Nishuda. The hour with Father Hamilton had merely sharpened Susette's sense of futility, of not belonging. Suddenly she stopped short. "Listen, Wihe!" The spring night had exploded into shrill rhythmic cadence.

It's *hákugthi*," said Susette, "the whippoorwill, his first call of the season. You know what the old men say? If you hear the *hákugthi's* first cry and shout to him, the number of calls he sends back is the number of years you are going to live. Shall I try it?"

Susan's eyes were round and fearful. "No!" she gasped. "You wouldn't dare!"

Susette stood very still. Superstitions, the Waxes called all such things—taking out the bundles, going to the hills at the sound of the first thunder, not going around a fireplace, not touching things that were tabu to your own clan, never looking at a sacred bundle, never combing your hair at night or whistling in the dark for fear of ghosts. Heathen notions they thought them—then paled if a black cat crossed their paths or they broke a mirror. The whippoorwill was silent. Would she dare to cry out, to challenge some ancient mystery for knowledge of the future? A Waxe would dare, but not an Indian. Which was she? Both—or neither? Suddenly the conflict within her became unbearable, like a bow stretched almost to breaking. She lifted her head.

"Ho!" she cried. "Ho, there—you, *hákugthi!* Ho, ho!"

Horrified, she waited in an agony of suspense, Susan clutching her hand in terror. It seemed ages before the shrill cadence came again, over and over, repeated so many times they lost count.

"You—you dared!" the child whispered.

"Yes," said Susette. "I dared."

She felt a strange relief, not because she had flouted superstition but because she had yielded to it. In that moment of desperate waiting she had known herself to be all Indian, inheritor not only of fears but of things beautiful and glorious. Once, if only for a moment, she had regained her identity.

For a little while that spring she was almost at peace with herself. The meadowlark returned to sing, "Winter will not come back!" It had rained, the thunder had spoken and the lightning had flashed. The old men had taken out their bundles. They had gone to the high hills to blow smoke and to pray: "Thou who causest the four winds to reach a place, help thou me!" She had seen, and she had heard, and life was good.

It was 1876. To enforce its policy of segregation government ordered all Indians to be contained in their reservations by January 31. All failing to comply would be hunted down by troops as enemies. In that "Moon When the Snow Drifts into the Tents" the Omahas returned from their last buffalo hunt.

They had left with high hopes. Though the winter hunts were chiefly for pelts, not food, that of the previous summer had yielded almost no meat, and the tribe was hungry. Southward the hunters had gone, toward Omaha, then turned west to the Platte and up along the Elkhorn, for the great herds had swung south in the winter from time immemorial. They had found remnants of the herds, yes—carcasses strewn over the plains, rotted and frozen, the freshest of them poisoned. They had had to hold their dogs on leash to keep them from eating the tainted meat. Decimation was almost complete. The hunters had nearly starved to death, would have if the army from a fort in the area had not given them salt pork, an unfamiliar food which made them sick. Straggling back to the villages, both horses and hunters were themselves little more than skin and bones.

"Lucky I killed my first buffalo two years ago!" Young Frank, nineteen, could afford to be cheerfully philosophical. He had been on a hunt three times and had been a runner once. "Now some of the boys will never get a chance." He made a wry face. "Never have to cut the beast open, either, and eat the raw liver with the gall over it!"

It was only the young who could be cheerful. There was wailing that night in many lodges, especially those of the Inkesabe Clan, which had furnished the *wathon*, leader of the hunt, for centuries. "If the last Inkesabe was an infant in its mother's arms" the saying went, "it would be carried to lead the people in the *wanonthe*, surrounding of the herd." There was no rejoicing among the women who stripped meat from the few lean carcasses and jealously hoarded every precious particle of flesh and bone and hair and hide and sinew. Inshtathabi (He Who Has Eyes), the last *wathon,* sat outside his village, a blanket over his head, and refused food or drink until at last he fell senseless.

No more hunts? They had been told the day would come. Joseph had told them, yet somehow they had not believed. It was the beginning of deprivation and suffering. For centuries their economy, their whole way of life, had revolved around the buffalo. They had never received rations from the government, like many tribes. Now the once thrifty and prosperous Omahas were reduced to poverty. But distress of mind far exceeded that of body. It was more than the end of an era. It was the dissolution of a proud and ancient culture. The sustenance which Wakonda had given "from every quarter" had failed. Had he become powerless? Then what hope for his people? Was he angry? But how could he be appeased when every sacred rite designed to win his favor was dependent on the gift he had taken away?

As if this were not enough, the year saw also the dissolution of tribal government. Chieftainship lost its meaning. The sacred tribal circle was abolished. The new "Council" consisted of a small number of chiefs who could be called together easily by the Agent, in whom all governing power resided. All that belonged to the past was as unstable as the ever-shifting sands bounding Nishuda, the Smoky Waters.

Yet, as always, the Omahas remained peaceful, compliant. Not so certain tribes of the Sioux, whose treaty giving them the seemingly worthless *Pahé thabe*, Black Hills, "forever" had been violated a hundredfold when gold was discovered in its grim wasteland. They both refused to sell their sacred land and failed to obey the edict. On February 1 these "hostile" Indians were turned over to the military for "such action as the Army might deem proper." General Sherman, he to whom good Indians were always dead, was sent to implement the order. Rumors of the boldness of Sitting Bull and Crazy Horse and Gall and Spotted Tail, who dared resist the Waxes, reached the Omahas and kindled fresh fires of opposition to Joseph, fires soon fanned by currents of similar defiance in more friendly tribes.

With no buffalo meat, hunger was rife, even in Joseph's house. Susette begrudged herself what food she did eat, for there was barely enough to go around. Sometimes there was nothing in the house but grated corn, from which Mother made bread. Though Father had a large farm and worked his fingers to the bone, he was compelled to sell only to the Agent's trader. How prosper when one had to sell wheat at forty cents a bushel when it was selling for ninety just off the reservation, and then be paid, not in money but in goods—calico, coffee, sugar, pork? Seeing little children pick kernels of corn from the ground to eat, Susette choked on her own food.

She choked, too, on resentment. In that same year the Agent built an infirmary for the tribe for $6,000. It was tribal money, paid for their land, yet the tribe was not consulted. They had no use for an infirmary. Few in the tribe were ever ill, and they would have been ashamed to let anyone take care of their sick for them. Several leaders asked that it be used as a school, but no attention was paid to their request. It stood empty until a white man moved into it. Still Susette's attempts to teach were unsuccessful. After the Agent's refusal she had written to the Commissioner in Washington but had received no answer.

Frank, Rosalie, and Marguerite were attending the day school. They came home laughing at the poor English one of their white teachers used. "He says, 'The boys is coming to schoool,'" Rosalie imitated with disgust. "Those of us who went to the House of Teaching know better than that!" But they knew the inept teacher would not be dismissed. He had been hired by the Agent and took care not to offend him. He was to remain in the school for five years.

Susette was heartsick over her father's worries. She spent all the time possible at home, knowing that more than any others of the family she could understand his sense of desperate urgency. His concern was not only for the Omahas, but almost equally for the Poncas, whom White Swan, Standing Bear, and other chiefs were struggling to educate in white men's ways. Joseph had never learned to read and write. In May, the "Moon for Planting," he dictated to Susette a letter to his brother White Swan.

"My brother, I have some news to send you, but not good. The Otoes came up here to visit us. Instantly, upon their arrival, the whole tribe got together and had a council. I did not hear all that was done, but I know it is the same thing I have been hearing for ten years. The Otoes told them that all the Indians where they came from sent word that trying to be like the white people is very bad, that all who tried to do it were badly off, but that those who had stayed in the Indian customs were doing well. They should go back to their old ways. It was too hard.

"The Chiefs' Party believed what they said, and they are determined more than ever to resist any step toward advancement. I think, however, that all of the Young Men's Party turned their backs on them."

Then Joseph quietly summed up the tenets of his philosophy:

"There are some good things," he dictated simply, "by which we live:

1. The God above made this world and gave it to us to live in.

2. The white man has been sent to teach us how to live.

3. God has made the earth to yield her fruit to us.

4. God has given us hands to work with.

"Look back on the lives of your fathers and grandfathers," he continued. "Then look at yourselves and see how far you have gone ahead, and seeing this, do not stop and turn back to them. Look ahead, and you will see nothing but the white man. The future is full of the white man, and we shall be as nothing before him.

"Do not think that if anyone cheats you or does you wrong, you will do the same to him. Look out for yourselves. Take care of yourselves. From your brother, Joseph La Flesche."

A month later, in the "Moon When the Buffalo Bulls Hunt the Cows," excitement swept through the tribe like a strong hot wind. War cries which for decades had been nostalgic echoes of the past became vibrant with long-suppressed emotion. Men and boys shouted them in a burst of exultation, while women beat their hands against their mouths and made the tremolo.

"*Hi-yay! O-we yah! Hi-yay-ay!* It's a good day to journey!"

News had come of the Battle of the Little Big Horn. "Long Hair" Custer who had built the Thieves' Road into the Black Hills, had been utterly destroyed with his regiment. Who could tell? Perhaps the flood-tide had turned. Men of the Chiefs' Party were exultant. This should show the Waxe-lover Joseph that the old ways were not dead!

Joseph shook his head sadly. The triumph, he knew, would

be short-lived. He was right. Before the summer was over the white man returned in the full fury of vengeance. Since the Sioux rebels remained out of reach, peaceful villages were burned, their people massacred. The Black Hills were taken forcibly, regardless of the treaty, the Sioux moved against their will to a new reservation on the Missouri. And Joseph was again the butt of bitter jibes.

"*E tha a betheh!* And you would like us to be like these Waxes, who kill the innocent, who break their promises and steal?"

But misfortune was soon to strike nearer home.

It was 1877, in the first month, the "Moon When the Snow Drifts into the Tents." The two Poncas who brought the news were half dead with cold and weariness, their horses stumbling, sweating, yet rimed with frost. In "Joe's Village" they were helped to the ground and led to Joseph's house. So portentous of ill news was their appearance that the usual formalities for greeting visitors from other tribes were for the moment forgotten.

"White Swan—your brother Standing Bear—" demanded Joseph of the older man. "Is it one of them? Death?"

"Not—death." The man could barely speak. "The tribe is—all well and—safe—now. But—" he choked.

"*Nonshtán*, stop, don't try to tell us. Rest first. The news will wait."

The two visitors were led to piles of buffalo robes, and slept. It was dusk when they woke, and the oil lamps were lighted.

"Come and eat," said Joseph, the Indian's perennial expression of hospitality.

Susette helped serve the food. She recognized the older visitor as Big Snake, Standing Bear's brother. The other was a mere boy, scarcely past puberty, and she learned that he was the youngest of Standing Bear's sons. Strange, she thought, to bring so young a lad on such a long hard journey in the dead of winter—or was it? Once an Indian youth would have welcomed snows, cold, biting winds, long freezing miles of travel, but in these days, since the end of the hunts, boys were growing soft. Few even went on the Vision Quest. Was this lad, perhaps, different? As he sat, bent ravenously over his food, she could not see his face.

Big Snake was ready to speak. The room had silently filled with leaders of the Young Men's Party, Two Crows, Wajapa, Dubamoni, No Knife, Thangeska, and others. It was like one of the old council circles, except that there was no glowing central fire, only the big potbellied iron stove. The pipe was passed, solemnly, clockwise around the circle. Susette, seated in the shadows, studied the big Ponca's face, and sighed. The anger was still there, just as she remembered it, the impatience, but something had gone. The dark eyes no longer smoldered. They were tired eyes, full of resignation rather than revolt.

"It began some weeks ago. All was well in our villages. We have many new houses. We make a good living from our farms. Our children are in school. We have a church. You know how it is with us. Time was when we were so harassed by the Sioux that we asked to move to your reservation to live. Your chiefs were willing."

There were nods of assent. "*A-sha-tun-ah-tha,*" said Joseph. "It is so."

"But that time is past." Big Snake made an impatient gesture. "The harassment has ceased. We are content with the land given us by solemn treaty. It is our home. It has been ours for generations. *But—now—*"

The words were like drum beats, rousing the circle to tense alertness.

"One Sunday we went to church, as usual. The minister spoke words we will never forget. He said he had heard we were to be sent from our homes far to the south, never to return. He was sorry for us, since we had been honest, industrious, had just got ourselves nice houses and farms. He couldn't help us, could only pity us. God would help us, he said. We must trust him."

It was hot in the room, but Susette shivered. Something evil seemed to have crept in, filling the place. As Big Snake continued his story, she relived it with him, sat huddled with a crowd of Poncas in the church and heard some men who said they came from Washington—an Inspector and some others— say they had been ordered to take the whole tribe to Indian Territory. She moaned and swayed and beat her breast with the women. She saw Standing Bear rise, heard him speak.

This land is ours. We have never sold it. We have our houses and our homes here. Our fathers and some of our children are buried here. We have kept our treaty. We have learned to work. We will not sell our land. Here we will live, and here we will die.

"Ou-daa! A-ou-daa!" A wave of exultant approval swept around the circle. "It is good!" "Our brother Standing Bear spoke nobly!" "The Waxes cannot take away your land!" "You have your treaty!"

Big Snake shook his head. His massive shoulders seemed to shrink into themselves. "*Dho*, yes. We have our treaty." His voice was hard and bitter. "And ten years ago, we learn, the Waxes made another treaty which gave all our land to the Sioux!" There were wails of shock and disbelief. "Yes, I tell you it is true. So did the Delawares and the Cherokees have their treaties. And where are they now? In the land 'Toward the Heat.' So do the Cheyennes and the Arapahoes have their treaties. But they will all be in the Indian Territory before the year is out. Wait and see. And," he added with ominous emphasis, "*you also have your treaty.*"

The silence could be felt, like a burst of coldness.

"And what did the Inspector say?" asked Joseph quietly.

"What you'd expect. That the Indian Territory was a much better country than ours. That we could raise more grain there and not work so hard. That if we once saw it we would not want to stay in our own country. That the Great Father would pay much for our land and give us all we needed down there. Then—he proposed that some of our chiefs go down and look at the land. If they did not like it, they might stay where they were. And so—it was agreed. Ten of our chiefs have gone, White Swan and my brother Standing Bear among them. The Inspector went with them and paid their way on the Iron Road."

The silence broke in a swift surge of relief. *Ou-daa!* Then it was not such a disaster. Big Snake had frightened them all for nothing. The Poncas need not be moved unless they wanted to be. And of course they would not. Uneasiness dissolved in a mood of hilarity. Blankets drawn tight about the shoulders were loosened. An atmosphere of warmth dispelled all coldness. No, not quite all. Susette was still shivering. "*Wait and see.*" As Big Snake repeated the bitter words, they kept echoing in her ears.

Her gaze clung to the face of the big Ponca. Even the anger seemed to have drained out of it, and, like Standing Bear's on that other day, there was nothing left but stolidity, resignation.

Then her eyes were drawn as with a magnet to the face of the boy beside him, and she felt a swift upsurging of warmth. Here was the anger, the impatience. It bristled with rage and purpose. The young eyes flashed fire. The two scalp locks over each ear peculiar to Ponca boys of his father's band stood out like sharp little horns. Bright Eyes did not know his name, but she wanted to give him one, this youngest son of Standing Bear. She thought, Mona-xaga—"Bristling with Arrows"? No. Inshtatheamba, her own name, was better, for it meant not only "Bright Eyes" but "Lightning Eye." Yes, Lightning Eye. No matter what his real name, he would always be that to her. Something in herself kindled in answering flame. She sensed that she and this boy were somehow akin. He would never be patient, resigned, in the face of injustice. As long as he lived, the Poncas—yes, and all other wronged Indians—would have a champion.

3

Wait and see. The winter days lengthened with no lessening of the imprisoning cold. Like the silent frozen Nishuda, the whole world seemed locked in waiting. Joseph waited anxiously, the worried lines in his face growing deeper, his limp more pronounced. The tribe waited in an agony of impatience, knowing that what happened to the Poncas today might happen to them tomorrow. Susette waited, dutifully running the treadmill of each day but getting nowhere.

Reading the rules governing the reservation one day, she made a discovery. There was a provision that any qualified Indian was to be preferred over a white person for any position in the Indian service. She knew it was no use to approach the Agent again. Her letters to the Commissioner all remained unanswered. But she decided to try once more. She wrote again to the Commissioner, quoting the provision in the rules and adding, "It's all a farce when you say you are trying to civilize us, then, after we educate ourselves, refuse us positions of responsibility and leave us utterly powerless to help ourselves. Perhaps the only way to make ourselves heard is to appeal to the American public through the press. They might listen."

More waiting, with little hope of a reply! Still no word came from the Ponca chiefs who had been taken to inspect land in the country "Toward the Heat."

"Suppose," worried Mary, "the white men have taken them and left them in a strange place where they cannot find their way home!"

"Nonsense!" Susette could not help laughing. "Impossible for the government to treat the chiefs of a nation with whom it made treaties in such a dishonorable fashion! It might cheat them," she admitted, "but at least it would treat with respect men with whom it hoped to make another treaty."

It was in the "Little Frog Moon" when the eight men arrived at the Omaha Agency. "The Ponca chiefs!" "You should see them!" "*Tha-eh-teh-wa-the*, pitiful!"

Joseph and Frank and Susette rode the three miles to the Agency, buffeting a cold March wind spitting needles of snow. In spite of the shocked reports they were unprepared for the sorry spectacle. The eight chiefs were haggard and emaciated. Their clothes were soiled and torn. Their moccasins were worn through and their feet swollen and caked with clotted blood. At sight of White Swan, eyes red-rimmed, features gaunt and barely recognizable, Joseph exclaimed in horror. "*Kagayho*, brother!"

It was many hours before they heard the whole story. The Poncas were made welcome in houses and lodges, given sweatbaths, provided with clean clothes and new moccasins. The horses, which had been given them five days before by the Otoes, in the south of Nebraska, were cared for. White Swan and Standing Bear came to Joseph's house, ate, slept, and were finally able to talk. Silently a group of villagers assembled, filling the small room. Susette sat beside Mary in one corner, clutching her mother's cold hand. It was Standing Bear who spoke.

"These men, the Inspector and another, came to us on our reservation. They said, 'We will take you to see the new land. If you like it, you can see the Great Father and tell him so. He will buy your land here and pay you for it. If not, you can also tell him so.' Because they would not believe us when we said we would not sell, we went, White Swan and I and the other chiefs. This Inspector showed us three pieces of land. They were not good. The water was bad. The ground was stony. A great many people there were sick. We told the Inspector that we would not come. He grew angry and told us that if we did not agree to come he would go off and leave us there to starve. He would not take us back home. We said it would be better for ten of us to die than that the whole tribe, all the women and children, should be brought there to die. I sent the interpreter and told him that he had brought us far from our own country on the cars and if he would not take us back he should at least give us money to pay our way. He said he would not give us one cent of money. We asked if he would take us to the Great Father, as he had promised. He replied that the Great Father had nothing to do with the matter. He would not take us anywhere. We could stay there and die."

The small room was stifling from the heat of the pot-bellied stove and the warmth of many bodies. The only sound was the crackling of wood. Even the walls seemed to be holding their breath.

"We went again and told the Inspector, if he would not take us back or give us money, to give us a paper that we could show to white men and tell who we were, so they would not think we were hostile and intended to steal. He replied that he would give us nothing, not even a paper. Now there were two very old men with us, who could not travel on foot at all. I sent and told the Inspector we would walk back, but these two old men could not walk and he must care for them. We could not carry them on our backs, and he must take them. He took these two old men and went off and left us. None of us had a cent of money, and we had no interpreter, so we could not speak a word to any man. The next morning we started on our long journey."

There was sound now in the room like a great long-drawn breath released in a single sigh. Susette made no sound. Her breath seemed frozen like the rest of her body. Though tears were streaming down Mary's cheeks, her own eyes were dry. Only her ears seemed alive, absorbing every calmly uttered word.

"It was winter. We started home on foot. White men were

suspicious of us, they thought we were vagabond Indians, who will travel around stealing. We slept out on the prairie without shelter. Sometimes we barely lived till morning, it was so cold. A few nights we found haystacks to sleep in. We had nothing but our blankets. We took the ears of corn that had dried in the fields. We ate it raw. The soles of our moccasins wore out. We were barefoot in the snow. Every day we traveled we grew weaker and weaker and had to go slower. It took us just fifty days to reach the Otoe Agency. The last few days we could walk only a few miles. When we got there we found that the Inspector had sent word to the Agent there to have nothing to do with us, that we were bad Indians and should be driven off. But when the Agent saw how hungry we were and looked at our bleeding feet, he took pity and gave us food and shelter. When we told him what had happened he was astonished and said he would write a letter to Washington. The Otoes gave us horses and provision, and after five days more—we are here."

Coldness dissolved into hot emotion. Suddenly Susette was all Bright Eyes. She wanted no part with the white men, even their God. Especially their God. If there was a God, he must have created Indians for the sole purpose of torturing them. But—no. She remembered the kindness of the Christian women who had taught her, taken her into their homes, paid for her education, and she could not wholly disbelieve. They had talked of America's ideals—justice, law, freedom for all. All, she understood now, bitterly, except the first Americans.

Freedom—when you had to have a pass to step off your reservation? Law? Remember the time Father had a horse stolen by a white man and saw him working it? He had gone to the Agent, but the Agent could do nothing. "You could go and steal it back," he had told Father seriously. Two Crows had had fourteen working horses stolen from him in the last few years, all by white men. No law to protect the Indian!

"They cannot make us go," insisted Standing Bear with dignity. "We have our treaty."

The next day the eight chiefs met in Joseph's house to consult together about the best way to avert the tragedy. Susette was there, and Father Hamilton. It was decided that a telegram should be sent immediately to the Great Father. Hamilton wrote it, with Susette's help. It read:

"To the President of the United States: Was it by your authority that the men you sent to take us down to the Indian Territory to select a home, left us there without money or interpreter, to find our way back as best we could? And did you tell them to say to us, if you don't select a home here you shall be driven from your present homes at the point of the bayonet? Please answer, as we are in trouble. We have been many days in falling back as far as the Omahas; tired, hungry, shoeless and footsore, and with hearts and spirits broken and sad."

Seven of the chiefs set out for the Ponca reservation on horseback. John Springer, an educated Omaha, went with Standing Bear to Sioux City to send the telegram. They stopped at the first station on the railroad and dispatched it. It cost $6.25.

"Ask him if anybody could stop it before it gets to Washington," said Standing Bear.

The operator laughed. "No! If they did, they would lose their jobs!"

The two men went on to Sioux City and told the story to the editor of a newspaper, the *Sioux City Journal*, and he promised to publish it. Then John Springer gave Standing Bear money and put him on the cars for Yankton. Presumably the telegram arrived in Washington, but no notice was ever taken of it. The matter had already been decided. The previous year a provision had been inserted in the Indian appropriation bill authorizing the Secretary of the Interior to use $25,000 for the removal of the Poncas to Indian Territory. This had been done without consultation with the Poncas, and the arrival of the Inspector on their reservation in January 1877 had been their first intimation of the action. All their bitter opposition and appeals were disregarded. On April 12, 1877, an order was given to force their removal, with army troops if necessary.

It was necessary. When Standing Bear joined the other chiefs and they arrived at the reservation, they found soldiers already there, also the Inspector who had taken them to Indian Territory. Threatened with removal at the point of bayonets, ten families of half-breed Indians had already loaded their belongings into carts and been carried away. But the rest of the tribe had remained adamant. They would not move until their chiefs came back.

"When we got there," Standing Bear later related what happened, "we asked the Inspector why he had done this thing, and he got very angry. Then we said to him, 'We did not think we would see your face again after what has passed. But here you are.'

"We said to him, 'This land is ours. It belongs to us. If you want money, take all the money which the Great Father is to pay us for twelve years to come, money paid for the land we sold under our treaty. You may have it all, if you will go and leave us our lands.' Then when he found that we would not go, he wrote for more soldiers to come.

"Then the soldiers came, and we locked our doors, and the women and children hid in the woods. Then the soldiers drove all the people to the other side of the river, all but my brother Big Snake and me. We did not go. And the soldiers took us and carried us away to a fort and put us in jail. There were eight officers there who held council with us. The commanding officer said, 'I have received four messages telling me to send my soldiers after you. What have you done?'

"Then we told him the whole story. Then the officer said, 'You have done no wrong. The land is yours. They had no right to take it from you. Your title is good. But I am a soldier, and I have to obey orders.' He said "I will telegraph to the President and ask him what I shall do. We do not think these men had any authority to treat you as they have done. When we own a piece of land, it belongs to us until we sell it and pocket the money.' Then he brought a telegram and said he had received an answer. The President said he knew nothing about it.

"They kept us in jail ten days. Then they carried us back to our homes. The soldiers collected all the women and children together; then they called all the chiefs in council; then they took wagons and went around and broke open the houses. When we came back from the council we found the women and children surrounded by soldiers.

"They took our reapers, mowers, hay-rakes, spades, plows, bedsteads, stoves, cupboards, everything we had on our farms, and put them in our large building. Then they put into the wagons such things as they could carry. We told them that we would rather die than leave our lands. But we could not help ourselves. They said they would make war on us if we did not go."

So it was that on May 21, 1877, the Poncas started on their long journey.

4

"We must go to meet them," said Joseph to Susette when the tragic news reached the Omahas. "The nearest point on their route of march will be *Uzha-ta-thon*, which the Waxes call Columbus."

The Agent was understanding. One look at Joseph's ravaged face convinced him that this was an emergency. Without objection he issued the pass.

With tears streaming down her face Mary packed the parfleche bags containing food, blankets, and other supplies for their journey. A pack horse was loaded with tent, poles, and other baggage. But heavier far than any baggage was the burden of tribal grief for the unfortunate Poncas, messages and gifts for relatives and friends, and, unspoken but real as death, fear for their own future.

It was the "Moon in Which One Plants," called May by the white man. The Poncas had planted, still clinging to their belief that their treaty would be honored. Many had sowed their spring wheat, some had planted corn and made gardens. As they rode the seventy miles or so to Columbus, Joseph and Susette saw white farmers planting, fencing fields, building houses on lands which had belonged to the Omahas for countless generations. The new owners exhibited no friendliness, only surly looks and muttered curses as they road past. Once a farmer stood with gun leveled until they were out of range. Another unloosed a pair of ugly dogs which followed them for a mile barking furiously and nipping the horses' heels.

Fortunately there was no need of finding a camping place, for Joseph would stop for only a few hours' rest, more for the beasts than for themselves.

"We may be too late," he worried. "According to the report it is nearly seven days since they started."

He need not have worried. Seven hundred people, including sick, old, infirm, babes in arms, traveling a hundred miles, most of them on foot, heartsick and despairing, with earth and heaven conspiring with man, it seemed, to confound their misery . . . it was a wonder it did not take seven weeks instead of seven days. The Ponca agent who accompanied them, Major E. A. Howard, made a day-by-day report of the journey which he forwarded to the Department of the Interior. He called it the "Journal of the March."

"May 21st. Broke camp at seven and marched to Crayton, thirteen miles. Roads very heavy. The child that died yesterday was here buried by the Indians. . . . May 22nd. Marched to Neligh, twenty-five miles. Day was cool and the road high and comparatively good. . . . May 23rd. Light rain . . . terrific thunder storm of two hours duration, steady rain throughout the day. A child died, and several women and children were reported sick. . . . May 24th. Buried the child that died yesterday, giving it a Christian burial. Marched about eight miles, crossing the Elkhorn River about two miles below Oakdale. . . . Road fearfully bad and much time and labor were expended in making the road and bridges passable over the Elkhorn flats. . . . May 25th. Marched twenty miles, to a point on Shell Creek. No wood. . . . Weather cold, damp, and dreary. The Indians behaved well and marched splendidly. . . . May 26th. Heavy continued rain, which prevailed until ten. Marched eight miles farther down Shell Creek when, a heavy thunder storm coming on, we went again into camp. May 27th. Several of the Indians were here found to be quite sick, and having no physician they gave us much anxiety and no little trouble. The daughter of Standing Bear, one of the chiefs, was very low of consumption, and moving her with any degree of comfort was almost impossible. . . . May 28th. Marched seven miles, when we came to a slough confluent to Shell Creek . . . two hours cutting willow-brush and bringing a large quantity of wheat straw, with which we covered the road thickly . . . made about fourteen miles . . . May 29th. . . . In coming down on the flats, which extended for five miles between the Bluffs and Columbus, we found the roads almost impassable, owing to many deep miry sloughs. . . . Difficulties were finally overcome, and the train marched into Columbus at two, having made a march of about ten miles. . . ."

Joseph and Susette arrived in Columbus first. They saw the soldiers pitch their tents at Soap Fork; then during the next hours the long train of wagons, travoix, tired horses, weary travelers came straggling in. White Swan and his family were among the last to arrive, for *Itimi*, Aunt, had been sick, and Cousin Rosalie had a new baby. The meeting was bittersweet. Never before had Susette seen Father weep. Few words were spoken. They were not needed. Hopelessness, pity, fear, love . . . all have a language more eloquent than words.

They pitched tents side by side. The train would remain there, the Agent said, for two or three days. It was strangely like old times, on hunts and tribal visits, with little cooking fires burning, shadows flitting across the lighted walls, little groups huddled in tight circles. But, oh, so different! No orderly *huthuga*, no story telling, no romping of children, no ritual songs and dancing. Susette was wakened the first night by a man's wailing. It sounded like a death song. Soon others joined in the mournful dirge, all crying for the beloved land left behind. She slept no more that night nor on succeeding nights. The camp was restless, and there was much coming and going among the tents. Finally the tight knots of misery unraveled into words.

"They talked and talked," said White Eagle, the Poncas' head chief, "the Inspector from the Great Father and our Agent. Like water through a rotted skin flowed their words. We must go, they said. The Great Father would give us better land and much money. No, we said, it was our land. Our fathers were buried there. We would not go. But it was no use. We must give our answer at once. Would we go peaceably, or by force? What could we do? We had no guns, like the Sioux. We are a peaceable people. The soldiers were there threatening us if we refused. We met in Council. All night we sat. Early in the morning we went to the Inspector. We told him we would go. If that is giving our consent, yes, we 'consented.'"

"That same day they took us across the river," said White Swan. His voice held no bitterness, only dull weariness. "It was swollen with the rains and cold. So swift was the current that the goods had to be packed on our shoulders. The quicksand bottom made it unsafe to trust them to the backs of animals. Even the wagons had to be drawn across by hand. And the old and infirm had to be carried on our backs."

Susette closed her eyes and clenched her fingers. That pretty daughter of Standing Bear, Prairie Flower, body racked by lung fever, teetering through that icy treacherous water on somebody's swaying shoulders!

"There were not many goods," said Standing Bear. "We were told to take them all to the Agency. There were some things the government had given us—threshing machines, reapers, mowers. I suppose they had the right to take them back. But some things I had bought with the grain and stock I had raised and sold. These were mine, and no man had any right to take them away. However, I obeyed the order and took them all to the Agency. These were the things which were mine and which I had to leave."

Slowly, without emotion, like a child reciting a lesson, he began recounting. "One house. I built it with my own hands. It took me a long time because I didn't know how very well. It was twenty feet by forty with two rooms. Four cows, three steers, eight horses, four hogs, two very large ones. Five wagon-loads of corn, with the side boards on, about 130 bushels. One hundred sacks of wheat and one wagon load loose which I had in boxes. Twenty-one chickens, two turkeys, and one prairie-breaking plow, two stirring plows, two corn plows, a good stable and cattle sheds. Three axes, two hatchets, one saw, three lamps, four chairs, one table, two beds, one hay-knife, three pitchforks, two washtubs and washboard, one crosscut saw, one cant hook, two log chains, two ox-yokes, two ladders, two garden rakes, three hoes, one new cooking stove, one heating stove, twenty joints of pipe, two trunks, one very large, one valise. Crockery, knives, and forks, and a great many other things which I cannot now remember. These were mine, and they took them away. You know, and I know, that I shall never see them again."

Susette stared with amazement at the chief's passionless face. How could he speak so calmly! Her own blood was boiling. The long enumeration went marching through her head in hot pulse beats. Instinctively she looked around for Standing Bear's son, him whom she had named "Lightning Eye." But he was nowhere to be seen. Had the fire in him died also? In all the faces she saw nothing but hopelessness and acquiescence, not a spark of rebellion.

Perhaps there was an official sensing that resistance among the migrants was dead, for at Soap Fork Major Walker, who had accompanied the train thus far with twenty-five soldiers, under orders from the War Department, took leave and returned to Dakota. On the fourth day, early, camp was broken, and orders for march were given. Rosalie, White Swan's daughter, clung to Susette.

"I'm so frightened," she whispered. "Two babies have died already. You can't know how terrible it is, this marching, so many sick. What if my little ones—"

They were just leaving when Susette felt his presence, looked around, and saw him. In the few months since she had named him he had changed, grown, it seemed, from boy to man. The anger was gone—burned away, she thought, in the fire of consuming purpose. It was as if he had no further need for it. He stood straight and tall, head flung back, eyes aflame but a little remote, as if he had just come from a Vision Quest. He was still "Lightning Eye."

"It is our land," he said. He might have been speaking to them, to anybody, or to himself. "Wakonda gave it to us. They may take me away now, but sometime I'll go back. I'll win back from those Waxes what belongs to us!"

As they rode home Joseph and Susette barely spoke. There was nothing to say. Susette scarcely noticed the greening fields, the ugly scowls, the raised fists, the audible mutters of "Thieving redskins!" "Dirty savages!" Only in body was she riding home to the beloved hills by the Smoky Waters. In spirit she was with the 700 Poncas patiently trekking "Toward the Heat." Later she would relive their terrible journey more vividly as she read the Agent's faithful "Journal of the March." A few words and phrases and sentences would become etched in memory.

"June 2nd. Broke camp at seven and marched seventeen miles, going into camp near Ulysses. Road in bad condition.

"June 3rd. Some trouble getting started . . . marched eight miles . . . camp on Blue River. Many sick, one reported dying. Bad roads. Rained during afternoon. . . .

"June 5th. Marched fourteen miles, went into camp near Milford. Daughter of Standing Bear, Ponca chief, died at two o'clock, of consumption. . . .

"June 6th. Prairie Flower, wife of Shines White and daughter of Standing Bear, was here given Christian burial . . . wish to take official recognition of the noble action by the ladies of Milford, in preparing and decorating the body of the deceased for burial in a style becoming the highest civilization. . . . It was here that, looking on the form of his dead daughter thus arrayed for the tomb, Standing Bear was led to forget the burial service of his tribe and say to those around him that he was desirous of leaving off the ways of the Indian and adopting those of the white man.

"June 7th. Heavy rain . . . wind blew a fearful tornado, demolishing every tent in camp . . . some of the people taken up and carried three hundred yards. Several of the Indians were seriously hurt, and one child died the next day. . . .

"June 8th. Marched seven miles. Roads very bad. Child died. . . .

"June 9th. Put the child that died yesterday in the coffin and sent it back to Milford, to be buried in the same grave with its aunt, Prairie Flower . . .

"June 12th. Broke camp at seven and marched to within two miles of Otoe Agency. Crossed Wolf Creek with a part of the train, crossing very difficult; but the Indians worked splendidly.

"June 13th. After considerable time we succeeded in building a bridge over Wolf Creek out of drift-timber and succeeded in crossing the balance of the train. . . .

"June 14. Water-bound and had to remain in camp all day. . . .

"June 16th. Reached Marysville, Kansas. . . . During the march a wagon tipped over, injuring a woman severely. Indians out of rations and feeling hostile.

"June 18th. Broke camp at seven. Marched nine miles and went into camp at Elm Creek. Little Cottonwood died. Four families determined to return to Dakota. I was obliged to ride nine miles on horseback to overtake them, to restore harmony and settle difficulty in camp. Had coffin made for dead Indian. . . . Fearful thunder storm during the night, flooding the camp-equipage.

"June 19th. Storm left roads impassable. . . . Buried Little Cottonwood.

"June 25th. Broke camp at six. Marched fifteen miles. . . . Two old women died. . . .

"June 30th. Passed through Hartford and camped six miles above Burlington. A child of Buffalo Chief died. . . .

"July 2nd. Broke camp at six. Long march of fifteen miles for Noon Camp. An Indian became hostile and made a desperate attempt to kill White Eagle, head chief."

Poor man, thought Susette. It was natural. He blamed the chief for getting them into such trouble. A chief was considered bound to let his people come to no harm.

"During the last few days of the journey the weather was exceedingly hot, and the teams terribly annoyed and bitten by green-head flies. . . . The people were all nearly worn out with fatigue from the march. . . ."

So ended the trek of five hundred miles. And what did they find on arriving in the country where "all their troubles would be ended"? A wilderness without one provision of any kind for their care or shelter.

"It is a matter of astonishment to me," wrote Agent Howard in this same official report, "that the Government should have ordered the removal of the Ponca Indians from Dakota to the Indian Territory without having first made some provision for their settlement and comfort. . . . The result is that these people have been placed on an uncultivated reservation, to live in their tents as best they may, and await further legislative action."

Though at least four years had passed when Susette read the "Journal" and momentous things had happened, her ears still echoed with that sound of wailing in the night which was like a death song.

1

Strange that a year which brought such tragedy to some could bring to others satisfaction and fulfillment! Susette's letter to the Commissioner threatening to publicize the failure of the Indian Bureau to implement its policy of giving qualified Indians preference over white employes finally brought a reply. An officer had at last deigned to make inquiries, writing to the principal of the Elizabeth Institute for her qualifications. Miss Susan H. Higgins was always delighted to talk about Susette.

"Deserves highest praise," she had often said of her. "She was at my school for over two years. She had pleasant winning ways and exhibited a wonderful courtesy. She was grateful for the smallest favor." Her report on scholarship qualifications was equally favorable.

However, before she could be given further consideration, Susette was told she must pass an examination and send in a certificate from the school committee of Nebraska. This necessitated an examination in Takamah, which was outside the Omaha reservation. Hopefully, for she had been given permission to leave the reservation before, she went to the Agency and asked the Agent for a permit. She was refused. She returned home, lips compressed. She said nothing to the family, but presently, when both she and her pony were missing, Joseph knew where she had gone. She rode to Takamah, took the required examination, and returned with the certificate. Now, she was informed, she must produce another certificate, one of good character! This was fortunately forthcoming from the Agent, and she was appointed assistant teacher at the agency day school with a salary of twenty dollars a month, just half of what white teachers were receiving. But that did not matter. At last! She plunged into her chosen career with all the vigor and ardor of an impassioned crusader.

Government promises for new buildings to house the day schools had been slow in materializing. Susette was given a small house, old and crudely constructed, in which to gather her pupils. Since it was two miles from home, she moved into it and kept house by herself, glad to relieve Joseph's overcrowded household of this extra burden. With Father Hamilton's help she started a small Sunday School and managed to save enough out of her meager salary to purchase a little organ, which enabled her to teach music to both groups. The training of well-bred young ladies at the Elizabeth Institute had included instruction in playing simple tunes and singing.

Autumn came with a burst of triumphant gold, the bluffs flaunting a new blanket of russet and yellow embroidered with crimson sumac. Susette's own spirit soared with the clouds of geese and cranes and ducks skimming in from the north, and she tried to forget that they also were bound in inexorable migration for those lands "Toward the Heat." Even when in late October the moon turned watery pale, forecasting the fall rains, she felt no waning of elation. At last she was *doing something* to fulfill her dreams. She would have been completely happy except for the restlessness and fear pervading the tribe and the news which came at rare intervals from Indian Territory.

The Poncas were driven to devious methods of communication. Uncle Frank's letters were a medley of contradictions. Unable to write for himself, he was forced to depend on either the Agent or some educated tribal member employed secretly. Those letters written by the Agent told of the good progress and satisfaction of the tribe. How different from the others, which pictured a barren land, intense heat, dire poverty, rampant disease in an area where malaria was endemic, and listed the names of numerous dead and dying! Occasionally there would come a solitary refugee who had fled the deadly climate, bringing sorrowful news of the despair and anguish of all.

Hope sprang when in November 1877 it was learned that a delegation of eleven Ponca chiefs had gone to Washington to plead their case before the Great Father himself. Among them were the head chief White Eagle, Standing Bear with his brother Big Snake, Big Chief, and Joseph's brother White Swan. Surely now that the President was involved, justice would be done and the Poncas be permitted either to return to their rightful home or to share the Omaha reservation. As details of the journey slowly filtered through, hope flared, flickered, guttered out.

"This morning," reported the Washington *Evening Star* on November 8, "the western train of the Baltimore and Ohio railroad brought to this city Major E. A. Howard, agent of the Ponca Indians and a delegation of chiefs and principal men of that tribe. . . . They were conveyed to Washington House, where they were assigned comfortable quarters—a large room with beds and chairs."

Subsequent news gave evidence that public interest ran as much to bizarre details as to justice.

"White Eagle is big and tall and athletic, wears white shirt, blanket, and leggings with sides worked with beads, moccasins . . . armlets between shoulder and elbow. . . . Others wear figured shirt, Standing Bear boasting one with a fancy worked bosom . . . no headdresses . . . thick black hair . . . armlets and finger rings indispensable. . . . Formerly lived in Dakota, had log houses and frame buildings, own horses, farming implements, and schools. . . . Will call at white house tomorrow. . . ."

Saturday, November 10: "The Ponca chiefs had an interview with the President at four o'clock yesterday in the cabinet chamber at the executive mansion. . . . They were resplendent in paint, feathers, and gay blankets. White Eagle, Standing Buffalo, Standing Bear, and Big Chief made speeches, interpreted by Batiste Barnaby. The one burden of each was an expression of dissatisfaction at their present place of residence in the Indian Territory and their desire to move back to their old reservation. Each shook hands with the President and his official associates before commencing his speech and performed the handshaking ceremony again at the close.

"White Eagle, a fine looking warrior, who made the first address, said he wished to know upon what ground his people were moved away from the reserve on which they had been living and spoke of the losses of property—farm implements, houses they had built, ponies and other property, and said, 'When anyone gets into a bad place, he wants to get out and be where he was before, and that is what I want. It seems the worst Indians get the opportunity to see you before we do. . . .'

"Big Chief spoke last. 'I am dressed as an Indian now, but I have different principles. I was living on that old reservation, but all at once I was taken up as by a whirlwind and disturbed in my place just as I had learned to plow, and was made to take another road which is new. We are all perishing. In less than three months time over thirty people have died and many cattle.'

"The President, rising, remarked, 'I have listened attentively to what you have said. I will consider carefully and will let you know the result.'"

The *Evening Star* continued its résumé for the next week, reporting further meetings with the President, more speeches by the chiefs, their attendance at the National Theater where they saw "Pink Pajamas" and at church where they spoke at a missionary service, the decision of government delivered to the delegation by Commissioner of Indian Affairs Hayt. They could not go back to their old agency, which had been given to other people, but they should have as good land as the government possessed in Indian Territory. No, they could not be placed, as they desired, on the Omaha reservation. There was no room there for two nations. They would have larger and better lands in Indian Territory, and, anyway, the Omahas themselves must shortly be removed from the Missouri River. "The Commissioner concluded," reported the *Star*, "by saying that it was better that all the Indians should live together in an Indian state, and that White Eagle might some day be returned as their senator to the Capitol."

On Monday, November 19, the *Star* wished the Poncas godspeed in language surprisingly biased in their favor.

"Lo, the poor Indian! The Ponca delegation left Washington Saturday. Perhaps, as the Indian nature is not believed to be very sensitive, the novelty of the visit here makes up for the annoyance of being stared at and profusely hand-shaken, but as far as solid results are concerned, the Poncas probably felt that they have had only their labor for their pains. This tribe of Indians formerly occupied lands on the Missouri River, were Christianized, taught to cultivate their ground, and in spite of their contiguity to the whites, actually gained the reputation of being honest. They were enticed from their lands, or, if they speak truly, on the pretense that they were to live elsewhere only on trial . . . and were to return if they were dissatisfied. . . .They came here hoping to be removed to their old reservation; this hope failing them, they petitioned to be allowed to live with the Omahas. After being denied this and finding they must live in Indian Territory, they sent in a list of articles which they need to live in their new and unwelcome home, and are told that, though everything possible will be done for them, 'the great council of the whites (Ponca for Congress, we suppose) alone has power to grant them what they desire.' After this last repulse the copper countenance of the chiefs took on a deeper shade of solemnity. They do not, however, return to Indian Territory empty-handed. A copy of the President's speech has been furnished them, and each has been presented with a small sum of money to buy presents for his wife and children, and with a pocket knife. If they do not feel grateful for these favors and for the kindly feelings which everyone has expressed for them, they are entirely unworthy of the notice and encouragement of the 'great council', and as they are peaceable and honest and do not need to be coaxed by money and supplies to permit white soldiers to remain un-murdered, this may be the decision of the 'great council' concerning them."

2

Remote though they were from the Great Father and his 'council,' news of the meetings in Washington came to the Omahas in graphic detail. Susette heard it in stunned disbelief.

At Elizabeth she had devoured the Constitution and the Declaration of Independence. Starry-eyed, she had learned by heart a poem by a contemporary poet named Longfellow. "Thou too sail on, O Ship of State! . . . Our faith triumphant o'er our fears, Are all with thee . . ." Somehow she had convinced herself that at the core of government the ideals of democracy prevailed, that, if the facts of oppression could be made known to those in power, justice would prevail. Now she listened with stony eyes and compressed lips as her pupils parroted, "We the people of the United States, in order to preserve a more perfect union, establish justice . . . secure the blessings of liberty . . ."

Since the removal of the Poncas the Omahas had lived in a limbo of fear and uncertainty. Tribe after tribe had been removed forcibly to Indian Territory—Arapahoes, Pawnees, Osages, Cheyennes. Most of the militant resisters—Crazy Horse, Roman Nose, Red Cloud, Spotted Tail, Gall—were either dead or conquered. The surrender of Chief Joseph just a month before had virtually ended the government conquest of Indians. Now they were panic stricken.

"The Omahas must shortly be removed from the Missouri River," the Commissioner had said.

Strange! In his report for this very year of 1877 Commissioner Hayt stated: "Experience has demonstrated the impolicy of sending northern Indians to the Indian Territory. To go no farther back than the date of the Pawnee removal, it will be seen that the effect of a radical change of climate is disastrous, as this tribe alone in the first two years lost by death over 800 out of its number of 2,376." Yet scarcely was the ink dry on this report when the Commissioner made public a letter claiming absolute power over the bodies of Indians to remove them anywhere the government pleased.

Susette was outraged. This time she did not wait for the leaders to act. She wrote a letter to the Commissioner herself. "Because I am an Indian," she demanded, "can you order me to the Indian Territory, New Mexico, or any place you please, and I be powerless to appeal to any law for protection? If this is true, rather than live in dread of such a fate, I would go to Canada and live under the protection of the British Government, where no commissioner could lay hands on me."

But of course it was an idle threat. She would have gone with family and pupils to steaming jungle or burning desert rather than separate herself from them.

The promise made in the treaty of 1854 and confirmed in 1865, that the reservation should be surveyed so that the people might own their own homes and tracts of land, had finally been partially fulfilled in 1872, largely through the influence of the Village of Make-Believe White Men. The eastern portion of the reservation from the Missouri to the Omaha Creek had been surveyed into townships. Oxen and breaking plows had been bought with tribal money, and certificates had been issued to many for lots selected.

Now, alarmed, those holding certificates took them to the large white settlements nearby and consulted lawyers to find out their legal value. When they were told that the certificates carried no patent rights to the land their fear and sorrow passed description. It seemed that the government they had always trusted had betrayed them. Why build houses, plant crops, improve the soil, if any day they were to be marched at bayonet point "Toward the Heat"?

Susette shared all their frustration, if not their apathy. Good teaching was almost impossible. Again and again she asked for books and supplies—a register, a bell, an object board—and, though the Agent dutifully sent in her request, nothing was ever received. Since the money that would have paid for them belonged to the tribe, it seemed reasonable that she and other tribal members had the right to say what should be done with some of it. But worse yet were the physical conditions under which she had to teach. So old was the building that when it rained the floor was covered with water. When it snowed, the desks were wet with snow filtering through cracks in the roof. The children would have to sit in a damp room all day. Now that there were no more buffalo hunts, many families were without skins to make moccasins and too poor to buy shoes even if the traders had kept any in stock. Some of the children came five or six miles to school, walking barefoot through the snow, and as they walked to their seats Susette was horrified to see blood marks on the floor. On the coldest days she dreaded to see morning come, fearing news that some of the little ones had been frozen on their way home the day before. Still they came, though neither parents nor government compelled them to. The second winter there were eighty in the whole school, and many had to be turned away.

Though the Agency was only two miles from "Joe's Village," the children from there were at a further disadvantage. There was a slough between the two, and they had to pass through or over it. When it was very cold they could walk on the ice, but in spring and fall it filled with water. They had to sit down and remove shoes and stockings—if they had them—and wade through the ice-cold water and mud. On one occasion a little girl broke through the ice into the water. That day Susette was fortunately with them. The wind was blowing furiously, and the snow was blinding, but with the aid of the older boys she managed to get the child out, then traveled the nearly two miles back home with her, making her run so she would not freeze.

"Why," she demanded desperately of Joseph, "*why* doesn't government build us a bridge?"

But it was a useless question. She knew the answer. Several years before the Omahas had asked the Agent to send to Washington for some of their money for a bridge. Eleven hundred dollars had been sent, yet no bridge had ever been built.

The helplessness of the tribe was dramatized in daily experience. The white workers on the reservation were laws unto themselves. One day an Omaha went to a pasture for his horses. In the same enclosure were kept horses belonging to the government farmer, who happened to be after two of his own at the same time. The Indian came out of the gate first and as the farmer came out, one of his horses which he did not want ran out with him. "Drive that horse back," he called roughly to the Indian. The latter refused, reminding the farmer that he was the one employed to look after the horses. Presently the Indian was arrested for being saucy and impertinent. He was locked in the block house but broke out. When the Agent and his men caught him, he would not submit to arrest without a fight, but the soldiers, knowing the Indian was in the right, refused to take him.

Susette was at home when the Indian came to Joseph's house and told his story. He showed no emotion, no anger. The injustice might have been done to someone else. She listened and watched with mounting pity and dismay.

Months later she felt the same helpless indignation when within a stone's throw of Joseph's house a young Omaha boy of sixteen was stabbed by a white boy of thirteen. The white people in the settlements around the reservation wondered that the Indian had permitted it, being so much older and stronger. No Indian wondered. Had he defended himself by striking the boy and harming him, the whole tribe would have been punished. Troops might have been sent and war declared on the tribe. Susette's indignation was not directed toward the Indian boy. She admired his heroism.

Not all the Omahas suffered their wrongs in silence. Though most of their leaders could neither read nor write English, they were not inarticulate. Susette was often their interpreter. At their dictation she wrote innumerable letters to the President, the Secretary of the Interior, the Commissioner, with elaborate attempts made to conceal the writing from the Agent. Some of the tribe would go away on the prairie and conceal themselves. Another member of the tribe would seek her out and lead her unobtrusively to the hiding place, where the letters would be composed and written, then carried to the nearest settlement and mailed.

One for whom she wrote such a letter was Wajapa, son of Watunna's sister, whom the children of Joseph called *Winegi*, Uncle, and who was almost as dear to them as their own father. Though in build and feature he resembled Joseph, no white blood flowed in the veins of Wajapa. He was all Indian, with the pride of a noble race and the wisdom of centuries stored behind his broad forehead and kindly, whimsical, but piercing eyes. Though he bore the "civilized" name of Ezra Freemont, he much preferred his *nikie* name, which signified "Tribal Herald." Now about forty years of age, he was a staunch but reluctant supporter of Joseph's crusade of change. Sensing the doom of the old ways, for his children if not for himself, he had doggedly adopted the forms, if not the spirit, of the white man's culture.

"Even the snake knows when it must shed its skin," he commented cryptically.

And, though he still tilled his fields wearing leggings and breechcloth, and would do so for the next quarter century, each Sunday he sat in Father Hamilton's little Presbyterian church dressed as conventionally as a New England deacon, and his children—Mable, Nettie, Marguerite, Francis—were being reared side by side with Joseph's sons and daughters. In fact Mable, near her own age, was one of Susette's closest friends.

Taking dictation from this man who could neither read nor write, translating his words into English, Susette marveled at his wisdom, his honesty, his simple fluency. For the letter Wajapa composed, addressed not to the President or the Secretary or the Commissioner, but to all white Americans, would have done justice to a scholar. Long afterward she would preserve its full text in a little book of Omaha literary treasures.

"My Friends: As I am thinking of you today, I send you a letter of a few words. . . . As to our being in this land, God put us here, and so we are here. Before the white man came hither, we thought it was our land. But when the Great Father said the land was to be sold, it was sold, and a very small part remains to us of all that used to be ours. And now the white people wish to take that from us! They wish to send us to a far-off land. It is very hard for us . . . like killing us. . . .

"It has been said, 'You are to have white soldiers reside among you.' But we know the soldiers. We have had them, so we know them. They act as if they were the only human beings. And whatever Indian woman they wish to dishonor, without taking her at all for a wife, they dishonor her, and they treat us as if we were hogs and dogs. We do not want them. . . .

"You think that all Indians are alike, but we are not alike. . . . We are all of different nations. You whites too are of different nations. We wish to live. We wish to become citizens. . . . As we wish to live, we are working for ourselves, yet we have fared very hard this year. The heat was so great that our wheat was withered, and did not bring more than thirty to forty cents a bushel. We are just as if we had not made anything at all for ourselves. . . .

"We have tried working and know very well that it is good, so we desire it. As we write this letter to you, God is sitting with us, as it were; therefore we hope that the white people will stop talking about our land, or against us.

"We wish to keep what is ours, so we petition you, and your people too, who are helping us, we pray to you, and you who are on the other side, we pray to you also. Have pity on us Omaha Indians. . . . Wajapa."

3

The Omahas were almost as fearful and distressed for the Poncas as for themselves. The 500 miles between were bridged by letters, gossip trickling into the Agency, the straggling refugees who manage to escape the new land and make their way back to their friends. These the Omahas kept carefully in concealment until they felt they could safely be absorbed into the tribe.

Always the news was disheartening. The Poncas had been a sober people. Hardly had their tents been pitched in the new country when whiskey dealers from Baxter Springs, across the border in Kansas, began peddling liquor among them. Dispirited, destitute, the Indians were easy victims. There was a Kansas law against such traffic, but, when the Poncas' agent attempted to bring the peddlers to court, the Kansas judge declared the law unconstitutional and freed the prisoner.

After the debacle in Washington they sought the only solution possible. Having been promised a choice of land in Indian Territory, they asked for a more favorable location. Permitted to examine other sections, they chose an area on the west bank of the Arkansas River, on both sides of the Salt Fork, part of the tract obtained from the Cherokees in the treaty of 1866. In July the tribe made the journey, the sick and aged carried in wagons, others walking through heat varying from 95 to 100 degrees. Though there was no loss of life during the eight days' trek, both people and animals approached exhaustion.

"The land was good," White Eagle said, "but in the summer we were sick again. We were as grass that is trodden down, we and our stock. Then came the cold weather, and how many died we did not know."

Though the new country was promising, it was not home. They had arrived too late to plant crops. During that second intolerably scorching summer they were unsettled and homeless. Huddled at first in a single tent village where at least there was a sense of tribal community, they were soon scattered over the reservation by the Agent, possibly to encourage a sense of land ownership and responsibility, more likely to discourage group rebellion. Malaria had taken severe toll. Already over 150 of the 800 people had died, and scores more were suffering from chills and fever. Scarcely a family was left which had not mourned its dead. Separated from others, a whole family might be sick and no one else know. In some families persons would die and the others not be able to bury them. They would drag them out with a pony on the prairie and leave them for the vultures. Men would take sick while trying to work and die in less than a day. No wonder a spirit of hopelessness and lethargy pervaded the tribe! Even the bravest chiefs—White Eagle, Big Snake, Big Chief, Standing Bear—felt like slackened bows, quivers empty of arrows.

What to do? Standing Bear was tortured with questions. "Should I gather up my people, send them on ahead, keep my warriors in the rear, and try to retreat to the mountains, and if the soldiers come, all of us die fighting? . . . No, I do not want to fight the soldiers. They have treated me kindly, the officers often taking my part. And my warriors are too sick to march or fight. . . . No, I see nothing ahead but death for the whole tribe. Where is Wakonda? He has failed us."

Except for his only surviving son, he would have lost faith entirely. But the boy's courage, his burning zest for life were contagious. He had gone to school on the old reservation, listened to the teaching of missionaries, learned to read from their Book. Wakonda was good, the youth passionately insisted. He cared for people. He would not let evil men have their way forever. He was a God of justice, the white men's book said so. Humbled, but still brooding, Standing Bear listened while his son prayed and read to him from the New Testament. The boy would gather a few in a tent and talk to them, telling them the right way to live as well as he could. As long as the fire blazed in the boy's eyes and the young voice remained unfaltering, Standing Bear could not quite lose hope.

Autumn came, bringing surcease of the torturing heat but not of sickness. Worst of all was the sight of little children. They would moan and moan, and there was no way to help them. Winter . . .

And then something happened which drew the slackened bow taut, closed his fingers on a sharpened arrow. His son sickened and lay dying.

"Please, Indadi." The fevered eyes were imploring. "Take my bones back and bury them there by the Swift Running Water where I was born. Promise me?"

Standing Bear trembled. His sluggish blood quickened. His shoulders straightened. He looked steadily into the rapidly filming eyes. "I promise," he said clearly.

Before the four days of mourning passed he began swift and secret preparations. First there was the planning with family.

"*Ou-daa*, it is good," agreed his wife, packing the parfleche cases even as she wept. "My mother is buried there, my grandmother, and another child. Our boy was a good boy, and we must do what he asked us. My heart is broken. Even before this, my eyes were full all the time with tears, and ever since I came to this place there has been an ache in my heart." She stopped packing long enough to gather two of her grandchildren into her arms. "If we stay here, these little ones will die soon too."

Now the scattering of the tribe was an advantage. In the nights when the wailing was silent Standing Bear could visit the tents of his relatives and friends far from the watchful eye of the Agent. He would take with him, he decided, only a small party, and if the soldiers came after them they would not fight. Whatever they did to them, it would be no worse than staying in this land of heat and death. The party included only about thirty persons, seven of them sick. They slipped away on the night of the second of January 1879. They had a few wagons, several wornout horses, a small quantity of rations, and among them all just twenty dollars. Standing Bear had ten, and Tazahba ("Buffalo Chip") had ten. In one wagon was a box containing the body of Standing Bear's son.

"We will go first to our friends the Omahas," the chief planned.

They were ten weeks making the journey. For the first twenty days Standing Bear fed the party on a dollar a day. After that there was no more money. For two days they were without food. Then he went to the house of a white man and motioned to him to follow him. He did so. Standing Bear pointed out to him the sick. Though the man did not seem to understand, he noticed how gaunt and poor were the ponies. He went off and came back with his boys, bringing hay and a big bag full of corn. They took some of the corn, shelled and parched it. The man watched and, seeing the children eat ravenously, understood. Presently he brought flour, meat, and coffee. After that other white people befriended them. Some gave bread, some coffee, others meal or flour. Only in two places were they refused food, and the Waxes there seemed to have little themselves.

Standing Bear kept his party far out in Kansas and frequently changed his course, fearing pursuit from the Agency. Even the Waxes in these parts seemed very poor. The weather was cold, for these were the "Moon When the Snow Drifts into the Tents" and the "Moon of Storms." It was a journey of incredible hardships for this band of thirty, many of them women and children, some sick, all weak and half starved. But courage was high. Anticipation helped allay their shivering on freezing nights. Their scanty food was flavored with the spice of freedom. They were going home.

It was in mid-March, in the "Moon When the Geese Return," that they finally reached the Omaha reservation, and the sky above the rushing Smoky Waters was alive with soaring wings.

4

Susette knew something had happened when her pupils came to school that morning. She knew also that the children of the white employees knew nothing about it. A Waxe could not hide a secret like an Indian. In the darker faces there was no sign of betrayal, just a tightened wariness which only one of themselves could detect. It was the sort of silent language which all peoples employ when their country is occupied by hostile strangers.

"What is it?" whispered Susette in Omaha, leaning over the desk of an older boy, ostensibly to help him with arithmetic.

"Poncas," he whispered back. "Came. In night."

The day dragged. She was as anxious for school to be over as her Indian pupils. Fortunately it was a Friday, so she would be expected to go home. She felt like pulling up her long skirts and running, and it took all her will power to walk with the sedate decorum expected of a school teacher nearly twenty-five years of age. Marguerite and Susan came to meet her, Susan, still only fourteen, setting a skipping pace that left the less impetuous Marguerite behind. Susan was the active, aggressive one of the four sisters, just as Rosalie was the most intellectual, Susette the most retiring, and Marguerite by far the most beautiful. Watching Marguerite come along the road, Susette was struck anew with her maturing loveliness. The heartshaped face with its high brow and huge dark eyes could surely compete with the youthful Nicomi for that title of "The Beautiful Omaha." Oh, both these girls, when they went to the Elizabeth Institute later this year, would fit into its strange exciting world as she, the shy Susette, had never done. Susan would dance gayly through every activity, always a leader with her piquant liveliness, and Marguerite, though a bit lazy when it came to mental discipline, would capture all hearts with her gentleness and beauty. A pity, though, that Rosalie also could not have the benefit of more schooling—Rosalie, with her wide, alert, eternally questioning eyes and keen hunger for knowledge!

The girls could hardly wait to share the news, but discreetly, for the road between Joe's Village and the Agency was well traveled, by Waxes as well as Indians. Fortunately few of the government employees could speak the tribal language, but caution was observed even when Omaha was spoken.

About thirty Poncas had come in the night, several families. No, Uncle White Swan was not with them. Many were sick. They had all been taken care of. Standing Bear and his family were in Joseph's house. They were going on to their old reservation, just stopping here to rest and get provisions.

"You say—Standing Bear and his family? Susette was instantly alert. "Did his son come with him?"

Yes. In fact, that was why he had come, to take his son back to the old country, where all his people were buried.

Even then Susette did not understand. "You mean—I don't see—"

Susan's eyes were wide with excitement. "He's in a box, sort of a trunk, and it's on a wagon, hidden under a blanket, in our barn. His son's bones, Standing Bear says, that he promised to take back and put in the old burying ground."

Susette's limbs kept moving steadily, but she felt as if some life had gone out of them. So—it was gone, that spirit that had flamed with a white-hot ardor so akin to her own. What a pity! Yet perhaps in his death he was a better champion of his people's cause than if he had lived. At least he had inspired some of them to action.

Joe's Village looked as usual. No one would have guessed that thirty strangers, plus goods, wagons, ponies, had been absorbed into houses, barns, corrals. But within the walls of Joseph's house there was bustling excitement—smells of food cooking, supplies being assembled and packed in parfleche bags for a journey, worn sandals and ponies' halters being mended, a half dozen strange children underfoot. The Poncas, it seemed, were determined to resume their journey before daybreak.

But Joseph had other ideas. He persuaded Standing Bear to call the men of his band together that night for a council in his house. One by one they drifted in, faces hidden in their blankets, until a dozen of them were assembled in a council circle. With them came leaders of the Omahas.

After the pipe had been passed and the guests properly feasted, Joseph spoke persuasively. "Listen, brothers, my friends. Your homes have been destroyed. Your fields are not plowed. You have no plows or tools to work with. Stay here with us, at least for awhile. We have land broken on which you may plant. We will lend you seeds and tools. Some of your band are sick. They should not travel farther. We speak the same language and have always been one people. Stay with us."

There were nods and murmurs of approval from members of both tribes. However, as Standing Bear shook his head, all fell silent. He was a commanding figure, topping most others even when seated. For his council meeting he had donned his chief's dress, a red blanket with broad blue stripes, a wide beaded belt, a necklace of bear's claws. His long black hair boasted a single eagle feather. They had not come this far, he insisted, to be overtaken and sent back before they reached their goal. Had they not taken pains to avoid settlements, other Indian agencies? Let the sick stay here if they must, but let all able-bodied braves return with their chief to their own land.

The other Poncas were no blind followers. Even Yellow Horse, Standing Bear's brother, shook his head. They were tired. For the first time in many weeks they were warm, their stomachs were full. The reasonable suggestion of Joseph exerted strong appeal. Moreover, as he went on to tell them, he believed it would be possible for them to remain on the reservation without making their presence known at the Agency. The Agent knew few of the tribe by name or face. To Waxes all Indians, it was said, looked alike. He spoke no Omaha. A few educated Omahas who acted as interpreters, Joseph's own daughter among them, were his sole means of communication with the tribe, and all were to be trusted. This was the beginning of the planting season. Many of the tribe who lived at a distance cultivated fields on the river bottoms, and it was their custom to live in tipis just above the river during this season. Several had already been put up near Joseph's house. The Poncas should occupy them, be given fields to till, and remain until they had raised enough food to take them safely to their own land.

It was so decided. Even Standing Bear was persuaded of the wisdom of the decision. Before morning the guests would all be encamped in the tipis. Only two Waxes would be told that the eleven hundred or so population of the Omaha tribe had been suddenly increased by thirty, Father Hamilton and Reverend J. Owen Dorsey, a missionary who had spent many years among Indian tribes and who was at present on the Omaha reservation making a study of tribal history, language, and customs.

Susette slipped out of the house. It was dark, but the stars were clear and bright, and she made her way to the barn without difficulty. She stood in the door accustoming her eyes to the darkness, until vague shapes appeared. She moved among them until she found Standing Bear's wagon. Most of his possessions had been taken inside, and the wagon was nearly empty. Her hands groped until they found the long rough wooden box, and rested on it.

"All that youth and fire," she thought with a blazing anger, "nothing but a few bones in a box!" Oh, it wasn't fair! He should be climbing high hills, blowing smoke to the four winds, riding hard across the prairie, fighting to win justice for his people. "Sometime I'll go back," he had vowed with that lightning flashing in his eyes. "I'll win back from those Waxes what belongs to us!" *Dho*, he would go back. He would keep his vow. He would win back just enough of his own land to lie in.

She went out and looked up at the stars, as on the night after her beloved Louis had died. In the face of death, she thought, as when she heard the first thunder, she would always be an Indian. *Wah-cunh-munthi*, the Milky Way, made a broad bright path across the sky.

5

Everything went as planned. The Poncas were given tools, seed, land on the bottoms, and those not too sick to work either plowed or planted a little wheat. Those too sick to move were cared for by men of the two medicine societies, the Pebble and the Shell. Though the *waxewakega*, the white man's sickness, which he called malaria and which they had brought back from the hostile land, was unfamiliar, they treated it like other attacks of chills and fever, with rest, sweat baths, purgation, liquid diet, and decoctions of red grass which for generations had been favorite febrile remedies. Since the Waxes themselves had made little progress in treating malaria since the borrowing of cinchona bark from Peruvian Indians in the seventeenth century, and the use of quinine as an effective remedy was still nearly a dozen years away, they could have observed some of these ancient treatments with respect and profit.

It was on a Sunday that the blow fell. Susette was at home. A band of soldiers came riding into Joe's Village, headed by Lieutenant Carpenter from General Crook's garrison, stationed in the fort at Omaha. They stopped at no houses, rode straight to the clusters of tents outside the village. Shocked and helpless, the Omahas watched them go. Not a person in the village but knew what they wanted. Without stopping to watch further, Susette left the village and started along the path to the Mission. Forgetful of decorum, she pulled up her long full skirt and ran full speed. If anyone could help the Poncas now, it was Father Hamilton and Dr. Dorsey.

Why? How? Who? Had the agent from Indian Territory pursued the fugitives, after all, or sent spies after them? Had their own Omaha agent betrayed them? Of course they had known that he must discover their presence eventually, but they had trusted that he would accept the situation as a *fait accompli*. Later they were to discover that it was indeed their own agent. He had sent a telegram to the Department of the Interior in Washington: "Thirty runaway Indians are here on my reservation. What shall I do with them?" Secretary of the Interior Schurz had known exactly what to do. He had wired an order to General Crook at the nearest army post to have the runaways arrested.

Lieutenant Carpenter went into one of the tents and through his interpreter told the occupants, not unkindly, that he had been sent to take them all back to Indian Territory. In the tent was Long Runner, one of the malaria victims, too sick to work.

"No!" he cried. "I would rather die than go." Stumbling from his bed, he started for his gun, in another part of the tent, whether to challenge the soldiers or to use it on himself no one knew, perhaps least of all himself, but before he could reach it the soldiers had handcuffs on him. When they entered another tent a woman, also sick, started up from her bed and drew a knife, but was easily kicked to one side.

Standing Bear soon came running. Even without his chief's regalia he was a commanding figure, and the Lieutenant recognized him as a leader. The chief tried to protest through the interpreter. He had always been a friend of the whites. Once he had found a poor white soldier on the plains in midwinter, with both feet frozen, and nearly starved to death. He had carried him in his arms to camp and taken care of him for weeks until he died.

"And now," he said hotly, "you, a soldier, come here to drive me from the land of my fathers."

When Susette and the two missionaries arrived on the scene, the Poncas had already been rounded up. Father Hamilton's protests were useless.

"I have no choice, sir," the Lieutenant told him regretfully. "I have had my orders, and they must be obeyed. They are to be taken to the fort in Omaha."

"But—surely you can see that this is a harmless, defenseless band! How can their presence here among their friends possibly be construed as a hostile act against the government?"

The Lieutenant was sorry but firm. The Poncas had broken the law by leaving their reservation without permission. Orders had come from Washington.

Hamilton persisted. It was obvious that many of them were sick, in no condition to be moved. The Lieutenant assured him that the utmost care would be taken to make their journey comfortable. The sick would be transported in wagons and the trip taken in short stages. Surely they would be much better off in the fort where they could have proper medical attention than in these tents, subjected to the magic and superstitions of savage medicine men! Tonight they would be housed at the Agency, under guard of course, and the journey would begin early in the morning.

"We have committed no crime," was all Standing Bear would say, "and done nothing wrong. Why does the government treat us in this way?"

Back in her small room at the Agency school Susette spent a sleepless night. The silence was like that of the four nights after death. The air was heavy with the burden of unreleased pain. But scarcely had the sky paled when the world sprang alive with sound—soldiers shouting, ponies whinnying, wagons clattering, children crying. And now came the wailings, helpless protests of a people being driven from their home into a strange land. Like the Jews, thought Susette, taken away to exile in Babylon.

"By the rivers of Babylon, there we sat down,
    yea, we wept, when we remembered Zion.
    We hanged our harps upon the willows. . . .
How shall we sing the Lord's song in a strange land?"

She dressed quickly and went out. The whole tribe, it seemed, had gathered to share the misfortunes of the Poncas. Father Hamilton was there with Dr. Dorsey, both renewing their efforts to avert the removal but able to do nothing. Joseph was there, looking somber and careworn. He would blame himself, thought Susette, for urging them to stay. The white government employes were there, looking as indignant and distressed as the Indians.

"That poor man in handcuffs," the wife of one of them confided to Susette. "He was off by himself, and the soldiers forgot to feed him. I took him some breakfast. There he was, shaking with chills, and so sick he couldn't eat!"

The Agent was there, obviously a little bewildered and apologetic for the trouble he had unwittingly caused. After all, he had merely requested methods of procedure. He would have been quite willing for the runaways to remain. What were thirty more poor heathen savages among eleven hundred?

The soldiers were not brutal, but efficient. Order and speed were essential. The journey to Omaha would be slow enough, with half the travelers sick and the majority on foot. They could not expect to make more than ten or twelve miles a day. And they might well have 500 more to go to get the poor devils back where they belonged. They did not relish the job, but orders were orders. The sickest ones, some unable to sit up, were bundled into the few rickety wagons, all but one woman, who was obviously too ill to be moved and had to be left in the agency barracks. All was ready at last, and the Lieutenant issued a sharp command to move. Better to end this weeping and wailing and blubbering as soon as possible. An unwelcome job, and it seemed an unnecessary one. Why couldn't the government have left the poor devils alone? It was the principle of the thing, he supposed. You couldn't let them get away with anything. You had to show them who was boss.

Dr. Dorsey wrote a letter to Colonel Meacham, editor of the *Council Fire*, who was at the time in Washington.

"I saw them leave today," he said in part. "All but the prisoner [Long Runner] went about half a mile in advance of the soldiers without a guard and without a struggle, save that *which was going on in their own hearts*. The appeals to me were touching. Said Standing Bear: 'My friend, you know us. We can't live down there where the Great Father put us. So we came here to live and work the land.'" The letter begged Colonel Meacham to see the Secretary of the Interior and Commissioner and appeal to them in Standing Bear's behalf.

Eyes dry, Susette watched them go, Standing Bear walking

straight and tall at the head of his band, behind him the rickety wagon bearing the rough wooden box. His eyes too were dry, his rugged features as rigidly inscrutable as if carved from bronze. He had managed to change into his chief's bordered blanket, belt, and necklace. The single upright eagle's feather rose proudly over his impressive six feet and more of height.

She went back into the schoolroom, where the pupils were already beginning to assemble, and set about the task of lifting them from savagery to civilization, using as her tools the white man's language, the white man's history, the white man's credo of freedom and democracy. But she was there only in body. In spirit she was trudging mile after mile toward a strange hostile country, rebellious and helpless. If only somebody could do something!

Three

1

Thomas Henry Tibbles was a crusader. Had he lived in other eras he might have faced Nero's lions, or stormed the citadel of Jerusalem with Godfrey, or been roasted for heresy in the Spanish Inquisition. In his own era, however, he found no dearth of adventurous causes.

At age eleven he ran away from a tortured existence as a "bound-out" apprentice. At sixteen he was traveling West with an emigrant wagon train sent out by Henry Ward Beecher in the movement to make Kansas a free state. During one of their engagements he was captured by the enemy and sentenced to hang as an Abolitionist, saved just in time by the Free State forces armed with Sharp's rifles, jokingly dubbed "Beecher's Bibles." Seventeen bullet holes in his clothes, others in a shoulder, arm, and leg testified to his narrow escape. He spent some time in the Abolitionist movement under John Brown, but left him in disillusionment before Harper's Ferry. Next he took part in a crusade to rid the country of horse thieves, and in a set-to with Quantrell when he refused to tell the whereabouts of his friends, he was strung up again and saved only by their opportune arrival. During subsequent years he lived intimately with various Indian tribes, sharing their hunts, their battles, their village and camp life. So intimate and honorable was their relationship that the Indians called him "Father" instead of "Friend."

At seventeen he emerged from the wilderness, entered a private school, and later studied at Mount Union College in Ohio, giving talks on his experiences with the Indians to pay his way. At twenty-one he married an English girl, Amelia Owen, and, turning West again, became a newspaper man, holding every position from assignment reporter to editor-in-chief. He became a local preacher in the Methodist Church, bought a circus tent, and held meetings along the frontier, preaching while his beautiful and talented wife played a little melodeon and sang. As they traveled over Missouri for two years their tent was often attacked by gangs, and he preached always with a revolver lying beside his Bible. During these years he never owned a suit of clothing that was free from bullet holes. But, moving West again to Nebraska, he discarded all deadly weapons and was never shot at again.

Assigned as minister in Republican City, where he had once hunted with the Plains Indians, he found another cause to champion: The victims of the terrible famine of 1874, when armies of grasshoppers despoiled the country of every green thing except buffalo grass. Greedy speculators, fearful of frightening off new settlers, kept the newspapers from publishing the true facts. Many people were starving. Tibbles' effort to appeal to the American public for aid brought a storm of abuse, but he persisted. Finally he went to Chicago, appealed to the Board of Trade, raised a good amount of money, aroused public sentiment to aid the sufferers, and returned to find his name anathema to nearly all the eighty-odd newspapers in Nebraska. Other trips east yielded some $80,000 in cash and many carloads of supplies. The settlers were able to keep their homesteads, and Nebraska was saved from losing many years in her development.

Such was the man who sat in the editorial rooms of the Omaha *Herald* late on the night of March 29, 1879, getting his paper ready to go to press. To his surprise he looked up to see General George Crook, commander of the department of the Platte, enter his office.

Tibbles admired the General and considered him a close

friend. After Custer's defeat Crook had made possible a treaty which had prevented what would undoubtedly have been the greatest of Indian wars. He was one of the few white officers who had always kept his word to the Indians. The two men had a peculiar bond. Crook also had experienced the painful ordeal of initiation into the Soldier Lodge, which gave a unique understanding and appreciation of Indian life and culture. They were the only white men ever accorded the honor.

"*Ka-gay-ho*, hello, friend." Rising, Tibbles greeted the General with the Lodge's grip of friendship. He saw instantly that his guest was disturbed. "Sit down, friend. Get it off your chest. This is no social call, I can see that."

General Crook sat for some moments studying the editor, possibly considering what secrets it was safe to confide. He saw a figure of towering strength, a great shock of black hair, a ruddy face with square, determined jaw and eagle-keen eyes set deep beneath heavy projecting brows, a twinkle lurking in their steely depths. Satisfied, he leaned forward, pulling savagely at his big tufts of side whiskers.

"During the quarter century that I've been on the plains in government service," he confided, "I've been forced many times by orders from Washington to do most inhuman things in dealing with the Indians, but now I'm ordered to do a more cruel thing than ever before. I would resign my commission, if that would prevent the order from being executed—but it would not. Another officer would be assigned to fill my place. I've come to ask if you will not take up the matter. It's no use for me to protest. Washington always orders the very opposite of what I recommend."

He showed Tibbles an order he had lately received through the War Department from the Secretary of the Interior: "Thirty Poncas have left their agency in the Indian Territory without permission. I respectfully request that the nearest military commander be instructed to detail a sufficient guard to return these Poncas to the agency where they belong."

The General had sent soldiers to the Omaha Agency, where the runaways had taken refuge, and now these thirty men, women, and children, many of them sick, who had traveled hundreds of miles to go back home, were under arrest at Fort

Omaha, due to be returned to the hell of exile from which they had managed to escape. There was nothing he could do. Orders must be obeyed. But Tibbles was an editor of a daily newspaper. He was a fearless crusader for unpopular causes. If he would try to do something for these unfortunate victims of the despicable Indian Ring, Crook would stand by him.

After the General left, Tibbles kept on working. His chief was away, and it was his job as assistant editor to get the paper ready for publication. But while he slashed and blue-penciled, juggled headlines, leads, pictures, his mind veered off on tangents. Take up the cause of a few obscure redskins of a little-known tribe who had dared flout an unjust law? It would mean bucking the whole so-called Indian Ring, that network of despotic power whose tentacles radiated from Washington down through the obscurest Indian agency and held the destiny of every tribe, peaceful as well as warlike, in their strangling grip. It would mean an interminable fight, for if he once started he would never give up until he won or died. It would mean giving up his honorable position as a newspaper man, which had cost him five years of hard work at journalism to attain. But the question he asked himself began with "How?", not "If?" While the General was still talking, he had made his decision.

It was four in the morning when Tibbles sent the paper to press, and as he left the building the kindling of a spring dawn was streaking the east. He went to bed at 4:30, rose at seven, and immediately started on foot for Fort Omaha, four miles away. The Poncas were there, all right, their misery so palpable he felt its physical impact. Most of them were sick with malarial fever. He saw despair on every face. In one tent a sick child moaned piteously. In another a woman was wailing for the dead.

He found an interpreter and went to Standing Bear's tent. Though he knew many words common to the Plains Indian dialects, he needed help for real conversation. "I want to hold a council," he told the chief. "I want to print your story, so that white people can know how you have been treated. I am your friend. I want to help you."

But Standing Bear refused to talk. It would not be seemly, he explained with dignity, to talk with any one else before he held his council with "Three Stars," General Crook. The General might take it as an insult. The paper would not be printed until Tuesday morning, Tibbles argued, because no paper was published on Monday. Still the chief was adamant. Nonplused, Tibbles reflected. Suddenly he had an idea. He gave the chief the signs of the Soldier Lodge. Standing Bear recognized them instantly. His face lit up, and the two exchanged the grip of friendship. Immediately he called a council, and the editor was soon seated around a council fire with the chiefs and braves smoking the pipe of peace.

It was Sunday. While the people of the nearby city attended church, ate their ample dinners, enjoyed siestas, took leisurely strolls, read their newspapers, Thomas Tibbles listened to sermons as eloquent and profound as any preached that day in an Omaha pulpit. Outstanding among the speakers were Chief Tazahba ("Buffalo Chip") and Standing Bear. So deeply were the words incised on the editor's consciousness that he was later able to record them almost verbatim.

"I sometimes think," said Tazahba, his slow speech punctuated with graceful but emphatic gestures, "that the white people forget that we are human, that we love our wives and children, require food and clothing, that we must take care of our sick, our women and children, prepare not only for the winters as they come, but for old age when we can no longer do as when we are young. But one Father made us all. We have hands and feet, heads and hearts all alike. We also are men. Look at me. I am poor. These clothes are ragged. I have no others. But am I not a man?"

Some of the chief's words challenged reason as well as emotion.

"I have hands that know how to hold the plow handles and to sow the wheat and corn and gather it in. I have taught them that in the last few years. The greatest friend I have is the plow. The game is gone, never to come back. It has vanished like a dream when I wake from sleep. From the ground the Indian must now live. We taught our hands to hold the plow handles. We built houses. We raised stock. Now look at us. We are prisoners, and we have never committed any crime. Eight days ago I was at work on my farm which the Omahas gave me. I had sowed some spring wheat. I was living peaceably with all men. I was arrested and brought here as a prisoner. Does your law do that? I have been told since the great war that all men are free, that no man can be made a prisoner unless he does wrong. I have done no wrong, yet I am here a prisoner. Have you a law for white men, and a different law for those who are not white?"

Tibbles hesitated. He felt a dozen pairs of eyes fixed on him, keen as arrows, impaling him on their sharp intensity. What to answer? Words drummed through his mind. "All men are created equal . . . All persons born in the United States are citizens. . . . No State shall abridge the privileges or immunities. . . ." The long silence was broken only by the whimpering of a baby and the crooning of a mother.

"No," said Tibbles at last. "There is but one law for all alike."

"Then why," demanded Tazahba, "am I and my family held prisoners when we have committed no crime?"

The editor shook his head. "I cannot tell."

Another silence fell. The Indians sat smoking a huge tomahawk pipe and passing it one to another. From time to time one of the braves would speak.

"When I worked my farm we had three meals a day. When I am forced to live on the government we get but one. Why does the government insist on feeding me? I seem to be blind. I cannot understand."

"If we go back to the Indian Territory we will soon all die. It would be better to stand us in a line, bring the soldiers, and tell them to shoot us all. Then our miseries would be ended."

Said Standing Bear: "We had many good farms, some good houses, a school and church. But the Sioux made raids on us, stole some of our ponies, and killed some of our people. It was then proposed that we come down to the Omaha Agency. Both the Omahas and the Poncas signed a paper that we were to go. That is all the paper we ever signed."

The interpreter, Charles Morgan, an Omaha who read and spoke English fluently, turned a shocked face to Tibbles. "This is awful," he said. "These men are my friends. They are of my blood."

When Tibbles left the fort, the sun was setting. The city was four miles away. He had eaten nothing since morning, but he thrust his notebook in his pocket and started walking at a five-miles-an-hour gait. He had an idea, and there was no time to lose. By the end of the first mile it began to grow dark, and he knew he must make faster time to accomplish his purpose. He broke into a run and kept the pace for two miles and a half. He reached the Presbyterian Church just in time for the evening service and explained the situation to Mr. Harsha, the pastor.

"Could I speak to your people after the sermon?" he asked. "I believe Christian people can do something to stop this outrageous act."

Permission gained, Tibbles rushed to the Congregational Church to make a similar request of its pastor, Mr. Sherrill. He spoke there between the opening hymns, then returned to give his message to the Presbyterians. Both congregations passed resolutions requesting the Secretary of the Interior, the Honorable Carl Schurz, to rescind the order returning the Poncas to Indian Territory.

But Tibbles had only begun. That same evening he saw two other ministers. Mr. Jameson, pastor of the Baptist Church, was a friend of Schurz, and he willingly despatched a telegram. It read:

"Seven lodges of Ponca Indians, who had settled on the Omaha reservation and were commencing to work at farming, have, by your order, been arrested to be taken south. I beseech you as a friend to have this order revoked. Several churches and congregations have passed resolutions recommending that these Indians be permitted to remain with the Omahas. Some of the Indians are too sick to travel. Particulars by mail."

It was signed by Reverends E. H. E. Jameson; H. D. Fisher, pastor of the Methodist Episcopal Church; W. J. Harsha; and A. F. Sherrill.

At eleven o'clock the tired editor reached home, called for "a good square meal," shared the day's adventures with his always sympathetic wife Amelia, sat down and wrote out from memory the speeches of Ta-zah-ba and Standing Bear with other details, and at twenty minutes past five in the morning stumbled into bed . . . to be up again at seven.

General Crook's council with the Indians was scheduled for

ten o'clock. This time Tibbles hired a conveyance to take him to the fort. At sight of the strangely diverse group his eyes opened wide. There were the smartly uniformed officers, most of the Indians in shabby white man's dress, and, vivid as a tanager in a flock of crows, Standing Bear magnificent in full chief's regalia. Calm, sorrowful, impressive, dwarfing many of the soldiers, he spoke with a vast simplicity and dignity.

"I had found the white way was a good way," he said after telling the story of the removal. "I had often wished I could tell the Great Father how grateful I was to him for showing me and my people this new way. I always obeyed every order that was sent me. I never committed a crime in my life. Yet here we are—prisoners."

At the General's request he told why he and his band had fled from the Territory, about his dying son and his promise, and the incredibly long cold journey.

"I thought God intended us to live, but I was mistaken. God intends to give the country to the white people, and we are to die. It may be well, it may be well. I do not protest. But let our bones be mingled together in the earth where our forefathers lie, and on which we lived so many years and were happy.

"I want to go back to my old place north," he concluded piteously. "I want to save myself and my tribe. If a white man had land and someone should swindle him, that man would try to get it back, and you would not blame him. Look on me. Help me to save the lives of the women and children. Above all, if we must be sent back, first let me go and bury my boy. Let me keep my promise to him. My brothers, a power which I cannot resist, crowds me down to the ground. I need help. I have done."

With sad finality he wrapped his blanket about him and sat down.

"It's a downright shame!" burst out a young officer who sat next to Tibbles.

A soldier on the other side murmured, "Such orders as these always come through the influence of civilians. The Army isn't responsible for this."

There were more speeches from Ta-zah-ba and other chiefs,

but none equaling Standing Bear's in eloquence. General Crook listened in silence, lips tight but eyes smoldering, fingers pulling hard at his short chin beard.

"I have heard all this story before," he muttered when the Indians had finished. "It is just as they represent it. It has long since all been reported to Washington."

Turning to Standing Bear, he spoke through the interpreter. "It is a hard case, but I can do nothing. I have received an order from Washington, and I must obey it. They have all the facts. I might send a telegram, but it is likely to do more harm than good. You can stay here a few days and rest. Then you must go."

Standing Bear bowed, his craggy features inscrutable. Then he spoke once more. He understood. Whatever they said he must do, he must do. He had one more request. All his property had been taken away. If the Great Father ordered them to return to the land "Toward the Heat," should he not give them some money to pay their expenses and buy such things as they needed on the way? Half of his people were sick and would die on the way and must be buried. Could he not have money for expenses?

The General shook his head. "All we can do is to give you what rations you will require on the way down. You will be permitted to take all your stock with you, and you can go slowly." His lips tightened. "It is a very disagreeable duty to send you down there, but I must obey orders."

Tibbles returned to his office. He wrote out the Indians' speeches and General Crook's reply and had them telegraphed to different papers in New York, Chicago, Boston, and other cities. He wrote three editorial columns for his own paper. At three A.M. he stretched wearily on his bed.

"I fought for the liberty of black men with pistol and saber," he told his wife, "but I swear this fight for the liberty of the Indian, with only a pen for a weapon, is a damned sight harder on the body!"

Nothing to do now but wait. The first responses to his telegrams came from the *Chicago Tribune* and the *Missouri Republican*. Both were strong for the Poncas. Similar reactions followed from the New York *Herald, Tribune, Sun,* and many others. But no response from Secretary Carl Schurz, the one man who could free the thirty Indians. Tibbles knew he must find a new course of action. He took down from the shelf the Constitution of the United States and began reading the portions referring to personal liberty. Over and over he read them, especially the Fourteenth Amendment. "All persons born or naturalized in the United States . . . are citizens . . . nor shall any State deny to any person within its jurisdiction the equal protection of the laws. . . ."

All persons. But—would the courts consider an Indian a *person?* Did he have any rights under the white man's law? To find out there must be a lawsuit, and a lawsuit would take money, something he did not have. Money, no, but he had other assets. Once he had routed a battalion of border ruffians by a show of sheer bravado. Could he carry on a lawsuit the same way? He determined to try.

He knew a brilliant young lawyer, John L. Webster, who had been president of the Nebraska constitutional convention and whose opinions commanded respect. He went to see him and laid the case before him.

"I believe," he said eagerly, "we could make a writ of habeas corpus hold. What do you think?"

After considering the matter for a day the lawyer said, "This is a question of vast importance. The principles involved in it underlie all personal liberty. I am not satisfied that such a writ would hold, because of the peculiar relation of Indians to the government. But there ought to be power somewhere to stop this cruelty, and if it does not reside in the courts where shall we find it?"

He suggested that Tibbles try to secure the assistance of the Honorable A. J. Poppleton, chief attorney of the Union Pacific Railroad, without a peer in the legal profession in the state and an eminent orator. Tibbles did so, and after a day's consideration Poppleton rendered his decision.

"I believe you have a good case. It is true that these Indians have been held by the courts as 'wards of the nation,' but this writ was intended for the weak and helpless—for wards and

176

minors. A ward cannot make a contract, but it does not follow that the guardian can imprison, starve or practice inhuman cruelty on the ward. I will undertake the case."

Both lawyers offered to serve without pay. Haste was imperative—also secrecy, for the Poncas were likely to be taken south any moment. Judge Dundy, before whom the case had to be tried, lived 150 miles away. Moreover, he happened to be away on a bear hunt. They managed to reach him, however, with telegrams and he was asked to determine the place where he would hear the application. A petition for habeas corpus was carefully but hastily drawn up by the two attorneys and signed by the marks of eight Poncas—Standing Bear, Buffalo Chip, Crazy Bear, Yellow Horse, Cries for War, Long Runner, Buffalo Track, and Little Duck. There were many anxious moments, and one of the most apprehensive persons was General Crook, constantly dreading orders from Washington to start the Indians south, after which nothing could be done for them.

"The most anxious person I ever saw," commented Tibbles with a chuckle, "to have a writ served on him!"

So began the historic case of Ma-chu-nah-zah (Standing Bear) versus George Crook, Brigadier-General of the Army of the United States.

2

Spring was a mockery that year. The world, it seemed, should have been moving toward death, not life. Susette had always loved the "Moon When the Frogs Sing," when the sky above the Smoky Water was alive with rushing wings and the earth was bursting into life. But not this year. As always, the four grains of red corn were given to each household by a member of the Honga Clan, Yellow Smoke's band, and the ritual songs were sung. But who could tell if the hands which planted would be allowed to reap? And when the migrating birds came south again, would the Omahas have already gone before them to that dread country "Toward the Heat"? Even the shining treasure of each day's teaching had become tarnished.

"We hold these truths to be self-evident," she prompted her

history class one day when the Agent came to visit school.

"That all men are created equal," they dutifully responded in slow painstaking English, "that they are en-endowed by their Cre-a-tor with certain un-un—"

"Unalienable rights," she joined the chorus firmly. "That among these are life, liberty, and the pursuit of happiness."

The Agent nodded approval. "Very good, Miss La Flesche. I see you are instructing your pupils in the noble ideals on which our country was founded."

"*Your* country," she amended silently.

The Poncas were not the only ones who had suffered during the fall and winter.

"As so many of you have died, it is grievous, o ye people," Dubamoni had written to one of his Ponca friends. "We too are sick. Five men have died, and now others are likely to. We are much afraid of arriving yonder at a land in your neighborhood."

"Wacuce is dead," Thangeska had dictated a letter to another Ponca, "so is Cukamanthin. And White Feather's son, and many small children. We are poor and suffering. The Great Father does not give us even money annuities. And as to work we have done our best, but we are still below the mark."

Government, it seemed, wanted them to be idle, helpless. During the preceding winter Joseph, with several of his friends, had gone into the woods on the reservation where, living in a tent, they had cut trees to be made into lumber. With his children growing, he needed an addition on his house. But now, in the spring, when he was ready to use the lumber, the Agent said to him, "You cannot use that. It belongs to the government." So the Agent carried away part of it, and the remainder was left on the ground to rot.

"We work for ourselves because we wish to live," Joseph wrote to A. B. Meacham, editor of the *Council Fire*. "But this season we are in great trouble. Our wheat was withered last summer by the heat; therefore we did not realize from our wheat crop more than thirty or forty cents a bushel. Consequently it seems as if we had not accomplished anything at all for ourselves. . . . It has been just three years since we began to have tools, as we have learned that all tools that are your own are life-sustaining. And we know very well that we ought to work at various occupations, therefore we desire to do this. And when we write this letter to you God is, as it were, sitting with us; therefore we hope that you will not talk at all about depriving us of our land. To take away our land would be just like killing us. We wish to live. Pity us Omaha Indians!"

The fate of the Poncas hung over the tribe like a pall. After their arrest the Omahas gave up all hope for their friends, as well as for themselves. How soon could they expect to receive letters from the Indian Territory telling that Standing Bear and his band had returned? And how many of them would have died on the way? Then suddenly there was news. Dr. Dorsey came to Joseph's house waving a copy of the Omaha *Herald*. Someone had written an article defending the Poncas and claiming that their imprisonment was an outrage! Susette read the article with incredulous hope. Someone *cared* what was happening. The Poncas had a champion. Who? The article was unsigned. Presently another article appeared. It stated that the ministers of the churches of Omaha City had sent a petition to Mr. Schurz in Washington asking him to allow Standing Bear and his party to go back to their land on the Niobrara.

Hope flared. What would the Secretary answer? Dr. Dorsey brought other copies of the paper. "No news." Day after day he shook his head. Susette pored over each issue, hoping he might be mistaken. No answer ever came. Then suddenly there was news. Someone had brought a writ of habeas corpus for the release of Standing Bear and his party. Who could it be? The ministers? And what was this thing, habeas corpus? Susette was kept busy trying to explain. It was a right given to a person under the government Constitution. It meant that a person could not be put in prison or detained without a good reason, that a person had to be brought to trial at a stated time and proven innocent or guilty.

A *person*! The word echoed hollowly in her ears. What Waxes had ever considered an Indian a person? Missionaries, perhaps, to whom they were souls to be converted. Her teachers and friends back East, to whom they were objects of charity to be petted and trained and exhibited. But not Agents, not soldiers, not white settlers, certainly not government. To them Indians were savages to be tamed, pests to be exterminated, property to be exploited . . . never *persons*.

Items about the approaching trial continued to appear. The names of the two lawyers were published, and Dr. Dorsey wrote to them that he had information about the case which might be of use. Then at last they discovered who had written all the articles and instigated the court action. A letter came from Thomas Tibbles asking Dr. Dorsey to send him all the information available.

"You write him," said Dorsey to Susette. "Tell him all you know."

Susette wrote, in the fine slanting script and perfect English taught her in Elizabeth. Nearly a hundred years later it would still remain, firm and black as on the day in April 1879, when it was written. It was a faithful chronicle of all the events as she knew them. She enclosed the original copy of the telegram sent by the eight chiefs to the President and the statement Standing Bear had made in Joseph's house on their return from Indian Territory two years before.

"This statement," she concluded, "shows how much they trusted in the justice of the white people, believing that the wrong done to them had been done by only a few, and without authority. I do hope some action will be taken in the matter soon."

A petition was also prepared by leaders of the Omaha tribe "To the friends of the Poncas now held as prisoners at Omaha barracks." It requested the return of the Ponca tribe to the Omaha reservation. "They are our brothers and our sisters, our uncles and our cousins, and although we are called savages we feel that sympathy for our persecuted brethren that should characterize Christians, and are willing to share what we possess with them if they can only be allowed to return and labor, improve and provide for themselves where they may live in peace, enjoy good health, and the opportunity of educating their children to a higher state of civilization." It was signed by Standing Hawk, Yellow Smoke, Dubamoni, Wajapa, and sixteen other chiefs and braves.

The New York *Herald* called this petition "one of the most extraordinary statements ever published in America." It went on to say, "Many white men in Nebraska might have made the same offer without hurting themselves . . . but white men did not do it. Church members talked and petitioned, but not an acre of land did they offer. It was reserved for a band of heathen redskins, who have hardly yet forgotten the war-whoop, to emphasize that sympathy which civilization and religions have talked about—and only talked."

3

The impending trial drew sharp fire from Washington. On April 10 an Associated Press telegram stated: "The Commissioner of Indian Affairs says with reference to the habeas corpus case at Omaha, where a writ was served on General Crook, commanding him to show cause why he holds Standing Bear and other Ponca Indians as prisoners, that the United States district attorney has been directed to appear for the United States and endeavor to have the writ dismissed. He takes the ground that under the law, and according to repeated decisions of the Supreme Court, the Indians stand as wards of the Government, and are under the same relations to the government as minors to their parents or guardians; that the law forbids them to make contracts, and such contracts if made by them are void. No attorney has the right or can appear for an Indian unless authorized to do so by the Indian Department."

On the same day Commissioner Hayt published a letter addressed to Secretary Schurz defending the action of removal as a necessary sequel to the treaty giving the Ponca reservation to the Sioux, the Poncas being in danger of destruction from the proximity of their ancient enemies. He himself had visited the new Ponca reservation and found it far superior to their old location on the Missouri. He had found Standing Bear the only one among the chiefs grumbling, discontented, and showing a bad spirit.

"It is true," he admitted, "that during the first four months of their residence in Indian Territory they lost a large number by death, which is inevitable in all cases of removal of northern Indians to a southern location. . . . The removal of northern Indians to the Indian Territory was probably not good policy, but it was done in pursuance of laws enacted before the present administration came into power. . . . If the reservation system is to be maintained, discontented and restless or mischievous Indians cannot be permitted to leave their reservations at will and go where they please."

Standing Bear listened to an interpretation of this letter with mounting indignation. Though he could neither read nor write English, his understanding of its import was by no means deficient, and his comments lost none of their terse logic when translated. "The Commissioner says our lands were given to the Sioux. Who had any authority to give our lands to the Sioux? The land belonged to us, and not to the Commissioner or General Sherman. What would the Commissioner think if some man should give his land to the Sioux? He says we are not sick any more in Indian Territory. Look at these lodges. There are seven very sick people in them, out of our small party. Seven persons out of thirty very sick, and five or six others not well enough to work. There is the same proportion of sick in all the tribe.

"So the Commissioner says I show a bad spirit!" he continued bitterly but with a twinkle in his eyes. "Then he must have changed his mind." Going to a trunk, the chief took out a large roll of papers and picked one from the rest. "Read that."

It was issued from the Office of Indian affairs and dated December 18, 1877. "This is to certify that Standing Bear is a chief of the Ponca Indians . . . whose influence has been to preserve peace and harmony between the Ponca Indians and the United States and as such is entitled to the confidence of all persons whom he may meet." It was signed, "E. A. Hayt, Commissioner."

Tibbles laughed heartily. "He certainly gave you a good character!"

"No," said Standing Bear with dignity. "The Commissioner did not give me a good character. I got that by a long life devoted to the advancement of my tribe."

He showed other documents, one signed by a Ponca agent in

Dakota which called him "a reliable and trustworthy man, of industrious habit, and rare zeal in setting a good example to the Indians"; another by an army lieutenant calling him "civil, quiet and well behaved, a warm friend of the whites, and loyal to the government."

Standing Bear listened closely to the translation. "There being no way by which their request to be sent back north could be complied with without action of Congress in the matter," the letter stated, "they were permitted to make their own selection among the best lands in the Indian Territory." Smiling, he lifted his hand to interrupt. "No one asked the Commissioner to *send* me back north. All I wanted was permission to come. Now I am already north, and that difficulty is overcome. If the Commissioner can't send me north, he seems to know of a very quick way to send me *south!*"

He interrupted again at the statement, "Every effort was made, and large sums of money were expended to provide for their comfort, and they received a sawmill, timber and all appliances for building houses, as well as an abundant supply of cattle and agricultural implements . . ."

"*Ee tha a betheh!*" exclaimed the chief in disgust. "All the money we ever got was $6.25 a head! The Agency had plenty, but we never got it. All that about cattle and agricultural implements is untrue. Besides, I don't want the Commissioner's money. All I want is to be allowed to make my own living. I can take care of myself if they will just let me out of here."

Meanwhile Colonel Meacham, editor of the *Council Fire*, acceded to Dr. Dorsey's request to interview Commissioner Hayt and Secretary Schurz. They gave him a patient hearing.

"It's a sad case," admitted Schurz. "I feel deeply for the Poncas. They are peaceable and quiet, and I wish I could better their condition."

"But there is no use talking about the Poncas going north," asserted Hayt. "They must remain where they are in Indian Territory. We have expended large sums of money for them in their new home. They have become acclimated. They are there by law. They cannot be sent north without authority of Congress. Those who have left must be taken back. If we allow them to stay away, the others will follow."

"But if a mistake has been made," insisted Meacham, "*we*

made it. The Indian was in our power. He should not pay the penalty for *our* mistakes. Let us do right because it is right."

"Right," snapped the Commissioner, "is for the Poncas to stay where we have placed them. I admit it was a mistake to give the Sioux the Ponca country. This mistake was made by General Sherman before our administration began."

Meacham reported his failure to Dorsey. "The Commissioner insisted that the Poncas must return. I will make another effort. Ever yours, for God's children."

This letter also was read to Standing Bear. *Large sums of money . . . acclimated!* Yet mingled with his disgust was a smidgen of triumph. "Big Eyes" Schurz and his Commissioner had at least admitted that giving the Ponca country to the Sioux had been a mistake!

The soldiers detailed to guard the Poncas were fascinated by their prisoners. It was the first time many of them had been closer to an Indian than the length of a gunshot. They were discovering for the first time what "savages" were really like. Some surprising discoveries they made by observation: that Indians ate, slept, wept, joked, argued, suffered pains, exactly like themselves; that they preferred to be clean rather than dirty; that they loved their children and taught them remarkably good manners. Some information, however, had to be gleaned through questions and answers. Charles Morgan, the interpreter, was kept busy acting as go-between. At one point Standing Bear was asked to state his religious belief. Folding his arms and half closing his eyes, he spoke without a moment's reflection.

"There is one God, and he made both Indians and white men. We were all made out of the dust of the earth. I once thought differently. I believed there were happy hunting grounds, where there were plenty of game and plenty to eat, no sickness or death, and no pain. The best of the Indians would go to these happy hunting grounds. Those who were bad would never live any more. But I have learned that these things are not so, and that God wishes us to love him and obey his commandments, follow the narrow road, work for him on earth, and we shall have happiness after we die.

"When I was arrested by the soldiers and brought down here,

I thought for a little while that God had forsaken me, but now I see that perhaps it is the best thing for me and my people. He has been with me through all my wanderings, and has taken care of me. He has seen how I have been taken away from my land. When I have felt that I had no friends, I remembered that he was my Father. His people have been good to me, but the people of the devil are trying to send me to hell. They have tried to make me believe that God tells them what to do, as though God would put a man where he would be destroyed! God put me here, and intends for me to live on the land they are trying to cheat me out of. I pray to God every day for him to help me regain my rights, if I am worthy of it. He made me and the whites, and although we are of a different color, I think men's hearts are all alike. If I were to go back to my land today, the first thing I would do would be to fall on my knees and thank God for it."

The soldiers were impressed, especially Lieutenant Carpenter, who had made the arrest. After having the prisoners in his charge for some weeks, he concluded his written statement with these words:

"From my personal knowledge of these people I consider them further advanced in civilization than any other tribe west of the Mississippi, with the single exception of the Omahas, to whom they are related. The men are industrious and willing to work, at anything they can find to do. The children conduct themselves well, and the women are modest in their demeanor and neat in appearance and domestic habits.

"Fort Omaha, Nebraska, May 8th, 1879."

Four

1

The "Moon When the Frogs Sing" waned, waxed slowly into the "Moon in Which the Tribe Plants," but among the Omahas there was little zeal for planting. Hope for the future was as tenuous as the tiny silver sickle which portended such faint promise of the harvest. No one really believed that the new developments in Omaha, exciting though they were, would avert the threat of removal for either the Poncas or themselves. No one, that is, except Susette. Even Joseph could not share her optimism.

"Take care, daughter. Hope that climbs too high has so much farther to fall. We have been betrayed too many times to expect justice from the Waxes."

"But this time," she argued, "we are not pleading ourselves. It is Waxes who are pleading for us. And these articles are being published all over the country. For the first time the *people* will be learning about the injustice done to a tribe of Indians. In the East there are many good Christian people who believe in freedom and justice for all and who will make their voice heard. I've been there, and I know."

"*Oui*," replied Joseph cannily. "But I have been to Washington."

The trial was to be held before Judge Dundy on the thirtieth of April. Dr. Dorsey, who had some influence at the Agency, obtained permission for Susette and Joseph to attend. They went to Omaha with Dorsey and Willie Hamilton, the missionary's son, who for the last six years had been employed to run the Agency store. He had been called as a witness in the case by Standing Bear's lawyer, Mr. Webster. There on the eve of the trial Susette met Thomas Tibbles.

At first she was awed and startled by his bigness. She felt swallowed up, drowned in his towering strength. Then, as she lifted her eyes, awe changed to fascination. The deeply bronzed face framed by the heavy shock of hair reminded her of a lion's, but a benevolent lion's. The steel-gray eyes which had stung more than one enemy with rapier sharpness held soft blue glints, and the stubbornness of the square chin was negated by the full smiling lips. She felt an instant kinship with this man who had so surprisingly espoused an unpopular cause; also a profound relief, as if a burden borne for many years had been lifted. This man inspired confidence as no one else had ever done except her father, and of late years, since he lost the chieftainship, Joseph had evidenced a weakness of decision which had left her feeling curiously alone. "Lightning Eye," she thought again as on her first meeting with the son of Standing Bear, and, as then, the idea of the shared name increased the sense of kinship. Yet somehow the very strength of the man was disconcerting. One felt that part of one's will, one's personality, could easily be absorbed into his indomitable purpose and vitality.

"So this is Inshtatheamba," he said with obvious appreciation. "Bright Eyes."

Susette flushed. How had he known her Indian name? Surely she had signed her letter "Susette La Flesche."

Later she visited Tibbles' home at 19th and Leavenworth Streets and met his wife Amelia and his two little girls, May and Eda. She was charmed with Amelia, lithe, vivacious, with big brown eyes, youthful red cheeks, and the most beautiful dimpled hands she had ever seen. The parlor with its flowered carpets, lace curtains, horsehair sofa, and chairs with rose and grape carvings brought a pang of homesickness, forcible reminders of the wonderful two years she had tried hard to forget. As always in the presence of strangers, she felt shy and tongue-tied, but Amelia soon put her at ease, plying her with questions about the poor Poncas and expressing hot indignation for their treatment. It was evident that Tibbles' wife was heartily in sympathy with his crusade for justice.

A committee had been formed of the Omaha ministers and other aroused citizens, and a meeting was held prior to the trial in the small hotel where the group from the reservation was given lodging. To Susette's intense embarrassment she was requested to attend, the only woman present.

"Ask Miss La Flesche," said Willie Hamilton when asked to tell what he knew of the case. "Her uncle, White Swan, is a Ponca, and she knows far more than I do. She can also interpret for her father, who speaks little English."

Susette shrank back, terrified. She felt impaled on a barrage of probing eyes. When she tried to speak, her voice was little more than a whisper. But the glances, the nods, were encouraging. These men were friends, an incredible assembly, white men anxious to help her people. She was soon leaning forward and talking eagerly, telling the story as she knew it. They asked questions, and she answered them, clearly and without embarrassment. In fact, she had forgotten herself completely.

There! It was over at last. The eyes were still upon her, but they seemed appreciative, no longer probing. Heads were nodding. She sank back in her chair, utterly exhausted but intensely relieved. She must have helped the Poncas' cause a little. She had no idea that the appreciative eyes, the nodding heads bespoke not only an increased awareness of the rights of the Poncas, but, even more eloquently, an admiration of herself.

2

It was morning of April 30, 1879. The courtroom was filled to the walls, a motley assemblage: the city clergy in their black frockcoats; men and women of every class and station, some concerned, some merely curious, many dressed as well as for a funeral or a formal lecture; several lawyers, Messrs. Webster and Poppleton for the relators, District Attorney Lambertson for the government; General Crook in the elaborate full-dress uniform which he seldom wore, looking more like a pleased spectator than a defendant up for trial (fortunately the order from Washington to return the prisoners forthwith to Indian Territory had been unaccountably delayed); Judge Dundy, impressive in his court robes and aura of judicial dignity; Standing Bear, somehow eclipsing both General and Judge in his colorful formal regalia; several of his leading men in their hopelessly tattered clothes.

Susette sat beside her father in one of the rear seats, trying to make herself as inconspicuous as possible. She wore her best dress, a black poplin with white ruching at the neck, made by Miss Read's dressmaker at Elizabeth, but, looking at the stylish women around her, she knew it was hopelessly outmoded. Not that it mattered. More important issues were on trial this day than details of dress. Did an Indian have any right of appeal under the white man's law? Could he avail himself of the rights guaranteed by the Constitution of this country where he had been born and had lived long centuries before the Waxes came, or must he be treated like a minor child, a slave—worse, a piece of property, subject to any rules the government might choose to make for him, and him alone?

Susette looked long and hard at the judge who must make this momentous decision. He was a bronzed, vigorous man who looked as if he would have been more at home on his favorite horse than on the bench. Even his loose robe looked too small for him. It was easy to picture him as the ardent horseman and hunter Tibbles had described him, harder as the lover of good books. But his eyes were keen, his lips firm, and his chin strong. He could be depended on to administer justice as he saw it. But—could there be justice under the white man's law for the Indian? She sat ramrod-straight and tense. What happened in this courtroom might well determine the destiny of her people, not only Poncas but all Indians, for generations to come, perhaps forever.

The trial began. It was the contention of the Indians' lawyers, Webster and Poppleton, that Standing Bear and the other Indians had the right to separate themselves from their tribe if they chose and avail themselves of the protection of United States law like American citizens—in other words, that they were "persons" with the right of freedom guaranteed by the Constitution. It was the contention of the government attorney that no Indians could separate themselves from their tribe, that their right to a writ of habeas corpus should be denied on the ground that they were "not persons within the meaning of the law."

Willie Hamilton was sworn on behalf of the relators, represented by Standing Bear. Webster questioned him at length. In answer Hamilton presented the bare facts of the case: the arrival of the Poncas at the Omaha Agency, their number, the property they brought with them, the land they had been given to break, their sickness, the willingness of the Omahas to give them land to cultivate. He was cross-examined by District Attorney Lambertson, who attempted to prove that Standing Bear and his party had absconded with government property.

"What did they live in—tents?"

"Yes, sir, they brought their tents, I think."

"These tents were provided by the government?"

"These tents were made by themselves."

"These wagons were furnished by the government?"

"Yes, sir. They brought their wagons with them."

"Did they have citizens' clothes?"

"They had."

"These clothes were also provided by the government?"

"Some were, sir, and some were not."

"Some of them wore blankets?"

"Some wore blankets, pants, and vest, and some wore Indian clothes throughout."

"Those blankets—were they provided by the government?"

"Some of them—yes, sir."

Lambertson elicited certain facts in his cross-examination: that there were 1083 in the Omaha tribe, with about 1,500 acres of wheat planted; that no annuities had been paid them for three years; that the government furnished them nothing but farm implements; that at present they had no chiefs, and that the Poncas were independent of their authority. He attempted to prove that the Poncas had their own chiefs, to whom they professed allegiance and to whose authority they were still subject.

Standing Bear was examined by Mr. Webster, through Willie Hamilton.

Lambertson protested. "Does this court think an Indian is a competent witness?"

Susette became rigid. The whole case might well hang on the judge's answer.

"They are competent," replied Judge Dundy crisply, "for every purpose in both civil and criminal courts. The law makes no distinction on account of race, color, or previous condition."

She drew a long breath and relaxed. For the first time since the trial began she felt a surge of hope.

Mr. Webster put questions to Standing Bear through Hamilton. He asked about the old reservation, how they lived, what labor they performed, what success they had.

"Ask him what they were doing up there to become like white men."

Judge Dundy interrupted. "What sort of white men? You had better limit that a little."

"Well—" Webster smiled appreciatively—"civilized white men."

A titter went around the courtroom. Susette relaxed still further.

Mr. Webster attempted to let Standing Bear tell his own story of life in the Indian Territory, but Lambertson objected. "I want questions put to him, and let him answer the questions." In the subsequent inquiry there were many more objections, counsel for government insisting that the only issue was whether the Poncas had dissolved their tribal relations. Nevertheless, Standing Bear managed to divulge some salient facts.

"He says," interpreted Hamilton, "when I got down there, I saw the land, and the land was not good to my eye; some places it looked good, but you kick up the soil a little, and you found lots of stones. It was not fit to farm. When we got down there we heard we were going to get clothing and money, but I have not seen it yet. I couldn't plow, I couldn't sow any wheat, and we all got sick and couldn't do anything. One hundred and fifty-eight of us died. Two of my children died. I thought to myself, God wants me to live, and I think if I come back to my old reservation he will let me live. What have I done? I am brought here, but what have I done? It seems as though I haven't a place in the world to go, but when I see your faces here I think some of you are trying to help me, so that I can get a place sometime to live in, and when it comes my time to die, to die peacefully and happy."

Here the Indian's voice became so loud and emphatic that Judge Dundy rapped his gavel. "Tell the witness to keep cool," he ordered mildly.

The examination continued.

"Ask him," said Webster at one point, "when they left the tribe whether they intended to stay away from the tribe."

"He says he told them if he ever came back it would not be to stay, that he wanted to go to a place where they could all work and earn their own living. He says in his travels he has seen a great many white people, and he finds them all working wherever he goes, farming, building houses, and they have cattle and all they want to eat, and he thinks if he has a chance he can do just the same."

The relators rested their case, and, the government having no further evidence to offer, the Honorable J. L. Webster began his argument for the Indians.

"How," he asked, "did the government get titles to land?" In three ways, by discovery, by conquest, and by purchase. It could not claim title to this land by discovery, or by conquest, for it had never been at war with the Ponca tribe. It had never purchased the land, therefore the title to it remained with the Poncas. He then gave a thorough study of questions relating to Indian tribes as separate nations, the effect of the Fourteenth Amendment, the use of the army in the control of tribes, and he claimed that there was no law for the removal of the Poncas to Indian Territory, or for keeping them there by force, or for returning those who had escaped, and asked the absolute discharge of Standing Bear and his party. Webster occupied about six hours in the delivery of his argument.

That night Standing Bear was intensely worried. He had been permitted only to answer leading questions, and of course he had understood nothing of the other proceedings. After asking many searching questions, he begged Tibbles to ask Judge Dundy to let him speak as he wished in court, like the lawyers.

"Was Standing Bear ever admitted to the bar?" asked Judge Dundy with a smile when Tibbles tendered the request. Yet the reporter knew, and told others, that the Indian would have a chance to speak.

The courtroom was crowded to the walls. Lambertson opened his argument with high commendation for Messrs. Webster and Poppleton, who had volunteered their services in defense of those helpless Indians. He claimed that Standing Bear was not entitled to the protection of the writ of habeas corpus, not being a person or a citizen under the law. He was very eloquent. The Honorable A. J. Poppleton followed. He traced the history of the writ from its origin and claimed that it applied to every *human being*. The arguments ended, Judge Dundy announced that he would hand down his decision later. Then only the few persons nearest the bench heard what followed.

The marshal came close to the Judge, who murmured, "Court is adjourned." Facing front, the marshal declared even more softly, "Hear ye, hear ye! The Honorable District Court of the United States is now adjourned." Then Standing Bear was told he might speak.

The Indian rose, towering in his impressive, colorful regalia. He held out his hand—so long that Susette, holding her breath, felt almost ready to burst. Finally he looked up at the judge and spoke quietly.

"That hand is not the color of yours, but if I pierce it, I shall feel pain. The blood that will flow from mine will be of the same color as yours. I am a man. The same God made us both."

He turned so that he half faced the audience. It was so quiet that Susette was conscious of the sound of her slowly exhaled breath. She reached out and clasped her father's hand.

"I seem to stand on the bank of a river." Standing Bear's voice was louder and more tense. "My wife and little girl are beside me. The river is wide and impassable, and behind are perpendicular cliffs. No man of my race ever stood there before. There is no tradition to guide me." He waited, motionless, for Hamilton to translate. "A flood rises around us. I look despairingly at the great cliffs. I see a steep stony way leading upward. I grasp my child's hand. My wife follows. I lead the way on the sharp rocks while the waters rise behind us. I see a rift in the rocks and feel the prairie breeze again on my cheek. I turn to my wife and child with a shout. We are saved! We will return to the Swift Running Water that pours down between the green islands. There are the graves of my fathers. There again we will pitch our tipi and build our fires."

Susette glanced around the courtroom. She saw General Crook leaning forward, his hand over his eyes. She heard a woman sob. Then with a leaping of her pulses she saw that there were tears on Judge Dundy's face.

"But a man bars our way," continued Standing Bear in a loud voice, turning again toward the Judge. "Behind him I see soldiers as numerous as the leaves of the trees. They will obey that man's orders. If he says that I cannot pass, I cannot. My wife and child and I must return and sink beneath the flood. We are weak and faint and sick. I cannot fight."

Looking up into the Judge's face, he said quietly, "You are that man."

There was a moment's tense silence, then the whole courtroom burst into life. There was prolonged applause. People rose to crowd to the front and clasp Standing Bear's hand. Among the first to reach him was General Crook.

3

There followed days of almost unbearable suspense. Joseph and Susette could not go home. They had to wait for the verdict. With General Crook's consent they moved into one of the lodges inside the fort where Standing Bear and his party were held prisoners. Susette felt, first excitement, then impatience, finally despair. Surely if the verdict was favorable, it could not take the Judge so long to make up his mind. He did not look like a man of indecision. Standing Bear's wife, another Susette, put her to shame. She went about her daily tasks, caring for her orphaned grandchildren, cooking the food provided by the soldiers, patiently, calmly, as if each new day might not tip the balances between life and death.

Meanwhile Judge Dundy was engaged in a task which challenged all the knowledge and legal skill of his judicial career.

"During the fifteen years in which I have been engaged in administering the laws of my country," he was to describe his quandary, "I have never been called upon to hear or decide a case that appealed so strongly to my sympathy. But in a country where liberty is regulated by law, something more satisfactory and enduring than mere sympathy must furnish and constitute the rule and basis of judicial action."

He studied all the treaties made by the government with the Poncas, especially that of March 8, 1859, by which the tract on the Niobrara was set apart for the *permanent* home of said Indians, the government agreeing to protect them during their good behavior. He went into the origins and history of the writ of habeas corpus, considering the claim of the district attorney, arguing from English law, that only the *free subjects* of the state came within the benefit of such beneficent laws. And he decided, "This only proves that the laws of a limited monarchy are sometimes less wise and humane than the laws of our own good republic—that whilst the Parliament of Great Britain was legislating on behalf of the favored few, the Congress of the United States was legislating in behalf of all mankind who come within our jurisdiction." He discovered that the habeas corpus act described applicants as "persons" or "parties," not as citizens. He even consulted Webster as to the definition of a "person"—"a self-conscious being; a moral agent; especially a living human being; a man, woman or child; an individual of the human race."

"This is comprehensive enough," he decided. "It would seem to include even an Indian!"

He studied the legal history of expatriation, for the case rested on the proven evidence that Standing Bear and his party had informed the Ponca agent of their purpose never to return to their tribe, but to disband as a clan, go to work, become self-sustaining.

"Whereas the right of expatriation is a natural and inherent right of all people," declared an Act of Congress, dated July 27, 1868, ". . . therefore any declaration, instruction, opinion, order, or decision of any officer of the United States which denies, restricts, impairs, or questions the right of expatriation, is declared inconsistent with the fundamental principles of the republic."

He studied the statutes relating to the governing of Indian country and the powers conferred on the Commissioner of Indian Affairs, in time of both peace and war.

"The Poncas," he wrote firmly, "are amongst the most peaceable and friendly of all the Indian tribes . . . If they could be removed to the Indian Territory by force and kept there in the same way, I can see no good reason why they might not be taken and kept by force in Leavenworth, or Jefferson City, or any other place which the commander of the forces might, in his judgment, see proper to designate. I cannot think, and will not believe, that any such arbitrary authority exists in this country."

These conclusions, and many more, Judge Dundy included in his final statement. It was a little more than a week before he was ready to render his decision and call the court to order. Again the courtroom was filled to the walls, and people had to be turned away. Again Susette sat beside her father, so tense that the muscles of her neck and back were constricted in pain. As the Judge read his long statement her eyes never left his face. She followed every sequence of the intricate argument, one of the few Indians who could understand its English or comprehend its meaning. Even many of the Waxes present became restive, having come more from curiosity than from interest in the legal aspects of the case. Standing Bear sat immobile as stone, unable to understand a word.

"The reasoning advanced in support of my views leads me to conclude—" said the Judge finally. He cleared his throat and rapped with his gavel. The room sprang to attention."—First. That an Indian is a *person* within the meaning of the law of the United States, and has therefore the right to sue out a writ of habeas corpus in a federal court or before a federal judge, in all cases where he may be confined, or in custody under color of authority of the United States, or where he is restrained of liberty in violation of the Constitution or laws of the United States.

"Second. That General Crook, the respondent, being the commander of the military department of the Platte, has the custody of the relators under color of authority of the United States, and in violation of the laws thereof.

"Third. That no rightful authority exists for removing by force any of the relators to the Indian Territory, as the respondent has been directed to do.

"Fourth. That the Indians possess the inherent right of expatriation as well as the more fortunate white man, and have the inalienable right to 'life, liberty, and the pursuit of happiness,' so long as they obey the laws and do not trespass on forbidden ground. And—

"Fifth. Being restrained of liberty under color of authority of the United States, and in violation of the laws, thereof, the relators must be discharged from custody, and it is so ordered."

The audience rose *en masse* to its feet. Such a shout went up, Tibbles reported later, "as was never heard before in a courtroom." Again General Crook was the first to reach Standing Bear and congratulate him.

An Indian is a person.

Few people in the courtroom that day understood the full significance of that decision. Judge Dundy's written opinion was one of the great civil rights documents of all time, a landmark in American history. The two lawyers understood it, for it was the goal toward which all their skill and tireless effort had been directed. Tibbles understood it, but knew that it was only the first skirmish in a long and harrowing battle. The district attorney understood it and considered appealing the case, but, reading the judge's brilliant, exhaustive essay, decided that he would let well enough alone.

The Indian Bureaucracy, both in Washington and in its tentacles stretching far across the nation (that vast entity known to many as the "Indian Ring") understood it all too well. If implemented, it might well threaten the whole reservation system. It would negate the right of unscrupulous thieves who had been robbing and oppressing Indians, maddening them to violence, making fortunes out of selling them rotten wheat, shoddy merchandise, poisonous whiskey—all with the risk of no penalty from law. If the Poncas could leave their reservation at will and assume the rights of citizens, the whole system would be in danger.

Standing Bear understood only that he need not go back to Indian Territory, that he was free. A few days after the decision, General Crook received an order from the Secretary of War ordering the discharge of the prisoners. Standing Bear was warned, however, that he and his party could go anywhere they pleased, *except on an Indian reservation.* "There" the lawyers warned, "you could be arrested as an intruder."

Here was a quandary. They could not go back to their old reservation, at least according to the present court decision. They could not live on the Omaha reservation. Standing Bear decided to encamp his party somewhere outside the bounds of the Omaha reservation on United States territory. There he would set his men to work immediately chopping wood to sell to the nearby townspeople.

On Sunday, the day before the party was to leave, Tibbles went to the fort to bid them good-bye. The chief said he had something to say that he did not wish anyone else to hear. The editor, Standing Bear, and the interpreter went out on a little hill to one side.

"When I was brought here a prisoner," the chief said in part, "my heart was broken. I had no friend in all the big world. Then you came. Sometimes, in the long days while I have been here a prisoner, I have come out here, and stood on this hill and looked toward the city. I thought there is one man there who is writing or speaking for me and my people. I know if it had not been for what you have done for me, I would now be a prisoner in the Indian Territory, and many of these with me here would be in their graves. I owe all this to you. I can never pay you for it. While there is one Ponca alive you will never be without a friend. You are my brother."

Standing Bear then led the way to his lodge and, opening a trunk, took out a war bonnet, a tomahawk, and a pair of beaded buckskin leggings. "These leggings are for you," he said, "the tomahawk for Mr. Webster, and the war-bonnet for Mr. Poppleton. Please take them and tell them I sent them to them."

"Why not come with me to the city and present them yourself?" suggested Tibbles.

Standing Bear was glad to go. First they went to the home of Mr. Webster, and the chief, holding the tomahawk, delivered a short speech which expressed not only gratitude but sentiments of profound wisdom.

"Hitherto, when we have been wronged, we went to war to assert our rights and avenge our wrongs. We took the tomahawk. We had no law to punish those who did wrong, so we took our tomahawks and went to kill. If they had guns and could kill us first, it was the fate of war. You have gone into the court for us, and I find that our wrongs can be righted there."

Stooping, the chief placed the tomahawk on the floor at his feet. Then, standing erect, he folded his arms with great dignity, and said, "I lay it down. I have no more use for it. I have found a better way."

He stooped again and, picking it up, placed it in the lawyer's hands. "I present it to you in gratitude. Keep it in remembrance of this great victory."

At Mr. Poppleton's house he presented the magnificent headdress, an ancient war bonnet, and spoke with the same simple eloquence and dignity.

"If I had to pay you," he concluded "I could never get enough to do it. I have here a relic which has come down to my people through many generations. I do not know how old it is, perhaps two or three hundred years old. I desire to present it to you for what you have done for me."

It was a rare treasure, the most venerable object in the tribe's possession. Somewhat resembling a wig, it had been worn only by the head chief at their most weighty councils. One of the occasions was at the signing of the first treaty, about 1817, made between the Poncas and the government of the United States.

Poppleton accepted the gift with deep humility. He had been more than repaid, he told Standing Bear, for what he had done, by his satisfaction in rescuing the chief and his people. Later he would be offered vast sums of money for the chief's gift by curiosity-hunters, anxious to secure such a treasure at any price.

"No," the lawyer would say to one and all, "money could not buy it."

The lawyers' work might be finished, but not Tibbles'. He had hopelessly involved himself in another unpopular cause. The battle had only begun. What of the remaining Poncas, stranded and dying down in Indian Territory? What of the

Omahas, in grave danger of reprisal from government because of the help given their runaway kindred? What of all the other tribes still subject to the whims of a capricious and all-powerful clique in Washington? He had long discussions with Webster and Poppleton and General Crook, and they mapped out a plan of action. Judge Dundy's decision had paved the way for other skirmishes in what would doubtless be a long legal battle. Money must be raised. Tibbles learned with dismayed resignation that he was marked for this task. He resigned his comfortable position as editor of the *Herald* and began the herculean task of amassing evidence to gain national support for the cause.

4

Back at teaching school, her post having been capably filled by Rosalie in her absence, Susette felt a tumult of emotions— triumph at the outcome of the trial, fear for the fate of the Omahas, a sense of let-down after a drama of intense excitement. Joy over the release of Standing Bear was diluted by concern for Uncle Frank and his family, still exiled in that netherworld "Toward the Heat." If only he had joined Standing Bear's party! Would anyone tell him of the trial and the possibility of freedom? No use writing. Letters must pass through the hands of the Agent. If only it were possible . . .

The impossible happened. Tibbles came to the reservation. The Omaha Committee wanted to send Joseph and Susette to Indian Territory to visit White Swan, to ascertain the condition of the tribe, to tell them of the court decision. The Commissioner and Secretary of the Interior were publishing claims that the Poncas were happy and well cared for, that they already had eighty houses constructed, and that they were well contented with their lot. The Committee wanted to find out if this was true. Expenses for the trip would be paid by them, and they wanted Joseph and his daughter to start at once.

"If our Agent permits," agreed Joseph.

"He will." Tibbles tossed his black lion's mane. "With the sentiment in Omaha what it is right now, just let him try not to!"

It was May. Joseph and Susette traveled by railway to

Wichita, then spent four days more proceeding by stage to the Ponca reservation. As they journeyed south, the heat grew more intense, the country more barren. As they approached the new settlement, Susette exclaimed in dismay. *"Na he!* Look!"

On either side of the path ahead, as far as they could see, were small mounds, each marked by a rough upright stone. Graves! But—all these—and the Poncas had lived in this new area only since last July! When Standing Bear had spoken of all the deaths, they had been only a number. Now suddenly they became persons—men, women, and children whose names and faces she had known.

Soon they came in sight of tents gleaming white on the prairie. There were no roads and few paths between them. It might have been a hunting camp, with the tipis pitched only for the night. One almost expected to see them dismantled at any moment, with the people on the move. But—no, it was not like a hunting camp, with the tents arranged in orderly formation in a circle. Here the tents were far apart, in groups of two of three, so separated that there could be little community life among them. Scattered among the tents were six rough little houses, the only buildings visible except—yes, there of course were the Agency buildings, with the big handsome Agent's house look-ing strangely out of place among the tents.

People soon clustered around them. There were shouts of welcome, tears, eager upturned faces, but not the ones they were seeking. "My brother—White Swan?" asked Joseph.

Someone pointed toward a group of tents and a small shanty some distance away on the prairie, and they went toward them. As they drew near, Susette saw a woman sitting in the door of the shanty. Not—surely not her Cousin Rosalie, this thin drooping figure looking so old and careworn! But the thin face lighted, the figure straightened and came running toward her, arms outstretched.

"Wihe—Sister!"

Soon the family were all gathered about them, Uncle Frank, Rosalie and her children, Cousin Susanne, Uncle's wife, who rose from a sickbed inside the shanty, looking more like a skeleton than the buxom aunt Susette remembered. It was a joyful yet sad reunion. Susette tried to hide her shock at sight of the gaunt faces, the shabby clothing, the makeshift shanty, bare except for a few blankets and heaps of skins. Uncle had been so proud of his neat house on the Niobrara, with its tight walls and glass windows and store-bought furniture.

"Daughter," he said now in shamefaced apology, "all we can offer you is a seat on the floor. Our chairs were all taken from us when they took our land."

Susette glanced hastily about the small eager faces, surreptitiously counting, assuring herself that Rosalie's children were all there. All those graves . . .

"My children have all been sick," her cousin was to tell her in the many conversations they were soon to have, "but they are better now. Scarcely a family in the tribe but has had to mourn some loved one, but Wakonda has been good to us, and none have died. As it is, we tremble day and night for fear our turn has come. All we think of is sickness and death."

"See how far apart our tents are from each other?" she asked once. "The Agent ordered us to do it, because he was afraid we would join together and break away and return to our own land. When the sickness commenced, it would be days before we heard of the deaths of dear friends who might live in the next tent. There were not enough well to take care of the sick, and some died of thirst in their fever because there was no one to bring them a cup of water. One woman died with her baby in her arms. They were almost the last of the family, and there was no one to bury them except two little girls, one seven and one nine. They dug a hole in the ground, dragged the bodies into it, and covered them with earth."

Rosalie, it seemed, could not get enough of talking. She was like a stream, long frozen, suddenly released in a torrent. "On the first piece of land we were taken to the ground was covered with water more than half of the time, and was so rocky that when it rained the water washed away the bones of our dead. For three months we were without almost anything to eat. Most of our horses were either stolen from us by white men or destroyed by disease, which attacked both man and beast. We had to sell our few remaining ponies to keep from starving."

Joseph had many council meetings with the chiefs, White Eagle, Standing Bear's brother Big Snake, and others. No news of the trial had reached them, but a spirit of revolt was sweeping the tribe. Many were already planning to follow Standing Bear's example. The Agent, aware of rebellion and probably apprised also of the developments in Omaha, was on tenterhooks. It was rumored that he had sent for a contingent of soldiers. Susette was shown wagons at the Agency, earmarked for the Indians but undelivered because the Agent was afraid members of the tribe would run away as soon as they received them.

Joseph's narration of the trial, the judge's decision, and Standing Bear's release was like a torch set to dry tinder. It meant they were all free to go, and some were for setting out immediately.

"No, no!" Joseph protested. "That is why we were sent, to keep you from risking all our friends hope to gain for us." He told them of the suit Mr. Tibbles planned to bring against the government with regard to their land and pleaded with them not to act until this suit was decided. Then and then only could they go back to their own land in safety. "Promise me," he begged White Eagle, the head chief, "promise me you will do nothing until you hear from the lawyers, who will be conducting the suit, that you have been set free!"

White Eagle, White Swan, and the other chiefs promised, but, though the Agent was fully aware of these developments, he remained wary and suspicious. While Joseph and Susette were still there, two of the chiefs were arrested and confined at Fort Reno, on the ground that they were stirring up strife and keeping the tribe in a state of dissatisfaction.

Joseph and Susette dared stay no more than a few days, for fear their own presence on the reservation might be challenged. They left all the provisions they had brought with them except the bare necessities for their return home. Even as they rode away they saw preparations being made for the arrival of the expected soldiers. But they had accomplished their mission. They could tell Thomas Tibbles just what conditions were among the Poncas. Eighty good houses, contentment, indeed! And they carried with them a letter from Khe-tha-ska, White Eagle, which would give Tibbles and the lawyers clear, written authority to take legal action for the stranded Poncas as well as for those who had escaped.

The letter was a masterpiece. Susette knew, because she had written it at his dictation and transcribed it into English. It related all the dealings of the chiefs with the agents who came to remove them from their lands, the possessions taken away from them and those they had brought with them, the deaths of persons, oxen, horses.

"When people lose what they hold dear to them," it concluded in part, "the heart cries all the time. I speak now to you lawyers who have helped Standing Bear, and to those of you who profess to be God's people. We had thought there were none to take pity on us. I thank you in the name of our people for what you have done for us through your kindness to Standing Bear, and I ask you to go still further in your kindness and help us to regain our land. You cannot bring our dead back to life, but you can yet save the living.

"When I went to see the President and told him how we had been wronged, he said that those who did the deed were gone, and it was among the things of the past. I now ask him once again through this message, which I send to all the white people of this land, to rectify this mistake. When a man desires to do what is right, he does not say to himself, 'It does not matter,' when he commits a wrong.

his

"Khe-tha-ska, X (White Eagle)"

mark

Tibbles started East in June, on a tour of newspaper publicity and lecturing designed to finance the long campaign in the courts which might make it possible for the Poncas, Omahas, and all other Indian tribes to live where and as they chose. In Chicago a big public meeting netted $600 for the cause, sent immediately to the Omaha clergyman acting as treasurer for the Committee. Tibbles was careful not to handle any such funds himself, for already the Washington officials were instigating a scurrilous campaign against him in newspapers across the country.

In Boston he secured the support of Edward Everett Hale and Wendell Phillips, the famous Abolitionist orator. At a meeting attended by poets, historians, scientists, lecturers, chaired by the city mayor, with Phillips listed as the principal speaker, Tibbles was invited to make an opening speech. So nervous that his shaking hands dropped all his carefully prepared papers, he suddenly kicked them aside.

"I take it this audience doesn't wish to hear me read from those official documents. They're at the service of any person present. What you wish is to hear some salient facts on which you can form a judgment. If any statement seems doubtful, you all know where to find the government documents to solve the doubt. I make no assault on any individual. I assault a system. If the angel Gabriel were President of the United States and he should select his cabinet from the courts of heaven, neither he nor his cabinet could prevent the wrongs against which I protest—so long as the present system is in force."

He went on the reveal its evils, as illustrated by the injustice to the Poncas, and proposed as remedies the allotment of land "in severalty" to the Indians, so that the removal of a tribe would be impossible; the recognition of Indians *as persons* under the protection of the courts. The response was overwhelming. After the meeting the crowd surged forward to shake his hand and pledge assistance. Afterward Wendell Phillips took him to dinner.

"You must go on with this work," he told Tibbles earnestly. "I made my fight for one race, the Negroes, and I feel that you are called to make the fight for the Indian race. But don't be deceived by the enthusiasm of that audience. I know the Indian Ring. Your hair will be gray before the first law is passed that does away with the present system."

Laughing indulgently, Tibbles ran his fingers through his unruly mane of thick black hair. With the intoxication of the evening's success still quickening his blood, the prophecy seemed absurd. He could not guess that after four years of the terrific battle yet to come, when he was only forty-three, it would have turned snow-white!

5

Never, thought Susette, had a summer seemed so long. With the school closed there was little to do. She helped Marguerite and Susan prepare for their coming year in Elizabeth, made over some of her own clothes (gifts of Eastern friends) to fit them, donated her small horsehair trunk for their use. She tried to share their excitement, describing once more the spacious school buildings, the luxuries of Eastern living, the chatter and pranks of the carefree schoolgirls. But it all seemed remote, unreal. This was reality, this constant uncertainty, this teetering between hope and fear, home and exile.

It was the season of the hunt, sacred as the Moslem's pilgrimage to Mecca or the Christian's to Jerusalem. But the tribal circle was broken. There were no more chiefs. The tribal council was now a band of puppets. The ancient rituals were fast becoming empty words, devoid of meaning.

Yet habit and loyalty were strong. It was the time for thanksgiving, Hedewachi, the ceremony which for generations had been observed after the hunt, "when the plum and cherry trees were full of fruit and all creatures were awake and out." Now, dutifully, stubbornly, the tribe repeated so far as it was possible the ritual of centuries. They made a circle, pitching their tipis as in the *huthuga*. The old men who knew the songs dusted off their drums. Ancient war bonnets, embroidered leggings, beaded garters, bone and bead necklaces, robes of soft fine deerskin, were taken from caches. The Sacred Pole was borne from its tent to the center of the circle.

"*Zwawa iba iba ba che!*" sounded the call. "I bid you come and rejoice!"

A "powwow," the white people from surrounding farms and towns dubbed this spectacle which had become an annual event, using the Indian word applicable, they thought, to any tribal gathering. And they flocked to witness it, fascinated by its brilliant colors, its strange "barbaric" rhythms, repelled yet intrigued by its "savage" content. The first wariness and suspicion of agents, fearing such conclaves might foment rebellion, had tempered to amused tolerance. "A good way for them to work off their bellyachings!" Father Hamilton, of course, and other missionaries frowned on such vestiges of "heathen" customs, and Joseph, his dutiful disciple, followed his example.

Not all his children, however. Not his son Frank, who took every opportunity to delve into tribal history. He was into the circle at the first sound of the drums, leaving it each day with face streaming sweat and seamed with dust. Though Frank agreed with his father that the tribe must move into new paths, it was with reservations. "Yes, but let us save the old as we move into the new."

And not Susette. Though out of loyalty to Joseph she watched from a distance, her blood sang with the ancient cadences, and under the full calico skirt her feet moved to the rhythm of the drums. She felt exultant, yet indescribably sad. The songs were of things past. The dances celebrated victories no longer possible. It was like watching a ghost dance. Yet it must not be lost. Oh—Frank was right! Father was wrong. Surely there was much in this rich heritage from the past worth saving—beauty, reverence, acknowledgment of the unity of all creation. And—it was *theirs.*

The elation of the trial had given place to depression. She felt incredibly helpless and remote, stranded in a backwash, while strangers were fighting for her people. If only there was something she could do!

And then suddenly there was. With horrified fascination she read the letter which Dr. Dorsey brought from the Omaha Committee.

"No!" she gasped. "Oh—no, I couldn't!"

"Of course you could, my dear child. You know all the facts. The Committee was most impressed with the letter you wrote Mr. Tibbles, and some of them heard you speak. Do you realize what an honor they have paid you? It's probably the first time such an invitation was ever extended to a woman, certainly to an—" He stopped, embarrassed.

"To an Indian woman," he had almost said.

"I know." Her voice was no more than a whisper. Speak in a great Omaha church? Stand up on a platform before hundreds of people? "I—I couldn't," she repeated, choking.

"This Bishop Clarkson of the Episcopal Church," continued Dr. Dorsey, "is a very influential man, and he seems most anxious for you to speak. This is an opportunity to plead the cause not only of the Poncas but of the Omahas and all Indians. And there's probably not another Indian woman in the country who has the training and ability to render such a service. You *must* do it, my dear."

Thomas Tibbles returned to Omaha from his Eastern tour, a few silver hairs already threading his black mane. The trip had yielded considerable funds, aroused public opinion, and drawn much personal abuse. The endorsements he had carried with him from the Governor of Nebraska, General Crook, Bishop Clarkson, fellow journalists, and many Omaha clergymen had been balanced by vituperative comments planted by Washington officials in all the city newspapers. He had even been accused of personal dishonesty in handling funds, which, fortunately, he had never let pass through his hands.

But on return he discovered a situation which made all such difficulties seem mere trivia. Standing Bear had disappeared from the Ponca camp! Tibbles went there posthaste and held a council with the other Ponca men. A man speaking the Dakota language, which the chief could understand, had appeared in camp and told Standing Bear that Mr. Riggs, the missionary to the Santees, and Mr. Tibbles had sent word for him to go back to his home in Dakota on the old Ponca reserve. Being shown a letter purportedly from Tibbles, Standing Bear had started off without hesitation. If he was permitted to arrive there, the whole cause might be lost. Tibbles immediately went on to the Omaha reservation.

"I know you have two fast horses," he said to Joseph. "I want to borrow them. It may not be too late to head him off."

At four in the morning he started for Niobrara City, rode for 120 miles in eighteen hours, and caught up with Standing Bear late that night where the chief had camped before trying to cross a dangerous river. Tibbles brought him back to the camp outside the Omaha reservation. A narrow escape indeed! He sent a letter to *The New York Times* describing the incident.

"When I see the Indian so deceived," he said in conclusion, "his confidence betrayed, his faith in the white man used to ruin him, I take a good deal of satisfaction in believing there is a hell."

The Ponca Committee had been busy. Bishop Clarkson was planning a big meeting in one of the large Omaha churches and, to Tibbles' surprise and somewhat to his consternation, he had persuaded the Indian Girl, Bright Eyes, to speak. A woman in a church pulpit! Congregations were more conservative than their leaders, and St. Paul's injunction of female ecclesiastical silence was rigorously observed. And—an Indian! With the Nebraska legislature urging expulsion of all Indians from the state, unfavorable publicity might jeopardize all the public support the trial had aroused. Besides, he remembered, this Miss Bright Eyes was a shy little thing—great dark expressive eyes glowing like candles, a pretty oval face and trim figure, a voice so low and timid one had to listen closely at first to understand.

He went to the meeting with great apprehension. The church was crowded, even to its outer steps. Several ministers, including Bishop Clarkson, were on the platform, their combined ecclesiastical dignity somewhat eclipsed by the presence of Standing Bear, who, even in citizens' clothes, was of dominating mien and stature. Tibbles had to look twice to discover the shrinking little figure in black which looked lost in one of the great plush chairs. Yet when "Miss Bright Eyes" was introduced, the big audience rose with one accord to its feet, clapping and waving handkerchiefs.

His heart sank. It was just as he had feared. As she stood there, a tiny shape half hidden by the high pulpit, her fear could be seen and felt. She was visibly trembling. Like a little bird caught in a net, he thought, torn between pity and dismay. Yet there was something graceful and appealing about her obvious fright, and never once did she lose her dignity. The huge dark eyes gazed at the audience without wavering. The trembling figure remained straight as an arrow. For a full minute she stood while the audience settled back in their seats, first expectant, then uneasy, finally obviously embarrassed and distressed. Tibbles could not have told which of his two emotions was stronger, pity for the girl or dismay over this embarrassment to the cause. The Committee should have known better.

Then she began to speak. Tibbles straightened, stared. He could not believe his ears. The voice, low as he remembered yet rich and vibrant, carried clearly to the back pews, even to the crowded steps outside. Hastily he reached for a pencil and began taking notes. Later he would record her exact words as he remembered them.

"Why should I be asked to speak? I am but an Indian girl,

brought up among the Indians. I love my people. I have been educated, and most of them have not. I have told them that they must learn the arts of white people and adopt their customs, but how can they, when the government sends soldiers to drive them about over the face of the earth?"

Except for the compelling voice not a sound could be heard.

"The soldiers drive Standing Bear and his wife and children from the land that belonged to him and his fathers before him—at the point of the bayonet, and on the way his daughter dies from the hardships of the journey. The Christian ladies of Milford, Nebraska, come to the Indian camp, pray for the dying girl, and give her Christian burial. Oh, the perplexities of this thing they call civilization! Part of the white people murder my girl companion, and another part tenderly bury her, while her old father stands over her grave and says, 'My heart breaks.'"

The girl's voice broke also, faded to silence. She swayed slightly and reached for the pulpit. Thinking she was about to faint, someone sprang to her side and helped her to a chair. She had broken down, but not, as Tibbles had feared, from shyness. In fact she had completely forgotten herself. Her failure under stress of emotion stirred the audience as no polished speech could have done. They went wild. Women wept, men shouted. Some even forgot the place and the Bishop's presence and swore loudly. One prominent Omaha citizen could be heard clearly above the hubbub.

"If I were Standing Bear," he yelled, "I would let the courts go hang. I'd take my tomahawk and scalping knife and follow the trail of the Secretary of the Interior. Then I'd settle the thing right there."

The girl's dramatic success stirred the Omaha Ponca Committee to an alteration in plans. Tibbles had already signed a contract with a Boston lecture bureau for the appearance of himself and Standing Bear at a series of meetings in that city. Now the committee insisted that he add Miss Bright Eyes to the party. Reverend Joseph Cook, a noted Boston lecturer who had been visiting in Omaha and had met the girl, was an enthusiastic proponent of the idea. Tibbles was at first reluctant. It would add much to the expense, and the main object of the campaign was to raise money for the cause. But, when it was further suggested that she not only speak herself but act also as interpreter for Standing Bear, he immediately saw the advantages. Of course the chief must have an interpreter. The girl had already had experience in the East. With mounting excitement he constructed the picture: Standing Bear, tall, impressive in his chief's regalia; this beautiful shy Indian girl in her modest black dress, thrilling great audiences with her magnetic eyes, her graceful figure, her vibrant voice, her first-hand knowledge of facts, her emotional concern. She *must* go.

"No, no, no, NO!" If Susette had been horrified before, now she was panic-stricken. She couldn't, she wouldn't, she refused even to consider the possibility. She was weak with relief when Joseph greeted the proposal with utter disapproval. An unmarried Indian woman travel hundreds of miles, lodge in strange cities, appear in public and on platforms—in the company of males not members of her family? Unthinkable! With profound thankfulness she returned to her teaching.

Then suddenly tragedy struck the Omahas. The shadow of fear which had stalked them for years turned into monstrous substance. It was learned that a bill to remove the Omaha tribe to Indian Territory had actually been introduced in Congress. The Department of the Interior was implementing its claim that all Indian tribes, regardless of their treaties, were completely under the control of Congress. Tibbles renewed his urging that Susette be allowed to go East and tell her story. Haste was essential. Public opinion must be roused to combat such legislation before it was too late. Even titles to allotments already made could be rendered invalid, since no certificates of possession had actually been issued. Every possible means of pressure must be exerted.

Susette suffered tortures of indecision. She was Queen Esther, challenged to flout regal authority to save her people. No—worse! She was Iphigenia, chosen for sacrifice as a propitiation for somebody's sins. Perhaps, even more pertinent to the problem, she was Jacob wrestling to the finish with some relentless compulsion within herself. Finally she went to her father.

"I have to go. You must see that, Dadiha. I would never forgive myself if I didn't do everything possible. Nor would you."

Joseph too had been wrestling, with guilt as well as fear. There had been a clause in one of the treaties, the Agent had informed him, which gave government the power of removal without the tribe's consent. Joseph had been appalled. This had not been so interpreted to him before he signed. Now, at Tibbles' further urging, he gave his reluctant consent.

"My daughter may go East to lecture," he agreed, "provided that her brother Francis, Woodworker, goes with her."

Frank agreed with alacrity. His marriage to Alice Mitchell two years before had terminated after a year of disillusionment. He did not consider the child born to them his own. Now twenty-two, a striking replica of his handsome father, keenly intelligent, he welcomed the adventure with all the eagerness of a young brave going on his first hunt.

Accompanied by Reverend W. J. Harsha, pastor of the Omaha First Presbyterian Church, the party left for the East in mid-October—Tibbles, Standing Bear, Susette and Frank La Flesche—a strangely assorted quartet destined not only to change history but to be linked one to another with bonds of loyalty, romance, fellowship, antagonism, joint purpose, which would change all their lives.

Part Three

Ironic! As an Indian living among Indians, she had been for many years Susette La Flesche. Now, journeying in the white man's world, she had become again Inshtatheamba, Bright Eyes. She had wanted to use her formal name, but the newspapers would not let her. "Bright Eyes" was too quaintly appealing to the public, and it described her too well.

"No such interesting squaw has appeared since Pocahontas as the young woman who rejoices in the above appellation," commented the *Lady's Journal*, "as pretty a name as was ever devised. Bright Eyes has taken sober Boston captive."

"Lovely and winning," reported another Boston paper, the *Woman's Journal*, "refined, of great intelligence, and with singularly sweet, graceful, and simple manners. There is unusual dignity and elegance in her talk in private, and a sense of the value of words that is remarkable, and is perhaps explained by the fact that Shakespeare is almost the only book she owns . . . never bitter, never vindictive. She is calm, but full of animation and a very deep feeling."

Doubtless the public would have preferred her to conform to the popular conception of Indian apparel—skins, porcupine quills, moccasins, beaded head band confining long glossy braids. But fortunately it was decided that all three Indians should dress for the most part in "civilized" fashion. Wood-worker, as usual, should wear what were called "citizens'" clothes. It was Tibbles' idea that Standing Bear should do the same, showing that the Ponca Indians were making an effort to adopt the ways of the whites. But, no. Whenever he spoke in public, as a chief Standing Bear must appear before the audience in his appropriate apparel—blanket heavily adorned with bead work, necklace of bear's claws, leggings and moccasins—everything but paint. He would pack his costume in a suitcase and carry it to the hall, then retire and don official regalia before making his speech. People became so accustomed to this dress that the press would have raised a ruckus had there been a change.

The party went first to Chicago, where they spent a week speaking to large audiences, attending numerous receptions, meeting many dignitaries, shaking a multiplicity of hands. There were luncheons and dinners, many of them formal. Though Standing Bear had seen nothing of white men's ways except while a prisoner in Omaha, he never made any mistakes in behavior. How, someone asked him, had he learned white men's customs so quickly?

"When I sat down at a table for the first time," he replied, "I watched what the others did and kept just a little behind, so I would make no mistake."

But occasionally his own customs intruded to cause personal distress. The first dinner at the Palmer House in Chicago was attended by Bishop Clarkson, Reverend Mr. Harsha, and two or three distinguished Chicagoans. Anxious for Standing Bear's welfare, Tibbles gave the waiter a quarter and said, "The old chief can't speak a word of English. See to it that he has plenty to eat; with a good supply of roast beef, well done. Indians detest rare meat."

The waiter complied. As soon as one slice of roast beef disappeared from the chief's plate, another took its place. Tibbles, immersed in conversation, felt a touch on his arm and looked into an agonized face.

"What am I to do? I can't possibly eat any more, and I have no way to take it away."

Tibbles instantly understood. With Indians courtesy demanded that a guest either eat the food given him or take it away when he left. If not, the host was insulted. He hastily assured the chief that further gorging was unnecessary.

For Bright Eyes every public encounter was sheer torture. After the debacle of her first speech in Omaha, she never attempted again to speak from a platform impromptu. Not that words did not come freely after the first terrifying onset of shyness had passed, but emotions were somehow more controllable when reduced to black and white.

There were times, however, when she could allow her emotions full play without fear of breaking down. One came during an interview with a reporter from the Chicago *Inter-Ocean*. It was an informal meeting in the hotel room, with chairs drawn together in an intimate circle. She had been reading a book of poems and kept it open on her lap.

"Just what is your mission on this tour?" asked the reporter of Standing Bear, whom he was to describe as a "man of powerful frame, every inch a savage, and three score years have not whitened a hair nor bent his head." Easily and with swift precision Bright Eyes interpreted the chief's reply.

"You may wonder at my traveling. When a weaker man is oppressed, he goes to a stronger. I am traveling to find someone to help me. I owned a field, and the land was mine. It belonged to me and was dear to me. We had lived on our lands hundreds of years. . . . If you white people had been treated as I have been, you would not like it. If anyone had taken hold of you and forced you to another country that you did not want, you would not like it. . . . I was driven down to the Indian Territory against my will. I did not like it, so I broke away. You ask why I did so? I wanted my women and children to live. That is all."

"And you—" the reporter turned to Bright Eyes—"what do *you* want?"

Composedly she closed the book of poems and folded her hands, one slender finger marking her place. She said quietly, "To make known the wrongs done to my people."

"And what specific wrongs do you complain of?"

"We, that is, the Omahas," she replied, "complain that we have nothing to say about the way in which our money should be expended. We have an annuity of about eight or nine dollars apiece, the price of our land, and the Agent invests it for us in what the government thinks we need."

The reporter raised his eyebrows. "Do you want each person to draw his share and spend it as he pleases?"

"Oh, no. It is better invested as a whole for the good of the tribe, but we want some attention paid to our wishes in the matter. For example . . ." She told of the building of the infirmary, left empty until a white person moved into it, of the books she had needed for her school, and other incidents.

"But," the reporter asked negligently, "I take it you don't claim there is any personal violation of proprieties by the agents?"

"Yes, I do." The bright eyes flashed fire. "What right does an Indian agent have to open a letter I may write or receive? You say it isn't done. Oh, yes, it is, every day. . . . If we have no rights, what does the Fourteenth Amendment mean? Are Indians the only people in this country who have no rights? Have the United States authorities the legal privilege to come into this room, arrest me, put me under guard of a soldier, and send me back to my reservation?"

The reporter straightened and began to scribble furiously.

"Your soldiers," blazed Bright Eyes, "are just kept to fight the Indians and quell disturbances that the Indian Department has caused. Then, if an Indian kills a white man, you go and kill all the tribe you can find."

"Oh, but our soldiers only kill Indians in open battle," interrupted the reporter mildly.

"They kill men, women, and children, and you cannot deny it. It is true."

"But Indian women fight like tigers, it is reported."

"So do white women when their homes are attacked, their husbands killed, and their children murdered. All history from the beginning applauds the courage of women who, when necessity demanded, were ready to fight to the end for their homes or their country."

The reporter's manner had changed. He was no longer the impersonal, indulgent listener, slightly amused by the unexpected fire and eloquence of this demure young female. These were the days when the Utes were being driven from their Colorado reservation following their attempts to prevent encroachment on their land and false charges that they were destroying forests. In September soldiers had been sent under General Thornburgh to quell the supposed uprising. In spite of the efforts of Nicaagat (Jack), a Ute chief, to prevent war, the soldiers advanced, shots were fired, Major Thornburgh and some of his soldiers were killed, and many more Utes had died in what they believed to be a desperate effort to save their reservation from the encroachment of greedy miners and politicians desiring to push them off their twelve million acres of land and remove their entire tribe to Indian Territory. For weeks newspapers had been full of the gory details of Indian barbarisms and of the valiant organization of white militia units to wipe out the "red devils."

"But," protested the reporter hotly, "you are more barbarous in war than we, and you shock the public by the acts of atrocity upon captives and the bodies of the dead."

"Scalping, you mean, I suppose," returned Bright Eyes scornfully. "Don't you know that the white men taught Indians that? It was practiced first in New England on the Penobscot Indians. The General Court of the Province of Massachusetts offered a bounty of forty pounds for every scalp of a male Indian brought in as evidence of his being killed, and for every scalp of a female or male Indian under twelve years, twenty pounds."

She was still Inshtatheamba, but the name should have been given its other translation, "Lightning Eye." Though her voice remained low and resonant, it held a searing heat.

"You never get but one side. We have no newspapers to tell our story. I tell you the soldiers do things with the prisoners and the dead as horrible as any Indian could think of. And your people are almost always the aggressors. Let me tell you a case I know of." She told an incident which had happened on the reservation not long before. "Two young white men met an Indian with a basket of potatoes. One of them said, 'I would like to be able to say when I go back East that I had shot an Indian.' The other dared him to shoot this one. He drew a revolver and shot him. The Indian was an Omaha, one of my people. Oh, I tell you, if he had been a Sioux or a Cheyenne, you would have heard from it. But we know we would gain nothing by protesting or resisting, so nothing was done."

The reporter was silent, unable for the moment to think of a suitable response. When he spoke again, the amused indulgence was gone from his voice. "Well—and what do you propose to do?"

Bright Eyes did not hesitate. "I propose that you white people treat us on a platform of plain honesty and let us be citizens. We now are farmers and are doing well. We want to stay on our land, which was deeded to us by formal treaty, and we want assurance that we can live under the protection of the law like other Americans."

The reporter faithfully recorded most of the interview, with no more than the usual errors in minor detail. "The young lady is a daughter of White Eagle, the old head chief, and no blood but that of the Omahas flows in her veins."

Other newspapers designated her as a Ponca, as a daughter of Standing Bear, as "a fine type of the aboriginal race," and as a "thorough young lady."

2

Though the press was largely favorable to the expedition, there were exceptions. While Tibbles' own paper referred to it as "Standing Bear's Holy Crusade," the rival Omaha *Bee* dubbed it "Tibbles' Bear Show." One Chicago journal commented that "the appearance of Standing Bear in the Chicago churches at this time, so soon after the defeat and death of Major Thornburgh and others of his command by the Utes, is an exhibition of 'cheek' not to be tolerated."

But the Boston *Advertiser* countered firmly, "The Poncas are not the Utes and are no more responsible for what the latter have done than the men of Massachusetts are responsible for the assassination of the Chisholms and of Dickson in Mississippi. Standing Bear is not asking for funds to make war. He asks merely for means of prosecuting a case in the courts to determine whether Indians cannot be protected by the laws of the land, as other people, white and black, native and foreign born, are."

In fact, it was Boston, "hub" of literary excellence, democratic leadership, and avant-garde thought (as well as the source of that ancient scalping edict), which became the focal point of the campaign. The party had intended to spend more days in Pittsburgh, but there Tibbles was greeted by a telegram from Mr. B. W. Williams, of the Boston Lecture Bureau, urging him to board the first train for the "hub" city. They were to be the city's guests for a week at the Tremont House.

They arrived by the Boston and Albany railroad at six A.M. on October 29 and went at once to the hotel, where they breakfasted, rested briefly, and at eleven o'clock were honored at a huge reception in the hotel parlors, attended by the mayor, the city council, many prominent ministers and other dignitaries.

"Bright Eyes," the papers reported, "a handsome young woman of twenty-three, wore a mantilla coat and black velvet bonnet, neatly trimmed with beads."

She felt as if her small hand had been crushed in a vise and her head tossed in a winnowing basket, but she smiled dutifully, and her eyes never lost their brightness. It was a relief when Mayor Prince announced that there would be no speeches, only introductions.

"Please tell Standing Bear and your brother Woodworker," he told Bright Eyes, "that the people of Boston are glad to welcome them, that their wrongs are known here, and that Standing Bear and his people should be patient and do nothing to excite a feeling against them, as a determined effort to bring their case to the attention of the courts is being made."

She relayed the message, and the chief said he would like to say something.

"This morning," she interpreted his words, "when I see you all, although I have felt sad all along, I feel no longer sad. It seems I have come to a place I can call home. I ask you all for your help."

Weary, yes, but intoxicated with hope and excitement! The battle seemed already half won, and with how little effort! There was to be another big reception in the evening, with speeches, but Bright Eyes for once felt little apprehension. A spirit of exhilaration pervaded the team. Even Frank, who had been sober and taciturn of late, forgot his grievances. He had been eyeing with disfavor actions and glances on the part of Thomas Tibbles toward his sister which, he felt, smacked of too great familiarity. A pat on the shoulder, a prolonged handclasp, an arm across the back of a chair—male gallantry, fatherly solicitude such things might seem to Waxes, not to Indians. Once, during an interval of jolly give and take, he had even pulled her down on his knee! When Frank protested in private to Bright Eyes, she had only laughed.

"Nonsense! He is only being kind and fatherly. No one was ever more devoted to his wife than Mr. Tibbles. Haven't you seen his face light up when he talks of his beloved Amelia? And doesn't he write her a long letter every day?"

Frank had agreed, but only halfheartedly. Perhaps, too, he had been a bit resentful because throughout the tour he was being relegated to a minor role. True, he sat on the platform with the others, interpreted often for Standing Bear in informal conversation, was noted by reporters as "Zon-the-tah, Wood-worker, brother of Bright Eyes," "a handsome young man of commanding height and determined expression," but the spotlight was always on the other three. His English was not good enough for speeches. He was there merely as a chaperon, a guardian, for his sister. Very well. If that was his role, he would play it to the limit. Now, however, after the morning's triumph, he was as exuberant as the rest of the party. Meeting later in the afternoon, they were lighthearted to the point of levity, laughing at the merest nothings, especially at the jokes of Standing Bear, who had revealed a surprising and delightful capacity for drollery and humor. He was a chronic punster. Strange that some of life's most exhilarating hours should prelude its most tragic!

It was at five o'clock that Mr. Williams came to the room where the party was gathered. He looked stunned. In his hand he held two telegrams. "I have some very bad news," he told Tibbles, "both for you and for Standing Bear."

Shocked and incredulous, they learned that Tibbles' wife Amelia, suddenly stricken by peritonitis, had died and been buried that very day; and that Standing Bear's brother, Big Snake, had been killed on the Indian Territory reservation.

Bright Eyes was doubly distressed. Already she had learned to love the charming and sympathetic Amelia. And Big Snake, so huge and powerful of build, but so gentle of temperament that he was known in the Ponca tribe as "the peacemaker"! What could have happened? Had there been fire beneath that calm resignation, a volcanic core of anger that had suddenly exploded?

Unable even to speak, Thomas Tibbles went to his room and flung himself on his bed. Standing Bear bore his grief in complete silence. Even later, when he learned the full details of his beloved brother's murder, he would maintain the same stoic calm.

Encouraged by the court decision in favor of Standing Bear, Big Snake desired to test it for himself. He asked permission of Agent William H. Whiteman to go north to join his brother, and was refused. Since coming to their present reservation many of the Poncas' horses had been stolen by white settlers. Hearing that the Cheyennes were willing to give them some of their horses as replacements, Big Snake again asked permission to leave the reservation, this time to visit the Cheyennes and procure the horses. Again he was refused. Very well, he would go without permission. Taking with him some thirty Poncas, he traveled the hundred miles to the Cheyenne reservation.

Whiteman immediately reported this defiance by "renegade Indians" to the Commissioner of Indian Affairs in Washington, who through the Secretary of the Interior ordered General Sherman to return the "renegades" to their own reservation as quietly as possible. Sherman immediately decreed that: "The release under writ of habeas corpus of the Poncas in Nebraska does not apply to any other than that specific case."

Returned to his own reservation, Big Snake was a marked man. Whiteman secured an order for his arrest and imprisonment. The Indian was summoned to the agency on a pretext, surrounded by soldiers, and accused falsely of threatening the agent's life. Big Snake calmly denied the charge, threw aside his blanket to show himself unarmed, and defied arrest. He would rather be killed. When the soldiers approached him with handcuffs, Big Snake pushed them away. One of the soldiers struck him in the face with his gun. He was knocked down, back against the wall. When he straightened up, a gun was fired, and he fell down dead.

Though Standing Bear had yet to learn all these details

through the eye-witness account of a fellow tribesman, Hairy Bear, he already knew enough. Big Snake could have committed no crime. His murder, to be dubbed by the Department of the Interior the "accidental shooting" of "a bad man," could have had but one purpose: the punishment of a close relative for the rebellious behavior of Standing Bear himself, and the serving of notice to all Poncas left in Indian Territory that further resistance would meet with swift and deadly retribution. It was a bitter lesson that no Indian would soon forget.

Standing Bear finally broke his long silence. "I want to go home. They will kill my wife and little ones next."

Hardly had the words been spoken when he negated them by his action. Going to Tibbles' room, where the reporter lay in stunned prostration, the chief knelt beside the bed, laid his hand on his friend's head, and began to pray aloud in his own language. Presently Frank entered and acted as his interpreter. Later, when Thomas Tibbles wrote his own life story, Frank would help him remember the chief's exact words.

"*Kagayha*, my friend. You have lost the one you love most. I knew her too. She was beautiful and good. Your heart is very sad. A wife is closer to a man than a brother. We both suffer, but remember those others who suffer and die in that strange land. Don't go back home. Don't stop trying to help my poor people. They have no one to help them but you. Many husbands have seen their wives die, down in that hot country. They have no missionary to tell them of the good words God has spoken to those who have trouble. You can read God's book, and kind people will say words to comfort you. You suffer greatly but they suffer more. Promise me that you will not forsake them."

And what could Thomas Tibbles do but promise?

The reception was all arranged and must go on. It was due to start immediately. The committee well understood the impact of the double tragedy, but they felt that the cause must transcend even such exigency of grief. "You must appear at the meeting," they told Tibbles, "and each of you must say at least a few words."

No! Tibbles would go, but he could not speak. It was impossible. Again it was Standing Bear who, gently but firmly, spoke the necessary words.

"I am older than you, my friend, and I have suffered more. Now my brother, as well as most of my children, is dead. He did not die of disease, but was cruelly murdered. All these things I bear. Your wife was dear to me. I know how sore your heart is, but do go to the meeting and say one word for those who suffer and die with no one to pity. If you can do that, it will make your burdens lighter, not heavier."

The reception in Horticultural Hall on that evening of October 29, 1879, received generous and favorable press coverage. Mayor Prince presided.

"On the platform," reported the Boston *Advertiser* the following day, "were the members of the committee and the three Indians. Standing Bear wore his civilized costume until just before the time for his speech, when he left the room and entered in his chief's official dress. His dignified figure showed to the best advantage in the picturesque costume, which was really handsome with its full draperies and strong colors—red, green, and goldwork predominating. Mr. Tibbles explained that the wearing of the costume was really a matter of importance with an Indian chief when he spoke in public, etiquette demanding it, just as military regulations commanded that an officer should wear his uniform on certain occasions. The chief spoke with great animation and earnest eloquence, using vigorous gestures. His language sounded much like any other foreign tongue we cannot understand. It seemed to be made up of short syllables and was not in the least unusual or disagreeable to the ear. The plain, simple interpretation of Miss Bright Eyes showed that it had a deal of natural eloquence, and its pathetic directness made a deep impression. Miss Bright Eyes read her address from manuscript in a modest, natural manner, and with a sweet, girlish, and expressive voice which quite won the hearts of her listeners."

Modest, natural manner! . . . No one knew the terror which made her limbs shake and her hands clench on the closely written pages. Every public appearance, it seemed, took a greater toll of her strength and will. Yet tonight, as always, she held the great audience spellbound.

"I come to you with gladness in my heart and to try to thank you, for here, after a hundred years of oppression, my people have for the first time found public sympathy, and, as soon as the truth of their story was known, help was given them. In the name of my people I thank the press of Boston."

In simple but dramatic language she recounted the events of the past two years as she had lived them—the journey of the ten chiefs, their return in the dead of winter, the long trek of the tribe, her visit with Joseph to Indian Territory.

"This Ponca case is only a single specimen among hundreds of others." As she neared the end her voice came near breaking. "We are thinking men and women. . . .We have a right to be heard in whatever concerns us. Your government has driven us hither and thither like cattle, and because poor human nature, unable to bear such treatment, retaliates in the only way open to it to free itself you call us savages and lay on us still more heavily that which we hate, the yoke of bondage . . .

"Your government has no right to say to us, Go here, or Go there, and if we show any reluctance, to force us to do its will at the point of the bayonet. An Indian does not want to cultivate a piece of land, fence it in, build him a house, furnish and stock his farm, and just as he is ready to enjoy the fruits of it, to have it taken from him and be sent with his family to a southern clime to die.

"Do you wonder that the Indian feels outraged by such treatment and retaliates, although it will end in death to himself? Oh, I wish I could tell you the story as it should be told! . . ."

As she finished, she scarcely heard the thunder of applause, and her fingers trembled as she was presented with a beautiful wreath of flowers.

When Tibbles' turn came, he did not spare himself. He continued to recount the wrongs done to the Poncas. There was one thing, he said, of which England could boast and of which the United States could not; that all men protected by the British flag were equal before the law. The young lady and her brother on the platform were really slaves, subject to the dictation of one man, and at the order of that man, the Commissioner of Indian Affairs in Washington, a guard of soldiers could carry them prisoners anywhere that man wished.

He sat and listened to the other speeches, shook hundreds of hands, heard encouraging plaudits from the committee, knew that the reception crowning their first day in Boston had been an astounding success.

"But the only thing I remember about it," he wrote later, "is that next day all the Boston papers printed long accounts of it. My mind was not at the meeting. It was living over, moment by moment, eighteen hard, brave, wonderful years that now were done."

3

Not for a hundred years had Boston, hub of progressive thought and cradle of independence, been so shocked and aroused by an infringement of human liberty. Crowds thronged to halls and churches to hear the details of the Ponca tragedy, to applaud the exotic visitors, to shake their hands, to sign petitions, to donate to the fund solicited by the Boston Indian Committee for the projected court actions. Newspapers head-lined each day's event—meeting, reception, luncheon, tea, soirée—and editorials waxed eloquent. If the party ventured on the street, they were endlessly accosted by strangers wanting to shake their hands.

The city's cultural life yielded gladly to the interruption. On November 3 the Reverend Joseph Cook, scheduled to deliver the one hundred and thirty-first lecture in the Boston Monday lectureship at Old South Church, preluded his discourse by an exhaustive discussion of the Ponca case.

"Call the roll of the ghosts which flit through this building," he began. "John Adams, John Hancock, Joseph Warren, George Whitefield, George Washington. I venture to say there is not one of these historic souls that does not sympathize with this Indian chieftain."

He was able to speak even more eloquently than most, having been an eye-witness at the Omaha trial and having heard the story first hand from Bright Eyes. He told it again with all the persuasion and emotional impact of a brilliant orator.

"Now everybody knows," he reasoned, "or ought to know, that the lands of the Poncas were granted to them in Dakota in exactly the same form of words by which the lands of the Union Pacific railway have been granted to the corporation running that iron construction." If a part of the land granted to the Union Pacific had been by some mistake of haste at Washington ceded afterward to some Indian tribe—say the Sioux—he demanded, would there not have been a swift rectification of the mistake by the courts?

But all of Dr. Cook's lengthy reasoning and eloquence affected the audience far less than the simple speech of Standing Bear, delivered a few words at a time and interpreted by the small figure in black standing at his side.

"I would like to say a few words to you all here. . . . I have received sad news. . . . My brother has been killed. He was trying to do just as I did—to break away from that land. My brother did no wrong against any one. . . . He was arrested and put in jail, and because he resisted they killed him. . . . It is hard for me to speak today, and I cannot say much more. . . . I feel sad, but I think of my family. They are all alone on the prairie in a tent. The cause of all our troubles is the agents and the government officials. That is all."

The lecture of Dr. Cook on "After Emerson—What?" was to all concerned, Dr. Cook included, an anticlimax.

Standing Bear was never at a loss for words, and he spoke with no apparent preparation. Had he been able to write, he probably would not have used a single note. Yet his skill in adapting himself to each situation was almost uncanny. Once, at the invitation of Henry Mason, of the Mason and Hamlin Organ concern, the party visited the manufacturing establishment. Mr. Mason asked Tibbles if the chief would say a few words to the two to three hundred employees. Tibbles consented with some trepidation. All the chief knew of white civilization was what he had seen from the car windows and a few days spent in Washington and Chicago and Pittsburgh. They went into a large hall where the men were assembled, still clad in the aprons and paper caps they wore at work. Standing Bear stepped on a small box and looked over the crowd for a full minute before beginning to speak. Then he proceeded with a glibness which took all of Bright Eyes' ingenuity to interpret.

"Your faces are white and mine is red, but one God made us both. Why should we not always have been friends and helped each other instead of killing one another? My tribe never killed a white man. The bones of 700 of my young men lie bleaching on the plains of Dakota, who lost their lives in defending the poor white men of Nebraska who live near the Sioux. I came from the far away country to ask justice for my people. I see that you are a great people. I have been thinking what made you great.

"My friend and I got on the cars at Omaha," he continued, "and we rode all night and nearly all day faster than any horse could run. We came to a great city. My friend took me to the top of a very high house. One one side there was water, but on all the other sides were houses and houses as far as I could see. Then we rode a day and a night more, and he took me to the top of a hill. And as far as I could see there were houses and houses. Then we rode a day more, and we came to a great river, and we went across it in a boat. It was night. We rode a long way in a carriage, and on either side were houses and houses. Then we came here, and the Governor took me to the top of your big council house, where your own chiefs meet to make your laws, and as far as I could see there were houses and houses. Then I began to understand why the white people were so great. They work. Every brick in all those houses was made by some man's hands. The white people are rich and great, and men like you are the ones who make them great. I have seen your great chief, but it is you who make your country great."

Tibbles marveled. Did any labor leader, he wrote later, ever make a more appropriate speech to a band of working men?

As the tour continued, Standing Bear learned many subtle nuances of diplomatic approach which a professional lecturer might have envied. And never did he lose his innate dignity, his poise, his proud yet humble self-confidence.

One evening there was a great meeting in Music Hall, said to have the largest seating capacity of any building in the country. Every seat was taken long before the designated hour. Aisles were crowded, the corridors and stairway jammed, the street for a block each way a mass of surging people vainly trying to get in. On the platform with Standing Bear were the Governor of Massachusetts, the city's mayor, Dr. Edward Everett Hale, Dr. Alcott, and other distinguished citizens of Boston.

"There are around me the wise men of your city," said

Standing Bear at the end of his speech. "I think how little I know and how hard it is for me to learn. If I know anything, some white man must tell it to an interpreter and then the interpreter must tell it to me, but since I have been traveling with my friend here [turning to Tibbles] I have learned many things."

One thing he did not have to learn was that instinctive courtesy which enabled him to adjust so amazingly to the manners of another culture. Many of Boston's most refined citizens commented on his correct deportment, whether on public occasions or at the select dinners and receptions given in his honor. Gallantry was as native to his nature as pride and dignity. He learned to close all his speeches with a compliment to the ladies, using a new one every night.

"When the white people came to this country," he said on one occasion, "the Indians were turned over to the army. For years the army did what it liked with us, and we had war and bloodshed. Then the Indians were turned over to the politicians, and they appointed our agents and rulers. That was a hundred times worse, and we had continual war. Then your great General who never talked [U. S. Grant] turned us over to the churches and divided us up among them. We still had war and bloodshed. Then they turned us over to some man in Washington. He came from a country beyond the great water where there never were any Indians [Carl Schurz] and we have had war and bloodshed ever since. Now I ask you to turn us over once more. Turn us over to the ladies, and they will not murder us or drive us from our lands."

He was cheered as never before, and some of Boston's most distinguished females pressed forward to shake his hand.

The women of Boston were as ardent promoters of the cause as the men. One, who remained anonymous, donated funds to make up the $3,000 deficit in the city's quota on the condition that Secretary of the Interior Schurz would endorse the movement. This was only one of the continuous assaults being leveled at the Secretary by concerned citizens of Boston. As early as September Mr. Edwin Atkinson had appealed to him in an open letter in the *Advertiser*. Other editorials had assailed him for insisting that Inspector Colonel C. E. Kemble had received from the Poncas their consent to be removed to Indian Territory. But now he was fated to a scourging which was to crack wide open his hitherto dignified and evasive façade—and from a woman.

4

She came to the hotel one morning early in November asking for an interview with Thomas Tibbles. She had written an article for publication which she wanted him to check for accuracy. He did so with the greatest praise, instantly recognizing her rare intelligence. It was a little later that Bright Eyes met her.

She first noticed the woman's hands. They were very white, shapely, and well kept, and they enveloped both of her own small ones in a firm yet gentle grasp, communicating a warmth of vitality which set her nerves tingling. Raising her eyes, she saw a round fair face, fringed by blonde curls turning gray, and blue eyes that drew her gaze like magnets. She knew instantly that this was no casual encounter.

"My dear," said the visitor, "you have given me a new purpose in life. You and I will work miracles together. You will see."

Bright Eyes read the article with mounting wonder and enthusiasm. Though the signature "H.H." meant nothing to her, she knew that the writer was no amateur. It was a brilliant, clever, lucid presentation of the Ponca tragedy, written as only a professional author, imbued with intense feeling, could create.

"It's—wonderful," she marveled.

Such was Bright Eyes' first meeting with Helen Hunt Jackson, destined to become not only her closest friend but one of the most powerful spokesmen of all time for the rights of the American Indian.

Mrs. Jackson had come from her home in Denver to Mt. Desert Island, Maine, in the late summer, her major object being attendance at the seventieth birthday party of Oliver Wendell Holmes, postponed from August 29 to December 3. Her mild interest in Indians had been sparked by a visit to an Indian camp at the age of twelve, when she had been both fascinated and repelled. Frequently she had applied to Indians in general the common adjectives of "loathsome," "abject," "hideous." Visiting Boston, she had found the city in a ferment of righteous anger and the mayor heading a committee of aroused citizens soliciting funds for the Poncas. Among the supporters of the cause was the editor of the Boston *Advertiser*, for which she often wrote literary reviews. At his urging she had attended one of the big public meetings at which Standing Bear and Bright Eyes had spoken, and—her life had been changed. She, who had always despised women with hobbies, whose writing had never championed Blacks or temperance or women's suffrage, who had had strong prejudices against the sight of women on a lecture platform, had found a cause to which all her remarkable talents should henceforth be dedicated. She, who had joined in the severe criticism of Longfellow for "using the silly legends of the savage aborigines" in his *Hiawatha*, was about to become a near fanatic in her espousal of their rights.

From that day Mrs. Jackson was an almost constant companion of the Ponca party. She accompanied them on most of their speaking tours around New England, spent hours poring over the official documents Tibbles had assembled and many more hours in the public libraries accumulating facts and figures. She was soon writing articles for the numerous magazines and newspapers to which "H.H." was a popular contributor. Her summary of the Ponca case published in the *Independent* concluded with an appeal for funds to be sent to the Indian committees—either to the Omaha Committee, endorsed by Nebraska's Governor Albinus Nance and consisting of the Right Reverend Robert H. Clarkson, Reverend A. F. Sherrill, Reverend W. J. Harsha, Mr. Leavitt Burnham, Mr. W. M. Yates, and Mr. P. L. Perine; or to the Boston Committee, of which Mayor Prince and Mr. Eben D. Jordan were treasurers. She appealed to all her friends who would listen. According to Joaquin Miller, it was she who persuaded Wendell Phillips to take the platform for the Indians as he had for the Blacks. She began bombarding Secretary Schurz and Commissioner Hayt with both letters and press attacks, so satiric and stinging that even the tough skin of government was irritated, for she could dip her pen in acid as well as in honey.

Mrs. Jackson was present at the Cambridge home of Mr. H. O. Houghton, senior member of the Riverside Press, when Henry Wadsworth Longfellow first met Bright Eyes and presented to her a copy of his *Hiawatha*.

Bright Eyes had been told the poet would be there. A dinner reception was always a little frightening, but this one was terrifying. Actually meeting face to face the poet whose writings she had always loved so much! What would one say? He had given the world an idealized, romanticized conception of an Indian woman. Surely she, the prosaic reality, must give his roseate image a severe let-down!

She was almost glad when a traffic snarl held up their carriage and made them late, though it would make their arrival even more conspicuous. Her limbs felt like lead as she started up the long walk to the house. Suddenly the door was flung open, and she saw him standing there waiting. He looked just as she had pictured him—white flowing beard, a poet's sensitive features, brilliant far-seeing eyes. Other faces, figures were crowded around him, filling the wide hall behind, but she saw none of them. At the foot of the steps, to her dismay, Thomas Tibbles dropped behind and, giving her a little push, made her go on alone. Her feet dragged, but the eyes drew her upward like magnets. One step more. He came forward, clasped her hand between his two strong ones, and drew her up to his level. She felt the keen eyes study her intently, seeming to probe into her innermost being.

"This"— she heard the words like a far-off echo—"is Minnehaha."

Still holding her hand, he led her through the group crowding the hall—many of the literary notables of Boston—introduced her to his daughters, then took her away to a quiet corner, where they sat and talked for a long time. It was not hard, once the first agony of shyness had passed. The most famous people, she had discovered, were often the easiest to talk with. He asked her many questions about herself, her family, the tribe, the Poncas. Now in his early seventies, he seemed more like a delightful and lovable grandfather than a great poet.

"Your friend Standing Bear looks sad," Longfellow commented at one point in their conversation.

"Yes," said Bright Eyes, her face grave. "He feels much

sadder when he is in homes like this. It makes him more conscious of how different it is for his people. In public places he does not think of it so much."

Afterward Longfellow said to Thomas Tibbles, "I've been a student of the English language all my life, and I would give all I possess if I could speak it with the simplicity, fluency, and force used by that Indian girl."

This was not their last meeting. After that Longfellow appeared at least once on the platform with Bright Eyes. Someone gave her an autograph album, a popular hobby of young ladies of that era, and one of its earliest and most treasured entries was by the poet. He wrote:

> "From the wigwam he departed,
> Leading with him Laughing Water;
> Hand in hand they went, together
> Through the woodland and the meadow;
> Left the old man standing lonely
> At the doorway of his wigwam,
> Heard the Falls of Minnehaha
> Calling to them from the distance,
> Crying to them from afar off,
> 'Fare thee well, O Minnehaha!'"

Cambridge, Dec. 3,   Henry W. Longfellow
    1879

1

Helen Hunt Jackson was only one of the remarkable women who became Bright Eyes' close friends. Another was Miss Alice C. Fletcher, a noted anthropologist connected with the Peabody Museum in Cambridge. Though a short, plumpish little woman with a dumpy figure, she was all soft curves and gentleness, and Bright Eyes was enchanted by the beautiful contours of her head, her shining eyes, her lilting voice. She had been studying Indian customs for years, she told Bright Eyes and Thomas Tibbles, in books and museums. Now she wished she might visit Indian tribes in their own lodges, actually living with them, observing their customs—especially those of the women and children—at close range. Would they help her?

"Did you ever camp out?" demanded Tibbles bluntly.

"No, never."

"Then I doubt if you could stand such a trip. You'd have to sleep on the cold ground. The food would be strange. You'd meet storms on the open prairie and get wet to the skin. Sun and wind would blister your hands and face. You never could endure it."

"Yes, I could," she insisted.

She was so stubborn that Tibbles reluctantly agreed to take

her—"sometime, perhaps." He hoped the half-promise would never materialize.

Frank found their new acquaintance enthralling. Suddenly all his intense interest in Omaha customs and traditions was accorded an eager and attentive hearing. To this highly intelligent woman, many years his senior, he was not only an adult, but a respected authority. She asked innumerable questions, listened enraptured to his stories of the Sacred Pole, the Tent of War, the legends of creation. He described his hunts, his visit to the secret Shell Society, the treatment of one of his sick friends by members of the Pebble Society. She was fascinated. Frank's moodiness vanished. He had suddenly become a valued member of the expedition.

The party remained in the Boston area more than a month, feted, banqueted, lionized, speaking almost daily. Bright Eyes' energy was taxed severely, more because of her innate shyness than for lack of physical stamina. The receptions were terrific ordeals. She came close to fainting more than once. After two or three hours patiently shaking the hands of an apparently endless line of strangers, her own small hand would feel crushed to painful pulp. Usually someone from the committee would stand close by her and warn the guests, "Please don't squeeze her hand. Shake it gently." But this only mitigated the agony.

"Please, just stick to the lecture platform," urged Tibbles. "Don't try to keep all these social engagements."

But she only replied earnestly, "When the people come and hear us talk, they go away and forget, but if they come to a reception and I shake hands with them, they will remember longer and will do what they can to save us. If we cannot get the protection of the law, we shall be driven from our reservation, and then what will become of my father and mother and my sisters, to say nothing of all the others?"

She felt burdened with guilt as well as responsibility. As with Standing Bear and Big Snake, her very participation in this rebellion against the government might endanger members of her own family and tribe. The attacks of officials were becoming all the time more bitter and angry. She dared not shirk a single opportunity for serving her people as long as there was breath in her body.

Though the writing or revising of her speeches was a constant chore, their delivery became increasingly easier.

"After being on the same platform with Longfellow, Oliver Wendell Holmes, and Wendell Phillips, all at the same time, I was never quite so frightened again. If I could speak before them," she confessed merrily, "I could speak before anybody."

There were many high points in Boston. At another meeting in Horticultural Hall on November 10 the Governor presided. Bright Eyes told again the story of the Poncas' removal, emphasizing the force and robbery which had accompanied it. Tibbles read many extracts from documents containing statements of the government admitting that the Poncas had been wronged. Reverend E. E. Hale showed how the clause for the removal of the Poncas had been slipped into a general appropriations bill, and how they were removed by force. He emphasized the need of money to carry Standing Bear's case to the Supreme Court. Tibbles stated the legal status of the case, three suits being necessary to dispose of all the points at issue and give the Poncas possession of their old lands.

The following Saturday Fisk University Jubilee Singers gave a concert in the Berkeley Street Church for the benefit of the Ponca cause. The house was packed. There were storms of applause and many encores for the talented black musicians. For the last selection Bright Eyes and Woodworker mounted the platform at the right, Tibbles and Standing Bear on the left. As the singers rendered "Home, Sweet Home," many eyes, gazing at the homeless chief, were "dimmed with tears."

Reported the *Advertiser*, "The scene of emancipated slaves extending their sympathy and help to the wronged, outraged, and long oppressed Indian was one to touch the hearts of all men."

One of the most important meetings was held in the Merchant's Exchange at one o'clock on November 25. It was one of the largest gatherings of Boston businessmen ever held in that building. There were nearly 500 present, three-quarters of whom stood during the entire meeting.

"That so many busy men," reported one newspaper, "at such a busy time of the day, should have assembled shows how deep is the sympathy felt in Boston with the Indians, and indignation at their treatment."

Colonel Atwood, secretary of the Board of Trade, called the meeting to order, and Mr. William H. Lincoln, one of the most prominent members, gave an introductory statement, after which Lieutenant Governor Long presided. Bright Eyes, the only woman in this assemblage of men, spoke with even more clarity and emphasis than usual. She had written her speech especially for the occasion, and it abounded in caustic and trenchant sentences. She was learning from her new friend Mrs. Jackson the possibilities of dipping one's pen in acid.

"The tribe has been robbed of thousands of dollars worth of property, and the government shows no disposition to return what belongs to them. That property was lawfully theirs. They had worked for it. The annuities which were to be paid to them belonged to them. It was money promised by the government for the land they had sold. I desire to say that all annuities paid to Indian tribes by the government are in payment for lands sold by them to the government, and are not charity . . .

"For the last hundred years the Indians have had none to tell the story of their wrongs. If a white man did an injury to an Indian, the Indian had to suffer in silence, or, if exasperated to revenge, the act of revenge has been spread abroad through the newspapers of the land as a causeless act, perpetrated on the whites, just because the Indian delighted in being savage . . ."

Here she told several stories of injustices she knew of: a government farmer sent to teach the Indians how to plow and plant, who had fenced in a piece of land, caused the Indians to till it, then, when they expected a share of the crop, kept it all for himself; a Pawnee brave who, trying to make a government employee understand that he needed some powder for shooting troublesome blackbirds, reached out to touch a jeweled flask hanging by the man's door, whereupon the latter, misunderstanding his intention, picked up a broadax and at one blow chopped off the Indian's arm and cut into his side; an Omaha man who had been missed by the tribe and found murdered in a white man's pigpen; the Indian youth stabbed by the younger white boy, but daring to make no protest.

The last meeting in Boston, at noon on December 3, was held in Faneuil Hall, the "cradle of liberty," where Bright Eyes became the first woman in its history to make a speech. Would people come there at that hour? The committee was doubtful. It was a hazardous experiment. But the house was filled, all the seats in the galleries occupied, as well as much of the standing room on the floor. Longfellow was one of those in the gallery. Again businessmen had left their offices, women flocked from their homes. Mayor Prince presided. Mr. Lincoln read a letter from President Seelye of Amherst College stating that Seelye had been in the House of Representatives when the bill authorizing the removal of the Poncas had passed and that with his own hand he had inserted the clause providing that removal should not take place without the full consent of the Indians. There were many speeches, including one by Wendell Phillips. Bright Eyes and Standing Bear each spoke briefly, "with the same dignity and forbearance," reported the papers, "which have been so noticeable whenever they have appeared before the public."

The month in the Boston area had been amazingly productive. A good start had been made toward raising the $10,000 deemed necessary for court procedures. Many groups had officially passed the resolutions formulated by the Committee, of which the most important were:

"1. That Congress should pass a law under which patents must be issued to Indians for lands, making the homesteads of Indians inalienable for life and free from taxation for a period of years, long enough to permit them to become civilized and fairly acquainted with their responsibilities, before they can freely dispose of their property.

"2. That the laws relating to Indian affairs should be so revised and enlarged that the Indian may become amenable to civil laws . . .

"3. That the questions raised by the recent decision of Judge Dundy . . . should be precisely determined by the Supreme Court."

The end of this skirmish brought no surcease, only a girding for fresh battle. Though Bright Eyes was becoming weary almost beyond endurance, she knew there was to be no respite from speaking, smiling, eating, handshaking, writing, interpreting, *ad infinitum*. For beyond Boston there were New York, Philadelphia, Baltimore, and all their surrounding areas. And beyond them Washington, where the last battle of all would be either lost or won.

2

"Cut hair," announced Standing Bear suddenly soon after the party's arrival on December 5 at the Fifth Avenue Hotel in New York. He started determinedly toward the hotel barbershop.

"No, no!" Hastily Tibbles summoned Frank to reason with him, but to no avail. Standing Bear would not only have his hair cut, but he would not wear his chief's regalia again. In short, he was done with making a dramatic spectacle of himself. Tibbles was at his wits' end. The fight with Washington was becoming more and more heated. Newspapers would play up such a change in costume and attention would be drawn from the real issues of the case.

"Wait! Keep him here," Tibbles told Frank and went posthaste to fetch Mrs. Helen Hunt Jackson, who had come with them to New York. As distressed as Tibbles, she went immediately to Standing Bear's room with Bright Eyes. In the past weeks she and the chief had become staunch friends. Her reasoning powers were effective. Presently she came to Tibbles with the good news that Standing Bear had promised not to have his hair cut.

"But only until we get to Washington," he explained to Tibbles, "and I have made my last speech."

The party's New York debut was at a reception on December 7 at the Fifth Avenue home of Josiah M. Fiske, who, with Mr. William H. Lincoln of Boston, was directing the New York campaign. Lincoln, a member of the great shipping firm of Messrs. Thayer and Lincoln, which controlled more tons of shipping than any other firm in the country, had been from the first a leader in the crusade.

"Standing Bear," reported the *Daily Tribune*, "is a large powerful man with long black hair, fastened over the ears with small rings. . . . Zon-the-tah, Woodworker, is an intelligent young man with a broad, pleasant face, is educated, and speaks good English. Bright Eyes, his sister, is a young woman of medium height, slight figure, with pleasing manner and graceful bearing. She speaks perfect English, and her voice is gentle

242

and well-modulated. . . . She wore a well-fitting dress of black silk with a white ruff at the throat, and black lace around the neck fastened by a gold lace pin. Her shining black hair was fastened neatly in a braid. . . ."

Fascination with the appearance of the cast continued to vie with newspaper interest in the drama itself.

"A tall, swarthy, aquiline-featured young Indian," the New York *Telegram* described Frank. "He wore a neat, dark-colored walking suit . . . has short hair parted fashionably over an inner angle of his left eyebrow." Bright Eyes was "petite, willowy, with olive complexion, wondrous eyes, face oval, nose delicately nostriled, hair in a coil behind her head, voice filled with pathos, musical . . . a black merino dress with black silk facings, trimmings, and fringe."

"A little woman," *The New York Times* commented two days later. "She wore a stiff felt hat with a feather, a tight-fitting basque, a dress of dark cloth, a ribbon about her neck fastened with a red coral pin."

Relying on the doubtful fashion sense of male reporters, one might think she had a dozen outfits, instead of a couple of plain black dresses varied by scarves, collars, ribbons and simple jewelry!

Some descriptions of her appearance and demeanor were less flattering. According to an interview recorded in *Frank Leslie's Journal*,

"Bright Eyes, the eloquent daughter of the Poncas, lounged, after the fashion of Sarah Bernhardt, in a large easy chair in a cozy parlor of the Fifth Avenue Hotel. She was attired in a blood-red morning wrapper, which draped itself in willowy curves over her lissome form. At her neck hung an ivory cross; on two of the slender fingers of her left hand were rings of plain gold. Her face is a delicate oval, her complexion olive, her hair the color of a raven's wing. Her eyes are black and lustrous. She is eighteen years of age, two of which were spent at school in New Jersey, during which she learned to speak English quite accurately. She received me with indolent grace."

On a copy of this interview kept in his scrapbook Tibbles was to write later: "This interview is an entire fabrication. Not one word of it was ever spoken by Bright Eyes."

Already the campaign was aiming its thrust toward its goal in Washington. The *Times*, which described the reception, reported also that Senator Hoar of Massachusetts "introduced a resolution instructing the Committee on the Judiciary to inquire whether any, or what, legislation is necessary to enable the Ponca Indians to prosecute in the courts of the United States their claims for land, under treaties and statutes . . ."—and it was adopted.

Another sharp thrust came out of Boston that same week with the publication of *The Ponca Chiefs* by Messrs. Lockwood, Brooks and Company. Though it appeared under his favorite pseudonym, "Zyliff," the author was Thomas Tibbles. It gave a full history of the Ponca case, with all the papers filed and evidence taken in the trial of Standing Bear before Judge Dundy. Its dedication, written by Wendell Phillips, read in part: "To the people of the United States—those who love liberty and intend that this Government shall protect every man on its soil, and execute justice between man and man . . . is respectfully dedicated as a fair specimen of the system of injustice, oppression and robbery which the Government calls 'Indian Policy.' . . ." He continued with a scathing denunciation of this policy, charging the government with being "incompetent, cruel, faithless, never keeping its treaties and systematically and shamelessly violating its most solemn promises."

Bright Eyes wrote the introduction, stating that "these are the facts concerning some of my people. . . . Many of these things came under my own observation."

"It is a little thing, a simple thing," she concluded, "which my people ask of a nation whose watchword is liberty; but it is endless in its consequences. They ask for their liberty, and law is liberty. 'We did not know of these wrongs,' say the magistrates. Is not that only the cry of 'Am I my brother's keeper?'? For years the petitions of my people have gone unnoticed, unheeded by all but their Creator. . . . Thank God it was only indifference and not hatred which withheld from an oppressed and unfortunate race, justice and mercy. . . . Inshtatheamba (Bright Eyes)."

Could it be that the resurrection of this book in a fresh printing exactly ninety years later would signify a continued pertinence of these accusations after almost a century?

"Did Bright Eyes really write that sentence herself, that 'law is liberty'?" asked Helen Hunt Jackson, who was reporting the book's publication for the New York *Daily Tribune.*

"Every word of the introduction," replied Tibbles, "just as it stands. I was astonished when I read that sentence. I looked up at her and said, 'How did you get at that? What made you say, "Law is liberty"?' She was sitting by the window. She pointed to the people going up and down the street, and said, 'I see it here. I see all people coming and going as they like. They can go to Europe if they like. That is being free. And it is because they have law to take care of them that they can do it.'"

"And what writer on political economy," wrote H.H., "has made a stronger or a better argument than this? And what could be more profoundly touching than the thought of this Indian girl herself, liable to arrest at any moment, as a 'ward' of the United States Government, absent without cause from the 'reservation' appointed for her tribe—sitting at her window, looking out on the hurrying city crowds, and thinking, not of the gayety, the beauty, the novelty of the spectacle, but simply, 'I see all people going, coming, as they like. That is being free.'! Shall we give to this long wronged race the 'liberty' for which they ask—the 'liberty of law'?"

Articles similarly signed by H.H. were bombarding the press these days. Letters from her acid-dipped pen were needling Secretary Carl Schurz into increasingly irate but dignified replies. These letters also were published in the newspapers.

"How many people know," she demanded again and again in the New York *Herald Tribune* on December 15: "That for any white man, other than the one licensed reservation trader, to sell anything to or buy anything from an Indian on a reservation is an offense punishable by a fine of $500 . . .?

"That Indians living on reservations have the right to cut hay for the use of their live stock, but are invested with no proprietorship in such products of the soil as will authorize them to charge and receive compensation for hay cut and used by white persons therein duly authorized by the Government? Under the operation of this law 1800 cords of wood were cut down last winter on the Ponca reservation and sold to army contractors by order of Mr Hayt, Commissioner of Indian Affairs. . . .

"That an Indian cannot be legally punished for an offense committed against an Indian? In two years the Winnebagoes stole over 100 ponies from the Omahas and passed the ponies along to the white man who had hired them to steal them. . . .

"That (in the Ponca case) the Department claims that 'it is an open question whether it is worthwhile to make any effort to restore to them the lands of which they were robbed, because it would be 'a mere vindication of a right to a piece of land'!"

The article listed in all ten "How many people know's" in deadly sequence, with chapter and verse from official documents to verify every one.

At last Secretary Schurz' dignity was cracked. His bitter reply, telegraphed to the *Tribune*, made Helen "wild with delight." One by one he defended or denied every one of the ten allegations she had made.

Schurz' argument in his correspondence with Helen followed the line of his other statements to the press defending the department's action in the Ponca removal. A mistake had been made, but the department was doing everything in its power to indemnify the tribe for their losses. (Except correct the mistake, Helen reminded him grimly.) The Poncas could not bring suit in the Supreme Court. No Indian could sue the United States in a state or federal court. Therefore there was no reason for well-meaning but misinformed people to be contributing to such a relief project. To solve the problem he advocated legislation transforming the Indians' tribal title into individual titles, inalienable for a certain period. The money already collected, he advised, might well go to educate Indian children.

Helen immediately began exhaustive research in the Astor Library in New York on the whole Indian problem, concerned with the unjust removal of the Utes, the Cheyennes, in fact all the northern tribes, as well as the Poncas. With each new discovery of an injustice, she would write another article, meeting every return bombardment with documents and signed statements from the reports of the Indian Bureau. And slowly her writings were growing into the manuscript of a book.

It was unfortunate that Carl Schurz (dubbed "Big Eyes" by the Indians) became involved in this Ponca tragedy, because he was in reality one of the more progressive administrators of the

so-called "Indian Ring." His "solution" for the "Indian Problem"—self-supporting agriculture, education, allotment of
lands in severalty, eventual treatment, like other inhabitants,
under the laws of the land—were in accordance with proposals
put forward by Tibbles himself and the friends of the Poncas.
Schurz had inherited both the Ponca dilemma and the corrupt
system of administration. Yet, while admitting that a tragic
mistake had been made, he refused to rectify it. Therein lay his
vulnerability to the mounting barrage of criticism.

3

Though attacks on Tibbles and his party from Washington
grew more and more personal and vindictive in the press, New
York publicity was largely favorable to their cause. Thomas
Nast, the famous cartoonist, became their champion. One day
Standing Bear, passing a newsstand, recognized a clever carica-
ture of "Big Eyes" Schurz, gave the newsboy a quarter for a
copy, and returned triumphant to the hotel, where he borrowed
a pair of scissors from the barber and carefully cut out around
the lines of the grotesquely elongated face, then asked Tibbles
to paste it in his scrapbook. It suited the chief's sense of humor
to a T. He would open the scrapbook again and again, laugh
and laugh.

"Bigger the eyes, less see," he quipped delightedly.

Mrs. Jackson aided the campaign in other ways than by her
pen. She enlisted her friends the Bottas to entertain the party at
an "evening at home."

"Professor and Mrs. Botta at home, at eight o'clock, to meet
Standing Bear and Bright Eyes and some members of the Indian
Commission," the invitation read.

The Bottas' weekly receptions were symposiums of the
literati. Emerson called their home "the house with the expand-
ing doors." Professor Botta was an Italian scholar and translator
of Dante, his petite wife a schoolteacher turned poet.

By now Bright Eyes was becoming accustomed to these
sorties into high society. She entered the house in 38th Street
with all the poise of a seasoned debutante, not at all fazed by an
assemblage which had often included Poe, Margaret Fuller,

Bryant, Bayard Taylor, Horace Greeley, Longfellow. After many of the houses they had visited, this one, with its floors covered with Chinese matting rugs, its marble head of Dante, its good pictures, its books, was a relief. It gave one room to breathe. A relief, too, not to have to speak, only to interpret.

"She was pretty," reported one of the guests, "picture-book type both in face and clothing, a really possible and acceptable Minnehaha. Standing Bear gave the usual talk about the Father at Washington, the Great Spirit, and the White Brothers, which his wife [sic!] translated, going so fast that it appeared she must have learned the little piece by heart."

Bright Eyes was sorry when they had to go on to another house. She would like to have stayed and heard the Professor read from Dante's sonnets.

The public meetings followed the same pattern as in Boston. At the first one in Steinway Hall the audience filled the lower hall and part of the gallery, but seemed small compared with the huge crowd attending their farewell in Boston. Reverend Dr. Henry W. Bellows presided, and the venerable Peter Cooper was among the distinguished persons on the platform. Here again the press was interested first of all in the persons of the city's exotic guests.

"Bright Eyes is a little woman about twenty years of age, not over five feet in height," reported the *Times*, "of tawny complexion, pleasant features, and has a very feminine voice and manner. . . . She speaks English fluently and seemed to be possessed of considerable information and intelligence."

Four days later Chickering Hall was crowded to overflowing, with every seat taken and all the standing room occupied around the walls. Resolutions similar to those passed in Boston were received with acclamation. Meetings were held almost daily in churches around New York. Only once was Bright Eyes refused permission to speak in a church. (It had happened once before in Chicago.) Both ministers refused because she was a woman, but they had no "conscientious scruples" against her interpreting for Standing Bear, even on a Sunday!

Through December and January newspapers in the New York area seized on the team's exploits with relish: the New York *Independent*, *Times*, *Tribune*: the Brooklyn *Times* and *Eagle*; the Jersey City *Journal*.

In Brooklyn, at the Church of the Pilgrims, Bright Eyes read a letter from seventy members of the Ponca tribe containing thanks and appeals for help. After a meeting at the Y.M.C.A. in January $2,000 were sent to Bishop Clarkson in Nebraska, gifts of prominent men including J. M. Fiske, William E. Dodge, and Cyrus W. Field. One meeting in Dr. Storrs' church in Brooklyn brought donations of $350. In Montclair, New Jersey, portraits of Standing Bear and Bright Eyes and copies of *The Ponca Chiefs* were sold for benefit of the cause. In Jersey City hundreds attended a meeting in the Tabernacle in spite of a severe storm.

But by far the best attended and for Bright Eyes the most exciting was the meeting in Elizabeth. Wonderful to be reunited with Marguerite and Susan, already more at home in the sophisticated atmosphere of the Elizabeth Institute than she had been after months! Humbling and satisfying to see the pride in Miss Read's eyes! Miss Higgins looked exactly the same as ever, in her black dress with high neck and ruffles over the shoulders, the pug on top of her head neat as always, the eyes behind the nose-pinching glasses sparkling with just a hint of tears.

Early in February the party went on to Philadelphia, staying at the Bingham House.

"A dusky Indian maiden and two braves," reported the *Record* on February 2 under the heading *"red skins in a pulpit,"* "sat on the platform of the West Arch Street Presbyterian Church yesterday moaning. Before them was one of the largest congregations which had ever gathered in that edifice. . . . This vast throng had gathered to hear from Indian lips the story of Indian oppression by the white man. . . . Bright Eyes, who has scarcely seen eighteen summers, has a pretty face, lighted up, as her name would denote, by sparkling and sometimes coquettish eyes. She was attired in a black silk dress, trimmed with fringe, cloth jacket, upon the collar of which rested an ivory cross, and a hard felt hat trimmed with silk and a blue and yellow bird. Her hair behind was tied with a bow of yellow ribbon."

Over and over she read her different speeches—the Ponca story, her difficulties as a teacher, injustices she had known and experienced—each repetition draining a little more of her energy. Finally she evolved her own carefully constructed statement of her own beliefs.

"The solution of the Indian problem, so called, is citizenship. Like all great questions which have agitated the world, the solution is simple; so simple that men cannot understand it. . . .

"When the Indian, being a man and not a child or thing, or merely an animal, as some of the would-be civilizers have termed him, fights for his property, liberty, and life, they call him a savage. When the first settlers in this country fought for their property, liberty and lives, they were called heroes. When the Indian in fighting this great nation wins a battle it is called a massacre; when this great nation in fighting the Indian wins, it is called a victory.

"After the Indian is prevented from earning his own living and from taking care of himself by this system of nursing and feeding—although I have heard it reported within the last few years that whole tribes have been found in a state of starvation—he is reported to be incapable of taking care of himself, and would starve if the government left him alone. It was because Standing Bear was trying to take care of himself that this powerful government sent out its armed forces to carry him back to a land from which he had fled because the terror of death was on him. . . .

"Why did the government do this? Because the Indian is a child, thing, or ward, and must be taken care of and fed; moreover, he left that strange land without permission from his father, master, or guardian, whichever you will. But the government feeds them. Was it feeding them when it took from them their land and carried them to a strange, unbroken country, reeking with malaria, there to live in canvas tents and likely to starve because their great father, master, or guardian failed to issue to them rations for three months? . . . This system has been tried for nearly a hundred years and has only worked ruin for the Indian. . . .

"Set aside the idea that the Indian is a child and must be taken care of, make him understand that he is to take care of himself as all other men do, give him a title to his lands, throw over him the protection of the law, make him amenable to it, and the Indian will take care of himself. Then there will be no more wars in trying to settle the Indian problem, for there will be no problem to settle."

It was a blessing she could not know that forty-four years would pass before Congress would confer citizenship on all Indians born in the territorial limits of the United States, and that over ninety years later her people would still be struggling to retain their few poor parcels of land and fighting for a government policy which would give them, not charity, not paternalism, but "some measure of the adjustment they had enjoyed as the original possessors of their native land."

Three

1

Speeches, receptions, luncheons, teas—they were but trifling hardships beside the ordeal which now faced Bright Eyes. With the rest of Tibbles' party she was summoned to Washington to testify before a special committee of the Senate investigating the removal of the Poncas. Emotionally drained, physically weary often to the point of collapse, she nevertheless must alert all her faculties to meet this supreme test on which life or death might depend. They went to Washington on February 10 and appeared before the committee seemingly for days on end.

The testimonies of Secretary Schurz, Commissioner Hayt, Inspector Kemble, and others were extremely damaging to the cause. Even Bishop Hare, a friend of the Indians, did not help, stating that fear of the Sioux, who now considered the Ponca land their own, had made life for the Poncas unbearable in Dakota without the promised government protection.

"So it appears," asked Senator Dawes, "that government took the Poncas away to keep the Sioux from hunting them?"

"Yes, it may be looked at in that way. You know the Indians have a common saying, "The better we are, the worse we are off.' Indians who kill and steal are likely to be well provided for.''

However, it was reported by *The New York Times* at about this time that the Sioux had not wanted the Ponca lands and had never occupied them.

If Bright Eyes was forced to summon her last slight reserve of strength when she appeared before the committee on Friday, February 13, she gave no sign.

"BRIGHT EYES EXAMINED," reported *Washington News and Gossip.* "At a meeting of Senator Kirkland's special committee . . . Bright Eyes was examined with reference to her knowledge of the causes leading to the removal of the Poncas and their conditions in the Indian Territory. . . . Her attention was called to a paper purporting to be signed by heads of nearly all the Ponca families, requesting the President to remove them to a new reservation in the Indian Territory. Bright Eyes exclaimed: 'Why, White Eagle has told me a dozen times that he never signed any such paper! That is monstrous!' Standing Bear was then shown the paper. He had it interpreted, smiled incredulously, made several gestures of disgust, accompanied by expressive 'Ughs,' and finally said, 'That's the white man's way. They write one thing and tell us another.'"

Bright Eyes explained that the only paper the chiefs believed they had signed was one agreeing that they be sent to the Omaha reservation.

Senator Dawes of Massachusetts, who conducted much of the investigation, was a staunch friend of the cause. In his cross-examination of Inspector Kemble, who had removed the tribe to Indian Territory, the latter was forced to admit that most of the outrages inflicted on the Poncas had been perpetrated on his own responsibility.

Both Tibbles and Bright Eyes became targets of increasingly violent and vituperative attacks. Tibbles was accused not only of distortions of fact and misuse of funds but of unmoral conduct in one of his preaching appointments. Bright Eyes was equally maligned. The Agent, who had come to the Omaha reservation in 1876, took all her accusations of injustice as personal insults and called them outright lies. "A BAD CASE OF BRIGHT EYES," his denunciations were headlined in several papers. Roof of her schoolroom leaking? Well, perhaps just a little, around the stovepipe. Children coming to school without shoes in the snow? Pure romance. Shoes had been provided for every child. Going into the prairie to write secret letters? What a fabrication!

"Which only goes to show," Bright Eyes commented coolly, "how well we pulled the wool over his eyes."

An article by Barclay White in the Philadelphia *Press* on February 13 declared many of her statements to be untrue. No person of her name had been an assistant teacher during the last two years. And the Omahas had not the slightest reason to complain of poverty.

Two days later Bright Eyes defended herself in the Reformed Episcopal Church of Philadelphia. Here again the press was more interested in appearance than in substance. She had worn a dark plain dress with a white lace scarf at the throat. Standing Bear appeared in the streets wearing an ulster, with side pockets and strap. He kept his hand in the side pockets as he walked and left the strap hanging as thousands of young men did. He smoked cigars. His long black hair was tied with strings at each side, and he had a small bunch of jet black whiskers on his chin.

In Washington again Bright Eyes was invited to the White House and spent an informal evening with President and Mrs. Hayes, in the company of Senator and Mrs. Dawes. The President had a long conversation with her, asking many questions.

On February 16 Senator Dawes introduced a bill, S. 1298, providing for the confirmation of the Ponca Treaty of 1869 and the return of the tribe without delay to their Dakota reservation, restored in the same condition as when they left, and the appropriation of $50,000 to enable the Secretary of the Interior to carry out the provisions of the act.

But the bill was merely referred to a committee, to be buried there for months. The battle with the Indian Ring had merely been intensified in fury. Early in March White Eagle and Standing Buffalo were called to Washington, but neither Bright Eyes nor Standing Bear was allowed to see them. And when Woodworker went to call on them, he was told it was necessary to get permission from the Secretary of the Interior. They were virtually state prisoners.

White Eagle was before the senate committee for three days,

and near the close of his vivid and impressive testimony he was questioned as follows:

"Are you willing to live down there in the Indian Territory if the government will take as good care of you as it can?"

"I would be afraid to trust the government again. Promises have been made me that we would be well taken care of, but they have not been kept."

"If the government should do as it promised and take good care of you, would you be willing to stay in the Territory?"

"No, sir, I would not stay there."

"If the government were to pay you a fair price for your lands in Dakota and fix your people up in the Indian Territory as well as it could, would you be willing to stay there?"

"No."

"Why not as well stay there if you can have a fair price for your lands in the old reservation as to go back and live on them?"

"What good would it do us even if we lived in fine houses and were fixed up with plenty of good things by the government and we were all to die? Better to go back to the old reservation and not have so good houses, and live in them and have health."

"What makes you want to go back to your old reservation?"

"Because the Indian Territory is no place for us. We love our own land."

But the officials of the Indian Department were even more adamant in their opposition. Their battle with Helen Hunt Jackson had undoubtedly intensified their bitter determination to resist pressure. From January to April of that year she devoted all her remarkable literary talent to the Indian cause, circulating petitions and tracts, bombarding newspaper editors, army officers, ministers, congressmen, college presidents. The *Independent*, *Tribune*, and *Times* were filled with her stinging columns. When she assailed Schurz, Hayt, and Kemble, they retaliated with attacks on Tibbles. Scurrilous accusations in the Omaha *Bee* were reprinted in the Boston *Post*. But the Boston Committee remained staunchly loyal to him and repeatedly published counter statements vouching for his character and giving their unqualified support.

There were exceptions, however. Mr. Perry Smith, Boston philanthropist and historian, who had been one of the initial supporters, deserted the cause. He believed that Inspector Kemble was a "much maligned Christian gentleman."

Some of the Boston Committee expressed their support of Tibbles in a more tangible way. A letter from L. R. Cabot on March 8 said: "I and a few friends have contributed $680 to bring your daughters here and put them for a year in school in Elizabeth. Mrs. Jackson has promised to receive them in New York, to see that they are provided with articles of dress. It will leave you time to devote to the cause."

A worry even more distressing than the scurrilous lies was lifted from Tibbles' mind. He was used to the attack of enemies. But the duties of sole parent and crusader were in constant conflict. May and Eda, in the temporary care of an aunt, were now assured of the best possible schooling.

An equally grateful person for the support of the Boston Committee was Joseph La Flesche. A letter he wrote to Mr. W. H. Lincoln at this time when a bill had been introduced in Congress by Senator Saunders of Nebraska to remove the Omahas to Indian Territory appeared in the Boston *Advertiser*.

"My dear sir, I will say a few words to you, friend. I was sick in bed when your letter dated the 5th February was received, and so could not answer it. My friend, I thought of God, and then I thought of you all. I seem to be kneeling at your feet, thanking you for all you have done for us. I think God's light must shine through you all. Friend, I thank you so much for helping my child, and I know you all pity me. . . . For fifteen years I have thought of this work which you are doing for us now. I could not do anything, because the agents seemed to hold me back. . . . Friend, God knew all that I wanted to do, and it seems to me he sent Mr. Tibbles just when I wanted help the most, saying, this man shall do what you want done; you have not the strength. . . . You can have my daughter to help you as long as you want her help. . . ."

"And these," commented Mr. Lincoln in a spirited article appended to this letter, "are the beings who must get out of the way of advancing 'civilization' or be exterminated!"

For weeks, months, the Ponca party shuttled back and forth between Eastern cities—to Boston again; to Philadelphia, Carlisle, Norristown in Pennsylvania; to Wilmington, to Baltimore. In Philadelphia the Society of Friends became active sponsors of the Ponca cause. Over and over Bright Eyes was greeted as "Minnehaha," the "Beautiful Indian Maiden," and a legend was born, to be enlarged, repeated, revived again and again through coming years. Some would even say that she had been the inspiration of Longfellow's poem, apparently unaware that it had been published when she was but a year old and conceived long before her birth. In fact, she would never be quite able to establish her identity apart from that of the "Indian Maiden."

Intending only to be kind, the thoughtless public had no idea of the grueling burden their attentions were imposing on her. No one, seeing the vivacious, smiling young woman in public, shaking her small aching hand, could guess that later she might lie motionless on a couch, wan and pale almost as in death. But to all her companions' protests she had but one answer.

"The lives of my father, mother, brothers, and sisters, and of thousands of other Indians depend on the success of this agitation. Everthing else has failed for a hundred years. It is better for me to die than that all the Indians should be exterminated."

There were invigorating interludes, oases in the desert of weariness. In April she met again some of her beloved teachers from the Elizabeth Institute.

"For every great work God raises up a worker," wrote Miss Nettie C. Read in the ubiquitous autograph album. "The Jews had their Moses; the slaves their Lincoln; if it is that the Indians are to have their Susette La Flesche, be very humble. . . ." Of course the tribute must be salted with gentle words of warning!

C. H. Read, aged seventy-seven, was less moralizing. "May the life which providence seems to have marked out for you, dear Susette, be more brilliant and crowned with perfect success in behalf of your injured people."

Susan H. Higgins merely wrote her name.

Bright Eyes treasured these entries even more than those with more famous names: Oliver Wendell Holmes, who quoted from "Build thee more stately mansions, O my soul"; Wendell Phillips, who wrote, "The Lord bless you and give you to see the rights of your race protected, in the land that holds the graves of their fathers"; George Crook, Brigadier General, U.S.A.: "Bright Eyes has accomplished more for the benefit of her race than their combined effort within my recollection"; John T. Morgan, who on March 16, 1880, vied with Longfellow in contributing an original poem:

"Yes, bright are the eyes and regal the grace
Of Inshtatheamba, true queen of her race,
As she pleads for her people, with spirit elate
   With a soul's earnest prayer
   That a nation must hear,
From the doom of the slave she will rescue them yet."

Marguerite was able to travel with Bright Eyes to some of the meetings. One evening in mid-April they were together in Baltimore at the Central Presbyterian Church and again in Wilmington, where they received guests in the parlor of the Clayton House. The company of Marguerite, excited over invitations to visit Eastern friends during the summer, was as stimulating as a dose of medicine, though what Bright Eyes needed most urgently was rest.

Thrilling also was a visit to Hampton, Virginia, where General Armstrong, in charge of the Agricultural and Normal Institute, was enrolling a number of Indians in the school. Government had agreed to give $150 for each of fifty more Indians to be educated there, and $15,000 was to be raised for a new schoolhouse. Wonderful! Already Bright Eyes visioned the long succession of Omaha youth, some in her own family, who would be taking advantage of this educational opportunity.

But excitement was no antidote for weariness. She might literally have died under the pressures but for a fortunate intervention. The party were traveling to Baltimore when a Boston woman, Mrs. Hemenway, also on the train, noted their utter exhaustion.

"They must have a few days' rest," she telegraphed the Boston Committee, and sent money to give them ten days' vacation at Old Point Comfort.

Even this respite could not restore the party's flagging energies. It was decided by the Committee that they should go home to recuperate. Tibbles, Bright Eyes, and perhaps Woodworker, would return in the fall for more lectures. Not Standing Bear. He was through. He was going home—at least, almost home. The runaway Poncas had been assigned a few hundred acres of unclaimed land near the mouth of the Niobrara.

The morning after the final appearance of Standing Bear before the Senate committee in Washington the chief came to Tibbles with a look of immense satisfaction.

"No more speech," he said clearly.

"No, no more speeches," replied Tibbles.

"Have hair cut," said Standing Bear, making straight for the hotel barbershop. There he took a seat and motioned to the barber to cut his hair. At breakfast he appeared at the table with short hair and a complete suit of "civilized" clothes, looking every one of his seventy-two-plus inches the normal, dignified, if heavily tanned, American gentleman.

"What will the chief have?" the waiter asked Tibbles as usual.

This morning Standing Bear was his own master. "Bifsteak," he replied immediately.

3

Dust! Returning to Nebraska, they could not believe their eyes. In Omaha it swept about in clouds, hiding the sun, stopping noses, gritting between the teeth, reddening the eyes, seeping through every crack in the houses, flavoring every particle of food. The drought, they were told, had been going on for three months.

"This part of Nebraska," Tibbles reported to the Boston *Advertiser* over his pseudonym "Zyliff," "has been settled for over twenty-five years, but no one ever saw anything like this before. Yesterday, all day long the wind blew a gale. Solid banks of dust dashed along the streets. About six P.M. there was a calm—then in the south a dense black mass rose up, as if the prairie had been ground into fine powder and then spouted out by volcanic force. . . ."

A lady from Boston was staying in his hotel. As she saw the great black mass moving toward the building, she turned ghastly white and clutched a chair. The dust struck the side of the hotel like a huge sea wave.

"What *is* it?" she gasped, rigid with fear.

Tibbles recalled the excruciating puns of Standing Bear and resorted to one even worse. "Prices out here are subject to violent fluctuations," he remarked dryly. "This is only a sudden but general 'rise' in real estate."

Another consequence of the white man's subjection of the prairie! He was denuding it not only of its herds of buffalo and its tribes of Indians, but even of its long centuries of grass-grown soil!

It did not seem like home. Bright Eyes viewed with dismay the brown rolling hills, the sluggish murk of the beloved Smoky Waters. It was the "Moon in Which the Tribe Plants," but even red kernels dispensed with the prayers and chants of centuries would not take root in powder.

However, even dust could not dim the excitement of Rosalie's marriage in June to Edward Farley, the hard-working thirty-year-old son of an Irish immigrant family which had settled in Indiana in the 1850s. The ceremony was performed by Father Hamilton at the old Mission. Bright Eyes signed the marriage certificate as one of the four witnesses. She viewed the slender, erect, shining-eyed young bride of nineteen with affection, pride, and a bit of envy. It would be simple, pleasant, to settle in one's own house on the reservation, to raise children who might synthesize the best elements of two cultures, to *live* a crusade rather than fight for it. Even if the pending bill was passed by Congress and the Omahas were transferred *in toto* to Indian Territory, Rosalie, married to a white man, would be safe.

Yet Bright Eyes knew that life for her could never be simple or wholly pleasant. This was home, yes. She was glad to be back. But she had returned to it only in body. In spirit she was in a half a dozen places. . . .

In Washington, where on May 31 the Senate Committee,

after a full investigation of the Ponca business, reported their conclusions to the Senate, both the majority and the minority agreeing that "a great wrong had been done," but where the opposing parties were still involved in bitter dispute. After hearing all the witnesses, including the chiefs, agents, inspectors, missionaries, citizens, and the Secretary of the Interior himself, the committee, consisting of five senators, unanimously agreed:

"That the Poncas were one of the most peaceable of all the Indian tribes, that they were dwelling upon a reservation which they had occupied ever since they were known as a tribe, under words of absolute grant from the United States . . . that without their knowledge and without compensation and without a shadow of complaint against them as a tribe, the United States . . . undertook to remove them from their home and provide for them elsewhere, and Congress authorized their removal to the Indian Territory if they should give their free consent to such removal; that the government, failing to obtain such free consent, removed them by force and lodged them in a hot and inhospitable climate; that they have suffered greatly from the time of their removal and have been greatly diminished in numbers; that they are at the present moment discontented, discouraged, and disheartened, and are making no progress toward self-support; that this proceeding on the part of the United States was without justification and demands at the hands of the government speedy and full redress."

And she was on the Niobrara, where Standing Bear and his runaways were joyfully recreating a new life and where the bones of his son were resting at last in land once owned by his fathers. . . .

. . . In Europe with Helen Hunt Jackson, who, exhausted by her three months of grueling research on the treatment of the Indians, on May 29 had sailed on the steamship Parthia, leaving her manuscript with Colonel Higginson to proofread . . .

. . . And, most discomposing of all, she was down "Toward the Heat" with Thomas Tibbles, who had been sent by the Omaha and Boston committees to ascertain the present condition of the Poncas in Indian Territory and apprise them of what was being planned. Though she did not learn the details of his journey until much later, she knew that any white man venturing on the Ponca reservation was in danger of arrest and that Tibbles especially was a marked man. It was well that she did not learn the full story until the worst danger was past.

Arriving at the reservation on Salt Creek, Tibbles and his interpreter, Henry Fontenelle, discovered that many of the Ponca chiefs had gone to visit the Cheyennes, and they set off after them. Warned that orders had come from Washington ordering the arrest of any person sent by the Omaha Committee, they went at top speed, confident that their horses could outrun any at the Agency. Through the dry red burning country they rode, suffering from heat and thirst. They met the returning Poncas by the Cimarron River. Though the Cheyennes had shared with them their scanty stores of food, White Eagle and his band were hungry. Tibbles drove one of their wagons to a trader's store, bought flour, salt pork, coffee, and sugar, and took great satisfaction in watching them eat. In council he tried to explain what had happened in Washington.

"You may be able to return to your own land," he assured them, "if only you don't sign any papers that will give up your title to it."

Pitifully grateful, they insisted on calling him, not "friend," but "Great Father," for he had proved himself more deserving of their highest homage than the President.

Before dawn on June 21 a runner came warning that a white man with police was coming. Fontenelle advised Tibbles to make a wild dash for the Kansas line. Arrived in Caldwell, Kansas, Tibbles fell sick and nearly died, probably from the tainted water of the thick brown streams. In Arkansas City a Ponca made him understand by sign language that the agent was scouring the country for him with a large force. To avoid trouble he hired a horse and rode back into the Territory, planning to stop at a ranch northwest of the Nez Percés' encampment which lay west of the Ponca reserve. He wanted to meet Chief Joseph, who had been sent there after the government deprived him and his tribe of their Idaho land, in direct violation of the terms of Chief Joseph's surrender.

"The ranch you want," he had been told, "lies about fifteen miles inside the state line." But the route, a faint trail, was beset with difficulties. Once his horse plunged into quicksand, and he managed to winch it out by means of a pocket knife, two poles cut into a "plainsman's windlass," and sheer ingenuity. Then, forced to spend the night in the shelter of his horse on the prairie, he was bombarded first by a terrific storm, then by a stampede of terrified Texas longhorns, from whose path he just managed to escape.

Arriving at Chief Joseph's camp after a day of rest at the ranch, he found that the chief had gone out on the reserve. A messenger was sent after him. But before Joseph could arrive, an armed Nez Percé Indian rode up and told him through an interpreter, "I have been ordered to arrest you. A white man will be here shortly."

The white man came and ordered curtly, "You're the man I want. Stay where you are until further orders, or you'll get badly hurt." He rode away. Tibbles tried to send a telegram to Mr. Webster by the interpreter, but the latter was afraid to risk the anger of the Agent. The Indian remained to guard Tibbles until the white man returned with three heavily armed men, who ordered him to mount his horse and ride with them to the Ponca reserve. Arriving there, he was lambasted verbally, accused of wanting to start a war in which white women and children would be murdered and scalped and, when he showed his fury, was threatened with shooting.

"You're a dirty coward," he told the Agent contemptuously. "Any man who will abuse an unarmed prisoner is a coward."

Then, as often during his seemingly charmed life, his luck turned. Ponca Agent Whiteman, apparently deciding that he was the innocent tool of the real villains, the Omaha lawyers, invited him to supper, entertained him with his ladies, and sent him to the Kansas border with an escort of police. There, however, he was warned by order of the Agent: "If you ever come back into either the Ponca or the Nez Percé reserve, you will be treated a lot more roughly."

"MAKING MISCHIEF AMONG INDIANS," headlined *The New York Times*, and quoted a letter from Agent Whiteman to Commissioner Trowbridge: "I have to inform you that on the 15th inst., during my absence in Arkansas City, Mr. Tibbles of Omaha, accompanied by an Omaha Indian as interpreter, came to this reservation in the night and sought, by promises and bribery, to induce the Poncas to give up their present home and leave (a few at a time) and return to their old home in Dakota. . . . I am credibly informed that Mr. Tibbles went into the Ponca camp disguised as an Indian squaw, with a blanket around his shoulders, and that he swore the Indians to secrecy, warning them never to disclose the fact that he visited the Agency. . . ."

William H. Lincoln hastened to reply to this diatribe in the Boston *Advertiser* of August 8, giving long quotations from Tibbles' letters describing the expedition and asserting that he was acting under the authority of the Omaha committee and with the advice of eminent counsel.

"The movement to secure justice to the wronged tribe," he concluded, "has, strange to say, encountered the determined opposition of the Secretary of the Interior, and this hostility has been conducted by means most unfair and disreputable. Affairs are now reaching a critical point, and it appears the press of the country is to be filled with despatches conveying entirely wrong impressions. . . . But a just and righteous cause will not be destroyed by such weapons."

Many who knew Tibbles laughed merrily at the absurd picture of the tall, broad, bewhiskered male masquerading in an Indian woman's dress. Not Bright Eyes. She knew all too well the power of such fanciful jibes to influence public opinion. She breathed a sigh of relief when, after Tibbles' life was threatened in Arkansas City, Mr. Webster sent him a wire to "Come home."

He had secured for the lawyers the information they needed, confirming the Poncas' despair, their poverty and bad housing conditions, their longing for their old home. But the incident gave further proof of the fierce resistance of the Indian Ring to any efforts to restore the Territory Poncas to their own reservation. The battle had only begun.

All that summer Bright Eyes was in close touch with the Omaha committee, and in tribute to her contribution John L. Webster wrote in her autograph album on August 2: "The Law shall soon come to know the rights of the Indian race, and the Indian race to feel the beneficence of the Law."

Yet, while she roamed far places in spirit, never had she felt so much a part of the life about her. Every detail of the familiar tribal world etched itself on her mind with sharpened clarity—a baby tied straight to its board, a small sister shaking over it a rattle-gourd filled with seeds; little girls playing *konci*, tossing plum seeds from a wooden bowl; little boys playing hunt and killing their first buffalo; a death wail plaintively greeting the dawn; the sound of a muffled drumbeat; the Oldest Grandmother telling eight-year-old Carey the story of the Sleeping Elk.

"These things are *ours*," she thought, "and they are passing away so swiftly! Somebody must do something. They must not be lost."

Feverishly, as if she had no time to lose, she began drawing again, sketching everything that reminded her of her childhood—faces, costumes, tipis, travoix, ponies, cradle boards, buffalo meat drying, children at play. And with the drawing she started writing.

"You have the gift," her friend Helen Hunt Jackson had told her. "You're a born writer. Use it, not just for these speeches, important as they are. Write about the things you know. Show these poor deluded white people that Indians are not savages. Let our children know how Indian children live."

Now suddenly she knew that Mrs. Jackson was right. She must create for herself. She wrote a story for children and called it "Nedawi," after her own great-great-grandmother, Nedawin, Nicomi's grandmother. A child who read the story would learn much about Indian life, how the tribe was organized, how a family lived in a tipi, the clothes a child wore, the food she ate. But—would white children want to read it? More doubtful, would any paper want to publish it?

She signed it "Bright Eyes" and sent it away, as Mrs. Jackson had suggested, to a children's magazine in the East called *St. Nicholas*. Wonder of wonders, a letter of acceptance came, and, still more incredible, a check in payment!

Mrs. Jackson had made much the same suggestion to Thomas Tibbles. "A popular book of fiction, why not? I don't know enough about Indian life to do it."

With his usual precipitate energy Tibbles was already at work on such a book, collaborating with William Justin Harsha, son of the Omaha clergyman. It would be a novel called *Ploughed Under, the Story of an Indian Chief*. Bright Eyes was furnishing much of the material, and she wrote the introduction, pointing out the distorted images which white people held about the Indian and making a plea for his recognition as a human being. The cases of injustice cited, she stated, were not at all exaggerated.

"The huge plow of the 'Indian system,'" she concluded, "has run for a hundred years, beam down, turning down into the darkness of the earth every hope and aspiration which we have cherished. . . . What sort of harvest will it yield to the nation whose hand has guided the plow?"

1

Autumn 1880 found Bright Eyes again touring the East. The Boston committee insisted that her presence was essential for the future success of the campaign. Accompanied by members of the committee, she and Thomas Tibbles again toured the whole area, following the same grueling schedule of lectures, receptions, luncheons, teas, dinners.

Enthusiasm continued to run high. At a meeting at the Berkeley Street Congregational Church in Boston on November 14 many were unable to gain admittance. Governor Long made a brief address on the present condition of Indians in the country with respect to their status as citizens and what it was hoped to attain by bringing certain cases before the courts. Edward Everett Hale spoke. Tibbles gave a brief report of what had been accomplished during the past year on the Ponca court case and of his visit to Indian Territory. Bright Eyes, as usual, gave an earnest and spirited address. She told of a tribe of Santees who had schools and churches, native ministers and school teachers, even a newspaper in their own language, whose editor was an Indian. Men of the tribe lived in houses and were self-supporting. Yet there was a bill before Congress to have this tribe removed to Indian Territory.

"But," her eyes flashed, "they will fight before they go."

Government, she continued, proposed to civilize her people by penning them up, setting soldiers to guard them, and allowing them the advantages of no civilization save their own.

"I lived seventeen years among my own people and never saw a man drunk," she declared, adding with pointed irony which sent an audible titter around the assembly, "until I came East."

By a curious—could it be called coincidence?—Boston newspapers published on the day of the meeting a dispatch from the Indian office stating that the exiled Poncas in Indian Territory were well and happy and were anxious to come to Washington to "sign away their rights" in Dakota. Similar press releases from Washington had preceded other public meetings designed to discuss the Indian problem. Had the chiefs actually signed such a petition? The Poncas were cut off from all communication with the outside world. No voice could reach them openly except at the pleasure of the Agent or of an ignorant interpreter who was his tool.

"I know that interpreter," Bright Eyes said scornfully after reading the dispatch. "I have known him all my life. He is a Pawnee who does not speak good Ponca or good English. He is an orphan boy my parents once took in and fed. The very idea that they want to come to Washington to 'sign away their rights'!"

In spite of the powerful opposition some progress had been made. Questions were pending in the courts relating to the right assumed by the Department of the Interior to hold Indians as prisoners, and to transfer them from place to place by force; concerning also their rights of property and of citizenship. There was a hope, but only a hope, that the bill reported by Senator Dawes the preceding spring might be passed, restoring all that remained of the tribe to the place and possessions they had held for generations.

Again Bright Eyes spoke in church after church, in Worcester, at Meeting House Hill, Unitarian; in Dorchester, where Senator Hoar also spoke; at Harvard Church, Brookline; at Tremont Temple; at the Portland, Maine, City Hall.

On December 18 President Hayes appointed a commission to hold a conference with the Poncas and ascertain all the facts of their removal and inquire into their present condition. Its members were Generals George Crook and Nelson A. Miles, William Stickney of Washington, and Walter Allen of Boston. Bright Eyes and her friends were much relieved. These were all fair-minded men who would see justice done.

Some of the Ponca chiefs were to be brought to Washington. Uncle Frank—White Swan—was among the names listed. It was arranged that Bright Eyes should go to Washington and see her uncle at the earliest opportunity, as soon as he arrived, to acquaint him and White Eagle with all the action thus far in their behalf and to forestall any precipitate statements, which the Indian Ring might persuade them to make before they had a chance to consider the possibilities. By now the cause had many friends in Washington. One, a Mrs. Claflin, was a woman of some prominence.

The chiefs arrived on December 21, and Bright Eyes went immediately to the hotel where they were staying and asked to see White Swan. Sorry, she was told, the chiefs were tired after their journey and could see no guests.

"But—this man is my uncle," she protested.

Sorry. Orders had been given.

This was a Tuesday. The following day she went to the hotel again, and again her request was refused. That day, December 22, a release was given to the press and appeared the following day in *The New York Times.*

"The Ponca chiefs, who asked permission to visit Washington, arrived here yesterday, and this morning Secretary Schurz held a council with them in the presence of General George Crook, Mr. Stickney, and Mr. Walter Allen. The chiefs declared unanimously that they desired to remain in the Indian Territory and to make permanent homes there; to sell their Dakota land, and to acquire title to their reservation in the Indian Territory. They said further that there had not been any sickness among them for a year. They were emphatic in declaring that they wanted Mr. Tibbles and the other white men, who had been trying to get them back to Dakota, and thus interfering with their working and becoming prosperous, to let them alone henceforth. . . . The chiefs here represent every band in the Ponca tribe."

Bright Eyes was appalled—yet not surprised. The strategy of the Washington officials was as transparent as glass. They had known she would influence her uncle and tell the chiefs facts the Department did not want them to know. It was the worst Christmas she had ever spent, in spite of the efforts of her Washington friends to make the day pleasant. As soon as the holidays were over she went again to the chiefs' hotel, this time accompanied by Mrs. Claflin, and she was admitted. Of course. The chiefs had already signed the papers agreeing to the Department's desired statement. Now that it was too late for her influence to affect its plans, she was permitted to see her uncle.

It was a happy yet tragic meeting. Wonderful to exchange family news, to learn that her aunt and cousins were all alive and well! Heart-wrenching to share the knowledge that there had been hope for a return to their own land.

"Why—oh, why couldn't we have known all those things before!" exclaimed White Swan piteously. He looked smaller and thinner than ever, the lines in his face etched deeper.

On December 28 Bright Eyes and Tibbles attended a meeting conducted by the special committee of the Senate concerned with Ponca affairs, with Senators Kirkwood and Dawes conducting a hearing. The chiefs were called to testify.

Said Standing Buffalo, "We waited for three years to get our own back again, but it was like climbing a wall. There is nothing to take hold of."

"We decided finally it was impossible," said White Eagle. "Impossible," he repeated the word sadly three times, yet the interpreter gave it only once.

Agent Whiteman was present at the hearing. Bright Eyes could see that the chiefs were terrified of him. Each time they spoke they would look at him, and his stern face gave full proof that he had instructed them what to say. She could hardly wait until her turn came to be questioned.

"I know they want to go back to Dakota," she testified clearly. "Not one of them is satisfied to live anywhere else. But, since the unprovoked murder of Big Snake, they are afraid they will be killed unless they acquiesce in the wishes of the Interior Department. I object, moreover, to the present arrangement, because the lands promised our people in the Indian Territory are the property of the Cherokees, and are not for the United States Government to bestow."

She stated further that, in proof of her assertion that the Poncas were kept under strict espionage by the Department, she had twice called at the Globe Hotel to see her uncle, one of the chiefs, and each time was refused admittance.

"And today," she averred fearlessly, "when my uncle White Swan was asked by you if he would not rather go back to Dakota, the Agent looked at him so hard that I could see the perspiration standing on my uncle's brow, and you heard his evasive reply."

Tibbles was even more explicit in his testimony, declaring that the letter received by Schurz purporting to express the chiefs' willingness to cede their Dakota lands was reported only in part, and the suppressed portion would have expressed an entirely different viewpoint. Moreover, he accused Joe Esau, the Pawnee interpreter who wrote the letter, of being the agent's tool.

"I heard him say last summer," Tibbles said, "'He is my meat.'"

Reverend J. Owen Dorsey, who had been engaged by the Department of the Interior as interpreter for its interviews with the chiefs, was also called. His testimony confirmed all of Bright Eyes' suspicions.

"On Saturday evening," he said, "when we reached the house of Secretary Schurz, Mr. Haworth, the Indian Inspector and one of the prime movers in the plot, said to Mr. Schurz, after alluding to this alleged refusal to let Bright Eyes see her uncle, 'I have arranged that she shall not see them till after the business is settled.' The papers were to be signed the following Monday.

"Moreover," he continued, "at the council held on Friday evening, it was remarked by one present, 'I understand that Bright Eyes is expected here.' Another said, 'Who asked her to come?' Then it was said that she was very sharp, and if she gave but a word to her uncle it would go—that is, from him to all the rest."

Dr. Dorsey later revealed another enlightening fact. White

Eagle, before signing the paper declaring his willingness to remain in the Indian Territory, had made a short speech to Secretary Schurz.

"For three years I fought against you in mind. I wish to go home to my own land, but it is impossible to get ahead of you. So I have decided to sit still in the new land. We wish you to make our papers straight for us and to give us good papers, such as cannot be set aside. Then I will be sitting on a big stone, and I will not be afraid of you when I see you."

But this statement was not included in the dispatches which the Interior Department sent to papers all over the country. Included, however, was an accusation that Bright Eyes' declaration, that she was twice refused permission to see her uncle, was a falsehood, and she was styled "a phenomenal liar."

2

January was not all defeat and calumny. Bright Eyes' story of "Nedawi" appeared in *St. Nicholas* and was acclaimed by both friends and strangers as a genuine contribution to a new understanding of Indian life. But it was a modest literary triumph compared with the publication by *Harper's* of Helen Hunt Jackson's book *A Century of Dishonor,* certainly the most exhaustive exposé of white-Indian relationships yet to appear and an indictment of government Indian policy which would not be surpassed for nearly a hundred years.

Mrs. Jackson had returned from Europe in October to resume her feverish activity on behalf of Indians and to help with the editing of her book. Bright Eyes' delight in being reunited with her friend was exceeded only by her triumphant joy over the book's contents. At last justice for the American Indian was given full and eloquent expression.

The preface was written by the Right Reverend H. P. Whipple, Bishop of Minnesota, long a friend of the Indians, and the introduction by President Julius H. Seelye of Amherst College. The first chapter was simply a lawyer's brief on the original right of occupancy—the law of nations as to treaties and their violations. Mrs. Jackson had made an exhaustive study of all the law authorities in the Astor Library from Grotius and Vattel to Wheaton and Woolsey. Then came the main thesis: that in its treatment of Indians the United States Government stood convicted of violating the principles of justice which were the basis of international law. There followed a case history of government dealings with seven tribes, including the Poncas. At her own expense Mrs. Jackson sent a copy of the book to every member of Congress. No official attention was ever paid to it.

For Bright Eyes no triumph or satisfaction could fully balance the agony of the vicious attacks being made on her integrity. Her sensitive spirit cringed and quivered under each fresh assault. Not that she lacked defenders!

"Sincerity is stamped upon her features," wrote one reporter to whom she gave a reluctant interview. "Truth looks forth from her earnest yet sad eyes. One cannot look into her face without the keenest sense of the outrage that called this girl 'a liar.' A thousand Carl Schurzes could not make me believe it. Carl Schurz, who instinctively is a gentleman, must have been sadly misinformed, as well as passionately exasperated, to have brought so monstrous an accusation against this defenseless girl as to call her 'a phenomenal liar.'

"It is true that she was allowed and not allowed to see her uncle, White Swan, when he was in Washington. The inspector 'arranged' that Bright Eyes should see her uncle 'after' the business had been settled with the chiefs in the Interior Department. Every care was taken that she should not see him before. Twice in one day she was refused permission to enter his presence. After the Poncas had signed away their Dakota lands, the danger from this acute mind, this just spirit, was past, and Bright Eyes was invited to see her uncle. Therefore, when she said, as she did before, that she was not allowed to see him, she was published abroad as a 'phenomenal liar.'"

Only devotion to the cause and powerful determination kept her from running away and leaving the campaign for others to wage.

"When I left home," she confessed to the same reporter, "I felt very bitterly against white people, but I do not feel so now. I have found too many kind friends, too many warm hearts. Yet I almost despair for my people, there is so much to be done for them, so much injustice. I do not like this exciting life. I want to go back and live with my father, mother, brothers, and sisters. I want to serve my people. I want to study geometry and logic, that I may think more strongly and calmly for them."

No wonder she wants to study logic! thought the reporter. It needs all the faculties of her keen intellect, plus the skill of a trained debater, to combat the wily machinations of men capable of such accusations.

Some of her defenders were men in high places. At that time the Senate was discussing a proposal of the Department of the Interior granting severalty rights to Indian tribes. While such a measure was highly desired by Bright Eyes, Tibbles, and other friends, this particular bill had been sharply criticized by Bright Eyes. During the senate debate toward the end of January Senator Morgan of Alabama read a letter she had written which had called his attention to one of the bill's glaring defects.

"If an Indian desires to settle on a farm and improve it," the letter stated, "under the conditions of this bill he will have to get the consent of two-thirds of the tribe and wait for the permission of the President, the Secretary of the Interior, and the agents before he can take his homestead."

"It is an Indian girl who wrote this letter," commented Senator Morgan. "Perhaps senators may doubt her ability to do it, but if they will examine her testimony before the Ponca committee they will understand perfectly how it is that the young Indian woman has been able to comprehend a subject which seems at least to have defied the powers of senators from some time past."

Senator Hoar rose also to deliver a long eulogy of Bright Eyes before the Senate. It was probably the first time that a woman had ever been accorded such an honor.

The President's Commission on the Ponca problems made its report on January 25 after a thorough investigation. Not only had they interviewed the chiefs in Washington, but they had journeyed to Indian Territory and taken the testimony of others at the Ponca Agency. Then they had gone to Niobrara City and interviewed the more than a hundred Poncas who had escaped from the Territory, including Standing Bear.

"I can picture him," reported Mr. Walter Allen, who had

seen and heard Standing Bear the previous winter, "as he is this moment in his log hut in Dakota. They are very poor, these Poncas. Nearly all live in tents, but Standing Bear has a log house. In this he wears the white man's garb and looks like a hard-working farmer of New England. While last year the Poncas in Indian Territory cultivated but fifty acres of land and are almost supported by the government, the little band that straggled back to Dakota, with no help from the government, with but few cattle and implements, given them by private charity, have cultivated four times as much land as four times their number did in Indian Territory."

The Commission's report on January 26 was long but unanimously decisive. It revealed, as one historian stated it, "the incredible ineptitude, indifference, mismanagement, and neglect that had made the experience of the Indians needlessly disastrous and cruel." They found that the removal of the tribe to Indian Territory was "injudicious, without sufficient cause, and without lawful authority." It had resulted in terrible hardship, serious loss of life, and the illegal seizure of property. It declared that the Poncas had violated no condition of their treaty and that their rightful claim to their land still existed in full force. It affirmed that the Territory Poncas, discouraged in their effort to return and believing they could obtain a stronger title to the new land in the Territory, had signed the agreement to remain there in good faith and considered their action as sacred. The Commission made many recommendations.

On January 31 Senator Dawes delivered a long speech in which he read a petition signed by Standing Bear and thirty-one other Poncas in Dakota protesting the signing away of their Dakota lands by the Territory Poncas. "The land spoken of is ours as well as theirs, and they cannot dispose of it without our consent." They requested recompense for their losses and reimbursement out of the tribal funds for their portion of the annuities, denied them since they left the Territory.

There were long arguments in the Senate, Secretary Schurz presenting a strong defense of government policy. Arguments and accusations were bandied back and forth for more than a month. Fresh revelations of the injustices of the "system" abounded in the press.

Reported Mary Clemmer in the *Independent* on February 17: "A chief of an important bureau in the Interior Department said to me the other evening, 'I gave up thinking of the Indian question years ago, for its abuses and horrors are so sickening and hopeless; and they never can be lessened till the entire status of the Indian is changed. . . . I have known Indian agent after Indian agent who, with a salary of $1,500 a year in an incredibly short space of time amassed a fortune of hundreds of thousands of dollars. All out of the Indians, of course. I had an Indian friend. He said, referring to a new Indian agent: "A good man. He take only half." . . . Another, "A bad man. He gave only so much to Indian (measuring his finger nail), took all the rest himself." The point is that *all* belonged to the Indian.'"

Yet perhaps, as Mary Clemmer suggested in the same article, Secretary Schurz in his action on the Ponca "builded better than he knew.

"Already it has given to the nation the manhood of those twelve Ponca chiefs, who, without money or food, set their faces and toiled their way back to Dakota; it has given us the eloquence of Standing Bear, the devotion, the intelligence of Bright Eyes, the enlightened ardor of 'H.H.', the hot zeal of Tibbles, the mild and late enthusiasm of Dawes. It has given to Boston a mighty wrong to right, an added opportunity to display itself as the chief moral adjuster of the universe; and if, at last, through the wider knowledge, deeper sympathy, the imperative demand of the people, it shall secure to all Indian tribes the justice that is their due, the integrity of kindness that they never yet have had, the security of law, the rights of enlightened citizenship, *then* we may all thank God together that Carl Schurz did perpetuate 'a mistake.'"

3

"THE PONCAS. Final Settlement of the Vexed Question in the Senate," headlined a Washington dispatch on March 3.

At a motion of Senator Dawes an amendment was adopted appropriating $165,000 to indemnify the Poncas for losses sustained in consequence of their removal and for other purposes intended to ameliorate, make restitution, and promote their welfare. Provision was made to secure to them lands in severalty, on either the old or the new reservation, whichever each person wished, to provide stock and implements, schools, dwelling houses both in Indian Territory and in Dakota. Though Senator Dawes endeavored to extend the choice of reservation to each tribal member "hereafter," the Interior Department got its way. The phrase was interpreted as referring to the choice already made. Those now in Indian Territory would not be allowed to return to Dakota.

Boston breathed a sigh of righteous relief and so far forgot its recent battle with Secretary Schurz that he was honored at a great public dinner attended by many of the dignitaries who had been most articulate in their aspersions. Attending were Parkman, Longfellow, Holmes, President Eliot, Charles Francis Adams, Richard H. Dana, Jr., ex-Governor Talbot, Colonel Higginson, William Dean Howells, Thomas Bailey Aldrich—all this much to the disgust and indignation of the more hardy adversaries, like Helen Hunt Jackson.

"It is trying to human nature," she wrote one of her friends on March 23, "to see him [Schurz] posing now before the country as the chief friend and champion of the Indians. It is like Pharaoh masquerading around in Moses' robes."

Bright Eyes felt neither disgust nor indignation. Relief, yes. A certain satisfaction. But not triumph. The battle for the freedom of the Poncas had been won . . . and lost. Standing Bear was safe at home, the bones of his son forever mingled with the earth of his fathers. But Uncle White Swan, White Eagle, Standing Buffalo, and all the others . . . forever exiled. "How can we sing the songs of Zion in a strange land?" And her own people, what of them? Senator Saunders' bill to remove the Omahas was still pending, waiting perhaps for the Ponca agitation to die down for implementation.

Yet mingled with the partial relief and satisfaction were other emotions—the inevitable let-down after the race is won, the battle fought; the emptiness which must follow days replete with activity. When the tour was over—what then? "I do not like this exciting life," she had told the reporter. "I want to go back and live with my father, mother, brothers, and sisters. I want to serve my people." But—how? Go back to teaching? Certainly the Agent would never hire her again. Write little stories about a culture which was in imminent danger of annihilation? For months she had been in the thick of the battle. Retreat now to a safe bivouac while others remained at the front? It was here in the East that Indian policy was being made, not on a tiny reservation in Nebraska.

She envied Helen Hunt Jackson, whose fearless pen would always be freshly dipped to sear the public conscience. She envied Thomas Tibbles, who always was and always would be in the center of action. At the urging of Mrs. Jackson he had rushed through another book, a novel called *Hidden Power: A Secret History of the Indian Ring*, which would be published in June. Although actual incidents and names of persons and places were all fictionalized, it was a frank denunciation of the Indian Bureau. Beside the three books which Tibbles had produced in less than two years and Mrs. Jackson's monumental study, Bright Eyes' own little introductions and articles—even her speeches—seemed but toy darts compared with deadly stinging arrows. As the tour drew toward its end she became more and more restless and uncertain.

And then something happened, something so sudden and startling that it nearly took her breath away. *Thomas Tibbles asked her to marry him.*

He must have sensed her shock and amazement, for he loosed his urgent grasp of her two small hands and patted one of them with a gentleness unusual in such a robust man. As always when he was excited, his blue-gray eyes looked black as the pupils enlarged until they nearly covered the iris.

"My little dear, I'm sorry if I startled you. Don't answer now. Think it over. But—you must have known how I feel about you."

Had she known? She had tried so hard to explain to Frank that all Mr. Tibbles' small personal attentions had been but the customary gallantries of a Waxe gentleman or fatherly expressions of affection. Certainly they had been before his wife died. But—since? Had she been trying equally hard to convince herself? And—had she really wanted to believe it? Now, even while her mind felt frozen with startled incredulity, her blood leaped and raced in a most disquieting fashion. Had she feared—or hoped—that this very thing might happen?

There followed days of hard self-searching. Marriage! She had long since given up the idea. For she knew she belonged irrevocably to two cultures. She was too much Waxe to find complete satisfaction in life with most Indians, far too much Indian to live compatibly with most white men. But Thomas Tibbles, like herself, was an embodiment of the same two cultures. Did that mean that they could be compatible in a permanent relationship? The fact that he was fifteen years her senior was unimportant. Indians were accustomed to older men marrying much younger women. Nor was the presence of what Waxes termed "sexual attraction" an essential. Mates were often chosen by Indian fathers for their daughters, and such marriages were often more successful than one like Frank's, where the lovesick youth had hidden in the grass by the spring to play lovesongs to his sweetheart on the flute.

She needed no study of logic to weigh Thomas Tibbles' proposal with a coolness and maturity of judgment which considered its every aspect. Was it opportunity—or temptation—or pitfall—or destiny?

A life of excitement, of struggle, such as the last two years had been. . . . She hated excitement, yet what could have been done without it? A chance to continue the battle for justice in places of power and authority—yes, and of bitter personal assault. Possible submergence in a dominating personality. . . . Remember that uneasiness she had felt at their first meeting, as if her whole identity as well as her small hand could be swallowed up in his huge grasp?

In the end there was only one question: How could she serve her people best? As Bright Eyes, as Susette La Flesche, or as Mrs. Thomas Tibbles? Pondering this long and carefully, she gave her answer.

4

Never had spring on the reservation seemed more beautiful, family more beloved, home more desirable. Yet she felt not the slightest regret for her decision. It was a time of awakening, of adventure, of new life. The corridor above the Smoky Waters was alive with wings. On the bottoms the rich brown soil was feathered with new green. And Rosalie, ripe with the fulfillment of her first year of marriage, was having a baby.

Rosalie and her husband, Ed Farley had been living at the Mission, working in the boarding school, now under the auspices of the Presbyterian Board of *Home* Missions, since Nebraska had become a state. Under Father Hamilton's guidance a church had been formally organized, and both Rosalie and Frank, who was an elder in the church, taught in the Sunday School. For some time Rosalie had been one of the two women teachers in the school, and Ed had been the industrial teacher. Now, however, the Farleys' connection with the school had come to an end, and they had moved to a small house near the Agency. Frank, anxious to secure Ed's position at the school, was both indignant and frustrated when Mr. Partch, the Superintendent, refused him the job, explaining in his letters to Dr. Lowrie that it was not wise to have him as principal, since he was married. Fuming, idle, still caught in the snare of his unsuccessful marriage, Frank was becoming increasingly morose and purposeless. The knowledge of Susette's plans only aggravated his unhappiness. His dislike of Tibbles, sparked on the Eastern tour of 1879 and 1880, had not diminished.

However, the rest of the family gave hearty approval. Joseph, who had never been easy about his daughter's unorthodox and recently unchaperoned journeys, gave his relieved consent. "Uncle" Two Crows was equally agreeable. The three women of the household, having almost given up hope for this normal development, were overjoyed.

In fact, the news was received with elation by the whole tribe. Thomas Tibbles, savior of the Poncas, one of the few white men ever to espouse the cause of justice for the Indian, was a hero. The two tribal factions—Joseph's Young Men's Party and the conservative Chiefs Party—for the moment forgot their differences. Their champion was to become one of themselves. He would continue to fight for their rights. Already he had accomplished one miracle. Perhaps he would achieve another, bring to an end this terrible uncertainty and compel the Great Council

282

in Washington to pass the bill which would assure them possession of their lands forever.

To Bright Eyes' great relief Frank would not be obliged to attend her wedding. Senator Kirkwood, who had become acquainted with his ability as interpreter during the hearings of the previous winter, had just become Secretary of the Interior. He now offered the young Indian a position as copyist in the Department of Indian Affairs. Frank was jubilant. In June he left for Washington, glad to be relieved of responsibility, both as husband and father and as brother of the bride. He was entering not only a new life but what was to be a long and distinguished public career.

As the wedding day approached, Susette felt a bit remote from the whole proceeding, as if it were happening to someone else. A few of her women friends in the East had insisted on providing her wedding dress. She fingered its soft fabric of wool challis, its elaborate ruffles, laces, tucks, furbelows, with wonder, not untinged by faint regret. Secretly she shared the Oldest Grandmother's disapproving exclamations and sad shake of the head.

"*Na he!* Soft, yes, but not like an *unonzhin* of finest doeskin! And not a proper robe for a bride. How well I remember my own wedding tunic, all embroidered with dyed quill work and fringed, made by my mother, the daughter of the great chief Blackbird. And no white man's gibberish was there for me! I was wedded as an Indian woman should be, mounted on a pony and led by four old men to the lodge of my husband. *Dho*, and did not my husband boast through all the tribe that his bride bore on her flesh the 'mark of honor'! Not that I would want you to be wearing it, my little one. Those days are long past."

The dress was beautiful, from its high lace collar at the neck to its four-tiered ruffles which swept the floor. The tight-buttoned bodice with its long V-shaped wedge of fine lace flared into a hip-length jacket, its long sleeves edged with multiple trimmings of leaflike appliqués, ruffles, and lace. A wide panel of lace decorated the front of the skirt, which was draped at the sides into voluminous folds, caught up at the back to form a mass of graceful flounces, ending in a sweeping train. Other bands of lace edged the train, the folds, the jacket, the wrists, and lengths of silk ribbon peeped from beneath the flounces.

"Much too fine," said Susette, almost in shame, amending silently, "much too Waxe."

"So small," marveled sixteen-year-old Lucy a bit enviously, her head already buzzing with plans for her own marriage to an Omaha named Noah Leaming.

It was small indeed, fitting Susette's five-foot slenderness to perfection. Many decades later its age-yellowed fabrics would fit without the slightest alteration the childish contours of Thomas Tibbles' great-granddaughter, aged thirteen who would pose in it for a picture.

The wedding took place in the chapel of the Mission on July 23, 1881, the officiating clergyman being Reverend S. N. D. Martin, missionary to the Winnebagoes. Susette had only one regret, that Father Hamilton did not perform the ceremony. But at the time Joseph was having one of his occasional disagreements with his old friend, and Susette yielded to her father's wishes. The misunderstanding, as usual, would be shortlived. A few months later, and the beloved missionary would have been everybody's choice.

"The lion and the lamb," at least one of the witnesses must have thought, seeing the two standing side by side—the strapping groom with his leonine head and mane of graying hair, his wisp of a bride half lost in her laces and furbelows. But it was by no means a mating of strength and weakness. The huge hand enfolding the small one was indescribably gentle, and there was certainly no sign of meekness in the bride's shining eyes.

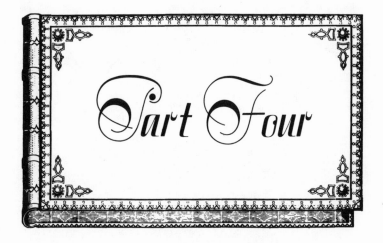

Part Four

1

Now that she was Mrs. Thomas Tibbles, the old problem of conflicting identities should have been solved. But, no. Even her name, most superficial of all the confusing elements, continued its ironic ambivalence. To her Indian family and close friends, she was now invariably "Susette." Indeed, "civilized" names were rapidly taking the place of Indian ones among younger members of the tribe. But to her Waxe husband she would always be "Bright Eyes." And Bright Eyes she was to the woman who arrived in Omaha in September 1881.

Alice C. Fletcher, the ethnologist, had kept Tibbles to his promise. His half-hearted "sometime" had become "now." Recognizing a determination equal to his own, he assembled supplies for camping, preparing to give this city-bred Easterner the taste of authentic Indian life she hungered for.

"I'll give her just two nights in a tent," he told Bright Eyes. "Well, maybe three. Then we'll bring her back to Omaha, put her in a hotel, and ship her back on the first train to Boston."

Bright Eyes only smiled and zestfully prepared for a long spell of traditional Indian living. She remembered Miss Fletcher's softly curved gentleness, but also her firm lips and snapping eyes. Not for nothing had some of the anthropologist's friends dubbed her "Your Majesty" because of her likeness to Queen Victoria.

After some weeks at the Mission Tibbles and Bright Eyes had moved to his house in Omaha, where he was earning a meager living with freelance writing, mostly for his former paper. A respite financed by this Eastern scholar, sufficiently prosperous to have made recent studies in Europe, was not unwelcome. But T.H., as both Bright Eyes and her family had soon learned to call her new husband, expected to be back home in a few days. The letters of recommendation Miss Fletcher brought with her from the Secretary of War, the Secretary of the Interior, the Postmaster General, and some reputable scientists did little to reduce his skepticism.

However, by the time they reached the Omaha reservation three days later skepticism had given place to reluctant respect. In spite of two days of solid rain, a sodden tent, and soggy food, Miss Fletcher remained cheerfully immune to discouragement. They took her to Rosalie's house near the Agency, and Bright Eyes sensed immediately a rapport of attraction between the two women. She brought Mary and Joseph to meet the visitor, and presently some of the leading members of the tribe came with their wives to call on her. With Bright Eyes acting as interpreter and guide, she returned their visits, seeming pefectly at home whether in houses, lodges, or tipis. She asked no questions, merely evinced friendliness, admired babies, devoured the constant offerings of food with apparent relish, and, if her keen eyes were noting every detail, her curiosity was unobtrusive. At first the people were reluctant to talk. Then— "Why are you here?" someone was bold enough to ask.

"I came to learn," she replied, "if you will let me, something about your tribal organization, your social customs, tribal rites, traditions and songs. I want to listen. And," she added simply, "I want to see if there is any way I can help you."

Listen . . . help . . . words as potent as "Open Sesame." People from outside did not usually come to listen. They came to tell. And *did* they need help! Faces immediately brightened. The men began talking, so long and so fast that Bright Eyes became exhausted interpreting. They told of their troubles. Their "land papers" given by the Great Father were not valid. They might be driven away "Toward the Heat" at any moment. What they needed were "strong papers." Could she help get them?

The little woman looked competent as well as sympathetic. "Bring me your 'land papers,'" she told them. "Let each one come prepared to tell me about your home and the size of land you have under cultivation. And come soon."

The news spread like wildfire. Each one who had papers brought them. She spent days recording each man's story of his struggle to cultivate his land. Then she began the far more difficult task of framing a petition to be sent to Congress.

Meanwhile, having won the people's confidence, she listened. Learning her interest in their history, customs, songs, rites—things most Waxes were anxious only to deride and suppress—they could not talk enough. Women brought her gifts, wooden bowls, horn spoons, thread sinews, tunics of buckskin beautifully embroidered with porcupine quills, treasures long hoarded in their parfleche cases. Even the old men, jealous of their tribal secrets, exhibited their sacred relics, revealed ancient mysteries, told the stories of "beginnings," sang their ceremonial songs. At night many gathered about a campfire, Bright Eyes and the visitor sharing a buffalo robe, while a number of Joseph's "citizens' party" stood or sat on the grass. They talked of the Great Father, President Garfield, recently shot and now fighting for his life.

"If they had sent him to us," said Kaga Amba, who had recently returned from Washington, "we could have cured him."

"If a man lives until the fourth day after he has received a dangerous wound," Joseph explained, "we think he is sure to get well, and we call that fourth day by a name which means 'the walking day,' because an Indian doctor makes his patient get up then and walk at least a step or two."

Others in the group began telling of cases where men of the Indian medicine societies had saved limbs which "the white doctors would have cut off," healed desperate wounds. But always, in every group, the talk would swing back to land titles.

The camping trip desired by the Eastern visitor had only started. Early one morning T.H., Bright Eyes, and the ethnologist set out in a light spring wagon drawn by two ponies on a journey which was to take them hundreds of miles to the north and west through what T.H. described later as "a steady series of rainstorms, broken whiffletrees, muddy roads, balky spells of a pony, thunderstorms during our night camping, and winds which burned our ethnologist's face to a blister.

"But," he added with what must have been sheepish wonderment, "that city-bred lady stood everything without one complaint."

With them on a third pony went Wajapa, the best possible choice for a responsible guide and companion. Now in his early forties, highly respected in the tribe, knowledgeable of Indian history and customs, he became for Miss Fletcher a rare source of information. To the children of Joseph he had always been Winegi, Uncle, and to their children for the next quarter century he would be Itigon, Grandfather. A pity, thought Bright Eyes, for such a specimen of Indian excellence to be saddled with the Waxe name of Ezra Freemont! But he had his own means of jolly retaliation. To Miss Fletcher's delight he gave her an Indian name from his own eagle family, describing the sweeping flight of the eagle high in the air. Bright Eyes tried in vain to translate it.

"How about 'Highflyer'?" suggested T.H. teasingly. And in spite of the ethnologist's chagrin Highflyer she remained, not unfittingly, for the rest of the trip.

They camped at the lower ford of the Niobrara, where the river was narrow and interspersed with islands, but with a frighteningly swift current and many shallows and quicksands. Soon after pitching camp they looked up the river toward the safer ford and saw a colorful caravan, men, women, and children, all in gay colors, bright against the brown prairie and river. On they came, in wagons and on ponies, Standing Bear, happily beaming, in the lead. His whole section of the tribe had come to meet them. The travelers must come across, he insisted, and have a meal in the new Ponca settlement. Wajapa stayed with the tent; Bright Eyes, T.H., and Highflyer mounted Standing Bear's wagon. Over the treacherous quicksands they rode, water at one time swelling almost to their knees, Standing Bear lashing the plunging horses until at last they reached firm ground. Though the chief's house was not yet finished, he served them a meal in his tent. Then the whole group assembled in a big shed to hear T.H. explain to them the final settlement of the tribe's affairs in Washington.

Tazahba drove them to the lower ford in his wagon, taking them over the first swift channel in a boat, then leaving them for Wajapa to carry them across in another boat which had been standing on the shore in the morning. But Wajapa stood helpless, shouting that the boat had been taken away. A predicament indeed! Stranded on an island in mid-river, with a long stretch of shallows and quicksand between them and the shore, and a chilly night coming on! Bright Eyes looked furtively at Highflyer. Surely this would end her enthusiasm for grass-roots research! But the visitor's eyes were still sparkling. "Well!" she said cheerfully. "What do we do now? Start wading?"

Tazahba appeared behind them, having suddenly decided that he wanted to make sure of their safe arrival in camp. Then Wajapa waded across. It was decided that the two women should be transported piggy-back. Tazahba, the taller of the two Indians, took Highflyer. Bright Eyes and T.H. were perhaps halfway across when she gave a sudden scream.

"Te unahe! Te unahe!" she shouted to Tazahba.

The camp was on fire! Fear of quicksands had been enough to inspire haste. Now the three men struggled with desperate urgency through the impeding water. By the time the two women were set down Wajapa was beating at the fire with a saddle blanket. It was soon extinguished, but much valuable equipment was lost. One more calamity for a trip which had seemed doomed to mishaps, especially for Wajapa. His pony, badly gored by a cow, had been left behind at the Santee Agency, so he had been obliged to make the last part of the journey on foot. Now, to his disgust, Standing Bear offered to lend, not give him a horse to continue the trip.

"He's no true Indian at all," Wajapa grumbled. "When did a traveler ever lose his horse by accident and come to an Indian friend without being *given* a horse!"

T.H. patiently tried to explain that Standing Bear's act was in full accordance with white men's customs. And wasn't Wajapa himself trying to live as nearly as possible like white men—

dress like them, cultivate his farm, live in a house, educate his children? And wasn't one of the Indian's greatest deterrents to progress his age-old custom of giving—horses to friends and strangers alike, possessions when a relative died, food to anyone and everyone whether you had enough for yourself and your family or not? But Wajapa was not convinced. Retreating to a solitary place, he yielded himself to that motionless, uncommunicative state which was as much an inheritance of traditional Indian custom as that of promiscuous giving, and which T.H. liked to call "the dumps."

So great was Bright Eyes' sympathy that she almost wished she could join him. For the first time since her marriage she sensed a gulf between herself and this man she had married. Of course he would feel as he did about giving. He was a Waxe. How could he possibly understand a communal loyalty which placed hospitality to strangers above even duty to family, which made an Indian share his last ounce of corn with another who was hungry, give until he had nothing left? Indians must learn the white man's way, she supposed, become selfish, in order to survive, but she felt an irreparable sense of loss.

It was this same traditional generosity which made them leave the Poncas. An Indian must place food before his guests whether they were hungry or surfeited, and the Poncas were poor. With every family extending constant invitations and compelled to set food before the visitors, which etiquette prescribed must be either eaten or taken away, their meager supplies would soon be exhausted. The party decided they must move on.

Tazaḣba went with them, knowing the language of the Brûlé Sioux whom they intended to visit next. He brought with him also a good Indian tent, which would not only shed water better than canvas but accommodate a fire inside, with its smoke rising straight through the hole at the top . . . and an even better treasure, his wife. Competent, far defter than any man at a hundred and one jobs—pitching tent, cooking, washing, driving ponies—always cheerful and smiling, facing cold, rain, wind, burning sun, all with the same equanimity and with no protection but her thin calico dress, she mitigated many of the hardships of their next six weeks of camping.

"Gaha," they called her much to her delight, an honorable title something like "Grandmother."

2

It was like living her childhood over again, thought Bright Eyes, as night after night they took their same places in the tent, listening to the stories and legends told by Tazahba, who, Wajapa declared, was the greatest of the three Ponca medicine men. The Highflyer listened with rapt attention while Bright Eyes interpreted, taking voluminous notes. She had an excellent chance for research that first week, for it rained days on end.

"Because you tossed some salt into the fire," accused Tazahba, "and made the Rabbit angry." But when he began invoking the Rabbit for forgiveness, Wajapa promptly made fun of his superstition, and Tazahba, who was a modest man, stopped his praying immediately.

It took the party a week to travel the 150 miles to Fort Niobrara. Their intention was to visit several Indian tribes. Runners had been sent ahead by the Omahas to the Poncas, and by the Poncas to the Sioux at the Rosebud Agency, to prepare the way. At the fort they were joined by Thigh, a Sioux Indian who would be their guide, and again rain and cold kept them huddled for hours in the tent around the fire. The three Indians talked and talked, Tazahba interpreting between Thigh and Wajapa, Bright Eyes relaying part of the conversation to T.H. and Highflyer. She was impressed anew by Wajapa's wisdom.

"I know that I myself can never really become like a white man," he said. "It wasn't for my own good that I cut off my hair, laid aside my Indian clothes, and put on white man's dress. I did it for my children, for they can and must become like the whites. If they don't, they'll die of misery and want."

It would take courage for Wajapa to hold to the new ways on their visit to the Brûlé Sioux, who disapproved of discarding the old customs and traditions. He could easily, thought Bright Eyes, put on blanket and breechcloth just for a few days, and thus be welcomed as a good Indian and probably be given horses and other gifts in abundance. But he rode north dressed in coat, trousers, and hat, just like T.H., as firm in his refusal to compromise his convictions as Joseph had been. Bright Eyes' affection for her "uncle" was heightened by a new admiration.

A Brûlé Sioux, tall and impressive in his blue blanket, came to meet them. They were taken to a large tent with a blazing fire in the center. "This is your house," said the Sioux, whose name as Ausapi. Almost immediately came the invitation, "Come and eat."

In a little log hut each of them was served with two or three pounds of boiled beef, three or four big biscuits, and a pint of very strong coffee. By now well acquainted with Indian etiquette, Highflyer regarded the mountain with horror. Just two hours before the party had dined on the plain.

"Tell the woman," said Gaha in a low voice to Bright Eyes, "that she need not eat it all. She can put what she doesn't want into my dish."

Back in the big tent they were soon invited to another feast, at the house of Ausapi's son-in-law. T.H. looked doubtfully at their belongings, heaped together on the ground.

"Is it safe," he asked, "to leave all those things lying there unguarded?"

Ausapi looked grieved. "There's not another white man within a day's journey," he replied, "except the Agent and his employees, and they never come over here."

T.H. felt duly rebuked. Though only an hour had elapsed since the last feast, they departed for another—the same food, the same quantities. Fortunately Gaha went along to absorb the surplus. After that Tazahba managed to explain without insult to their hosts that white people, being somewhat infirm, could not eat more than three meals a day, and the Indians of the party thereafter acted as their substitutes.

There was threat of trouble at the Rosebud, but not from the Brûlé Sioux. Highflyer was appalled by some of the injustices observed—lack of schools, no work at the sawmill, 6,700 Indians camped in uncomfortable canvas tents on sandy, barren land. She wrote notes, talked. It was inevitable that reports of her activities should reach the Agent, sole arbiter in that vast tract of land, with government troops at his disposal. T.H.

begged her to talk publicly only of her scientific research, but she refused to heed his warnings. One of the persons she talked with most frankly was a half-breed in the Agent's employ.

They were invited—or was it summoned?—to call at the Agency. The buildings were on a high sandy hill surrounded by a stockade. To speak to the Agent any Indian, even a chief, must stand outside and talk through an opening in the door. A white man came, unlocked the gate, and directed them to the office. But Highflyer had other intentions. The Agent's house was the proper place for him to receive a lady. To Ausapi's horror she walked straight to it and knocked—but in vain. She was forced to go to the office. Leading the way in, she introduced her companions.

"I have heard of you," the Agent said to Tibbles with marked disapproval. When Highflyer made some pleasant observation about the weather, he responded with doubtful humor, "I regulate everything here except the weather."

However, when she presented him with letters of introduction from some powerful friends in Washington, he changed his attitude, welcomed her cordially, and even gave her a key to one of the stockade gates. Any danger there might have been was at least for the present averted.

Later Ausapi told T.H. that the summons to the Agency had been a stern order, not an invitation. His fear of trouble unexpectedly averted, he wiped the sweat from his face with profound relief. Though he was a chief in the tribe and the Agency had been there for many years, this was the first time, he confessed, that he had ever set foot in the Agent's office.

Not only did Wajapa appear in "citizens'" dress throughout the visit, but at a big council of leaders in the band of young Spotted Tail, son of "Old Spot," he boldly ignored Tazahba's warnings by setting forth his views on the necessity for citizenship, land titles, and court decisions. Though the polite "Hows!" of approval were markedly unenthusiastic, Indian hospitality stood the test, and the crisis passed. Highflyer, less controversial for once in her speech, received a loud chorus of "Hows!"

During the days among the Brûlés she utilized her opportunities for study to the full. At a formal war dance in full dress performed for her benefit, even the prospect of a third huge feast within four hours failed to curb her enthusiasm.

"Oh, let's stay for another round," she kept begging. "I must study this thing."

A funeral some miles out on the prairie offered another opportunity. They sat in the place of special honor in the big tent lighted by a glowing pine-stick fire and listened to the chant of the official mourners, saw the dead man's horse and dog shot, all his property—blankets, clothing, tools, wagon, harness—given away, even the tent stripped of its contents, with nothing left to the family but the poles and tent cloth.

"You see," said T.H. afterward, "why white men insist that Indians have to get rid of some of these old customs before they can make any progress. This wholesale giving has to stop."

Again Bright Eyes felt that sense of estrangement. He was right, of course. Had not she herself felt puzzled and a little resentful when all of Louis' possessions had been given away? And yet—oh, let not the time come when they would become like so many of the Waxes, every man for himself, not for the good of the tribe! The loss would be irreparable.

No detail was too small for Highflyer's scientific interest. She kept Bright Eyes busy every spare moment of the day and often into the night, interpreting, explaining, telling stories, reminiscing. She was even trying to learn the Omaha language, stunned and baffled by its complexity of grammar—its use of particles as prefixes and suffixes, its shifting of accents, its modification of both verbs and nouns to correspond with the gender both of the person speaking and of the person spoken to.

"But—it's worse than Latin!" she marveled. "And then we white people think all your talk is either 'Ughs!' or smoke signals!"

A runner appeared with a secret message inviting T.H. to come and visit Sitting Bull. The chief had heard the party planned to visit the Yankton Sioux, across the river from Fort Randall, where he was being held a prisoner. It was a long and difficult trip, 140 miles through the wilderness. It took the party a week, for they were snowed in two days. They could buy no corn on the way, and there was not enough fodder for the ponies. Twice they had to camp without wood. But the gentle, city-bred woman from the East made no complaint. She might be a "blueblood" from Boston, but there was fiery red stuff in her veins.

The party was well received at Fort Randall, and T.H. was permitted to hold interviews with Sitting Bull at the camp where he was kept under strict guard. Bright Eyes went with him, interpreting Tibbles' words to Tazahba, who in turn translated them into Sioux for Sitting Bull. The latter told his pathetic story, his resistance to the white man, his exile in Canada, his return and surrender, in order to keep his people from starving.

"All I ever wanted," he said simply, "was to be left alone in the land God had given the Lakota."

He gave Bright Eyes a photograph of himself, saying, "My daughter, when we are relieved from this imprisonment and have our own reservation, come and see me again. Then I shall be prepared to make you the presents which your work for the Indians and your rank demand."

To their surprise he took a pencil and wrote his name on the bottom of it. The chief did not really know how to write, but he had asked someone to write his name, "Sitting Bull," and had copied it so many times that he could make the letters perfectly.

This was their last stop, and they returned to the Omaha reservation, where Alice Fletcher continued to collect data for the petition to be sent to Congress. It was finally framed and signed, each signature accompanied by the amount of land cultivated, stock owned, and persons dependent for support, together with personal remarks. Joseph was among the signers. His statement was the longest of all.

"It seems as though the government pushes us back," he said in part. "It makes us think the government regards us as unfit to be as white men. . . . We ask for titles for our children's sakes. . . . The reason you do not look upon us as men is because we have not law, because we are not citizens. We are strangers in the land where we were born. We want the law that we may be regarded as men. . . ."

On December 31 Alice Fletcher sent the papers to Senator Morgan of Alabama.

"I am sending a petition from fifty-five Omahas," she said in an accompanying letter, "asking that titles be given them to the lands on which they have worked and homesteaded. But for failure of this year's crops, which has caused many Indians to go trapping, there would have been more signers. One hundred families are away. About 200 men are working on their claims. . . . The signers stand as the true leaders of the people. . . . I feel keenly that the cold black lines cannot give you the picture. The little log house, hand made by a man who had not been taught by theory or observation how to rear a house . . . yet there it stands, and within it the mother sits, gathering her children close about her, while the fire crackles a sympathetic accompaniment to the father's story while he talks about his land, how he fell down every few feet when he first held the plow! No one showed him how to hold it. How his pony died in the furrows, too weak to pull the plow through sod. The fire that swept away everything, leaving nothing but the blankets in which the family fled. Open-eyed astonishment that cutting a tree should make it grow. Some weeks ago Indians gathered in the chapel consecrated this petition to God. Each day they come back to pray for titles to their land."

On January 12 Senator Morgan wrote that he had approved the petition and presented it to a Congressional Committee.

"Cannot my name be put on?" pleaded many of the returning hunters.

All that winter Miss Fletcher and the Omahas waited for a further response. Scarcely a day passed but some Indian would ride over the snowy hills to ask, "Any news from Washington?" Every day there was the same answer. "None." But Highflyer was not idle. She gathered some of the signers into a night school at the Mission, marveling at their dogged persistence as they grappled with arithmetic and tried to learn to read and write. Tibbles, Bright Eyes, and their friends in the East had a new and powerful ally. She was determined to fight the battle to its finish.

3

The Tibbles house in Omaha was not home. For both Susette and T.H. it was like standing outside the walls of a theater when an exciting drama was being played inside. All their interest and suspense centered in the reservation. Then, too, Tibbles' young daughters, May and Eda, were with them now. This had been their mother's house. Her gentle presence seemed almost as pervasive as her furniture, her personal belongings. Susette could sense the girls' resentment at this usurpation of her place by another woman, especially a woman of another culture. For a year after their mother's death they had lived with her beloved sister who, "for Amelia's sake," had spoiled them with tender ministrations. The year at Elizabeth had scarcely made them more amenable to parental discipline. When T.H. suggested that they sell the house and move to the reservation, Susette was unutterably relieved.

They moved into a house near the Agency, not far from Rosalie. Though the girls' sullen aloofness was still obvious and painful, at least Susette could now relate to them in her own world. The close relationships of family helped. Rosalie attracted all children with her warm personality, and her year-old Caryl, joined in July 1882 by twins, John Francis and Joseph, could not fail to soften the resistance of two adolescent girls. The return of Marguerite and Susan that same year helped even more to bridge the gulf. Susan, only a few years older than Eda, now age fourteen, became a well-loved companion, and Marguerite—

"You may tell your young folks," Eda was to write to Marguerite many years later, "that their mother was the most graceful thing I ever set eyes on, and the most beautiful."

Mary, accepting her daughter's stepchildren with the same largesse of love as her own grandchildren, was always there to soothe and reconcile. Although she did not speak English, little murmurs and gestures were sufficient to express affection and understanding. May especially would remember her quiet intervention when tempers flared and tensions between herself and Susette came close to snapping, when Mary's gentle touch and warm smile said more plainly than words, "Don't mind. It will be all right. We all love you."

That year of 1882 the reservation teemed with excitement. Dr. Dorsey was there, busily revising his notes in preparation for publishing his exhaustive study of "Omaha sociology." Two

Crows was assisting him, also Joseph, who the preceding year had gone to Washington to aid the ethnologist with similar research. Several of the younger members of the tribe were preparing to go to Hampton in the fall. Joseph was having another difference of opinion with Father Hamilton, who had become involved in Frank's quarrel with his wife's father, Prairie Chicken.

But births, quarrels, histories, even education, were nothing beside the pending legislation which would determine the fate of the tribe. A bill had been introduced in Congress for allotting the Omahas lands and issuing them patents. Miss Fletcher had gone herself to Washington and made many addresses before congressional committees, spoken in churches, in the parlors of leading citizens. But weeks passed, and no news came. However, though the suspense was agonizing, there was hope at last for a settlement. A new Commissioner in Washington, together with a new Secretary of the Interior, opened possibilities for a less rigid Indian policy. Agent George W. Wilkinson was cooperative. He wrote to Hiram Price, the Commissioner, that the Omahas "are a steady and reliable set of men who are trying to do what is right."

The bill passed both houses of Congress on August 7, 1882, and became law. For the first time since the beginning of the Ponca tragedy Susette felt the burden of worry lifted. She agreed with T.H. that Allotment was only a step in the solution of tribal problems, but at least the Omahas would not be driven away "Toward the Heat." T.H., strangely enough, did not seem to share her relief. Nothing could really be achieved, he maintained, until the Indians became citizens. Rosalie, almost as determined in temperament as her brother-in-law, did not agree. Laws did not change people's habits of thinking and living, and she felt that most of the tribe were not yet ready for the responsibilities of citizenship. To Susette's dismay, this disagreement was only the beginning of a rapidly widening rift between T.H. and her family.

A new spirit of hope and enterprise pervaded the tribe. The Commissioner of Indian Affairs reported that year that 119 frame houses were occupied by Omaha families, and that among the 1,193 members of the tribe 250 were accustomed to speak English and others were able to read it. Alice Fletcher's concern for the Omahas was only stimulated by the passing of the bill. Immediately she set to work on another project, sending more young people of the tribe to Hampton and Carlisle. She persuaded General Armstrong, director of Hampton Institute, and the Secretary of the Interior to open the school to married couples. Returning to the Omaha reservation that fall, she persuaded three such couples to go to Hampton, among them Minnie and Phillip Stabler and Lucy and Noah La Flesche, Noah having taken the name of La Flesche after their marriage. She herself accompanied the group to the school in Virginia.

The government also agreed to educate a number of Omaha boys whom she would select, but, when she rounded up the designated number, through a tangle of red tape the government refused to accept six of them. Nothing daunted, she went on a tour and raised the necessary funds herself in two months. Gracefully the government yielded the point, assuring her that "now you have raised the money, the Omaha boys will stay at Carlisle."

Susette knew many of these boys. Some had gone to the Mission School. Others she had taught at the agency school. Many came to ask her questions about life in the East. But one young man who came to her house one day was almost a stranger. She knew who he was, Thomas Sloan, and he lived with his grandmother, Margaret, an Omaha woman, who had been given an allotment back about 1870. His father, like her own, was part French and part Omaha. Her heart leaped strangely at sight of him. "Lightning Eye," she thought instantly, remembering the son of Standing Bear. They did not look alike, but in this youth's eyes there were the same fires of impatience, of fearlessness, even of potential anger. Again she felt that peculiar thrill of kinship. This youth also would never be patient, unresisting, in the face of injustice.

Like the others, he asked many eager questions, yet not the usual ones—what was life like in the East, what did people wear and eat, what did their houses look like?—but: What are these laws you and your husband are trying to get passed? What are the provisions of this Allotment Act? Is it going to be a good thing for the tribe? Why do the Waxes say we can no longer sing our songs and dance? What will become of all our songs and rites and traditions? What can we do so they will not be lost? Who will be our leaders after the old men are gone?

Susette answered him as well as she could, yet she knew he was still unsatisfied. What would the Eastern schools do to him? Would they give him answers—or raise more questions? She was not the only one who wondered, for all Indians, Omahas and others, did not regard this exposure to white men's ways in boarding schools as progress.

"I have seen the results of such schools," commented Sitting Bull in that same year. "The children who return are neither white nor Indian."

And a decade earlier another Indian had written to the Superintendent of Indian Affairs in Washington, "I feel that I belong to both races and yet to neither, and by turns am wronged, scorned, and rejected by each. In short, I am between two fires, and cannot get over either."

Two people—and yet neither! How well Susette could understand this conflict, which had been the very essence of her own life! And there was conflict even in her assessment of the conflict. For, while she fully affirmed the imperative of education for her people in the white man's culture, she knew well the price it must exact in lost identity. Bright Eyes . . . Susette. Never completely the one, never both. And now, she discovered, she had acquired a third personality, with possibilities of deep conflict both with the other two and with itself. For she was also Mrs. Thomas Tibbles.

4

In April 1883 Alice Fletcher was appointed a special agent to carry out the provisions of the new law allotting to the Omahas their lands in severalty. Frank La Flesche was coming with her to act as her interpreter and assistant.

The Omahas, overjoyed, awaited her arrival with eagerness. "When will she come? . . . Soon?" they kept asking Rosalie and Susette. Some of the older members of the tribe met in council. How could they best express their gratitude to this white woman who had labored for their cause with such success? They decided to pay her one of their highest tribal honors, perform for her the ancient calumet, or adoption, ceremony, breaking their traditions by giving it informally.

She came on May 12. The people were called to assemble, and many came together in a big earth lodge. The calumets, sacred pipes decorated with duck heads, were set up in their appointed places. When Miss Fletcher entered as the honored guest, the people fell silent. Three men rose and picked up the calumets and the lynx skin on which they rested; then, standing side by side, they sang softly the opening song, after which, turning to face the people, they moved from right to left, singing a joyful song and waving the sacred pipes over the heads of all in the assembled circle.

"Song after song they sang for their friend," Frank reported long afterward, "of the joy and happiness that would follow when men learned to live together in peace. When the evening was over they told Miss Fletcher that she was free to study this or any other of their tribal rites."

A privilege indeed! Few white people had ever been accorded such an honor or the opportunity to delve with such detail into the history and culture of an Indian tribe. Dr. Dorsey's exhaustive study entitled "Omaha Sociology," at this time in preparation and to be incorporated in the *Third Annual Report of the Bureau of Ethnology, 1881–1882,* would be fittingly sequeled two decades later by the even more detailed *Twenty-seventh Annual Report, 1905–1906,* which devoted all of its nearly 700 pages to the study titled "The Omaha Tribe," written in collaboration by Alice C. Fletcher and Francis La Flesche.

Her combining of this tireless research with her allotment duties was well illustrated by a slip of paper preserved among records of the period. On one side was her official appointment as a Special Agent of the Indian Bureau and on the other the notes of a song "made by Big Tobacco." She managed also to spark many activities for the betterment of the tribe—starting night classes in English, encouraging the women to create handcrafts and plant flower gardens. In all of these projects the daughters of Joseph—Marguerite, who was now teaching at the Mission; Susan, fresh from her two years at Elizabeth; and of course Rosalie and Susette—were her ardent helpers.

The La Flesche family cooperated in another of Miss Fletcher's ambitions. Since the resettlement of the tribe in the 1850s they had occupied only the wooded hills in the eastern part of the reservation. Having traveled on the new railroad which ran along Logan Creek in the western section, Alice Fletcher had been impressed by the fertility of the Logan Valley, so much more suited to agriculture than the hills on the bluffs.

"Choose lots in the western section," she now urged. Most were reluctant to leave the familiar territory. Move again? Leave far behind their beloved hills and creeks, the river on which their ancestors had traveled for generations—above all, the council ring and sacred High Place? Mr. Partch and others at the Mission also looked at the change askance, fearing that their missionary activities might be curtailed. However, when she began her work of allotment in 1883, Miss Fletcher pitched her tent in the Logan Valley, a surveyor and Frank La Flesche with her, forcing the men to go there to choose their lands.

"See?" Here she could use visual persuasion. "Isn't this better for farming than your old lands among the hills and forests?"

Joseph and his family were among the first to choose allotments in the Logan Valley. A new town called Bancroft had been laid out in 1881 just south of the reservation line. The La Flesches, Farleys, Tibbles, and others of Joseph's Young Men's Party took sections to the north and a little to the east and west of this new village. But it was due as much to the influence of Miss Fletcher as to Joseph's example that others of the tribe followed.

One day as she and her assistants were running quarter section lines, they came on a man standing on a section mound. "This is my land," he announced firmly, with a broad possessive gesture.

After the surveyor had described the tract by section, township, and range, and Miss Fletcher had recorded it, she shook the man's hand and said, "I congratulate you. Now build a house, barn, and granaries and cultivate this land."

Looking straight into her face and still holding her hand, the man said, "We have had agents to manage our affairs, but none have offered advice. My people are not prone to follow the advice of women, but I shall follow yours."

As the allotments were made, each adult or older child was made fully acquainted with the position and extent of his land. Laws of property and legal descent were explained. Those relating to children's rights were especially difficult and essential for them to understand, since in Indian custom the claims of children were secondary to lateral relationships.

In the midst of these weeks in the Logan Valley tragedy struck. The gallant little Easterner, who had endured months of tent living, cold, snow, strange foods, rickety wagons, and quicksands, was struck suddenly with rheumatic fever. Realizing the seriousness of her condition, Frank sprang into action. He hitched a pair of horses to the only available wagon, placed a mattress on the floor, lifted her into this improvised ambulance, and started across the prairie at a galloping pace to the Agency sixty miles away. The mad drive in the springless wagon was for the patient excruciating agony.

There was a small hospital at the Agency with a young, inexperienced doctor in charge. Under his treatment she recovered, but the doctor started the exercise for her rehabilitation too soon. She fell and injured one leg so severely that until her death it would be fixed at the knee at a grotesque angle. That summer of 1883 she spent several months at the Mission from July to October, with eighteen-year-old Susan, who was an assistant teacher at the school, acting as her nurse. A misfortune? It certainly seemed so at the time, and she fumed with impatience, yet out of it came benefits to the Omahas which would more than compensate for both her suffering and the postponement of her work.

"I recall a young girl," she wrote years later, "who watched beside my bed when I lay ill among the Indians. She told me how she desired to study medicine, that she might instruct her Indian friends in the laws of health and minister to them in sickness. I determined as I saw her mental ability that she should have her wish."

The episode was only an unwelcome hiatus in the duties of her assignment. Presently she was back at work, living again in a tent, registering the allotments, spending long hours conversing with old men of the tribe, writing down songs, legends, rituals, collecting many of the numerous articles and sacred tribal objects which would later comprise the huge Omaha exhibits in the Peabody Museum at Harvard. It was due to the admiration and confidence she inspired in the tribe, as well as to Joseph's influence and Frank's persistent efforts, that in 1884 the first of her major contributions, the Sacred Tent of War with all its contents, became the property of the Museum. On June 6 she wrote to Frederic W. Putnam, its director:

"The Sacred Tent of War was vital to the autonomy of the tribe. Without it citizenship was impossible; it gave rank to the tribe among other tribes and caused the Omahas to be feared by their enemies and consulted by their friends. The act by the keepers of the ancient symbols is without parallel and was done with a sober appreciation that a new era is upon the people wherein these objects have no place. . . .

"Today Ma-ha-thin-ga . . . put his sacred charge into the keeping of the Museum. . . . 'These . . . have been in my family for many generations, no one knows how long. My sons have chosen a different path from that trodden by their fathers.' . . .

"It was late in the afternoon when we reached his lodge, the sun had set. He was alone in the fading light, taking a last look at the ancient belongings. He lifted them into the wagon and said, 'They are all there,' and turned away. We too turned and left as the round moon rose over the valley."

That month of June 1884 was indeed one of change for the Omahas. The formal signing of the allotments began on the fifth and was completed on the eighth. A ritual was made of the act. Each tribal member made his or her mark in the presence of witnesses chosen by the signer. Papers were issued to 1,179 members of the tribe, 564 males, 615 females. They were days of triumph. The Omahas were now secure in their lands. Never again could government say to them, "Go here" or "Go there," or drive them away like cattle, as the Poncas had been driven "Toward the Heat."

Yet there was as much sadness as triumph. The allotments were as symbolic of change as the departure of the Sacred Tent of War. The old tribal unity was gone. The ancient Indian concept of "each for all" had given way to the white man's concept of "every man for himself." Land, the gift of Wakonda, free to all, had become property, like a man's horses, his blanket, his leggings.

Susette, watching the procession of new landowners approaching the table, signing, leaving, felt the sadness outweigh the triumph. She was not the only one. Suddenly she became conscious of the figure of an old man standing on a hill overlooking the scene. As he lifted his arm, the crowd sensed the urgency and authority of his gesture and became silent. In a loud voice he began repeating the speech made by Big Elk years before after his return from Washington. "I bring to you news which it saddens my heart to think of. There is a coming flood which will soon reach us, and I advise you to prepare for it. . . ."

The words pounded like drums, stamped like hoof beats, to the sad and bitter end. "Now, my people, this is all I have to say. Bear these words in mind, and when the time comes think of what I have said."

As the words ceased, the silence became even more profound, as if every one in the crowd held his breath, as if even the land and the sky and the four winds had stopped to listen. Then the old man again lifted his hand and shouted in a still louder voice, "My friends, *the flood has come!*"

1

Luxury—poverty, exultation—despair, triumph—failure, life—death . . . the years of the eighties held them all in that constant imbalance of conflict.

Again and again during the early years of the decade Bright Eyes went East with T.H. for lecturing. Although emotions over the plight of the "poor Indians" had somewhat cooled with the solution of the specific Ponca problem, her appearance in a city invariably fanned the fires of public interest and provided fuel for the committee's less dramatic crusade for legislative action.

She was welcomed now by many as a *person*, not merely a symbol. Especially in Boston, her literary talent was recognized by her firm friends among the writers' group. Whittier, Lowell, Holmes, Louisa May Alcott, Edward Everett Hale—all were her loyal admirers. Dr. Hale gave luncheons and dinners in his home so that she could meet other writers. Her Indian stories in *St. Nicholas*, *Wide Awake*, and other children's magazines, illustrated by her own clever drawings, were gaining favorable attention.

But satisfaction in her own small literary success was nothing beside her fierce joy in what Helen Hunt Jackson was doing. In their sorrowful parting Mrs. Jackson had promised to write one more book in the hope of rousing the American people to the injustices done the Indians. Then she had gone to California, having secured a government appointment through Senator Hoar to investigate the conditions and needs of the mission Indians.

"I have an idea for the book!" she wrote joyously in the autumn of 1883. "It flashed into my mind just this morning. And it cries to be written immediately!"

She returned to New York on November 20, and on the first day of December started to write. The book progressed at lightning speed. When *Ramona* appeared, taking the country by storm, Bright Eyes was wildly happy. Surely this romantic and tragic story of injustice would touch people's hearts as no factual account like *A Century of Dishonor* could ever do!

But joy plummeted to the depths of sadness when a year later news came of Helen Jackson's death. Bright Eyes shut herself in her room and wept all day, then mourned the passing of her friend for weeks, grief locked in a tight shell of silence. It was one of the times when she would have liked to be all Indian, able to vent emotion in unrestrained wailing.

After these Eastern excursions they would return, almost penniless, to the reservation. In the summer of 1883, when the allotment was being made, the family camped in a tent on the banks of the Logan Creek, moving back to the Agency that winter. For some months Eda and May lived and studied at the Mission school, now a boarding school for girls only. By the next summer T.H. had built a small house on Susette's quarter section of prairie, sod but with a good tight roof. Later there would be a central frame of two stories, extended on either side by one-story parts made of sod, the main part with a window and a door in front, a window in the gable, and one window on the side.

That summer of 1884, living in the tiny sod house, the family were literally hungry. True, there was corn to eat, but T.H.'s huge crop did not sell for enough to pay the grocery bills. Prices were being cruelly manipulated in the East against all Western farmers, so that the corn they had raised so hopefully, corn for which people in the nation's cities were starving, had to be burned for fuel.

"It's the political juggling with money at Washington," T.H. explained bitterly to his daughters. "Don't blame me." Already he was gritting his teeth for a new struggle on behalf of the underdog, this time the farmer and the industrial worker, which less than ten years later would embroil him in politics.

Eda, sixteen, and May, fourteen, did not care who was to blame. They were hungry. Sickened by the very thought of another ear of corn, they found some fish hooks, crawled out on a squared log that bridged the swollen Logan Creek and sat with their legs dangling, hands tense on their lines, eyes glued to the white roil of water.

"A bite!" exclaimed May with the rapture of a miner unearthing a gold nugget. She landed the fish safely and laid it on the log while she rebaited her hook. Calmly it flopped back into the water. There were no more bites, and the girls went hungry to bed.

Poverty, even hunger, was the least of Susette's worries. That winter T.H. was often traveling, gone for many weeks in the East, and she was alone with the girls. No Marguerite and Susan now to bridge the gulf between them! Mr. and Mrs. Joshua Davis, active members of the Boston Committee, had furnished a scholarship for Marguerite to go to Hampton for further study, and Susan and eleven-year-old Carey had gone with her. Rosalie's section was across the Logan Creek. She and Ed had moved their little house there from near the Agency. With three children (little Joseph had died as an infant, but Mary was born in 1884) she had little time for visiting, and Susette sorely missed her sister's calm and sensible influence. Joseph, first to build a frame house on the reservation, had been also the first to build a house in the Logan Valley, but it was far up the creek and on the other side. Shut up in a tiny house far from family and neighbors, with two teenagers who obviously resented her presence, Susette felt as imprisoned by loneliness and frustration as by the snows which often buried the door and lower windows.

The girls' antagonism was not wholly the usual aversion to a stepmother. Susette was conscious of other wider gaps— culture, generation, temperament. She was too young to be their disciplining mother, too old to share their youthful bewilderment like an understanding sister. It was to Rosalie that they often went, crying over some misunderstanding with Susette. "Don't you care," she would comfort, freely dispensing the affection which the more reserved Susette was unable to express. "She did not mean it. She is tired. Just don't care."

Yet long afterward May would write of Susette in a letter to Marguerite, "I owe her a great deal. She taught me to love good literature and to scorn the sensational and crude. One beautiful thing, Eda and I did not know we were poor. We appreciated the great things that had come to Papa and Susette and felt in some way that we shared them."

Strangely enough, the cultural gap developed in the girls a sense not of pride but of inferiority! Conversation in the home stressed Indians, the injustices done them, their lofty ideas of Wakonda and their unity with nature, their past history. White people, as they saw or heard about them, were usually intolerant, unjust, many times dishonest. For months they nursed a sense of guilt and frustration in silence. Then to Susette's chagrin and amazement May one day blurted, "I wish I'd been born an Indian!" Hastily she and T.H. began inculcating in his daughters a sense of pride in their own white race.

Life for Susette was both easier and harder when T.H. was at home. Tensions in the household relaxed, for the girls adored their father. His strong mentality dominated the place, just as his huge body seemed to fill the tiny house. The isolated little house became the center of world events, of political action, of the legislation T.H. was helping to shape for Congress. Yet his presence inspired restlessness, not serenity. He was no more fitted to the life of a farmer, especially the slow painful drudgery of wresting fruition from unbroken prairie, than was she herself to those contests in the public arena which were his meat and drink. He was built to wrestle with ideas, not stubborn soil, and his favorite tools were the pen and tongue, certainly not the plow and hoe. As May was to comment shrewdly long afterward, it must have been a tragic anticlimax to his life of crowds and excitement to "spend his days following a plow up and down"! Sensing his discontent, Susette felt guilt as well as distress. Was the gift of land she had brought him asset or liability?

If his presence reduced tensions in the household, it heightened them in the family. T.H. did not approve of certain developments on the reservation, and said so. Especially did he disapprove of the Farleys' action in what was called "the pasture."

There were thousands of acres of Omaha land still unallotted after the work of Alice Fletcher, land to be held in common by the tribe both for advancing cultivation and for allotments to future generations, land which was rapidly being encroached upon by white settlers disdainful of the claims of mere "savages." White men had long been allowed to graze cattle on the reservation by paying a fee to the Agent. These cattle were allowed to roam at will, often encroaching on the cultivated fields of the Indians. Alice Fletcher, concerned with the use of the land as well as the allotments, mulled the problem. Why not fence in their crops? she suggested. But this was a strange idea not only to Indians but to all Westerners. And there were no stones for walls and few trees for rail fences. She thought again. Then why not fence in the cattle, have a cooperative grazing program? Let the Indians put in their cattle at no cost, outsiders who wished to put in their herds pay a fee. A manager might lease the land, put up the fences, pay rent to the tribe, and divide the profits between them and himself. The Agent, George Wilkinson, gave hearty approval. Ed Farley was given a twenty-year lease on the unallotted land, and "the pasture" became reality.

Thomas Tibbles was unalterably opposed to this cooperative venture, even more violently opposed to a plan of voluntary self-government which some of the Omahas, including Joseph and Rosalie, were promoting. Citizenship, he insisted hotly, must come first. Only when the Omahas were citizens could all these other problems be resolved. Soon he was in explosive disagreement not only with most of the La Flesche family but with Alice Fletcher, who had helped formulate the tentative plan.

Susette was torn between two loyalties. While strongly supporting T.H. in his efforts to win citizenship for Indians, she trusted Joseph's judgment implicitly and felt that the experimental plan for self-government might well offer training for the responsibility of citizenship. But the emotional stress was far greater than the mental. To be held in suspension between two cultures—that had been painful yet somehow external. But to be separated from family—it was like having one's vital organs torn apart!

2

After that difficult winter of 1884 Susette was more free to travel with T.H. Though she still shunned publicity and every appearance on a platform drained nearly every ounce of energy, the frequent trips East were a relief from the increasingly agonizing tensions.

In 1885 Eda and May were going to school in West Point, boarding themselves on provisions their father brought or, in his absence, running up debts at the grocer's.

"It was slim going," recorded Eda. "I prayed one night as I never prayed before, that we might go to Lincoln to prep school. Within a few days Dr. Taylor, who used to be doctor at the Agency, was passing. We poured out our troubles to him. He told us his wife was taking university students to board, and he thought we might be able to help her enough to work our way." It was an arrangement which continued for several years, most happily.

Bright Eyes (for in the East she would always be known by her Indian name) continued to tell her story. Her beauty, her lovely voice, her impassioned sincerity aroused sympathy wherever she went. Though there were seldom the massed audiences which had been keyed to white-hot fervor by the Ponca tragedy, the lectures were well attended, and the committees in Boston, Hartford, Philadelphia, and other Eastern cities labored constantly for more just legislation and better conditions for the Indians.

Many friends established personal relationships with the tribe. Mr. and Mrs. Joshua Davis of Boston, who had provided scholarships for students at Hampton, came to the reservation and were invited to dinner at Rosalie's. "Though we didn't have a chance to get acquainted with them," wrote Rosalie to Alice Fletcher. "Mr. T.H. was in a terrible hurry to get off, so we didn't have much time." Mrs. John C. Kinney of Hartford, president of the Connecticut Women's Indian Association, wife of the editor of the Hartford *Courant*, worked hard on building plans for students returning from Hampton. Minnie and Phillip Stabler moved into the first house built by the women, called "Connecticut Cottage."

Bright Eyes rejoiced when both Lucy and Sue graduated from Hampton on the same day, May 20, 1886, Susan delivering the Salutatorian address on "My Childhood and Womanhood" and receiving a gold medal awarded to the senior passing the best examination. Even more thrilling, Susan was determined to study medicine and was accepted for the Woman's Medical College of Pennsylvania. It would take another generation, Alice Fletcher had said in 1884, before an American Indian could enter one of the learned professions. Now, just two years later, one of Bright Eyes' own family—and a woman!—was about to disprove the statement, entering medical school with the highest possible recommendations.

Yet with all her rejoicing Bright Eyes felt sadness, isolation, almost resentment. How could the tribe—her own family—have forgotten, and so soon, all that Thomas Tibbles had done for them? Didn't they realize that, except for his ceaseless efforts, none of these things would have happened? Yes, and she herself, who had surely helped to bring all these benefits to the tribe, was being ostracized by both her family and her people. But this knowledge brought only sadness, not resentment.

The battle was almost won. The Dawes Act, which constituted the major thrust of the eastern committees, was passed by Congress on February 8 and soon became law. It provided for the general allotment of Indian lands and would be amended during the next twenty years to apply to almost every tribe in the country. It authorized the President to divide tribal lands and assign 160 acres to each family head, eighty to single persons over eighteen and orphans under eighteen, and forty acres to each other single person under eighteen. Each Indian was to make his own selection, but, if he failed or refused, a government agent would make it for him. Title to the land was placed in trust for twenty-five years or longer, at the President's discretion. Citizenship was conferred on all allottees and on other Indians who abandoned their tribes and "adopted the habit of civilized life." Surplus tribal lands remaining after allotment might be sold to the United States.

The bill had its opponents, some of them thoughtful and genuine friends of the Indians. It would make an efficient tool, they argued, for the eventual separation of the Indian from his land and his relegation to even further pauperization. Others, not friends of the Indians, cannily foreseeing a future in which little would be done to encourage them in necessary skills, were heartily in favor. With Indians controlling nearly 135 million acres of land, if it was divided on a per capita basis, there would be thousands of surplus acres which would eventually be made available to whites, and, as soon as the trust period ended, thousands more which could be bought for a pittance.

Neither friends of the bill nor its opponents questioned its basic philosophy which, as one astute Indian was to comment eight decades later, "was to make the Indian conform to the social and economic structure of rural America by vesting him with private property." It assumed that all men were the same in their basic patterns of motivation and action, that merely by leaving their tribes and owning a piece of land, Indians would become exactly like the white homesteaders who were swarming over their old villages and hunting grounds.

Whatever its strengths and weaknesses, the Dawes Act instituted a government policy more humane than those which had preceded it; extermination, forced exile, segregation.

There were many meetings of celebration, especially in Boston. An invitation was extended to General Crook by the Boston Indian Citizenship Committee to attend a series of meetings in recognition of "your valuable services in behalf of justice to the Indians and their advancement in civilization and all the arts of peace" and signed by many distinguished names. The General's concepts of justice for the Indians were well known, as well as his championship of the Ponca cause. Even the Indians who had suffered his military dominance had words of praise: "He at least never lied to us."

"I wish to say most emphatically," he had stated, "that the American Indian is the intellectual peer of most, if not all, the

316

various nationalities we have assimilated to our laws, customs, and language. He is fully able to protect himself, if the ballot be given and the courts of law not closed against him."

In spite of his dislike of public appearances, the General accepted the invitation, arriving in Boston on February 23. Tibbles and Bright Eyes attended many of the meetings where he appeared and were often his guides or companions on his tours of the city. There were lectures at Old South Church, where the Collector of the Port, Mr. Leverett Saltonstall, introduced the General. There were trips to Springfield, to Wellesley College, to Wintonville, where both Tibbles and Bright Eyes spoke. From his arrival until his farewell dinner at Young's Hotel on March 4 the General delivered nearly one speech a day, telling only briefly about his campaigns, stressing over and over the uplift of the Indian.

"The Indian is a human being," the *Boston Post* reported him as saying on February 28. "The one question today on whose settlement depends the honor of the United States is, 'How can we preserve him?' My answer is, first, take the government of the Indian out of politics; second, let the laws of the Indians be the same as those of the whites; third, give the Indian the ballot. But we must not try to drive the Indians too fast in effecting these changes. We must not try to force him to take civilization immediately in its complete form, but under just laws, guaranteeing to Indians equal civil laws, the Indian question, a source of such dishonor to our country and a shame to true patriots, will soon be a thing of the past."

It was over. The last meeting had been held at Number 1 Beacon Street. The Tibbles' prepared to return home to their farm. Bright Eyes, wearied as much by success as by the strain of long battle, was infinitely relieved. Already it was the "Moon When Little Frogs Are Born." Soon spring would be coming to the prairie. Even at her new home, far from the Smoky Waters, the land would be stirring, the poplars and cottonwoods and willows kindling into smoky green and pale gold, the wings circling overhead. Her blood quickened. Then she looked at T.H., and her enthusiasm died. He was like a lion doomed to be shut in a cage. It was always so when a lecture tour was over, but this was worse than most. There might be no more lectures. For the moment he was a general without an army, a crusader without a cause. She sighed.

On the way home they stopped in New York for a few days, and Thomas Tibbles was suddenly rejuvenated. He burst into their hotel room. Major Pond, a well-known lecture-bureau manager, wanted him and Bright Eyes to lecture in England for a year! The steel-gray eyes turned sharply blue with excitement. The mane of white hair stood out like a sunburst about the craggy features, as if charged with electric energy.

Bright Eyes could only stare at him, speechless.

T.H. waited for neither questions nor objections before launching into further details. There would be a contract. Major Pond would send with them a manager to handle all the business arrangements. Their lectures would be classed in the area of ethnology, being dissertations on the life and culture of the American Indian. There would be few difficulties in the way of their going. The girls were comfortably lodged in Lincoln for another year. Nothing needed immediate attention at the farm. Of course they would have to give the matter careful consideration, however, before making a decision.

But Bright Eyes knew that already the decision had been made.

3

"Bright Eyes in England," T.H. was to caption Chapter Forty of his autobiography some twenty years later. He kept a careful record of the year they spent there, but one day after their return to America a freelance writer who wanted to write an article about Bright Eyes was left to do research with the various scrapbooks, and some time after he left the scrapbook containing all the newspaper clippings of the England trip proved to be missing! It was never found. However, T.H.'s memory was vivid, if not always accurate, in recalling names and dates. Since in the same autobiography he mistook the date of his marriage by a year, it was not surprising that in recollection he and Bright Eyes were touring England and Scotland during months when newspapers were recording their attendance at affairs in Boston, or that British and Scottish dignitaries were writing their names in Bright Eyes' autograph album when he remembered her as back home in Nebraska!

They sailed in May 1887 and encountered difficulties immediately on arriving in London. The agent sent with them decided that he preferred management of a London theater where some Americans were producing a play to promotion of lectures on ethnology. What to do? Bright Eyes, with relief, suggested that they return home, but T.H. would have none of it. He had brought with him some 400 letters from judges, congressmen, ministers, and especially from literary lights of Boston, to their personal friends in England. Hastily he perused them for possibilities. Two, from James Russell Lowell and Reverend Dr. Hitchcock, were addressed to the Reverend Dr. Fraser of the Presbyterian Church. Taking a cab, he drove at once to the cleric's church, obviously one of importance. Dr. Fraser, a distinguished and courtly gentleman, greeted him cordially and began reading the letter from Mr. Lowell. At the end he dropped his hands to his sides and shook his head.

"I cannot understand," he said despairingly, "how Mr. Lowell ever came to write me such a letter as this."

T.H. was thunderstruck. "Please," he said, "may I see that letter?" Reading it, he was even more perplexed. It said merely that Tibbles and Bright Eyes had lectured frequently in Boston, that they were Lowell's friends, that he had been delighted to entertain the young Indian girl in his home, and that Dr. Fraser would no doubt be glad to give his congregation an opportunity to hear her.

"Why—what is wrong? Why were you so surprised to receive it?"

"As Presbyterians," replied Dr. Fraser with some embarrassment, "we believe in the command that women should keep silence in the churches."

T.H. was also embarrassed, and after some awkward courtesies he left to do some business in the city. He did not return to their lodgings until after dark.

"Oh!" Bright Eyes sprang to meet him, her face eager. "There was the nicest old gentleman here to see me, so cultured and refined. He stayed nearly two hours. He wants us to speak in his church next Sunday night. He left his card and said that we never had received a heartier welcome anywhere in America than we would receive from his people."

T.H. stared at the card which bore the name of Dr. Fraser. "You're sure you're not mistaken, that you didn't get the cards mixed?"

"Of course not." She laughed merrily. "Only two people have called, and the other was the American minister, Mr. Phelps."

"But—there must be some mistake."

"No. He wrote on the back of the card. Look at it."

T.H. looked. There was the address of the church, the hour of service, and a request that he come fifteen minutes early for consultation.

He found Dr. Fraser in a private room, dressed in his clerical robes, walking up and down in obvious excitement. T.H. begged him to excuse them from speaking, explaining that he would never have presented the letter had he been acquainted with English customs. Dr. Fraser replied that he had had a long conversation with the "Indian Princess" and that she should speak in his church if it turned the whole kingdom upside down. He added that church law required him to hold two services each sabbath, but that a religious service was defined as consisting of a hymn, scripture reading, a text, sermon, and prayer.

"Please, sir—do not inconvenience yourself," protested Tibbles.

Dr. Fraser's lips tightened. "That Indian Princess shall speak in my church. It will not take more than ten minutes to go through the legal service, and after that the church shall be yours, whatever happens."

They went into the church, and the three mounted to the platform. Dr. Fraser announced a hymn, and one stanza was sung. He read two verses of scripture, announced his text, preached less than three minutes, and offered prayer. Then he came down from the high pulpit and introduced Thomas Tibbles. After the latter's address he presented the "Princess Bright Eyes from America."

While Bright Eyes was speaking, Tibbles whispered to Dr.

Fraser, "In America, after Bright Eyes has spoken, there are always a great many who come forward to shake hands. Will you be kind enough to make the introductions?"

"That is an American custom," the cleric whispered back. "You will never be annoyed that way in England."

But he was wrong. When Bright Eyes had spoken her last word, a woman came forward and kissed her on both cheeks. She was the sister of a Scottish duke. Since she was the highest ranking person in the room, it behooved others in the congregation to do likewise. Soon there was a crowd around her as large as any in America. Tibbles pressed his way to the side of Dr. Fraser, who was making introductions after the best American custom.

"I thought you said Englishmen never did such a thing as this," he could not help jibing.

The cleric threw up his hands. "You are upsetting us all at once. You are upsetting us all at once."

Tibbles listened with amazement as title after title rolled off the minister's tongue—dukes, lords, baronets. But none, he thought with both pride and wonder, possessed any greater dignity and poise than the "Princess Bright Eyes."

The next morning there were articles in the London papers that not only launched their debut as lecturers but assured their welcome in the highest strata of society. An English agent made them a proposition which they accepted, and thereafter they lectured up to five times each week for many months. Patiently Bright Eyes accepted the inevitable. The grueling ordeal had begun again.

But when the agent took advantage of this publicity and printed a supply of folders which featured the "Princess Bright Eyes," she rebelled. She would never again appear on the platform if she had to be given that title; all the printed matter must be destroyed. Friend of Lowell, Longfellow, Whittier, ardent reader of Emerson, Harriet Beecher Stowe and others of the liberal school, champion of freedom for her own people, she found the very idea of royal address repulsive.

"They may call me daughter of the head chief of an Indian tribe," she agreed, "but not 'Princess.'"

"But," argued T.H., "one must conform to the customs of the

country where one happens to be. I had to conform to Indian customs when I went among your people, even though white men ridiculed them."

Reluctantly she agreed, though still insisting that the hateful folders should be destroyed. In spite of her protests the title, with all its distasteful implications, was inescapable. Frequently when she entered a room where they were being entertained in London, all would rise and remain standing until she was seated, since she was considered to be of royal blood. Sometimes when this happened it was all she could do to keep from laughing. "Dirty savage . . . Princess!" What consternation if each group of name-callers could see and hear the other!

But Britain also, she discovered, was not averse to disparaging name-calling. At the time home rule for Ireland was the absorbing topic in all circles. At a dinner party given for her by one member of the nobility there were many titled persons present. One gentleman, who tended to monopolize her company, was a fierce conservative and tried to impress upon her the disasters that would follow the reelection of a home rule parliament and the continuing power of Mr. Gladstone. The Irish, he maintained, were the most depraved people on earth. She listened with the sympathetic attention which strangers always found so captivating.

"I am sure you tell the truth," she said finally. Then, smiling, but with a shrewd glint of challenge in her eyes, she added, "But hasn't Ireland been governed by England since Cromwell conquered it in 1650? And whatever the conditions are there, isn't England largely responsible for them?"

He looked at her in wonder, reluctant admiration, and in silence. Later he approached T.H. and asked, "How did that Indian Princess know when Cromwell conquered Ireland?"

Mr. Chesson, head of the Society for the Protection of Aboriginal Peoples, arranged for T.H. to attend a dinner at the Liberal Club, at which Mr. Gladstone would preside. The Prime Minister, who had expressed a wish to meet Tibbles, asked some pertinent questions about the American Indians. Why, he inquired, had the whites and Indians of the United States been constantly at war, while in Canada the race existed in even larger numbers and there had never been a war?

T.H. explained the differences in the systems adopted. The French in Canada had always treated the Indians as equals and intermarried with them. The English there had made them equal before the law, and in Canada the Indians could always come to court and have their rights tried, while in the United States the Indians were made "wards" of the government, could not make a contract, could not sue or be sued, so that their only means of redress for any wrong was war. He told of the appeal Bright Eyes had made and the legislation that had been secured, and the Prime Minister was impressed.

"In the end," he commented, "what you have accomplished will be of greater blessing to the white people than to the Indians."

The conversation then turned to the ideas of Indians concerning a Supreme Being and their belief in a future life.

"The main difference between them and white people," said Tibbles, "is that the white people *say* they believe in a future life, but the Indians have no doubt whatever about it. It is as real to them as the present life. Their word for the Supreme Being means 'the great mystery.'"

They spent a year in England and Scotland, stopping only a few days in hotels, entertained nearly all the time in private homes, sometimes with the nobility, sometimes with those of the middle class, occasionally with humble workers. Mingled with the signatures in Bright Eyes' autograph album from Boston, Philadelphia, Omaha, Washington, there appeared others from Glasgow, Birmingham, Edinburgh, London. Some were famous names, others memorable merely for some personal association. London appeared again and again: Henry S. Wellcome, the well-known chemical manufacturer and explorer; Francis Bennoch, 5 Tavistock Square; W. M. Ainsworth, Clapham Park; Eli Lemon Sheldon, an American with business interests in London; Arthur G. A. Bridge; F. W. Chesson. Reverend S. Fletcher Williams, pastor of Newhall Hill Unitarian Church, Birmingham, was a reminder of spirited conversations over the teacup.

Some of the memories were visual. G. Graham Thomson, of Werston Kilwinning, on the 1st of May 1888 drew a beautiful colored picture of a thatched cottage, "to remind Bright Eyes of her visit to Kilwinning." Rob Harvey of Glasgow made a colored drawing of Niagara Falls. Mary Reeve Issell of London inscribed her name on a music staff in the very center of the book. Annie S. Swan, the famous Scottish romantic novelist, decorated her autograph with a beautiful pen-and-ink sketch of the Bells of San Gabriel "from my Sketchbook." Thomas B. Marshall of Edinburgh made a poetic acrostic on her name, Inshtatheamba.

Only once was Bright Eyes persuaded to lecture on a subject other than that relating to the past, present, and future of her own people. The effect of liquor on Indians had made her a thorough prohibitionist, and she had become a friend of Frances E. Willard, the temperance crusader in America. Now Lady Henry Somerset, head of the temperance movement in England, kept begging her to lecture at least once on that theme. Finally she yielded. Lady Somerset hired a large London theater for the occasion. The audience was impressive, with many titled persons in attendance.

Perhaps it was a report of this success which made Frances E. Willard write to the Tibbles toward the end of their year in England, requesting them to go on around the world and deliver temperance lectures in Australia, Tasmania, and New Zealand. The World's Christian Temperance Union would take charge and arrange the whole tour. For T.H. it was undoubtedly a temptation. For Bright Eyes it was the extension of a prison sentence. But, if her going would help protect any people from this evil of drunkenness which the Waxes had brought to her own race, she was willing to go. However, she was infinitely relieved when T.H. decided that the plan was not feasible. When the year was over, they returned to the little house on her homestead claim near Bancroft.

Here disaster greeted them again. Not dust this time, but grasshoppers! As usual T.H. became embroiled on the unpopular side of the controversy. Scientists were fighting the plague on the premise that insects traveled and ate only during the day, spending their nights harmlessly in the fields. Not so, claimed T.H., and proved it. Taking a big kite, he coated it with tar, sent it high up into the sky after dark. When he pulled it down, there were hundreds of migrating grasshoppers stuck fast in the tar!

Grasshoppers were only one of the liabilities which for T. H. made farming distasteful. When an opportunity came to rejoin the editorial staff of the Omaha *World-Herald*, he seized it with alacrity, leased the farm, and sold the tenant all his stock and implements. That same year of 1888 Bright Eyes moved with him to Omaha.

She should have been used to change. Certainly one who had moved among the aristocrats and literati of Boston, London, and Edinburgh should not have felt timid about becoming part of a frontier town, especially one bearing the name of her own people. But she did. Here she was not the "Indian Maiden," the "Indian Princess," not even Bright Eyes. She was not Susette La Flesche Tibbles, possessor of her own homestead section. She was Mrs. Thomas Tibbles, wife of a newspaper editor. To some she was obviously "that half-breed wife of T.H." Not that such designations mattered, but with her lost identity there seemed to have gone also her chief purpose in living. Even Joseph made himself more at home in her new neighborhood than she did.

Though most of the family had begun to avoid her house because of their enmity toward T.H., not so Joseph. He came down to visit her soon after they moved. She was shocked at the change in him. The black eyes were still piercing, the full lips firm as a taut bow, but the shoulders were stooped, the cheeks a bit sunken, the limp more pronounced. His zest for adventure, however, remained unflagging. He must immediately explore the neighborhood.

"Don't go too far, *Dadiha*," she warned him. "You'll get lost." He still could not speak English, only French and several Indian languages.

"Don't worry," he replied, and started jauntily forth.

Later some of the neighbors came in, laughing. As a precaution he had nicked all the trees with his pocket knife as he went by!

4

"The Omahas' land is their own," wrote Alice Fletcher to a friend in April 1888. "I have secured industrial training for thirty-six and prospect of nine more at Carlisle and Hampton. The Omahas are on the eve of a new life."

Indeed they were. No one knew that better than Susette. Each time she visited the reservation, it seemed, a little more of the past had slipped away. For Miss Fletcher the changes were occasions for triumph..Susette, even though she knew they must come, felt a sense of indescribable loss.

"It is more than ten years," she wrote once, "since we went on our last hunt. The poles of the holy tent remain. There is no one who remembers the sacred words which were said at the feast preparatory to the start. We camp no more in the great circle. The habitations of the bands are mixed in inextricable confusion. Soon we can no more tell to which band we belong than can a Jew of today tell whether he is of the tribe of Judah or the tribe of Benjamin. A few of the old men only remember our laws and customs and try to keep them. The young are passing into another life."

It was in that same year of 1888 that for the Omahas the past irrevocably died.

One day Francis La Flesche sat smoking with Shudenathi (Yellow Smoke), keeper of the Sacred Pole, in the shade of trees near his house. They spoke of many events in the history of the tribe and of the important part which the old chief had played in them. After they had talked for some time, Frank said with sudden boldness, "Grandfather, why don't you send the 'Venerable Man' to some Eastern city where he could dwell in a great brick house instead of a ragged tent?"

The old chief softly whistled a tune and tapped the ground with his pipe stick. A slow smile crept over his face. "My son," he said at last, "I have thought about this myself, but no one whom I could trust has hitherto approached me upon this subject. I shall think about it, and will give you an answer when I see you again."

The next time Frank went to his house Shudenathi led him to the Sacred Tent and delivered to him the Sacred Pole with all its belongings. Frank received it with an awe not unmingled with fear. All the terrors of his youth rose up to chill his blood and make his hands tremble. It was the first time the sacred object had been purposely touched by anyone except its hereditary keepers. He felt as if he should go and be cleansed, or some terrible evil would befall him. With the utmost care and precautions this most sacred possession of the Omahas was shipped to the Peabody Museum in Cambridge, there to be treasured with other relics of a proud people's past history. Still the legend and songs connected with it remained a mystery known only to the chiefs of the Honga Clan.

Then one day in September Frank came again from Washington, accompanied by Alice Fletcher. They were filled with intense excitement for, under Joseph's urging, Yellow Smoke had promised to impart the legend of the Sacred Pole. The old chief came to the house. "It was a memorable day," the ethnologist later recorded. "The harvest was ended, and tall sheafs of wheat cast their shadows over the stubbled fields that were once covered with buffalo grass. The past was irrevocably gone. The old man had consented to speak but not without misgivings."

For a long time he smoked in silence, his deep-set eyes and sunken cheeks seeming to retreat into the shadows of the past.

"It is old," he said at last, "so old that no man living can remember how or whence it first came. And its words are forbidden to be spoken to any save those of the appointed clan, under penalty—under penalty of—who knows what evil?"

Joseph cleared his throat. "Grandfather," he said, "I will cheerfully accept for myself any penalty that may follow the revealing of these sacred traditions."

Yellow Smoke nodded. "*Ou-daa*, it is well, my son."

He began to speak, telling the old story of the finding of the Sacred Pole. As he talked, he continually tapped the floor with a little stick, marking with it the rhythm peculiar to the drumming of one invoking the unseen powers during the performance of a sacred rite. His eyes were cast down, his voice low, his speech deliberate. Alice Fletcher, flushed with excitement and triumph, wrote frantically.

Was it coincidence that very soon after this interview a fatal sickness fell upon Joseph La Flesche, that in a fortnight after only three days of fever he lay dead in the very room where the sacred legend had been revealed?

The funeral of the former head chief was the largest ever

known in that area. White men and Indians joined to honor him. He was buried in the Bancroft cemetery, in land symbolic of his life, white men's soil on the edge of the Indian reservation. The stone later placed on his grave bore the words:

INSTAMAZA
Iron Eye
Joseph La Flesche
Died Sept. 24, 1888
Aged 67 years
Last Chief of the Omaha Tribe

It was the end of an era. For Susette it seemed for a long time the end of her world. She had been in England at the time of Nicomi's death in March, and grief, though keen, had been tempered by remoteness. Now it assailed her with all the trauma of a first adult sorrow. It was Mary, always wise, strong, compassionate, who comforted her daughters, and out of the heartrending experience came for Susette one joyous emotion: a sense of unity with family. No misunderstanding, no disagreement, could destroy the affection and loyalty between herself and her mother and sisters. Ed Farley might refuse to shake hands with T.H., Frank might write scurrilous letters about him to Rosalie—and he did—but her sister would always be her beloved "Ro."

And Marguerite—lovely, laughing "Mag," "Migs," "Daisy" —could never be an antagonist. Susette felt toward this younger sister a fiercely protective, almost maternal affection, for she seemed especially vulnerable to the conflicts which must come to them all through the constant pressures of two cultures. In Marguerite's autograph album she had written her favorite lines from George MacDonald's "Within and Without":

"And should the twilight darken into night
And sorrow grow to anguish, be thou strong. . . ."

but she accompanied it with a delicate little drawing of a leafy

328

branch, each leaf bearing a letter of her own name, with a light and tender ditty:

"Mag is a sunflower
Mag is a daisy
Mag is the very gal
to set 'herself crazy.'"

Having graduated from the Normal Course at Hampton in 1887, her senior composition on "Customs of the Omahas" winning special honors, Marguerite had taken a teaching position in the government school. Now, after Joseph's death in September 1888, she was married to her Hampton sweetheart, Charles Felix Picotte, son of a French father and a Sioux mother. Charles assumed the care of the family allotments— Mary's, Nicomi's, Marguerite's, Carey's, Susan's—a huge responsibility even for a strong man, and Charles was not physically robust. But he flung himself into the farm labor with all his energy, raising record crops in 1890. Susette feared for her beloved sister. Could her Felix, as she called her frail young husband, bring permanent "happiness"?

Susette had no fears for Susan. There was nothing of the fragile dainty flower about Mary's youngest daughter. Tough, determined, dedicated, Susan knew exactly what she wanted. At a time when few white women dared to flout the prejudice against women physicians, Sue graduated in 1889 from the Woman's Medical College of Pennsylvania at the head of a class of thirty-three women, the first American Indian woman to become a Doctor of Medicine. She was one of six in the class to be chosen for added training in Philadelphia hospitals. Then she came home to serve as the government-appointed physician to the Omaha Indian School.

It was a triumph for the family, for the tribe, for the whole Indian race. Only one thing marred its perfection. Joseph was not there to see it.

Three

1

It was 1890, and a strange strong wind blew out of the west. It tore away the clouds which had long hidden the sacred Black Hills, Olympus of the Sioux nations, stolen by the white men for their gold, and revealed once again the ancient dwelling place of their God, Wakatonka. It sent old men burrowing into past treasures for sacred tribal bundles and young men climbing the high hills in quest of holy visions. It set women's fingers busy sewing shirts from tattered bits of cloth, to be painted blue with moons and stars and fringed with red, the color of life. It turned despair into hope, the certainty of defeat into the assurance of victory.

The message borne on the wind was of a savior, a Messiah, and, though the action of the drama was all Indian, its theme and language were all Christian. Christ had come to earth again, this time as an Indian, to redeem his people. He would appear in the clouds, and the faithful would be caught up to meet him. They would be joined with their loved ones who had died and now lived again. The evil-doers (white people) would be driven away. The Indians, God's people, would inherit a new earth, where there would be unspoiled green grass and unsullied streams and trees. The buffalo would return to roam the prairie, and once more the elk and deer and antelope would run wild. That the Messiah was a humble Paiute Indian named Wovoka was no deterrent to belief. Had not the Christ come first as a village carpenter?

Secure at last in the possession of their land, the Omahas heard these rumors with only mild interest. Not so the Sioux, who were desperate and half starving. Not only had they lost their sacred Black Hills, but they had been persuaded to sell other vast areas of their big reservation under threat that the government would take them away if they did not sell. Shunted away on small reservations with agencies far removed from each other—Pine Ridge, Rosebud, Crow Creek, Standing Rock—the once strong and warlike nations were subdued and helpless. To force them into the white men's mold of farmers, government officials had fathered the bright idea of cutting down the tribes' rations, to force them to raise crops.

"Fools!" fumed T.H., learning of this development via Susette via the Indian underground. "Don't they realize that even an expert white farmer couldn't raise crops on that land with the Sioux' poor equipment?"

The Sioux were as ripe for news of a Second Coming as the Christians had been under Nero. Eleven tribesmen of the Cheyenne River Reservation, including Kicking Bear and Short Bull, made the long trip west seeking the Messiah, and returned with reports of ecstatic visions, including the sight of crucifixion marks on Wovoka's hands, and with instructions for the sacred dance which would unite its participants with their risen dead and prepare them for life on the new earth. This "Ghost Dance," as it was soon called, kindled excitement like fire in dry prairie grass. Even Sitting Bull, in comparative exile up on the Standing Rock Reservation, had Kicking Bear come up and describe his visions, and, though the canny old chief had little faith in the new movement, his people were soon donning the sacred shirts and abandoning themselves to the rhythmic ritual. Government officials, always jittery at any sign of strange activity, were both shocked and alarmed.

"Savage, heathen, pernicious superstition!" denounced one agent, quite unaware that he had heard the same theological tenets propounded by Christian clergymen all his life.

It was the dance that frightened them. In spite of King David's scriptural example, the inheritors of Puritanism could not equate dancing with acceptable religion. And had not the war dance always been prelude to an Indian uprising? Remember Custer! Frantic warnings and appeals were soon speeding from worried agencies to military stations, especially from Pine Ridge, where a new agent was horrified by what seemed to be a sudden massing of Indians, all taking part in bewildering gyrations and weird incantations. Troops were soon on their way. Newspapers were printing avid headlines. Another Indian war was about to erupt.

"The paper wants us to go to Pine Ridge," T.H. told Bright Eyes one day in the late fall. "We're to be special 'war correspondents,'" he grimaced, "for the Omaha *World-Herald* and the Chicago *Express*."

She gasped in dismay. "War correspondents! But—"

"I know. The Sioux have no more intention of starting war than have the Omahas. But tell that to these city editors slavering for bloody headlines. Maybe we can counteract some of their stooges' cockeyed dispatches. It wouldn't be the first time," he added grimly, remembering his battles over the grasshopper episode.

They took with them Susan's husband, Charles Picotte, who knew the Sioux language. Arriving at Pine Ridge, in the far southwest of South Dakota, they found a startling situation. The place was teeming, not only with troops, but with other "war correspondents," all vying with one another to dispatch colorful "war news" to their various papers. Since no violence was occurring, details had to be manufactured—burning arrows fired into the agency buildings, soldiers being sniped at from ambush, orgies of human sacrifice such as had accompanied the ancient Sun Dance.

T.H. and Bright Eyes (she was always Bright Eyes, not Susette, when working with T.H.) chose to lodge in an Indian home instead of at the agency hotel. There they were visited by some of the leading Indians, who assured them that the tribes were all compliant as usual and had no thoughts of war.

"It's a peace dance," insisted some of their new friends who had made the long journey and talked with the so-called Messiah. "No one is allowed even to carry a weapon of war nearer than half a mile to the place where the dance is held!"

It was the new inexperienced agent, they declared, who had precipitated the tension at Pine Ridge. He had been a coward and a fool. When one of the dances was being held nearby, he had sent his Indian police to arrest the leaders. They had returned, saying it was impossible because there were hundreds of Indians there.

"Let them dance," they had advised. "They mean no harm. They will soon tire of it." In fact, as they well knew, many of the Indians from outlying areas had come to the vicinity of the Agency because they were half starving and hoped to be fed.

The Agent had lost his head. He had dispatched frantic wires to army headquarters demanding troops to quell a Sioux uprising. The Indians had viewed the influx with bewilderment and terror. *Why?* None of them had committed any crime—or had they? A whole tribe could be punished for a single man's misdemeanor. Many had fled to the Bad Lands, foodless and unsheltered, for refuge.

Bright Eyes went with her friends one night to a secret place to watch the Ghost Dance. It was a strange commingling of past, present—yes, and of future. Except for their "ghost shirts," with the blue figures and red fringes, it might have been any tribal group performing an age-old sacred dance, circling, wheeling, dipping, shouting, chanting, to the beating of drums and the rhythms of age-old songs, in the days before missionaries had frowned on such "heathen" practices or government had forbidden them. Yet this ritual celebrated no glories of an Indian past but the Christian's millennium of the future! Its motions simulated the tortures of a crucifixion, the triumph of a resurrection. Eyes filled with a fanatical hope scanned the sky for Messiah's reappearance in the clouds of glory. Arms lifted, limbs leaped in a frenzy of appeal to be caught up into the air to meet him. Voices in ecstasy foretold the triumphant reunion with the beloved dead and a new earth.

Bright Eyes was speechless with pity . . . and anger. It was a hopeless dream, of course. The new earth for which they yearned was really the old one, which was gone forever.

But—why must drums be muffled and voices muted? Why must they hide away like Christians in the catacombs to dance their ritual of hope? Had soldiers been waiting to arrest William Miller and his deluded followers when they had gathered in their white robes on a high hill to await the Second Coming?

2

Tensions mounted. Frightened by the massing of troops yet more than ever determined to carry on the prohibited Ghost Dance, Indians fled in greater and greater numbers to the Bad Lands, where many of them danced with fanatic zeal all day and far into the night. Though some food was smuggled to them from the pittance rations issued at Pine Ridge and Cheyenne River reservations and it was possible to eke out the supplies with a few rabbits and birds, the swelling number of refugees was nearly starving. When T.H. heard that among these refugees was the Brûlé Sioux Crow Dog, with his band, he immediately sent word to the chief to come to Pine Ridge as the military authorities had directed, promising that he would vouch for the band's safety.

Crow Dog came and camped with his band north of the Agency near old Chief Red Cloud's house. He soon came to see T.H. and Bright Eyes, as kindly, virile, noble of feature as they remembered from their visit to the Rosebud Agency in 1881. Now his big brown eyes were deeply troubled. He did not believe in the Messiah. He had gone to the Bad Lands out of fear of the soldiers.

"Many of my people hate me," he confessed, "even some of my own band, because I killed Spotted Tail."

T.H. knew the story. Goaded on by gossip and misunderstanding, the two Brûlé chiefs had become engaged in a deadly feud, and Crow Dog had shot his rival. He feared now that if trouble should arise he would be blamed and all his band would be killed. To add to his fears, several strange Indians had joined his band who were obviously bent on mischief.

"They keep their packs tied up," he worried, "and at night they sleep beside their horses. If they should kill somebody, I would be responsible."

Tibbles promised him that he would speak to General Brooke and ask him to send a guard of soldiers to arrest the potential troublemakers. But the General refused to accept the advice.

"It's my opinion," he replied brusquely, "that such a move would precipitate a fight then and there."

Had the advice been followed, it is probable that one of the great tragedies of American history could have been averted.

Tibbles' and Bright Eyes' commission as "war correspondents" grew steadily more precarious. Compared with the lengthy blood and thunder columns luridly headlined by other newspapers, their mild dispatches were stuff for Sunday School papers. When they persistently refused to manufacture news about a nonexistent war, their newspapers summarily cut off their expense account and ordered them home. But T.H. would not leave. Both he and Bright Eyes felt that their presence might aid in bringing about a peaceful solution to the problem. He kept speeding the true facts over the wires whether the papers chose to print them or not.

When he went to one of the railroad towns near the reservations to send his dispatches, he encounted other problems. He was an object not only of scorn but of dangerous revilement. These towns were growing rich on the war news. Reporters and other excitement hounds were jamming the hotels. Saloons were thriving. Army mules and horses had sent the price of hay soaring from near nothing to $25 a ton, and it was a heyday for gamblers, prostitutes, and other adventurers. But the boom was dependent on an outflow of exciting war news. When it was discovered that Tibbles was failing to create fictitious tales, he was as unpopular as when he had refused to suppress the unpleasant truths about the grasshopper famine. Once in Rushville he was so threatened by would-be assailants that he had to put his hand behind him as if reaching for a gun.

Tibbles' firm belief that the Indians intended no violent uprising was later confirmed by official documents of the period. Though some 3,000, led by Short Bull and Kicking Bear, were concentrated in the Bad Lands about fifty miles northwest of Pine Ridge, they had fled there in panic because of the inexplicable influx of soldiers.

Wrote Commissioner Morgan in his official report: "No

signal fires were built, no warlike demonstrations were made, no violence was done to any white settlers, nor was there any cohesion or organization among the Indians themselves."

Yet troops continued to pour in, cavalry, infantry, Crow Indian scouts, until there were 3,000 of them scattered at strategic points through the Sioux reservations. Fear precipitated every action—of the military concentration on the one side, of the mysterious implications of the Ghost Dance on the other. And fear harbors always the deadly virus of crisis.

Long a fomenter of resistance among the Sioux, Sitting Bull was blamed for all the present disturbances, including the Ghost Dance. On December 12 order was given for his arrest. Just before dawn on December 15 a band of Indian police surrounded his camp on the Standing Rock reservation, and, though the great medicine man yielded peaceably, some of his followers resisted, and there was an eruption of violence.

"Sitting Bull has been killed!"

The news resounded through the Sioux nations with the force of the rifle shot which had accidentally killed him.

"Oh!" moaned Bright Eyes in genuine grief. She remembered the great clumsy fingers painstakingly and with such childish pride shaping the letters of his name, the keen eyes full of hurt bewilderment. T.H. was less grieved than alarmed. The fabrications of Indian violence might now become reality. Threatened by the massing of soldiers, their beloved leader brutally killed, surely now the once-fierce Sioux would rise up in grief and wrath, declaring, *"Hoka hey!* It's a good day to die!"* But no; the hope of a coming Messiah was all-powerful. In the wastes of the Bad Lands, in secret enclaves on the outskirts of reservations, they danced with even greater frenzy, feet frozen to numbness, stomachs empty, but eyes burning red with fanatical hope. The few strong leaders left—Red Cloud, at Pine Ridge, Big Foot camped with his Minneconjous near Cherry Creek—had no illusions, either of a millennium or of successful warfare. All they wanted were food and safety for their people.

"There was no hope on earth," said Red Cloud, "and God seemed to have forgotten us. Some said they saw the Son of God; others did not see Him. . . . The people did not know; they did not care. They snatched at the hope. They screamed like crazy men to Him for mercy. They caught at the promise they heard He had made."

It was a strange, somber Christmas. Bright Eyes was desperately homesick. The family would all be gathering at Mary's or at Rosalie's. There were few holiday festivities. It was not a time for rejoicing. Yet at the Episcopal chapel near the Agency the rector, a full-blooded Sioux, led his congregation to celebrate the birth of Christ as usual. Attending the Christmas services, Bright Eyes found the room hung with greens, and across the chancel front, above the pulpit, a great banner triumphantly proclaimed: PEACE ON EARTH, GOOD WILL TO MEN.

She lifted her eyes to it gratefully. Surely it was a prophetic sign! The crisis would pass without the violence so many forces were trying to create. A blessing she could not know the scene that same room would be witness to in just four days!

3

Driven by fear and hunger and reassured by reports of peace at the Agency, the refugees were streaming into Pine Ridge from the Bad Lands. News came also that Big Foot, with over 300 of his Minneconjous, was on his way to Pine Ridge, where there were more abundant supplies and he might find food for the women and children. He had not the slightest intention of joining any hostile Indians or committing any depredations.

But Big Foot was on the list of "fomenters of disturbances" connected with the Ghost Dance, and his every action was suspect. Major Whitside was sent out with the 1st Battalion of the 7th Cavalry to meet Big Foot and accompany him and his band to Pine Ridge, taking them first to a cavalry camp on Wounded Knee Creek. Better, the Major was heard to remark, if he had been sent alone without troops, because any movement of soldiers was likely to alarm the Sioux at this time. But orders were orders. Knowing Whitside to be a man of long experience with Indians and of sound judgment, Tibbles did not accompany the battalion.

As expected, the Major encountered no trouble. On the afternoon of December 28 he met Big Foot and his band and, finding the chief ill with pneumonia and hemorrhaging, he transported him to Wounded Knee by ambulance, arriving at the camp about dusk. Big Foot was quite willing to go, explaining that he was taking his band to Pine Ridge only to assure their safety. On the advice of his half-breed scout, Major Whitside postponed disarming the band until morning. He assigned them a camping area, issued them rations, furnished them tents to eke out their meager supply, and sent a doctor to minister to Big Foot. It was a small band, numbering only 120 men and 230 women and children, and as the campground blossomed with little cooking fires, no scene could have looked more homelike and peaceful.

But Major Whitside was only a subordinate, and the higher echelons of the military were still jittery. General Brooke suddenly decided than an additional show of force was indicated. He ordered Colonel Forsyth with four troops of cavalry, Lieutenant Taylor with his company of Cheyenne scouts, and four pieces of light artillery to proceed to Wounded Knee to join Major Whitside.

T.H. was close to General Brooke's headquarters when he saw two orderlies run out, mount their horses, and start off full speed. Trouble? It must be, but where? It took him some time to procure an Indian pony, even a third-rate one, but two hours later he was hot on their trail. Night had fallen, but it was easy to follow the trail of four hundred soldiers even in the dark. He overtook Forsyth's troops just as they reached the north side of Major Whitside's battalion and were preparing to pitch camp.

"We expect no trouble," the officers whom he approached assured him. Was there a trace of disappointment, he wondered, in the disclaimer? This 7th Regiment was the one which had suffered such humiliating defeat under Custer. Could they be thirsty for vengeance? It was unlikely, for few of the present officers had served with Custer, and most of the men were raw recruits, many from the city slums, and wholly unexperienced as soldiers.

Remembering an Indian house a mile back on the trail, Tibbles retraced his steps, planning to ask shelter. The house was empty. After finding shelter and forage for his pony, Tibble crawled through a window. The weather was cold, but he found blankets to keep him fairly warm. Though Indians had been passing this way for many days, all doubtless hungry and cold, nothing had apparently been touched. Yet the newspapers were reporting wholesale thefts and vandalism! There was even a flock of chickens roaming the place, tempting game for the half-starved Indians! To pay for his shelter, he drew water from the well for the flock.

About eight in the morning he arrived at the camp on Wounded Knee. A formidable array of troops was now drawn up entirely circling the Indians and their makeshift village. On the south, across a deep ravine, was Lieutenant Taylor with his scouts. On a hill to the northwest were four Hotchkiss guns in the charge of Captain Illsley. Deployed in all about the Indian camp were eight troops of cavalry, one company of scouts, four pieces of light artillery (the Hotchkiss guns), a total force of 470 men, as against the total of 120 warriors in Big Foot's band. As Tibbles rode near the guns and was talking with Captain Illsley, a young lieutenant approached, his face grave.

"Isn't that a strange formation of troops," he inquired of the Captain, "if there should be any trouble?"

Tibbles thought so too. If any troops tried to shoot any Indian, they must fire straight toward some other army group enclosing the camp in a square.

The Captain only laughed. There was no possibility of trouble. The soldiers were merely a guard of honor to escort Big Foot and his band to the Agency.

"Rather a big escort," thought Tibbles grimly.

He rode along the north side of the square, where Colonel Forsyth had gathered the leading Indians of the band in council and was speaking to them through an interpreter. Big Foot, very ill, had been carried from his tent and now sat in front of it, the other braves grouped in a half circle about him. Indians were scattered all over the encampment, white persons here and there among them. One of the army captains was dickering with some of the Indians for souvenirs. All was peaceful.

"No need to wait," thought Tibbles. He had better get to the railroad and send his dispatch, such as it was. But he did not hurry. It was a perfect winter day, not a cloud in the sky. Even the hoofs of the ambling little pony made little sound on the snowy trail. Not a breath of wind was stirring. As he rode slowly along the frozen creek, the whole world seemed locked in peaceful silence. It was the quiet before the whirlwind.

Back at the council circle Colonel Forsyth finished his parley with Big Foot and his band and gave orders that the Indians be disarmed. They were sent to their tipis to get their rifles. Several were brought and stacked in a pile. Dissatisfied, the Colonel sent details of soldiers to search the tipis.

"They would go right into the tents and come out with bundles and tear them open," reported one Indian, Dog Chief, afterward. "They brought our axes, knives, and tent stakes, and piled them near the guns." Most of the rifles, the official report stated, were old and of little value.

"The search consumed considerable time," the report continued, "and created a good deal of excitement among the women and children, as the soldiers found it necessary in the process to overturn the beds and other furniture and in some instances drove out the inmates. All this had its effect on their husbands and brothers, already wrought up to a high nervous tension and not knowing what might come next."

Still the Colonel was not satisfied. He ordered that the men's blankets be removed and that they be searched for more weapons. One Indian protested, a medicine man named Yellow Bird, who went about blowing on an eagle bone whistle, urging resistance. Bullets would be unavailing, he cried, against the sacred "ghost shirts" that most of them were wearing.

"The bullets will not touch you!" he shouted over and over in Sioux. "The bullets will not touch you!"

The soldiers found two rifles. One belonged to an Indian named Black Coyote (or, as one report had it, Black Fox). Versions of what followed varied, depending on who gave them, whether white men or Indians. One said that he "drew a rifle from under his blanket and fired at the soldiers, who instantly replied with a volley directly into the crowd of warriors and so near that their guns were almost touching them." Another stated that the Indian stood waving the gun above his head, declaring that he had paid for it and it belonged to him, whereupon the soldiers spun him around and grabbed his gun. There followed a loud report, more like a crash than a shot.

"He hadn't his gun pointed at anyone," an Indian in the band said later. "He intended to put it down. And, anyway, he was deaf and didn't hear what they were saying."

"He was a crazy man," said another Indian, Turning Hawk, "a young man of very bad influence and in fact a nobody."

In fact, Tibbles was to learn, he was one of those same unruly Indians whom Crow Dog had wanted arrested. As General Miles admitted to him several days later, if General Brooke had heeded the advice, there would have been no tragedy.

Whatever the truth, death erupted. The first volley of the soldiers must have killed nearly half of Big Foot's braves, among them the chief himself, lying sprawled in grotesque contortion before his tent. As Tibbles and the young Lieutenant had foreseen, it also whizzed straight into the lines of Cheyenne scouts ranged on the opposite hill, sending them in pell-mell flight to escape the fire of their own forces. The terrified surviving braves leaped into action, some with knives or war clubs concealed under their blankets, and joined in bloody hand-to-hand combat with the soldiers. Outnumbered, most of them weaponless, their mangled bodies were soon strewn over the crimson ground.

At the first volley the Hotchkiss guns, trained on the Indian village, burst into fire, raking the tiny settlement. Screaming, the occupants of the tipis tried to flee toward a nearby ravine, but few reached it. The guns, pouring in two-pound explosive shells at the rate of nearly fifty a minute, mowed down everything in their range. One woman, Blue Whirlwind, received fourteen wounds, while each of her two little boys was wounded at her side. Within minutes 200 Indian men, women and children were lying dead or wounded on the ground, the tipis torn to pieces by the shells. The few survivors who managed to flee in wild panic were pursued by hundreds of maddened soldiers and raked by the fire of the Hotchkiss guns, now moved into position to sweep the ravine.

"We tried to run," said one surviving woman, Louise Weasel Bear, "but they shot us like we were buffalo."

"There can be no question," stated the *14th Annual Report of the Bureau of Ethnology*, "that the pursuit was simply a massacre."

Wrote Commissioner Morgan in his official report, "Most of

the men, including Big Foot, were killed around his tent, where he lay sick. The bodies of the women and children were scattered along a distance of two miles from the scene of the encounter."

Though the active attack lasted perhaps twenty minutes, the firing continued long after that, wherever a soldier saw a sign of life. It was estimated that nearly 300 of the 350 men, women, and children were killed. The soldiers lost twenty-five dead and thirty-nine wounded, most hit by their own guns.

Tibbles had ridden for about a half hour when he suddenly heard a single shot, then more, then a rattle of rifle shots, then the burst of Hotchkiss fire. Smoke rose behind him into the clear blue air. What did it mean? Trouble. Death to Indians, certainly. With that roar of guns, surely few would be left alive. He must ride hard to the Agency and break the news.

It was a dangerous ride. To keep his lazy pony going even at four miles an hour, he had to ply the whip. Knowing none of the leading Sioux wanted to fight, he had taken no weapon. Yet here he was, a lone white man, likely to encounter Sioux now maddened into hostility. Who could blame them?

Two soon overtook him on horseback. Fortunately they knew him and were friends. "Better turn back," they warned. "There may be bad Indians ahead." When he refused, they helped him along for a few miles by riding behind and taking turns lashing his lazy pony; then they turned off to the south, adjuring him in sign language to "Go! Go fast!"

Soon he was overtaken by three more Indians, in war paint, riding at full speed. Each carried a rifle. "Oh, well, a man can die only once," he told himself. But they gave him only a cursory glance and rode past, singing loud war songs. Presently two more groups rode by, naked to the waist, wearing war paint. He suspected that they were some of Crow Dog's "bad Indians." Why did they spare him? Who could tell? Perhaps they had seen him visiting Crow Dog in his camp.

The news had somehow gone on ahead. Five or six miles from the Agency he met swarms of Indians fleeing northward, on ponies, in travoix, a few in wagons. All were terrified. He talked with one man he knew, who had bundled his wife, two children, and a few supplies into a light wagon. They had been ordered through signals, the man said, to flee to the Bad Lands because the soldiers were going to kill them all.

"Go back home," Tibbles urged him, "or come with me to the Agency. I'll see that none of you are harmed." The man turned and drove with him.

Just outside the agency buildings they were overtaken by Lieutenant Preston of the 9th Cavalry, who had made the nearly twenty-mile ride in a little over an hour, one horse falling dead of exhaustion on the way. The one he rode was rimed with sweat.

"How long have you been here?" asked the Lieutenant sharply.

"I'm just arriving," replied Tibbles.

"Good." The Lieutenant had been sent by Colonel Forsyth to report the battle to General Brooke, and he wanted to be the first to break the news.

Tibbles also wanted to be first with a dispatch to the papers. Dashing off a brief account of the battle, he sent it off by a trusted messenger to the telegraph office in Rushville. To his satisfaction his account of the Battle of Wounded Knee was apparently the first to reach any newspaper in the country.

4

The settlement around the Agency was a maelstrom of panic and confusion. No one knew what to do or whom to trust. Was the Agent friend or enemy? Were the remaining soldiers there to protect or to kill? Some were fleeing from the Agency to escape. Others were fleeing toward it to find safety. Children's wails and women's screams mingled with shrill battle cries of "Hoka hey!" Ghost shirts, long the symbols of peace, were suddenly teamed with accouterments of battle, leggings, moccasins, full war paint.

"Come into the Agency buildings with us," one of the white women urged Bright Eyes. "The soldiers can protect us better there. These terrible savages!" Her eyes were wide with terror.

Always the choice, thought Bright Eyes. Waxe or Indian? These white women considered her one of them, the wife of that newspaperman Tibbles. What about her new Indian friends? Would they also think of her as a Waxe, one of those who could take away their guns and then shoot them down like buffalo? But this time there was no choice. At a time like this she was always an Indian. She thanked the woman and refused.

"Come," said her hostess, who could speak a little English. "People need help. Much frightened. Will listen to you."

They went about among the terrified women, trying to quiet their fears. Many were hastily piling goods in light wagons or on travoix or staggering under heavily loaded parfleche bags, prepared for flight yet not knowing which way to go. Bright Eyes spoke to them in English, and her hostess interpreted into Sioux. They urged the women to go back to their lodges and wait. They comforted crying babies, restored lost children to their mothers.

Suddenly even greater terror and confusion erupted. A Sioux warrior came riding down the main road from the north. He wore a ghost shirt, breechcloth, leggings, moccasins, and full war paint. As he rode, he shouted something at the top of his lungs. Though Bright Eyes now understood a little of the Sioux language, the meaning of the man's shouts evaded her.

"What is he saying?" she demanded of her hostess.

"He says," the woman replied calmly, "we must prepare for battle. Some of the Indians are going to shoot into the Agency."

It was not the Pine Ridge Sioux who were planning to attack, she wanted Bright Eyes to understand. It was the Brûlés who had fled to the Bad Lands from Rosebud under such leaders as Kicking Bear and Short Bull. They had always been more warlike.

Bright Eyes regarded her with amazed humility. Apologizing, as it were, for acts of retaliation by terrified people who had just seen their comrades massacred! Yet this Brûlé Sioux was human enough to warn both whites and Indians before the attack was made.

Unity seemed to have emerged suddenly out of chaos. The Indian women and children were all rushing together toward the agency buildings.

"Come!" Bright Eyes seized her friend's hand. "They

mustn't go there! If there's going to be an attack on the Agency, that's the worst possible place!"

Within moments she was standing on a box inside the converging group of women and children, white as well as Indian, her melodious but penetrating voice, used to dominating large audiences, compelling them to attention.

"Why do you come here?" she challenged. "These thin board buildings can't protect you from bullets. They'd go right through them. Go back to your log houses, go back . . . go back . . . back."

Again and again she repeated the words, waiting for them to be relayed by her interpreter. Already shots were being fired and shells dropping in the compound. She was still sounding the urgent warning when T.H. came pushing through the crowd to her side. Just then one of the army officers rode up on his horse and waved to T.H.

"Give Bright Eyes my compliments," he shouted, "and tell her the order is for women and children to retire to the log houses for safety and that she's requested to force them to go."

He started away, then wheeled. "And tell her she herself must stay in a log house. Stray bullets are flying all around here."

The gunfire was more effective than her warnings. With the help of T.H. and her hostess she was able to herd the Indian women into safety of their log houses.

"It's some of Crow Dog's bad Indians," T.H. told her. "They're lurking in a deep gulch on the north, a good place to fire into the Agency. The northern hills, too, are covered with Sioux on horseback. There must be 2,000 of them! But I'm sure they don't mean war. If they did, they could capture Pine Ridge in just twenty minutes, with the few soldiers there are here now and not the slightest sign of any orderly defense. I think they're just gathering there as a rear guard for the women and children if they need to flee to the Bad Lands."

T.H. went away to where the few troops were lined up, waiting, and sat down on a cracker-box to take notes. Occasionally a spent rifle ball would raise a cloud of dust not far away. He saw a soldier go by with a camp stove on his back. Suddenly the man's hat flew off. He took it off and looked at it, then began to run. There was a bullet hole through the crown. General Wheaton came by and advised T.H. to move, but he was not one to heed advice.

Neither was Bright Eyes. After seeing most of the women into their log houses, she roamed about to see what was happening. Later the same officer found her standing on a well-curb not far from the firing line, a vantage point for viewing the whole field of operations.

The group firing from the gulch was finally routed by the agency's force of protective Indian police, who, the new Agent had kept asserting, would be sure to join in any hostile movement by the Indians and murder everybody in the Agency. There was occasional firing until sundown, when the Sioux braves on the hills began to move northward, substantiating T.H.'s surmise that their presence had been for purposes of protection rather than war.

That night the weather turned bitter cold, forerunner of a big snowstorm and blizzard. The Indian corpses strewn along Wounded Knee Creek froze solid and would remain there for three days, after which they would be shoveled into a large trench there on the battlefield and buried . . . all but one tiny baby girl, snuggled under a blanket in the embrace of its dead mother. Colonel Colby, crossing the field and seeing the blanket move, would ride with it in his arms back to Pine Ridge, handling it as tenderly as if it were his own flesh and blood, then later take the baby home with him to Beatrice, Nebraska, adopt and educate the child.

Darkness fell early on December 29, the day of the massacre. About seven o'clock came the 7th Cavalry bringing long trains of dead and wounded soldiers in army supply wagons, their former loads left on the battlefield—bacon, rice, crackers, and other supplies—to remain untouched for days in that region of half-starving Indians. The wounded troopers and five wounded Sioux warriors were taken to the soldiers' quarters for treatment.

There came also forty-nine wounded Sioux women and children, piled into a few old Indian wagons. Major Butler, who was ordered to attend to them, could think of no place to take them. Finally Tibbles suggested that the Episcopal rector might lend his church for the purpose. With the rector's willing consent the seats were torn out and the floor covered with hay. Here they laid the rows of wounded, and here Bright Eyes soon came with her hostess to render what help she could.

At first she thought she could not bear it. The sights, the smells, were overpowering. She was sure she was going to faint. The concentrated agony in the room was palpable substance, twisting one's vitals. But there was no time for feeling or thinking, much less for fainting. Presently other women came to help, among them Elaine Goodale, supervisor of an Indian school on the reservation and a poet of some note.

They did what little they could, with their meager medical knowledge and the few supplies available—going up and down the gruesome rows, prying loose caked clothing as gently as possible, marveling when not even a moan escaped the tight lips; bandaging the worst gaping wounds with strips from an old sheet; keeping the half-frozen bodies covered with blankets. One beautiful young woman kept throwing her blanket off as she tossed in delirium. She had been shot straight through the hips. There were four nursing babies whose mothers had been killed, already too weak even to cry. No milk, of course, to feed them.

"If only I had Susan's knowledge and skill!" thought Bright Eyes. Or—"If only one of our medicine men were here with his healing roots and herbs and his sacred bundle!" But the only doctor was with the wounded soldiers.

The strangest thing about the whole scene was the silence. For all their agony not one of the women uttered a word, even a moan, of complaint. The only sound in the place came from a little three-year-old girl who lay beside the one unwounded woman, an old grandmother with a baby on her lap.

"*Min-nie, min-nie, min-nie,*" the child kept crying in a plaintive voice.

"She's begging for water," said Bright Eyes to T.H., who was standing by helplessly, looking half sick.

He went out and returned presently with a bucket of water and a tin cup. The child looked frightened at the approach of a white man, so he gave the cup to the old woman. The child snatched it as if dying from thirst. As she gulped it down, he was horrified to see it gush out, bloodstained, through a hole in her neck.

"I'm going to see if I can get the doctor," he told Bright Eyes, and rushed out.

He went to the agency hospital to find the surgeon, Major Hartsuff. To his surprise, although it was a zero night, he found the doctor caring for his sixty patients in tents! He told him about the terrible condition of the women and children and begged him to come.

"My first duty is to these wounded soldiers," the doctor replied, "but as soon as I can leave them, I'll come."

However, he gave T.H. some morphine to ease the pain of the worst sufferers and two bottles of beef extract for the four nursing babies.

"Make hot soup of it," he told him. "It might harm a white baby, but the Indians have thrived on meat for ages."

It was two in the morning when the doctor reached the church. He stood at the door looking in. Then he grew pale and sat down abruptly.

"What's the matter, Major?" asked T.H., thinking he looked sick.

The surgeon, who had attended wounded in battles all through the Civil War was indeed sick. "It's the first time I've seen a lot of women and children shot to pieces," he said thickly. "I—I can't take it."

He went outside and sat down on a log. T.H. went to an officers' tent near by and begged a cup of strong coffee which he brought to Major Hartsuff. Finally the doctor was able to reenter the church and minister to the wounded.

All this time the strange silence had continued, no crying out, not a groan, not even a sigh. It wasn't natural, thought Bright Eyes. Indians were not usually reticent about expressing pain and grief. Her hostess also was puzzled. Now, as the doctor approached them, they shrank back in abject terror. *Why?* One of the women reached out to clutch at her dress and spoke imploringly. Not understanding the Sioux words, Bright Eyes called her friend.

"What is she saying?"

"She says—*'When are they going to kill us?'*"

They looked at each other in horrified understanding. "Kill you!" Bright Eyes' friend was swift to explain. "They aren't going to kill you. The doctor is here to help make you well. White people do not kill prisoners and women and children."

"But they do," the woman protested. "We saw them. They killed all the others. We know they brought us in here to make a feast and then kill us."

So that was the reason for the strange silence. An Indian must not let his enemies hear him utter a sound of complaint. They must die as Indians should, proudly, silently. But once they were made to understand and were released from this obligation, they burst into loud groans and wailings. Which was harder to bear, wondered Bright Eyes, the outpouring of agony or the terrible silence?

She stayed there all night, doing what she could, until the new day dawned, almost the last day of the year—yes, and of an era. Even the dawn seemed more like an end than a beginning. The dream of the Messiah and a new earth was dead. The Indian was at last conquered, his age-old pride and dignity and ambition ground into the blood-soaked earth at Wounded Knee.

She looked up at the Christmas greens still festooning the church rafters and the banner hung above the pulpit. She was glad that most of the suffering women and children could not read the travesty of Christian brotherhood blazoned there above their bleeding, broken bodies:

PEACE ON EARTH, GOOD WILL TO MEN

1

Ten years! They flowed by at a pace as ever-changing as the Smoky Waters. The "Gay Nineties," they were to be called later. They were not that for Susette.

Wounded Knee marked a turning point not only in Indian history but in the lives of Thomas and Susette Tibbles. T.H.'s crusade for the Indians was finished. True, all Indians were not yet citizens. That was still a quarter of a century away. But T.H. was satisfied with what he and Susette had accomplished. Now his vast energy and passion for justice must be channeled to another cause.

This time it was Populism. The plight of the Western farmer, saddled with debt at the exorbitant rates of Eastern capitalists, cursed with poor crops through years of drought, politically dominated by the great railroad monopolies, was enough to stir the blood of any champion of the underdog. The organization of the People's or Populist party in May 1891 was a bugle call to action. Its national convention in Omaha the following year, nominating James B. Weaver of Iowa as its presidential candidate, roused T.H. to white-hot fervor. Its platform was a recital of the poor man's grievances "in the midst of a nation brought to the verge of moral, political, and material ruin. Corruption dominates the ballot box, the legislature, the Congress, and touches even the ermine of the benches . . . newspapers subsidized or muzzled . . . land concentrating in the hands of the capitalists . . . urban workmen denied the right of organization . . . fruits of the toil of millions stolen to build up colossal fortunes for a few . . ." T.H.'s new loyalty was to wax hotter and hotter through the years until, over a decade later in 1904, he would become the Populist candidate for Vice President of the United States.

While Susette shared this new interest, she was far more concerned with the problems of the Omahas, and, since she and T.H. came back to live on the farm early in the decade, she was a close observer, if not active participant, in all of them. One problem, long debated, was the status of half-breeds. Some Omahas declared that white men who settled on the reservation with their Omaha wives had no right to allotments. The matter was hotly debated at one council meeting. It was old Two Crows, always wise, outspoken, pithy in his pronouncements, who settled this question for the moment. As usual, he waited until the debate had waxed long and furious, then at the climactic moment rose to speak.

"My friends," he said in the purest Omaha of which only he was master, "I agree with you. None but pure blood Omaha have a right to this land. . . . Now you know that my family and Wajapa's are the only two families of pure Omaha blood in the tribe. All the rest of you have a little Ponca blood, a little Sioux blood, a little Ioway blood mixed in. Now all of you move off. Wajapa and I will keep it for the pure Omaha."

When Two Crows died not many years after Joseph, Susette was heartbroken. Not only had she lost a beloved "uncle," but the tribe was bereft of perhaps its most responsible leader. Even Wajapa did not possess his qualities of leadership. There seemed no one qualified to take his place, unless—Rosalie!

For Rosalie, to Susette's wonder and delight, occupied a position of amazing responsibility in the tribe. Not only was she the business head of the "pasture" project, attending to all the endless details of the leasing of the unallotted land, but she acted as contact person and interpreter, as well as adviser, for individual members of the tribe in their relations with the Council and the Agency. Though by 1890 she was the mother of six children all under ten (Louis had been born in 1885, Fletcher in 1888, and Marguerite in 1890), she found time not only for business supervision but for innumerable other activities— entertaining guests from the East, carrying on a voluminous correspondence, all in her beautiful even handwriting, helping Alice Fletcher with her exhaustive study of Omaha customs, songs, traditions.

But Rosalie and Ed, with their "pasture," encountered violent opposition and suffered continuous attacks by white speculators anxious to gain control of the tribe's unallotted land. In the same month that Susette and T.H. were at Pine Ridge, when Rosalie was preparing to make a new lease, a group headed by William E. Peebles was stirring up members of the tribe to demand more allotments, since allotted land could not be leased. Two years later Rosalie was fighting a suit brought by the same parties in the courts using fraudulent signatures of claimants. Susette was torn constantly between two loyalties— to T.H., who had always opposed the "pasture" and whose very name was anathema to Ed Farley, and to her beloved sister, whose judgment she might question but whose qualities of leadership she trusted and admired.

With Susan she had no such reservations. Graduating from the Woman's Medical College of Pennsylvania in 1889, Sue had returned to the tribe to become physician at the Government School; then the Agent, Robert Ashley, asked her to give medical service to other tribal members—at no increased salary, yet she spoke of it in glowing terms as a promotion, a wonderful opportunity to promote better health and improved habits of hygiene among her people. It was the beginning of long years of selfless service, traveling first on horseback, later in a small top buggy, all over the reservation, never refusing a call day or night, summer or winter, in every kind of weather.

When Charles Picotte, always frail, died in 1892 and Marguerite returned to the government school to teach, the two sisters cooperated in a long-term effort to educate the children of the tribe in the laws of health, the new habits and techniques of living which they had acquired through superior advantages of education and experience and which the Indian desperately needed if he was to make the whirlwind adjustment demanded of him by an alien, dominating society.

It was a herculean task. The Omahas were now under the

civil and criminal laws of the State of Nebraska. Their whole way of life established through long centuries had been disrupted. The white man, while destroying not only their means of livelihood but customs which had constituted an orderly and workable society, had done little to provide substitutes. New laws of marriage, involving licenses, legal, and, if possible, Christian sanction, had been suddenly imposed on a people whose experience with the white man's law and with Christianity was in many cases nil and at most but a generation in duration. Both Marguerite and Susan advised, explained, encouraged, helped young couples to plan weddings, older ones to legalize marriages made according to Indian custom.

Such efforts were only the beginning of long years of dedicated service which the two sisters were to render not only to the tribe but to surrounding communities. Later, as influential citizens in the new town of Walthill, to be built a few miles from the Agency after the turn of the century, they would become leaders in innumerable church and civic enterprises. Susan's "tall house" and Marguerite's beautiful home across the street would bring together the finest elements of two divergent cultures. Their children, Susan's two boys and Marguerite's two girls and two surviving boys, would mature into respected American citizens. And a fine hospital built by the Presbyterian Church and later bearing Dr. Susan's name would perpetuate the memory of her long years of professional service.

Susette was not jealous of her three sisters, she loved them too much for that, yet she envied them their opportunities of service. Her chief desire was to help her people. Now suddenly she seemed thrust into a backwater while the tribe, with all its successes, its discouragements, its problems, swept into the uncertain future without her. Though the family remained tender and loving, their distrust of T.H. made frank communication difficult, if not impossible. They suspected her of agreeing with him in all his strong convictions, while as a matter of fact she was becoming less and less certain of the right or wrong course of action on many issues. She was almost glad when the thrust of circumstance took her far away from the tribe and its problems.

The hard times of the early nineties gave the Populist party a boost of energy. In 1893 T.H. was invited to become a reporter in Washington for an Indiana weekly, the *Noncomformist*, and for a syndicate of weekly newspapers, most of them published by the Farmers' Alliance. While he reported for the House of Representatives, Susette became the correspondent reporting actions in the Senate.

The next months were a flood tide of rich and happy fulfillment. She wrote, she painted, she attended concerts and lectures, she visited art galleries, she enjoyed the stimulating company of old friends and new. Though many of her articles were in support of the tenets of the Populist party, they lacked the spontaneous verve and color of her stories of Indian life. Yet the writing of Indian stories brought regret and nostalgia, uncertainty for the future. She expressed it once in a story called "Omaha Legends and Tent Stories" for the children's magazine *Wide Awake*:

"How often I have fallen asleep when a child, with my arms tight around my grandmother's neck, while she told me a story, only I did not fall asleep till the story was finished. When thinking of those old days—so happy and free, when we slept night after night in a tent on the wide trackless prairie, with nothing but the skies above us and the earth beneath; with nothing to make us afraid; not even knowing that we were not civilized, or were ordered to be by the government; not even knowing that there were such beings as white men; happy in our freedom and our love for each other—I often wonder if there is anything in your civilization which will make good to us what we have lost. I sometimes think not, unless it be the wider, fuller knowledge of God and his Word."

Francis was in Washington, living in Alice Fletcher's house on Capitol Hill at 214 First Street. Miss Fletcher's niece, Jane Gay (later Jane Gay Dodge) was also a part of the household and accompanied her aunt on summer expeditions in Nebraska and Idaho, wearing a cook's outfit of long apron and sunbonnet and operating the heavy ungainly camera equipment. Together the three made extensive studies each summer on the Omaha reservation, slowly accumulating the words of tribal rituals. In 1891 Miss Fletcher had drawn up a paper legally adopting Francis as her son, but the relationship was never finalized since Frank refused to give up his name of La Flesche. He was becoming increasingly famous for his work in ethnology with the Indian Bureau. Through attendance at night school he won the degree of Bachelor of Law in 1892, and the following year his master's degree.

But Susette saw little of Frank and Miss Fletcher. Both disapproved heartily of T.H., Frank vocally, Miss Fletcher silently but in words often expressed in letters to Rosalie. Occasionally, however, Susette was invited to share in the research and add details. Her memory was keen, and she could recall legends and stories told by old members of the tribe almost word for word. To her great delight Miss Fletcher was compiling a book of Omaha rituals and songs. John C. Fillmore, a noted composer, was setting them down in musical form. In 1891 his son had spent two months with Rosalie and Ed on their farm. It had been a gigantic task collecting both the words and the music of the rituals, involving many hours of waiting for the old men to feel moved to make their recitations, and of meticulous recording both by Alice Fletcher and by Frank. And even after the tunes had been recorded, their rendition on piano or organ was but a poor echo of the original. In fact, it was impossible for a white person to even approach the effect.

"I have heard some of your finest singers," Susette wrote in that same story for *Wide Awake*, "but nothing I ever heard from them has touched me so profoundly as the singing of the Indians. The tears fill my eyes as I listen to their wild, weird singing, and I can never seem to tell myself why."

Songs, like the language, had been transmitted from one generation to another and never varied. Few were ever sung solo. Many were sung by a hundred or more men and women. The melody moved by octaves rather than harmonies, with the overtones strongly brought out; hence the Indians had a preference for a simple harmony of implied chords when their songs were rendered on piano or organ. Rhythm was a marked characteristic, as with all Indian music, and most songs presented more than one rhythm, a pulsation of voices adding a sort of inner rhythm to that of melody. In lovesongs, which frequently had long notes, the hand was sometimes waved in front of the mouth to break the continuity of sound. The time also varied. Often an aria might be in triple time, three-quarter, six-quarter, or nine-quarter, while the drum was played in two-quarter or four-quarter time.

John C. Fillmore and Alice Fletcher transcribed the Omaha Wawan Ceremony (*Wawan* meaning "to sing for someone"), a rite for the securing of peace between unrelated persons or groups. It was inevitable that the music, reduced to notes on a staff, even by the most expert of white musicians, should fall far short of the desired effects. Yet especially in one noble choral, harmonized for the piano, Fillmore managed to achieve a satisfactory rendition even to the Omahas.

"Now it sounds natural!" They nodded their heads in approval when it was played to some of them on a reed organ, the only instrument available. The words had little meaning for a white person—they were chiefly vocables—but to the Omahas the sounds had profound significance.

More than a decade later Alice Fletcher's and Frank's painstaking reconstruction of such songs and rites would be made the basis for numerous dramatic presentations. In one pageant Hartley B. Alexander would draw heavily on the Hedewachi Ceremony, and the music, arranged by Howard I. Kirkpatrick and featuring some of these Omaha songs, would long be called "The Sacred Tree of the Omaha." A worship service in St. Marks-in-the-Bouwerie in New York City would include a responsive reading taken from the Omaha ritual of the "The Child Introduced to the Great World at Birth." Of even more popular interest the well-known composer Charles Wakefield Cadman would ask Miss Fletcher for permission to use themes from her book of Indian songs for his "Four Indian Songs," including "Land of the Sky Blue Waters," "Far Off I Hear a Lover's Flute," "The Moon Drops Low," and "While Dawn Is Stealing." The first three would be based on Omaha songs.

"Good," was Susette's appraisal of all the work Frank and Miss Fletcher were doing to preserve the precious heritage of her people. Not that even their best efforts were truly satisfying. How, for instance, could one put into black and white the magnificent, soul-stirring Wawan Ceremony, with its four full days of ritual, its glorious color, its hundreds of voices, its

(Sung in octaves) Harmonized by John C. Fillmore for interpretation on the piano
♩ = 132 *With religious feeling*

The akede hiao tha
Ho tha kede hiao tha
The akede hia the he
Hiao tha kede hiao tha kede hia thehe

graceful pipe-bearers portraying the flying, circling, rising, and falling of the eagle, the feather appendages of the pipes moving like wings? What white person, playing the tunes on a piano, looking at the sacred symbols in the glass case of a museum, could possibly comprehend their meaning for a proud and ancient people, seeking unity with Wakonda and his world, peace with other tribes, and a safe journey across the straight red path of life?

One of the songs they transcribed, however, was fully satisfying. Frank wrote it on one of the pages of her album, recapturing all the happy memories of their childhood together and for a moment, at least, melting all the constraint which had risen between them:

Beneath, in his fine slanting handwriting, he wrote:

Dear Susette

This is a little song we have often sung
years ago in our play with the children of
the Winjahgue village. We used to form in a
single line and march through the village
singing this at the tops of our voices, following
the leader wherever he went, through vacant
houses, deserted mud lodges, the tall grass
and through mud puddles. Little beaded
moccasins would be a sorry sight when we got
through. I put it in your album to remind you
of the fun we used to have.

Your brother

Frank La Flesche
Washington, D.C.
Oct. 7, 1894.

Theodora Bates was eleven in 1894 when she first met Thomas Tibbles and Susette. Her older brother Herbert had just married Tibbles' daughter Eda. She would never forget her introduction to T.H. She was helping her mother prepare the wedding feast. Just as the guests were entering the dining room from the parlor, her mother was opening a bottle of homemade root beer. The cork flew out with a bang and hit T.H. in the chest. He gasped, threw back his head with a toss of his silver mane, and burst into laughter. "Well," he boomed, "it seems natural to be under fire again."

So vivid was that first impression that nearly a half century later, when Theodora Bates Cogswell, herself a writer, was preparing Thomas Tibbles' autobiography, *Buckskin and Blanket Days*, for publication, it was still fresh in her mind.

Susette was happy now in her relationship with her step-daughters and intensely proud of them. After college studies in Lincoln and St. Louis Eda had come back to teach in Lincoln, where she had met Herbert Bates, who already was revealing the scholastic and literary ability which would later result in many published writings, among them a volume of one-act plays and a new translation of *The Odyssey*. Eda, like her father, was more interested in finance and social problems, concerns which would later involve her actively in the League for Industrial Democracy. May, on the other hand, soon to become the wife of Chester Barris, was more like her mother in temperament, sensitive, giving and needing much affection, deeply religious. "May has made her life work Christian Science," Eda was to write Marguerite from her home on Long Island in 1928.

But for Susette and T.H. themselves life was unsettled and distraught. After their return from Washington in the summer of 1894 they spent some weeks with Rosalie. The small house bulged, for another boy, La Flesche, had been born in 1892, making seven children, yet Rosalie always made room for company, whether relatives like Uncle White Swan or Eastern visitors like Mrs. Kinney of the Connecticut Women's Indian Association, Alice Fletcher and her niece Jane Gay, Mrs.

Amelia S. Quinton, president of the Women's Indian Association, Miss Heritage, a friend Susan had made in Philadelphia, Mr. and Mrs. William Thaw of Pittsburgh, who had made large contributions for the tribe and established the "Thaw Fellowship" at the Peabody Museum to assist Alice Fletcher in her Indian research and publications.

Human relationships in the house would have been replete with tensions even without present complications: T.H.'s frustration because an expected editorial job did not materialize; Ed's and Rosalie's increasing problems with the pasture. William Peebles and his group of white speculators had encouraged squatters, most of them mixed-bloods unrecognized as Omahas, to lay claim to unallotted lands, since further allotment would withdraw more lands from tribal use and open them eventually to white ownership. Since T.H. had interested himself in the rights of mixed-bloods to gain allotments, even though he had no connection with Peebles and his ring, tension between him and Ed Farley was at an all-time high.

Susette was infinitely relieved when they moved back to the farm, living in three rooms which they had reserved when renting the house and land. Then came good fortune indeed. T.H. was invited to edit the *Weekly Independent*, a new paper which a group of men in Lincoln was starting, later to become the *Lincoln Independent* and the official organ of the Populist party. They were in Lincoln for the next five years, living in two different houses, both east of the capitol building.

These years should have been completely happy. She seemed to have resolved most of the old problems of identity, fitting comfortably into all three of her diverse personalities. Even the house furnishings typified the synthesis. The parlor and adjoining sitting room, cluttered with pictures, antimacassars, doilies, drapes, throws, hassocks, cushions, after the "civilized" fashion of the day, were an amalgamation of her varied life. Mingled with the chairs, tables, what-nots inherited from Amelia Tibbles' decor were mementoes from her many Eastern trips, gifts from wealthy friends. Prints of best-loved pictures shared the crowded walls with her own vivid paintings. On her reed organ stacked with photographs, the top row with Longfellow at the center was flanked at either end by likenesses of

Joseph and Mary. One corner of the room was completely filled with Indian handcrafts—a buffalo robe, blankets, woven belts and other fabrics, bead and porcupine quill embroideries, leather bags and pouches. Someone took Susette's picture as she sat on the couch covered with the buffalo robe, serenely smiling, her full dark skirt and shirtwaist with tight sleeves puffed at the shoulders all in the latest fashion, herself the living embodiment of the best features of two diverse cultures.

Work also was an expression of all three identities. As Mrs. Thomas Tibbles she wrote articles and editorials for the *Weekly Independent*. As Susette La Flesche she joined with Fannie Reed Giffen, a writer long acquainted with the Omahas, in preparing a little book to be published during the Exposition in Omaha in 1898. It was called *Oo-mah-ha Ta-wa-tha* ("Omaha City"), and of course any history of Omaha must be introduced with stories of the Omaha tribe. It contained stories told by Joseph and Mary—of Big Elk, of the prisoner being taken to St. Louis, of the death of Louis, illustrated by the little picture Mary had so lovingly treasured. There was much material about Iron Eye, his adoption by Big Elk and rise to chieftainship, his accident and dramatic act with cork leg and electric battery, his conversion to Christianity, his philosophy of life. There was a sketch of Standing Hawk. Most important, there was included the full text of the treaty of 1854 with sketches of most of its signers.

"If only the Oldest Grandmother were here to help!" thought Susette again and again. But Memetage (Madeline Wolf) had died in 1895 at age 105.

Susette's own big contribution was the illustrations. All her artistic ability and love of Indian life were concentrated in the drawings. There were two full-page pictures in color, one of a chief in war bonnet and one of a young Omaha girl. Little black and white sketches of Indian life opened and closed each chapter—a canoe in moonlight, a tipi, a baby on cradle board, feathered arrows, a page of picture writing, a travois loaded for the hunt, and of course, symbol of death, the arrow with an unstrung bow. In spite of serious illness in 1897 which sapped her strength and left her strangely upset emotionally, she pursued the task with relentless fervor.

The little book, only ninety pages, *Oo-mah-ha Ta-wa-tha,*

"by Fannie Reed Giffen, with illustrations by Susette La Flesche Tibbles," published by the authors in Lincoln, contained the note: "Illustrations by Inshtatheamba (Bright Eyes) are believed to be the first artistic work by an American Indian ever published."

The decade brought other changes to the family. Marguerite, who had taught at the agency school since Charles' death, married Walter Diddock, the agency's industrial farmer, a steady and industrious young man who would assure his wife and children a happy and prosperous future. Susan, to everyone's surprise, married Henry Picotte, Charles' brother, a young man likable and friendly but lacking the stability of his brother. He had once traveled with a circus and had developed habits oddly at variance with the rigid temperance ethics of Susan. Her two fine sons, however, were full recompense for any deficiencies of the husband, and Susan became even more active in tribal affairs, if possible, not only as a doctor but as interpreter, as adviser, as leader in the little Presbyterian Church in Bancroft and later in the new town of Walthill.

Frank was making a reputation as author as well as scientist. He had written a book about his schooldays at the Mission, called *The Middle Five*, but was having difficulty getting it published. Editors thought books about Indians should substantiate their preconceived notions of savagery and wildness. "This shows too little difference from *any* boy," one editor objected, which was precisely Frank's purpose in writing.

"They don't want to think of us as anything but 'wild Indians,'" Frank complained bitterly.

However, Miss Fletcher sent the manuscript to a friend, Bliss Carman, who was on the board of a Boston publishing house and had a realistic concept of the Indian problem. "The current vulgar notion of the Indian," he wrote her, "is enough to make angels weep." His publishing firm accepted the book, and it was published in 1900, with moderate success. Over sixty years later it would be republished by a great Midwest university as an American classic. Even then its dedication "To the Universal Boy" would challenge the popular concept of Indian history nurtured by Wild West shows and the "westerns" of movies and television.

Miss Fletcher was not so fortunate with another project for

the preservation of Omaha history, the securing of the Sacred White Buffalo Hide for the Peabody Museum. This was the skin of a small whitish buffalo with hoofs and horns intact, a row of shell disks fastened down the back. In 1897 Frank was able with his gramophone to record the songs from Wakonmonthi, its last keeper. At the same time Frank begged him to teach him also the songs belonging to the Sacred Pole, which he had once heard Wakonmonthi sing, but the old man refused. The songs did not belong to his side of the clan, and he was afraid he would not repeat them properly. The slightest mistake might bring misfortune to one of his children. But he agreed to give Frank the Hide. Only let him keep it one more winter, "until the grass should grow again." That winter, however, when the old man was at the Agency on business, the Sacred Hide was stolen. The following summer Frank begged him again for the songs of the Sacred Pole.

"Grandfather, I have been to the other side of the clan, to find someone who knew the songs, but the answer is always, 'I do not know them. Wakonmonthi is the only man who knows them.' Therefore I make bold to come to you again."

The old man looked up at the sky and muttered a prayer, then lighted his pipe and smoked it in silence before passing it to Frank.

"All that you say, my son, is true. Our people have entered a new life utterly unlike the old. All that gave me comfort in this lonely travel was the possession and care of the Sacred Buffalo, but rude hands have taken from me this one solace. For awhile I wept for this loss, morning and evening, but as time passed by tears ceased to flow."

Frank passed the pipe back to him, and he smoked for a long time with eyes fixed on the ground. When he had finished he spoke again, while cleaning his pipe. Yes, he would give the songs. He had abandoned all hope of the old customs ever returning. "As I sit speaking with you, my eldest son, it seems as though the spirits of the old men have returned. I feel their courage and strength in me, and the memory of the songs revives. Make ready, and I shall once more sing the songs of my fathers."

Hastily Frank adjusted his gramophone. The old man sang

with eyes closed, his voice as full and resonant as long before when Frank had heard the same songs in the holy tent. Watching him, he wrote later, was "like watching the last embers of the religious rites of a vanishing people."

There followed a long search for the White Buffalo Hide. There were rumors that it might be on sale at the Omaha Exposition in 1898, but they proved false. Then after months Frank and Miss Fletcher found that it had been sold to a man in Chicago. Efforts were made to buy it back, but the purchaser would not agree. Finally it was deposited with the Academy of Sciences in Lincoln Park.

The grief of the old man was pathetic. If only he had let the Sacred Hide go when Frank had asked him, that it might remain where it belonged, with the Sacred Pole! Sorrow shortened his life, and only once or twice more did he live "to see the grass grow again."

4

Yes, the years should have been happy for Susette. Why, then, did they seem to close about her in ever-tightening coils, constricting both mind and body into strange modes of thought and behavior? She who had always been so mild and kindly of speech, bursting into fits of temper and lashing out in anger against those she loved best! She could see the puzzled dismay and hurt in the faces of friends like Wajapa and the loving concern shown by T.H. and her mother and sisters.

Rosalie too was not well. She had frequent headaches and colds. After February in 1900 she had to spend most of her time in bed, and she did not live to see the new house Ed was planning to build for her that summer. On May 9 Susette received a wire from her second son, Frank, "Mama died this morning."

The family and tribe were not alone in their grief. White people of the community united with Indians in mourning her loss. Even papers like the Omaha *Bee* were eloquent in her praise: "She was a woman of rare business qualifications . . . but her influence among the Omahas was not due to her sagacity. . . . She was the resource of the poor, the sick, and the improvident. Her life was a benediction. Truly she was one of the most remarkable women of the state." Later when a town was settled on the new railroad near the southwest of the reservation near where she had lived, it was named "Rosalie."

It was Mary who again comforted her daughters. Though lonely, still living in the house Joseph had built on their allotment, she retained her serene faith and inexhaustible courage. But it was more than comfort which Susette needed. In her troubled spirit grief was mingled with a complexity of emotions—anxiety, helplessness, and, worst of all, guilt. She knew suddenly that this last had been with her for a long time, perhaps responsible for much of her mental unrest. She had dedicated her life to serving her people, then run away and left the hard work to others. Should she be down here writing about bimetallism and an income tax when she might be up there on the reservation doing—yes, doing what? For she was not Rosalie, the businesswoman, nor Susan, the trained doctor, nor Marguerite the teacher. When she tried to express something of her frustration to T.H., he only patted her shoulder and laughed.

"Nonsense, my dear! Don't you realize that you have done more for your tribe than anyone else in your family, even your father? Without you they would undoubtedly have been carted away to Indian Territory, lost their lands. There would have been no Dawes Bill, no allotment. I know the trouble with you. You're homesick."

Relieved that he had diagnosed her strange behavior, he took her back more frequently to the farm; then some time after Rosalie's death they moved there permanently, T.H. editing the *Independent* by mail and frequent trips to Lincoln. The result was satisfying. At first she was almost her old self, exulting in the closeness to nature which had made her childhood so happy and in the renewal of family relationships. There were often picnic suppers in the yard, with Susette presiding serenely over the table, and children—Rosalie's, Marguerite's, Susan's, Lucy's, Carey's—tumbling about in the grass. T.H. sometimes joined in their sports, looking like a great good-natured lion frolicking with lambs. He also found life on the farm exhilarating, so long as subsistence did not depend on agricultural labor. Unfortunately, however, he was not popular in Bancroft, probably because he was considered a radical. He could count only one person a real friend, John G. Neihardt, a young man working for J. J. Elkin, who ran an insurance and real estate business, as well as being an Indian trader. But Neihardt's real interest was literature. At nineteen his first book had been published, *The Divine Enchantment*, based on Vedanta philosophy, and now in his early twenties he was evincing the concern for Indian culture and problems which was to make him one of the foremost writers of his day. He and T.H. had many interests in common.

Susette's contentment was brief. Here, closer to the tribe and their problems, she became still more agitated in mind. Too many things were going wrong. Each Indian had his own allotment of land, yes, but more often than not he was failing to cultivate it, finding it easier to lease it to some more enterprising white man and live on the rental money. "Allotments are ordered," reported a paper at the Lake Mohonk Conference on the Indian in 1894, "not with reference generally to the Indian, but to the greed and demand of the white people about the reservation who wish to secure the surplus land."

The twenty-five-year trust period would expire in 1910. Susette could almost predict the result. Covetous white men like Peebles and his ring would be everywhere with enticing offers which few Indians could resist. Content oneself with a small annual stipend of lease money when what looked like a gigantic sum was there for the taking, to slip through one's fingers in exchange for the white man's liquor and baubles? For few, even of Joseph's carefully indoctrinated Young Men's Party, were like Wajapa, with his neat house, his well-cultivated fields, his cow, chickens, and pigs, his children sent away to Eastern schools, his frugality and profound commonsense. It was well she could not know that within the next few decades the original 300,000 acres given the Omahas by the treaty of 1854 would have shrunk to 30,000!

She was glad that Joseph could not wake from his dream of a sober, responsible people. "The whiskey business is horrible," Rosalie had written not long before her death. Even members of their own family had succumbed to the habit. Ed had once had to put his brother-in-law in a wagon and take him home.

Frank had been even more bitterly explicit in a letter to Caryl in 1901. "No one can deny that since the Omahas found it easy to get liquor they did more loafing and since they had the privilege of leasing their lands there has been more and more idleness, drunkenness and vice. For a time debauchery was rampant. There is no denying that these two things, the illicit traffic of liquor among the Indians and the indiscriminate leasing of their lands have done more harm than anything that happened to them in their history."

What, wondered Susette despairingly, had gone wrong? The trust period, they had believed, should have prepared the new landowners, through constant education and assistance from government, to handle their affairs with the same efficiency and incentive as their white neighbors. But instead of teaching, government had dictated. Instead of assisting, it had controlled. Instead of encouraging economic responsibility, it had doled. Even the money that legally belonged to a man was issued to him by the Agent in driblets, like a child's allowance, and by a process involving endless red tape. And waiting by the Agent's table, almost invariably, was a white creditor demanding payment for a note, perhaps for $25 or $30 when the Indian had borrowed but $15.

These "skinners," as the more canny, both Indians and whites, called them, were local men. Many were pillars of the community, even of the church, so respected that some went to the state legislature or even to Congress. They would not have thought of cheating their own kind. But it was always "open season" on Indians.

Citizenship would solve everything, Susette and T.H. had insisted. Once the Omahas had access to the country's courts, the protection of the country's laws, their worst problems would be solved. They had forgotten that the judges and lawyers of the courts were white men, the laws were made by white men, the "Little Grandfather" in Lincoln was a white man, and the "Big Grandfather" in Washington. And white men had learned through centuries of experience the complicated techniques of their laws and courts, often the means of manipulating them to their own ends.

"The Omahas went to bed as Omahas," one young member of the tribe had written in the *Red Man*, a paper issued at Carlisle, "and woke up as citizens."

Susette was heartsick. Sobering, chilling thoughts: Had she and T. H. been wrong in all they had accomplished? *Had the allotment been bad instead of good?* Would future generations condemn it as a mistake, as betrayal of their tribal identity, of the communal values which had been their most precious heritage? If they did, she hoped they would understand it had been the only way to save their land, to keep them from exile.

Then one day she had a visitor. It was the young man who had come to her some twenty years ago with such eager questions and blazing, knife-sharp eyes. He was a man of nearly forty now, but she knew him at once. Lightning-Eye, she thought again instantly, as an old memory leaped to her mind. Yes, in spite of the fact that this man was of mixed-blood and the son of Standing Bear had been a full-blooded Indian, the latter might have grown to look something like this had he lived—proud, fully mature, the fires of emotion still ablaze but contained and controlled, helpless anger honed to a fine edge of confident purpose.

"Tom Sloan," she greeted him cordially. "I have heard good things about you." For some years he had been a clerk at the Agency, during which time he had studied law and been admitted to the Bar of the State of Nebraska.

This time he had not come to ask questions.

"Grandmother," he said, giving her the customary salutation of respect, "you once shared with me your best knowledge and advice. Now I want to tell you some of the things I and many of my friends are thinking."

He talked for a long time, using language which would have done credit to any cultured and well-educated white man. Less than ten years later, as one of the six founders of the Society of American Indians and destined to become president of the organization, he was to give an address expressing some of the same convictions which he voiced to Susette that day.

"Early in the administration of Indian affairs it became evident that the Indian could not rely upon the statements of the Indian Service officials, the laws made by Congress for their protection, nor the treaties made between them and the United States of America. . . . The idea of the Indian Office seems to be that they are better fitted to handle all the affairs of the Indian than the Indian himself, or the other departments of a republican form of government. . . . The evil seems to be that the Indian Bureau administers as if the Indians were selected for their benefit, to exploit them, and not that they were created for the benefit of the Indian. . . . The representatives of the business people of the town adjoining a reservation desire that the land be obtained in fee, sold or otherwise disposed of, not for the welfare of the Indian, but to enable them, the white people, to develop business or trade. . . .

"In the administration of Indian affairs there should be such reforms as will give the Indian in hearings and investigations those rights which belong to him under the Constitution of the United States. That his property may be protected by regular court proceedings, and that when the court decrees certain rights, no Indian official be permitted to disregard the decree of the court and the law protecting the Indian, and not to violate his own oath of office to the detriment of the Indian. . . ."

Susette listened as the young man talked of injustices on the reservations and what he intended to do about them. "A lawyer," she thought with wonder and gratitude, "and an able one. An Omaha, yet with all the knowledge and experience and skill of a white man!"

That, she knew with a sudden flash of insight, was what she herself would like to have been. But who had ever heard of a woman lawyer! As unheard of as, just a few years ago, for a woman to become a doctor, like Susan, or to mount a platform and speak to crowds of people, as she herself had done! She felt a swift surge of relief and exultation. Her work was not ended, it was only beginning. Hers had been the task of trail-breaking. Others, like this youth with the "lightning-eye," would somehow make of it a new "red road of life" for their people. As long as there were spirits like his emerging, the future of the tribe would be safe.

"We can't depend on the white man to solve our problems," Thomas Sloan said finally, as if giving voice to her own thoughts. "We of my generation and of those to come must work together to understand our rights, to organize and fight for them, and to keep alive the values in our heritage worth saving. We must not let the Waxes take them from us. Perhaps sometime they will realize that they need them too. I, and some of the others I know, are willing to give our lives to the task. It was you who first started me thinking about these things, and I wanted you to know."

When he had gone Susette felt as if a great burden had rolled from her shoulders.

<h1 style="text-align:center">5</h1>

Susan's keen professional eyes detected the truth before the rest of the family. T.H. noted only that his beloved Bright Eyes was once more serene and untroubled in mind, and he took himself off, relieved of anxiety, to Lincoln, not knowing that as soon as he left she retreated in abject weariness to a couch and spent most of her days there.

It was 1902, and the Populist party was already looking toward the next election year. Though unaware as yet that he would be running as candidate for Vice-President, T.H. was heavily involved in politics as well as editing his journal. Populism had lost its great thrust back in 1896 when the Democratic party through its candidate for President, Nebraska's William Jennings Bryan, had adopted the plank of free silver, and it had been pronounced dying in 1900. But T.H. was never one to desert a cause until it was dead and buried, and he was fighting with all the tenacity of a cornered animal. Like many exponents of unpopular causes, he was a generation ahead of his time. Within three decades most of the tenets of Populism—the income tax, the direct election of senators, the social legislation—would become accepted national policies.

Bright Eyes (for these days somehow she wanted to be just Inshtatheamba) was glad to be left alone. She wanted to savor this springtime which, she knew as well as Susan, might well be her last. A pity, some might think, to die before one was fifty. Rosalie had been even younger, only thirty-nine. But Bright Eyes had no regrets. Since her talk with Thomas Sloan, she had been content.

There had never been a more beautiful spring. As Bright Eyes lay listening and watching, reality merged with memory. At the sound of the first thunder, Wakonda's summons, she saw the old men take out their sacred bundles, go to the high hills, and blow smoke to the four winds; saw them change into a boy climbing up and up, bound on his vision quest. He had the face of Louis—or was it the son of Standing Bear?—or Thomas Sloan with his blazing, knife-sharp eyes? Whoever he was, he was fasting, weeping, waging the eternal battle between man and his flesh—praying. "Wakonda, here, poor and needy, I stand. Come hither, haste, to help me!"

Here in the Logan Valley one could not hear the Smoky Waters, yet she heard them, swollen to a great flood, singing, bursting their earth bounds, sweeping in the full spate of their triumph toward some unknown and even more triumphant flood. She heard the rushing of wings and shrill honkings as the flocks followed the path of their seven couriers up the long sky corridor. Never had the feathery mist of the willows been more golden, the new cottonwood tips aglow with more magic fire. The crimson of cardinals, the sapphire glints of bluejays were brighter than she had ever seen them. She waited with an almost painful eagerness for the return of the "gone-down" birds, afraid they might come too late, and when she heard the first meadowlark flute loud and clear in Omaha, "It is spring, it is spring!" her sense of fulfillment was complete.

It was May, the "Moon in Which the Tribe Plants," when she became so desperately ill that she had to take to her bed. No keeping of the secret any longer. T.H. went no more to Lincoln but spent his days in blundering, ineffective nursing and much of his nights walking the floor like a caged lion. Susan came every day, often spending the night. One day toward the end of May she knew the end was very near. She asked Winnie, the devoted, competent young woman whom Ed had married sometime after Rosalie's death and whom they had all learned to love, to spend the night with her. Mary also was there, and they expected Jack, Rosalie's son. T.H. kept to himself in the front room.

"Always the odd one," commented Susan in a scornful aside.

"I don't blame him," said Winnie gently. "It would be hard for him to see his Bright Eyes go."

Her mind wavered toward the last. She would babble unintelligibly, then speak clearly and lucidly. Asking a question of Winnie and realizing that she had spoken in Omaha, she

apologized. "Sorry, dear, forgot you don't know our language."
She asked for the boys, meaning Rosalie's sons. Jack had gone
to the Agency, Winnie told her, but he might be coming by any
time.

When it was over, Mary, heretofore calm, yielded to abandoned weeping. It was as if all the grief for her many sorrows
had concentrated in this final agony of loss. Mingled with the
weeping was the wild Indian mourning wail, haunting and
plaintive as the death song she had once heard the captive sing.

"Where can I go
That I might live forever?
The old fathers have gone to the spirit-land.
Where can I go
That we might live together?"

She would not be comforted. Fortunately Jack came soon and,
though little more than twenty, took command of the situation
with wise proficiency. Taking his weeping grandmother in his
arms, he carried her to a rocking chair and sat rocking her,
murmuring comforting phrases and singing songs in Omaha
until she quieted. As soon as morning came he prepared for
departure. The son of Ed Farley did not intend to remain in
Thomas Tibbles' house, or let his family do so, longer than
necessary.

"Come," he said brusquely to the three women. "There is
nothing more we can do here now. I'm going to take you
home."

They went, reluctantly, after Susan and Winnie had performed the last tender ministrations for the beloved sister. So it
was that T.H. was left alone with his dead.

6

John G. Neihardt was touched and surprised when the
message came. Thomas Tibbles had asked his friend to sit up
with him during the night before his wife's funeral. Of course
he was glad to go. He well knew that he was one of the few
friends, perhaps the only one, that Tibbles had in Bancroft. But

where were his wife's relatives? He knew of at least a dozen. Surely they were the proper companions of a grieving husband!

He went to the farm some three miles north of town and found T.H. alone. All the rest of his life he was to wonder why. True, he had heard rumors of misunderstanding between T.H. and his wife's people, but this would seem to be a time for reconciliation, if ever. Neihardt knew many of the La Flesches and Farleys. Frank had given him a first edition of his book, *The Middle Five*. The Farley boys, about his age, were his close friends. He had met Mrs. Diddock, the wife of a cattleman, as well as the Farleys, through their business relationships with J. J. Elkin. He admired Dr. Susan tremendously. In fact, he liked them all.

But he liked Thomas Tibbles too. Though he had known him only a year, a close friendship had developed between them. The very qualities which made T.H. suspect and unpopular with the rest of the townspeople—fearless, often brutal candor, defense of the underdog, radical idealism—were the ones Neihardt most respected and admired. He knew T.H. to be a truly great man, but far ahead of his time, and so anathema to many of his contemporaries.

So the night began. Seventy years later John Neihardt, when he had become Poet Laureate of the State of Nebraska and one of the country's most famous writers of Americana, would remember it as the strangest, loneliest, weirdest night he had ever spent.

"Come," said T.H. soon after his friend had entered the house. He took him into the front bedroom where the still form lay on a bed, white cloths covering the face. T.H. removed the cloths and stood looking down, shoulders shaking.

"Look at her," he said softly after a long silence. "My Bright Eyes. Isn't she beautiful?"

John Neihardt looked. It was the first time he had ever seen Susette La Flesche Tibbles. The face was round, smooth, serene, the wings of black hair folded gently about it. "Like bird's wings," he thought, always the poet. She looked strangely alive. A faint smile seemed to play about the mouth. He had a feeling the eyes had just closed and would soon open, and he wanted to see them, knowing they must have been her most vibrant and compelling feature. It was a pretty Indian face, he decided, with character, if not beauty. But—yes, the man was right. Death had made her beautiful.

T.H. dipped the cloths in a basin of cold water, fresh from the deep well, and laid them over the face with slow caressing motions. (To keep it from changing color, thought Neihardt with sudden understanding. Obviously there had been no embalmment.)

They went back into the front room and sat down, and Tibbles began to talk, like a man in the moments of drowning, reminiscing about the past, especially of his life with Bright Eyes. He went on and on, then suddenly sprang up with an abrupt, "Let's go look at her again." Once more they went into the front bedroom with the basin of cold water. There was the same long tender inspection, then the dipping of the cloths, the replacing of them with the big caressing hands.

This went on all night, over and over, in the same strange sequence—the old man's garrulous reminiscences, the sudden "Let's go back and look at her again!", the return to the room with its flickering shadows, the dipping of the cloths, the covering of the still face. That night Neihardt heard the whole story of T.H.'s life with Bright Eyes—the defense of the Poncas, the tour with Standing Bear, the year in England—and he listened enthralled, knowing that he was being given intimate participation not only in an exceptional love story but in one of the truly dramatic sagas of American history. Sometimes T.H. would almost forget that Bright Eyes was dead. Relating some humorous incident, like a joke of Standing Bear, he would throw back his great head and laugh and laugh. Then, suddenly remembering, he would spring up, eyes dark with agony. "Come, let's go look at her again."

The night passed, and Neihardt returned to town. But not to forget. As long as he lived he would see the still face with its folded wings of hair, the shaking shoulders, the big hands so tender and caressing, dipping and changing the cloths; hear the words repeated over and over, "Isn't she beautiful? Isn't she beautiful!"

She was laid in the cemetery on the opposite side of Bancroft beside Joseph, Nicomi, and the Oldest Grandmother. Later a stone was placed on her grave bearing this inscription:

SUSETTE LA FLESCHE

BRIGHT EYES

Wife of T. H. Tibbles

1854–1902

SHE DID ALL THAT SHE COULD TO MAKE THE

WORLD HAPPIER AND BETTER

In the lefthand corner was engraved her own symbol of a life fulfilled and ended—an arrow poised for flight within an unstrung bow.

The author makes grateful acknowledgment to the following:

Mrs. Pauline Tyndall and Wayne Tyndall of the Omaha Tribe for invaluable help with research and for reading and criticism of the manuscript;

Mrs. Winona Porter for entertainment during visits to the Omaha Tribe and for help with research;

Mrs. Rosalie Boughn, niece of Bright Eyes, for sharing family reminiscences;

Mrs. Vivien K. Barris for sharing reminiscences, papers, and photos of the Tibbles family;

Mrs. Norma Kidd Green for permission to use source materials contained in her book, *Iron Eye's Family*;

Professor Carter Revard for his exhaustive reading and criticism of the manuscript;

Mrs. Mary Logan, a native speaker of Omaha, for help with the forms and meanings of Omaha words (Mrs. Logan was delivered by the sister of Bright Eyes, Dr. Susan La Flesche Picotte);

Mrs. Barbara H. Matthiessen and Miss Eileen Helicar for their exhaustive research in this country and in England;

Dr. John G. Niehardt for sharing his reminiscences of Thomas Tibbles and the Omaha Tribe, especially of the night before Bright Eyes' burial;

Curators of the Nebraska Historical Society, Lincoln, Nebraska; the Museum of the American Indian, New York City; the Peabody Museum, Cambridge, Massachusetts; the National Museum of Natural History, Smithsonian Institution, Washington, D.C.; the British Museum Archives, London;

The University of Wisconsin Press for permission to quote the following: From Francis La Flesche, *The Middle Five* (Madison: The University of Wisconsin Press, 1963 by the Regents of the University of Wisconsin), sections from pp. 127–129, and for permission to use the book as source material;

Doubleday and Co., Inc. New York, for permission to use certain direct quotations from Thomas H. Tibbles' *Buckskin and Blanket Days* and to use other details and incidents in the book as source materials.

BOOKS

Andrist, Ralph K. *The Long Death* (*The Last Days of the Plains Indians*). New York, Macmillan, 1964–1969

Ballou, Ellen B. *The Building of the House, Houghton Mifflin's Formative Years.* Houghton Mifflin, Boston, 1970

Brown, Dee. *Bury My Heart at Wounded Knee.* Holt, Rinehart and Winston, New York, 1970.

Carter, E. Russell. *The Gift Is Rich.* Friendship Press, New York, 1955

Clarke, Helen Archibald. *Longfellow's Country*, Chapter V, "The Lore of Hiawatha." Baker and Taylor Company, New York, 1909

Davis, Christopher. *North American Indian.* Hamlyn Publishing Group, Ltd., London, 1969

Deloria, Vine, Jr. *Custer Died for Your Sins, an Indian Manifesto.* Macmillan, New York, 1969

Dictionary of American Biography, "Bright Eyes," pgs. 46, 47

Dorsey, James Owen. "Omaha and Ponka Letters." Bureau of American Ethnology, Annual Report. Government Printing Office, Washington, 1891

———. "Omaha Sociology." Bureau of American Ethnology, Third Annual Report, Government Printing Office, Washington, 1884

———. "Omaha Dwellings, Furniture, and Implements." Bureau of American Ethnology, 13th Annual Report, Washington, 1896

——— "The Çegiha Language." Bureau of American Ethnology, Annual Report, Government Printing Office, Washington, 1890

Encyclopedia Britannica. *Inshtatheamba (Bright Eyes)*. Pg. 307

Farb, Peter. "The American Indian, a portrait in limbo." From *Man's Rise to Civilization as Shown by the Indians of North America from Primeval Times to the Coming of the Industrial State*. E. P. Dutton and Co., Inc. New York, 1968

Fletcher, Alice C., and La Flesche, Francis. "The Omaha Tribe." Bureau of American Ethnology, 27th Annual Report, Government Printing Office, Washington, 1905–1906

Foreman, Grant. *The Last Trek of the Indians*. University of Chicago Press, 1946

Fritz, Henry E. *The Movement for Indian Assimilation*. University of Pennsylvania Press, 1942

Giffen, Fannie Reed. With illustrations by Susette La Flesche Tibbles. *Oo-Mah-Ha Ta-Wa-Tha*. Lincoln, Nebraska, 189?

Green, Norma Kidd. *Iron Eye's Family, The Children of Joseph La Flesche*. Sponsored by the Nebraska State Historical Society, Lincoln, Nebraska, 1969

Haley, Pearl Patrick, *O'po of the Omahas*. Doubleday, New York, 1956

Harsha, William Justin. *Ploughed Under: The Story of an Indian Chief, Told by Himself. Introduction by Inshta Theamba (Bright Eyes)*. Ford, Howard and Hulbert, New York, 1881

Jackson, Helen Hunt. *A Century of Dishonor*. Reprint, Harper and Row, New York, 1965

Josephy, Alvin M., Jr. *Red Power: The American Indians' Fight for Freedom*. American Heritage Press, New York, 1971

La Farge, Oliver. *A Pictorial History of the American Indian*. Crown Publishers, Inc., New York, 1956

La Flesche, Francis. *The Middle Five*. Reprint, University of Wisconsin Press, Madison, Wisconsin, 1963

———. *The Omaha Tribe*. (With Alice C. Fletcher) Bureau of American Ethnology, 27th Annual Report, Government Printing Office, Washington, 1905–1906

Longfellow, Samuel. *Henry Wadsworth Longfellow*. Houghton, Mifflin and Co., Boston, 1886

McNickle, D'Arcy. *The Indian Tribes of the United States, Ethnic and Cultural Survival*. Oxford University Press, London, 1962

Mead, Margaret. *The Changing Culture of an Indian Tribe*. Columbia University Press, New York, 1932

Mississipppi Valley Historical Review. Story of the Ponca Removal. Pgs. 498–516

Mooney, James. *The Ghost Dance Religion and the Sioux Outbreak of 1890.* Bureau of American Ethnology, 14th Annual Report, Government Printing Press, Washington, 1892–1893

Neihardt, John G. *Black Elk Speaks.* University of Nebraska Press, Lincoln, Nebraska, 1932, 1959

———. *A Cycle of the West.* Macmillan, New York, 1949, 1961. University of Nebraska Press, Lincoln, Nebraska, 1953

———. *When the Tree Flowered.* University of Nebraska Press, Lincoln, Nebraska, 1970

Odell, Ruth. *Helen Hunt Jackson.* D. Appleton-Century Company, New York, 1939

Paxton, Frederick L. *Recent History of the United States.* Chapter XVII, "Populism." Houghton Mifflin and Co., Boston, 1921

Priest, Loring Benson. *Uncle Sam's Step-children, The Reformation of U. S. Indian Policy, 1865–1887.* Rutgers University Press, New Brunswick, N.J., 1942

Sandoz, Mari. *Love Song to the Plains.* Harper and Row, New York, 1961. University of Nebraska Press, Lincoln, Nebraska, 1966

Schmitt, Martin F. *General George Crook, His Autobiography.* University of Oklahoma Press, Norman, Oklahoma, 1946

Sheldon, Addison E. *Nebraska Old and New.* Lincoln, Nebraska, 1937

Slotkin, J. S. *The Peyote Religion, A Study in Indian-White Relations.* The Free Press, Glencoe, Illinois, 1956

Stabler, Eunice W. *How Beautiful the Land of My Forefathers.* Private Printing, 1943

Stone, Eric, M.D. *Medicine Among the American Indians.* Hafner Publishing Co., New York, 1962

Stoutenburgh, John L., Jr. *Dictionary of the American Indian.* Philosophical Library, New York, 1949

Tibbles, Thomas Henry. *Buckskin and Blanket Days, Memoirs of a Friend of the Indians.* Doubleday, New York, 1957

———. *Hidden Power: A Secret History of the Indian Ring.* New York, 1881

———. *The Ponca Chiefs.* Lockwood, Brooks and Company, Boston, 1880. Reprinted for the Omaha Posse of the Westerners by the Old Army Press, Bellevue, Nebraska, 1970

Vogel, Virgil J. *American Indian Medicine.* University of Oklahoma Press, Norman, Oklahoma.

Wagenknecht, Edward. *Longfellow: A Full-Length Portrait*. Longmans, Green and Co., New York, 1955

Pamphlets and Magazines

Frank Leslie's Journal, January 3, 1880. "Bright Eyes"

Look, June 2, 1970. "America's Indians: Reawakening of a Conquered People," William Hedgepeth

Nebraska History Magazine, Vol. XIII. No. 4. Pgs. 238–247. "Some Recollections of Thomas Tibbles," Charles Q. De France

———. Vol. XIII. No. 4. Pgs. 271–276. "Anecdotes of Standing Bear," Thomas Tibbles

New England Pictorial, February 1881. "A Sketch of Bright Eyes and the Ponca Question"

North American Review, 1881. "The Indian Dilemma—Civilization or Extinction," Carl Schurz. In *Annals of America 1876–1883*

Omaha World-Herald Magazine, July 30, 1961. "Nicomi—A Proud Nebraskan," Alice Wright and Grace Steinberg

"People of the Smoky Waters: The Omahas." Text by Steven Standing Bear. Photos by Ibahan

Presbyterian Life. "A Comeback for the Vanishing American," James W. Hoffman. Series of four articles, reprinted by Board of National Missions, United Presbyterian Church, U.S.A., New York, 1969

Reader's Digest, April 1970. "Our Shameful Failure with America's Indians," Edgar S. Cahn

St. Nicholas, January, 1881. "Nedawi," Susette La Flesche (Bright Eyes)

"The School Interests of Elizabeth," Elias D. Smith. Elizabeth, N.J., 1911

U.S. Congress. A Bill for the Relief of the Ponca Tribe of Indians. S. 1298. February 16, 1880

———. Senate Report No. 91-501. "Indian Education: A National Tragedy—A National Challenge." Government Printing Office, Washington, 1969

U.S. Department of the Interior, Commissioner of Indian Affairs, Annual Reports for 1879–1886

U.S. Treaty with the Omahas, March 16, 1854

U.S. Treaty with the Ponca Tribe of Indians, March 12, 1858. Ratified by the Senate March 8, 1859

Wide Awake, June 1883. "Omaha Legends and Tent-Stories," Mrs. Susette Tibbles (Bright Eyes)

Newspapers

Baltimore Sun, April 17, 1880. "Indians and their Wrongs. Address by an Indian Maiden"

Boston Daily Advertiser, 1879: September 16, 20; October 8, "The Indian War"; October 21, "The Indian Troubles"; October 24, "The Mission of Standing Bear"; October 30, "The Visiting Poncas," "The Public Reception," "Miss La Flesche's Address," etc.; November 4, "The Monday Lectures"; November 11, "The Poncas," Longfellow Episode; November 15, "Standing Bear"; November 17, "The Oppressed Poncas"; November 26, "The Poor Poncas," Merchants Exchange meeting, address by Bright Eyes; November 28, "The Indians," Schurz's statement; November 29, Standing Bear's reply to Schurz; December 3, "Indian's Rights," meeting in Faneuil Hall, "Carl Schurz and the Poncas"; December 6, "Broken Treaties"; December 10, "An Indian Reception"; December 24, "The Present Difficulties of the Indian Problem"

———. 1880: February 16, "The Ponca Indians"; February 17, "Prospect of Justice to the Poncas at Last"; February 29, "The Indian Problem"; May 25, "The Drought in Nebraska"; August 13, "The Indian Expulsion"; July 8, "Mr. Tibbles' Arrest"; November 13, "A Cause to be Remembered"; November 15, "The Ponca Petition"; November 19, "The Administration and the Indian Service"

———. 1881: January 26, "The Ponca Wrongs," "Bright Eyes Complimented"

Boston Herald, March 4, 1880. "The Status of the Indian"

Boston Morning Journal, October 30, 1879. "The Ponca Indians"

Boston Transcript, February 1, February 16, 1881. "The Ponca Question"

Boston Traveler. January 11, 1881, "Miss Bright Eyes"; March 2, 1881, "Bright Eyes"

Chicago Inter-Ocean, October 1879. Interview quoted in *Woman's Journal*, December 27, 1879

Christian Union, March 10, 1880. "The Indian Question," Susette La Flesche

Daily Graphic, New York, December 19, 1879. "Schurz' Indian." Picture of group

The Independent, December 18, 1879. "The Story of the Poncas," Colonel E. C. Kemble

Lincoln Sunday Star, December 11, 1932. Article on Susette

New York Daily/Herald Tribune, 1879: November 24. "Standing Bear of the Poncas"; December 6, 8, 10, "Seeking Redress in the East," "Indian Wrongs," reception; December 13, "Wrongs of Indians," meeting in Steinway Hall; December 15, "The Indian Problem," letter of "H.H.";

December 19, "Mr. Schurz on Indian Affairs"; December 28, "H.H.'s reply to Schurz"; December 29, "Wrongs of the Poncas"

———. 1880: January 17, "Justice to the Indians," meeting in Chickering Hall; March 12, "The Butchered Chief"

New York Times, 1879: August 22, "Schurz on the Poncas"; August 23, "Wrongs of the Poncas," Secretary Sherman's story; September 22, "Standing Bear enticed away"; November 28, "Secretary Schurz on the Indians"; December 9, "Is the Indian a Citizen?"; December 13, "For the Ponca Indians"; December 21, subscription in New York to press litigation.

———. 1880: January 17, "Rights of the Ponca Indians," meeting in Chickering Hall; February 10, Mr. Deering's Relief Bill; February 14, "Fraud in Removal"; February 15, E. C. Kemble's views; February 28, "The Indian Question," by Susette La Flesche; March 25, W. H. Lincoln's charges against Inspector Kemble; March 31, April 2, Poncas freed back to reservation; April 20, 30, Indian Bill passed in 46th Congress; May 2, 3, 8, 14, 20, Conference Committee's report; June 1, Congressional report; June 29, "Making Mischief Among Indians"; July 12, Tibbles' visit to Poncas; July 23, Senator Dawes' views; July 29, Poncas' title to land; December 3, Schurz on past and proper policy of United States toward Poncas; December 4, Ponca's rights to lands established; December 11, 20, Presidential Commission appointed; December 23, 25, 28, Ponca chiefs in Washington; December 29, "The Wrongs of the Poncas"

———. 1881: January 8, Poncas' return to Dakota; January 10, suppressed evidence on Poncas publicized by W. H. Lincoln and Bright Eyes defended; January 27, 28, "Poncas' Wrongs," Presidential Commission report; January 30, Poncas' testimony before Senate committee; January 31, Secretary Schurz charged with garbling facts; February 3, President Hayes' message to Congress; February 10, Secretary Schurz' reply to Senator Dawes on killing of Big Snake; February 23, Boston man's letter criticizing Schurz, July 27, Bright Eyes' marriage to T. H. Tibbles; August 18, 19, 20, Poncas in Dakota, successful attempt to secure land from Sioux; August 22, Ponca question settled by Secretary Kirkwood.

New York Sun, October 16, 1904. "Thomas H. Tibbles, a Man of Many Adventures"

Omaha World Herald, February 28, 1915. "When Instah-Muzzhe ('Iron Eye') Ruled the Omaha Indians in Nebraska," Eugene O. Mayfield; February 27, 1916, "A Life of Thrills" (article about Tibbles), Eugene O. Mayfield

———. February 1879–June 1879. Accounts of the Ponca tragedy

Philadelphia Public Ledger, March 6, 1880. "A Bad Case of Bright Eyes," statement of Agent Vore

Sioux City Sunday Journal, May 10, 1970. "Beautiful Land of the Omahas," Maxine Burnett; May 17, 1970, "Operation Bootstrap at Macy," Maxine Burnett

Washington Evening Star, 1879: November 8, 10, 12, 15, 17, 19; 1880: February 12, 13, "Bright Eyes Examined"; February 16, 17, "The Ponca investigation"

Woman's Journal, Boston. December 6, 27, 1879; November 27, December 18, 1880; May 14, 1881. Articles about Bright Eyes and the Poncas

Family Papers, Manuscript Collections, Museum Archives

Historical Society of New Jersey and library of Elizabeth, New Jersey. Papers of the Elizabeth Institute

Museum of the American Indian, New York City. *Thomas S. Tibbles family papers; Tibbles' scrap book*

Nebraska State Historical Society, Lincoln, Nebraska.
La Flesche family papers, containing: Susette's autograph album, Rosalie's diary; correspondence between Rosalie Farley and her sons, Rosalie and her brother Frank, Rosalie and Susette, Ed Farley and Frank, Frank and Caryl, Eda Tibbles and Marguerite; letters from Susan in medical college, 1887–1888; papers by Susan: "Primitive Farming among the Omahas," "Folk Tales of the Omahas," etc.
Books of Susette
Alice C. Fletcher papers
Missionary letters from workers at the Mission to Walter Lowrie, official of the Presbyterian Board of Missions: Charles Sturges, July 1856–February 1860; Reverend William Hamilton, 1856, 1866, 1868; R. J. Burtt, 1860–1866; Agent Furnas, May 29, 1866; Homer W. Patch, 1800–1883; John T. Copley, 1884–1887
Family pictures

Peabody Museum, Cambridge, Mass. Exhibits and artifacts of the Omaha tribe; Alice C. Fletcher papers and reports

Smithsonian Institute, Washington, D.C. Alice C. Fletcher and Francis La Flesche papers

Schlesinger Library, Radcliffe College, Cambridge, Mass. Jane Gay Dodge papers

NOTES

While most of the Omaha customs, rites, history, legends, language, music, medicine, societies, hunting, etc., are derived from general sources, such as Fletcher and La Flesche, *The Omaha Tribe* (referred to below as Fletcher), and Dorsey, "Omaha Sociology" (referred to as Dorsey), the following notes relating to specific incidents may be of interest.

i–v. Details of Bright Eyes' meeting with Longfellow are recounted in Boston newspapers, Tibbles' *Buckskin and Blanket Days*, and Odell's *Helen Hunt Jackson*.

PART ONE

Chapter One. Susette's reluctance to enter the tent is affirmed by family tradition. Details of Joseph's early life are supplemented by a sketch in *Oo-mah-ha Ta-wa-tha* and a paper by Wajapa. The incident of the falling of the pipes is related by Frank in Dorsey.

Chapter Two. Joseph's early experience with drunkenness and his organization of the police force are related in Fletcher. Two Crows' lapse from sobriety is detailed by Mayfield in "When Instah-Muzzhe Ruled." Susette herself related the story of the turkeys in "Nedawi." Susan's Notebook gives full details of farming operations. The incidents of desecrating the Sacred Pole and of Louis' pursuit of the buffalo really happened to Frank at a later time instead of to Louis (found in Dorsey, *The Ȼegiha Language*), but the author has taken the liberty of assigning them to this period for purposes of time and plot concentration. Susette relates the story of the little bird in *Oo-mah-ha*

Ta-wa-tha. Joseph's reluctance to permit the anointing of the pole is found in Dorsey.

Chapter Three. School details are derived from Frank La Flesche's *The Middle Five* and from missionary letters. Louis' death is described in *Oo-mah-ha Ta-wa-tha.*

Chapter Four. Joseph's display of his artificial leg and the electric battery is detailed in *Oo-mah-ha Ta-wa-tha.* The incident of the children and the Winnebago boy comes from *The Middle Five,* from which Joseph's speech is quoted.

Chapter Five. Josephs refusal to let his daughter be branded by the mark of honor is authenticated by Fletcher. His conversion to Christianity is related in *Oo-mah-ha Ta-wa-tha.*

PART TWO

Chapter One. Details of the Ponca troubles are found in Jackson, *A Century of Dishonor,* Chapter VI; Brown's *Bury My Heart at Wounded Knee;* Tibbles' *Ponca Chiefs;* Foreman's *The Last Trek of the Indians;* and many other sources. Hardships among the Omahas were related by Susette in her speeches and recorded in Eastern newspapers.

Chapter Two. Wajapa's letter is printed in *Oo-mah-ha Ta-wa-tha.* Susette's school problems and other incidents are detailed in her Eastern speeches.

Chapter Three. Details of Tibbles life are in his *Buckskin and Blanket Days.* His efforts for the Poncas are related in full in his *Ponca Chiefs.* Susette's letter to Tibbles is preserved in the family papers.

Chapter Four. A handwritten paper by Susette in the La Flesche papers gives details of her trip with Joseph to Indian Territory. Other sources as in previous chapters.

PART THREE

Chapter One. Full details of all speeches, meetings, etc., are given in the newspaper accounts. Incidents about Standing Bear are from Tibbles' "Anecdotes of Standing Bear" in the Nebraska History magazine.

Chapter Two. A description of Bright Eyes' visit to the Bottas is given in Odell's *Helen Hunt Jackson.*

Chapter Three. Mrs. Jackson's crusade for the Indians is also detailed in Odell. Tibbles' visit to Indian Territory is related in full in his *Buckskin and Blanket Days* as well as in Eastern newspapers.

Chapter Four. The date of Susette's marriage, July 23, 1881 (not 1882, as affirmed in *Buckskin and Blanket Days*), is confirmed by the County Judge of Burt County, Takamah, Nebraska. Her wedding dress is preserved in excellent condition by Mrs. Vivien K. Barris.

PART FOUR

Chapter One. A full account of the Tibbles' trip with Miss Fletcher is given in *Buckskin and Blanket Days*. Letters of Eda and May Tibbles describe life in the Tibbles home, and for many other details of family events the author is indebted to Green's *Iron Eye's Family*. Miss Fletcher's experiences with the allotment are detailed in her papers, in her *The Omaha Tribe*, and in Green. The incident of the man repeating Big Elk's words during the allotment is found in Fletcher.

Chapter Two. Details of Farleys' "pasture" are found in Green. General Crook's visit to Boston is described in Schmitt, *General George Crook*, and in Boston papers. Unfortunately exhaustive research in England failed to disclose corroborative evidence of the Tibbles' year spent there, but Susette's autograph album and a long account by Thomas Tibbles giving full details of the trip (much fuller than in *Buckskin and Blanket Days*) were treated by the author as reliable sources.

Chapter Three. The Tibbles' experiences at Pine Ridge, at the time of the Battle of Wounded Knee, are detailed fully in *Buckskin and Blanket Days*. Other details are found in numerous sources, such as Brown, *Bury My Heart at Wounded Knee*, the Fourteenth Annual Report of the Bureau of Ethnology, and contemporary documents.

Chapter Four. Again the author is indebted to Green for many family details. A sketch of the life of Thomas Sloan was furnished by Mrs. Pauline Tyndall, as were many touches of local color, Omaha customs and traditions, nature descriptions, and other pertinent details throughout the book. Sloan's speech is excerpted from Alvin M. Josephy's *Red Power*, pgs. 22 ff. A rewarding interview with Dr. John G. Neihardt elicited the details of the night he spent with Thomas Tibbles.

Index

About the Author

As an author, Dorothy Clarke Wilson has established an enviable record, with over seventy inspirational plays and seventeen novels and biographies published and an ever-growing following of devoted readers. In addition to her writing career, which began at the age of ten, she finds time for lecture engagements and travel. Her extensive travels in India and the Holy Land resulted in several books, including her well-known biography of Dr. Ida Scudder, *Dr. Ida*, published in 1959 and still in demand.

Some of her works have received exceptional recognition: *Prince of Egypt*, a novel, was winner of the Westminster prize for religious fiction in 1949 and was used as auxiliary material for the film "The Ten Commandments"; *Lone Woman*, the story of Dr. Elizabeth Blackwell, was a selection of Reader's Digest Condensed Books; and *Ten Fingers for God*, the story of Dr. Paul Brand, appeared in an abridged version in the monthly *Reader's Digest*. Many of her books are published in foreign languages; *Take My Hands*, the story of Dr. Mary Verghese, has been translated into over a dozen languages.

For *Bright Eyes* Mrs. Wilson spent some time on an Omaha Reservation studying Indian customs and culture and interviewing descendants of the La Flesche family; further research took her to Boston, New York, and London. In between her travels and lectures, she and her husband, a retired Methodist minister, enjoy the advantages of a university town—Orono, Maine.